Transformational Trends in Governance and Democracy

National Academy of Public Administration

Modernizing Democracy:
Innovations in Citizen Participation

Edited by Terry F. Buss, F. Stevens Redburn, and Kristina Guo

Meeting the Challenge of 9/11:
Blueprints for More Effective Government

Edited by Thomas H. Stanton

Foreign Aid and Foreign Policy:
Lessons for the Next Half-Century

Edited by Louis A. Picard, Robert Groelsema, and Terry F. Buss

Transforming Public Leadership for the 21st Century

Edited by Ricardo S. Morse, Terry F. Buss, and C. Morgan Kinghorn

Performance Management and Budgeting:
How Governments Can Learn from Experience

Edited by F. Stevens Redburn, Robert J. Shea, and Terry F. Buss

About the Academy

The National Academy of Public Administration is an independent, nonprofit organization chartered by Congress to identify emerging issues of governance and to help federal, state, and local governments improve their performance. The Academy's mission is to provide "trusted advice"—advice that is objective, timely, and actionable—on all issues of public service and management. The unique source of the Academy's expertise is its membership, including more than 550 current and former Cabinet officers, members of Congress, governors, mayors, legislators, jurists, business executives, public managers, and scholars who are elected as Fellows because of their distinguished contribution to the field of public administration through scholarship, civic activism, or government service. Participation in the Academy's work is a requisite of membership, and the Fellows offer their experience and knowledge voluntarily.

The Academy is proud to join with M.E. Sharpe, Inc., to bring readers this and other volumes in a series of edited works addressing major public management and public policy issues of the day.

The opinions expressed in these writings are those of the authors and do not necessarily reflect the views of the Academy as an institution. To access Academy reports, please visit our website at www.napawash.org.

This book is due for return on or before the last date shown below.

Performance Management and Budgeting
How Governments Can Learn from Experience

Edited by F. Stevens Redburn
Robert J. Shea
and Terry F. Buss

Foreword by David M. Walker

NATIONAL ACADEMY OF
PUBLIC ADMINISTRATION

TRANSFORMATIONAL TRENDS IN
GOVERNANCE AND DEMOCRACY

M.E.Sharpe
Armonk, New York
London, England

Library of Congress Cataloging-in-Publication Data

Performance management and budgeting : how governments can learn from
experience / edited by F. Stevens Redburn, Robert J. Shea, and Terry F.
Buss.
   p. cm. — (Transformational trends in governance & democracy)
  Includes bibliographical references and index.
  ISBN 978-0-7656-2232-7 (cloth : alk. paper)
  1. Public administration—Evaluation. 2. Organizational effectiveness. 3.
Administrative agencies—Evaluation. 4. Performance—Management. I.
Redburn, F. Stevens. II. Shea, Robert J., 1965- III. Buss, Terry F.

JF1525.P67P475 2008
352.4'39—dc22   2007022829

Printed in the United States of America

The paper used in this publication meets the minimum requirements of
American National Standard for Information Sciences
Permanence of Paper for Printed Library Materials,
ANSI Z 39.48-1984.

BM (c)   10   9   8   7   6   5   4   3   2   1

Contents

Foreword

The Honorable David M. Walker
Comptroller General of the United States

As we enter the twenty-first century, it is becoming increasingly clear that government needs to rethink what it does and how it does business. The United States is experiencing dramatic changes on several fronts, from the economy to the environment to national security. Unfortunately, we have a government that is based overwhelmingly on social, economic, and other conditions from the 1940s through the 1960s. As a result, our government is increasingly out of touch with both current and emerging challenges and is poorly positioned to capitalize on related opportunities.

Our continuing failure to prioritize government functions and target resources appropriately means that vital programs may be inadequately funded while under-performing and outdated programs receive excessive funding. Hurricane Katrina brought this point home in a painful way. Obviously, governments have a key role to play in planning for and responding to natural disasters. In the aftermath of Katrina, some agencies, such as the Coast Guard, did come through with flying colors. But others, notably FEMA, fell far short of expectations. Most Americans, including me, were shocked and disappointed by our government's overall inability to meet even basic needs in New Orleans and the Gulf Coast. At the same time, inefficient and ineffective contracting, disbursement, and other activities wasted billions of dollars.

The task of transforming government and aligning it with modern realities is even more urgent because of our nation's worsening financial condition and long-term fiscal outlook. The United States is deeply in debt, and that indebtedness threatens our government's future flexibility to act. With the retirement of the baby boomers getting closer, health care costs spiraling upward, and personal savings rates plummeting, we face unprecedented and increasing fiscal risks.

Our government's lack of fiscal discipline in recent years has not helped matters. Between out-of-control spending and several major tax cuts, federal deficits have returned with a vengeance. The unified budget deficit numbers, such as the $248 billion deficit in fiscal year 2006, get a lot of press coverage, although these numbers are far lower than our nation's operating and accrual-based deficits. Lower short-term deficits are better than higher ones, but our short-term costs are still too high.

Importantly, it is our government's growing liabilities and unfunded commitments that are the real problem. These include the present value of Social Security and Medicare's unfunded promises and potential payouts by government entities such as the Pension Benefit Guaranty Corporation or the National Flood Insurance Program. In fact, the estimated future burden to U.S. taxpayers has soared from about $20 trillion in 2000 to about $50 trillion in 2006. This translates into an IOU of about $440,000 for every U.S. household—and this bill is growing each and every day. Keep in mind that the median household income in this country is less than $50,000.

At the present time, the federal government is spending more than it takes in and charging the balance to our "national credit card," which has no express credit limit. Unless we change course, someone will ultimately have to pay the bill, along with compound interest, and that someone is our children and grandchildren.

Clearly, a crunch is coming. Long-term simulations from my agency, the U.S. Government Accountability Office (GAO), show that if we stay on this path, our government will eventually have to more than double federal taxes or slash many programs the American people now take for granted. Based on historical tax levels, by 2040, the federal government could be reduced to doing little more than mailing Social Security checks and paying interest on the national debt.

Over time, we will need to make tough choices on competing needs, whether it is homeland security, public health, airports and highways, border control, or natural disaster preparedness. Ronald Reagan once quipped that a government program is "the nearest thing to eternal life that we'll ever see on this earth." But the truth is that the status quo is not sustainable. Unless we start to scrutinize "the base" of government on a periodic basis, it is going to be increasingly difficult to finance existing programs that the American people strongly support, let alone respond to compelling new priorities and needs.

It is useful to reflect on how much things have changed in recent decades and how much they continue to change. For example, today's teenagers have little firsthand memory of the cold war, but microcomputers and HIV/AIDS have always been part of their world. We must strive to maintain a government that is effective and relevant to this and future generations—a government that is as free as possible of outmoded commitments and operations that can encumber the future.

Federal managers will have to make a case that their missions matter today and that they deliver real, outcome-based results. Credible performance information can foster meaningful debate on what we expect from government and how finite resources should be allocated among a broad range of federal activities.

This idea is hardly new. Since 1950, the government has made repeated attempts to better align spending decisions with expected performance, generally known as "performance budgeting." Most of these initiatives failed to shift the long-standing focus of federal budget process from spending dollars to getting results.

In 1993, Congress passed the Government Performance and Results Act (GPRA), which requires agencies to develop periodic strategic and annual performance plans and reports. GPRA also calls for performance plans to be linked to budgets. The idea is that with objective information on program spending and outcomes, federal managers will be better able to improve performance. These data would also be useful for congressional policy making, spending decisions, and program oversight. Because of GPRA's status as law, every administration and every agency head, regardless of party affiliation or philosophy, must follow its provisions. At the same time, the Office of Management and Budget (OMB) has yet to develop an overall executive branch strategic plan that meets the spirit of GPRA. Furthermore, we need to expand this concept to tax preferences, which, despite their "off-the-books" status, significantly affect the nation's bottom line.

In 2001, the Bush administration launched the President's Management Agenda, which focuses on five management priorities in government, including budget and performance integration. A central element of this initiative is the Program Assessment Rating Tool (PART), which OMB developed to provide consistent assessments of federal programs in the executive budget formulation process. PART is a standardized series of questions meant to serve as a diagnostic tool, drawing on available program performance and evaluation information to form conclusions about program benefits and recommend adjustments that may improve results. PART is not perfect, but it is a step in the right direction.

Performance-based budgeting can help government better assess competing claims in the budget by providing more precise information on program results. Performance information can help change the type of questions asked in the budgetary process. Policymakers may be prompted to ask such questions as whether programs are: contributing to their stated goals, well coordinated with related initiatives at the federal level or elsewhere, and targeted to those most in need of services. It can also provide insights into the outcomes being achieved, whether the return on investment justifies the costs, and whether program managers have the capacity to consistently deliver promised results.

Although performance budgeting can help to change the nature of resource debates, it is also important to understand its limitations. Performance information cannot be a substitute for difficult political choices. Since the founding of our republic, there have been conflicting views on the appropriate size and roles of the federal government and the need for various programs and policies. Performance information cannot settle that debate, but it can help move it to a more informed level—one that focuses on results as well as competing claims and priorities. In fact, it raises the stakes by shifting the discussion to what really matters: lives saved, children fed, successful transitions to self-sufficiency, individuals lifted out of poverty, reductions in fossil fuel emissions, and improvements in health care coverage.

Performance problems may well prompt budget cuts or program eliminations, but they may also inspire greater investment or reforms in program design and management. Conversely, even a program that is exceeding its performance expectations could be a candidate for cutbacks if it is a lower priority than other competing claims in the process. Poor evaluation results could also prompt greater investments in people and technology or perhaps redoubled management improvements if there is general agreement that the activity is critically important to the country.

Going forward, the information compiled by federal departments and agencies will be essential in assessing whether federal activities are meeting the needs of our rapidly changing society. Frankly, a top-to-bottom review of all federal activities is long overdue. Congress and the president need to decide which programs and policies remain priorities, which should be overhauled, and which have simply outlived their usefulness.

This effort would benefit from a set of key national indicators. These outcome-based measures could help to assess the United States' status, progress, and position relative to other developed nations on public safety, health care, housing, immigration, energy, and environmental issues.

Various international entities, including the European Union and the United Nations, now use key indicator systems. In addition, several countries—Australia, Canada, and the United Kingdom among them—and even some U.S. states and municipalities have been using indicators to prioritize and target public resources. It is time the federal government did so as well. GAO is working with the National Academies, the Organization for Economic Cooperation and Development, the International Organization of Supreme Audit Institutions, and others to help make key national indicators a reality in the United States and around the globe.

Given our long-range fiscal imbalance, I believe we must impose meaningful budget controls and broaden the time horizon of the federal budget process. The budget controls will need to be broader and tougher than in the past, not only because our fiscal situation is worse but because a tsunami of federal spending generated by the retirement of the baby boomers is racing toward our shores. The nation's fiscal challenges begin to escalate rapidly just beyond the ten-year budget projection period. As a result, new metrics and mechanisms are needed to help highlight the long-term implications of existing federal programs and new fiscal commitments.

We need better ways to describe and measure the range of fiscal exposures—from explicit liabilities such as environmental cleanups and federal pensions to the more implicit obligations in the life-cycle costs of capital acquisition or disaster assistance.

Social Security, Medicare, and Medicaid are not the only programs in the budget that present a very different cost picture beyond the ten-year budget window. For example, federal insurance can appear costless in its first year, but when an insured event, such as a flood, takes place, the budgetary impact can be significant.

Most critically, Congress must become more involved in this debate and the resulting decisions and follow-up activities. After all, Congress plays a central role in setting national priorities and allocating resources to achieve those goals. Without congressional buy-in, major management initiatives will not be sustained. Going forward, I am hopeful Congress will develop a performance assessment process to assist its oversight efforts. To help focus these efforts, in November 2006 I sent the incoming Congress a list of three dozen government areas needing additional oversight, from addressing the "tax gap" to reviewing our activities in Iraq.

I am a big believer in partnering for progress. With the range of challenges facing our nation today, our federal government cannot go it alone. Public officials have to show a greater willingness to reach out to their colleagues across government as well as to their counterparts in the academic, private, and nonprofit sectors, both domestically and internationally. I am delighted that the National Academy of Public Administration has provided this opportunity for individuals from various sectors to share their views on performance management, as well as related issues such as human capital strategy. I am hopeful that their submissions to this volume will help stimulate much-needed discussion on how best to achieve a more efficient, effective, economical, ethical, equitable, and accountable government in the twenty-first century.

Preface and Acknowledgments

This work is part of a series of edited books, *Transformational Trends in Governance and Democracy,* that captures the latest thinking in public management. The books collectively represent what we believe are fundamental, transformational trends emerging in governance and democracy. Each book addresses the questions: How is governance or democracy being transformed? What impact will transformations have? Will forces arise to counter transformations? Where will transformations take governance and democracy in the future?

The National Academy of Public Administration sponsors the series in partnership with M.E. Sharpe Publishing. Many of the chapters in the series have been contributed by academy fellows and professional staff. We have also drawn on leaders in public management representing different ways of thinking about the issues. I am editing the series overall, with well-known experts editing individual volumes. Initial books in the series are available at www.mesharpe.com.

Acknowledgments

We would like to thank Jenna Dorn, president of the Academy, and Howard Messner, past president, for their support and encouragement; Scott Belcher, executive vice president, for marshalling academy resources in developing and executing this project; Morgan Kinghorn, past academy president, for promoting the project widely across the institution; Bill Shields, vice president, for facilitating the project; Dan Spikes for editing several of the chapters; and of course, Ednilson Quintanilla for managing the production of the manuscript. The Academy would also like to thank M.E. Sharpe, especially Harry Briggs, Elizabeth Granda, Stacey Victor, and Anna Kaltenbach, for their assistance and encouragement in preparing this manuscript for publication.

Terry F. Buss

Performance
Management and
Budgeting

1

Performance-Based Management

How Governments Can Learn from Experience

F. Stevens Redburn, Robert J. Shea, Terry F. Buss, and
Ednilson Quintanilla

This volume is about the process by which governments hold themselves accountable to their citizens for performance. Or, it is about the development of institutions
that allow governments to learn from experience.

Accountability for Results

From one viewpoint, the effort to plan, budget, and manage government programs
based on explicit performance goals and measures is an effort to make government more accountable to its citizens for achieving promised results. In this view,
good government—a government responsible to the people—must have as its core
purpose the achievement of results for the people, taxpayers, whose money it uses.
Taxpayers expect government to offer programs that will provide basic services
that improve their lives. They also want their money spent wisely, effectively, and
efficiently. They will at some point hold the government accountable for results.

To properly hold governments accountable, however, taxpayers need clear,
candid, easily accessible, and up-to-date information about agency and program
successes and failures. The Bush administration, for example, has attempted to
improve the federal government's accountability by making more and more budget
decisions based on performance. The president's Budget and Performance Integration (BPI) Initiative[1] is an effort to ensure that dollars produce the best results
by helping decision-makers and the public identify which programs work well,
which are deficient, and what can be done to improve their performance. In some
cases, it may be necessary to reallocate funding to more effective programs. This
and other decisions about programs are ultimately made jointly by Congress and
the president, but the analysis of program performance can help the executive and
legislative branches make more informed decisions. To broaden and inform citizen
participation in these choices, federal agency and OMB career staff prepare formal
assessments of each program's performance that are made public and accessible.

Similar systems of performance and accountability are becoming the norm in

3

governments at the state and local levels, not to mention in developed and developing countries around the globe. Consider this: A web search on Google for "performance budgeting" yields 340,000 sites, for "performance management," 31,600,000 sites.

Learning from Experience

From another viewpoint, use of performance goals and information as a basis for public choice and program administration is an effort to enable government to learn from experience. Just as people individually and collectively learn from experience, so—it is argued—governments can improve their performance over time not by simple trial and error, but by systematically analyzing what works and what does not and translating this information into decisions about where to put their resources, how to manage, and how to improve program designs. Unlike people, however, governments do not necessarily possess the capacity to readily learn from their previous successes and failures. This capacity has to be consciously created. Some would argue that the effort to institutionalize government capacity to learn from experience is still in its infancy, and that failures merely highlight the need to get on with building this capacity.

Whether BPI, or its counterparts in other governments, are viewed as efforts to improve accountability or to create a capacity to learn from experience, results of this and other efforts can be measured in two principal ways:

- *Improved program performance:* Through the use of performance assessments, programs will have the information they need to improve their performance every year. The initiative requires each agency to identify opportunities to improve program management and design, and then to develop and implement clear, aggressive plans to get more for tax dollars every year.
- *Greater investment in successful programs:* Overall, scarce resources need to be allocated to programs that benefit the nation most effectively and efficiently. Program performance will not be the only factor in decisions about how much funding programs receive. However, policymakers equipped with information about program performance can consider performance to a greater degree in their decision making and invest primarily in programs that provide the greatest return on the investment of taxpayer dollars. If poorly performing programs are unable to demonstrate improved results, then that investment may be reallocated to programs that can demonstrate greater success.

The success of BPI and similar efforts can be judged over time by whether programs are becoming more efficient and more effective through implementation of meaningful improvement plans guided by assessment and evaluation and by whether budgets shift resources from unproductive programs to those that produce results consistent with their goals.

Many programs are demonstrating improved results. For example:

- In FY2005, the Social Security Administration improved the efficiency with which it processed claims by 2.7 percent. The gain in overall agency productivity meant that the SSA needed 2,155 fewer work years to complete its job. With each work year estimated to cost $73,700, this improvement in efficiency represented savings of approximately $159 million.
- In FY2005, the Arizona state legislature was on the verge of eliminating a $10.8-million drug treatment program that supplies psychotropic drugs to the seriously mentally ill. But the drug treatment program demonstrated not only that its 9,000 participants were benefiting from drug therapy, but also that the state was saving money by providing drugs to people who otherwise tended to end up in jail or hospitals. The legislature refunded the program.
- In FY2005, Mayor Michael Bloomberg ordered a review of New York City's tax incentive programs. Each program had to demonstrate—using outside consultants and researchers—that programs' results were significant enough to justify continued funding. In addition, programs would have to align themselves with the city's strategic plan.

How BPI Works

To many, the Bush administration's performance management and budgeting initiative is among the most sophisticated efforts in the field—although, as chapters 2 through 6 demonstrate, there is no shortage of ways to improve or reengineer it. In 2007, in its fifth year, it was also developing a track record against which to evaluate its effectiveness as a management tool. We focus this book on various aspects of BPI, including:

- Assessing performance with the Program Assessment Rating Tool (PART);
- Publishing a scorecard to hold agencies accountable for managing for results, addressing PART findings, and implementing follow-up actions;
- Communicating results to the public on *ExpectMore.gov;* and
- Coordinating program improvement through interagency collaboration.

We also include work from U.S. state and local government, and developed and developing countries, many of which have adopted some or all of these BPI techniques, have contributed to their further development and shaped them to their needs through their own efforts, or have taken very different approaches that can inform performance management and budgeting. We turn now to the central feature of BPI, the PART.

Comprehensive Assessment with the PART

How do we ensure that programs are improving every year? First, we assess their current performance. In order to improve program outcomes, it is critical to have a good understanding of how the program is currently performing. By 2007, the Bush administration had assessed the performance of 976 programs with the PART, representing 96 percent of the federal budget, or $2.5 trillion in spending.[2] As of March 2007:

- 17 percent of programs were rated *effective*
- 30 percent of programs were rated *moderately effective*
- 28 percent of programs were rated *adequate*
- 3 percent of programs were rated *ineffective*
- 22 percent of programs were rated *results not demonstrated.*

Note: in several contributions—chapters 2 to 6—to this volume, PART results from previous rating cycles are cited. A notation in each of those instances refers the reader to these results, the most recent at the time of publication. This information is also updated regularly on www.ExpectMore.gov, a public website designed to make transparent the evidence on which program assessments are based.

History of the PART

The federal government spends 2.7 trillion dollars on programs annually, but until the advent of the PART, no one had a uniform basis for assessing the extent to which these programs actually work. For example, were the taxpayer dollars the federal government spent on adult education actually improving the lives of adults? Were federal efforts to cure or reduce disease successful?

The Bush administration built upon prior efforts by creating the PART, an objective, ideologically neutral, and easy-to-understand questionnaire with which to assess program design, planning, management, and performance. Federal agencies and OMB administer the PART. Objectivity of PART ratings is paramount. When first launched, the test PART asked whether the assessed program served an appropriate federal role. The answer to that question would depend on the perspective of the person answering it, so the question was removed.

Reviews of the PART by public- and private-sector entities have often praised the transparency and objectivity of the process, while at the same time raising concerns that needed to be addressed. For instance, some reviews found the assessment to lack consistency in the answers to the same questions when applied to different programs. So OMB now audits all draft assessments to correct any obvious inconsistencies. Reviews also found that agencies did not always agree with the final assessment of their programs. Agencies can now appeal to a high-level subcommittee of the President's Management Council (PMC) to dispute answers with which they disagree. To address the conclusion by some reviewers that OMB and agencies were not doing enough to involve Congress in the assessment process, agencies are now required to brief and consult with their congressional appropriators, authorizers, and overseers before the annual assessments begin (Posner and Fantone focus on this issue in chapter 5).

Effective programs set clear performance objectives, develop realistic strategies for achieving those objectives, and continually review their progress to improve their performance. This requires an ongoing annual planning and review cycle integrated with the agency's budgeting cycle and with agency-level strategic planning processes.

OMB assesses strategic planning for individual programs using the PART. In judging the quality of a program's strategic planning, the PART assesses whether the program has a limited number of performance measures with ambitious and achievable targets to ensure that planning, management, and budgeting are strategic and focused. Sources and evidence for the assessment include strategic planning documents, agency performance plans/performance budgets and reports, reports and submissions from program partners, evaluation plans, and other program documents. While it is recognized that some programs have greater difficulty than others in developing quantitative performance goals, all programs are expected to have meaningful and appropriate methods for assessing their progress and demonstrating results.

In short, OMB judges the quality of a program's strategic planning effort by whether it produces realistic but ambitious long-term and short-term goals that permit the program's managers and others to assess whether it is making progress toward important outcomes. The quality of a strategic planning process therefore must be judged by whether it produces agreement and commitment to such goals.

A Short History of Performance Management and Budgeting

The history of performance management is exemplified by at least one new significant proposal advanced almost every decade, the PART being the latest advance. New approaches tend to acknowledge the shortcomings of previous models and address any critical public or political concerns. Federal interest in performance budgeting was initially manifested during the early 1920s, partly as a result of recommendations from the earlier Taft Commission of 1912. Rising government spending, and debt associated with financing World War I, led Congress to pursue a budget system that would also act as a tool for controlling federal spending. The Budget and Accounting Act of 1921 had a twofold approach: it delegated more definitive authority and responsibilities over the budget to the executive and established many basic measurements to facilitate greater congressional oversight. Prior to 1921, the federal government operated without a comprehensive presidential budget process. The earlier budgeting process, dominated by Congress, treated each bureau individually, which limited the analysis of overall federal budget priorities. The act of 1921 assigned responsibility for budget programming squarely on the executive, directing the president to provide Congress with expenditure estimates and appropriations necessary to operate the government. By placing budgeting responsibilities on the executive, a single office elected by voters and charged with policy implementation, Congress made effective use of the budget as a control mechanism. The act also created two new institutions—the Bureau of Budget, now OMB, and the General Accounting Office, now the Government Accountability Office (GAO). These offices were primarily charged with watchdog responsibilities. Congress intended for OMB and GAO to have discretion over bureaus and in the case of OMB to act as an extension of the president in developing a budget. Nevertheless, the reach of these policies was limited because they ignored the numerous dimensions of budgeting, including political priorities, constituencies, and external pressures, as well as other approaches that enhance the effectiveness of budget formulation.

While the policies of the 1920s improved spending controls, they failed to establish a comprehensive understanding of performance budgets. That task was taken up by the Commission on Organization of the Executive Branch of the Government (Hoover Commission), in 1949, which specifically called for employing performance budgeting throughout the federal government. For the first time, the commission's recommendations acknowledged that the value of performance budgeting consisted not in gathering data as an end in itself, but rather in using that information for budget and management decisions. The Hoover Commission opined that the federal budget should be based on the "general character and relative importance of the work to be done or upon service to be rendered, rather than upon the things to be acquired, such as personal services, supplies, equipment, and so on" (as quoted in Grifel 1993, 404). In short, this approach focused budgeting on workloads, unit costs, and functions as tools that help inform management practices.

The Commission recommended an extensive reorganization of the executive branch, enacted through the Budget and Accounting Procedures Act of 1950. The act of 1950 directed the president to present a budget to Congress showing "obligations by activities," a format that further institutionalized the system of measuring budget outputs. It also expanded the managerial powers of the executive further under the notion that the president needed to have substantial budget authority in order to implement policies effectively. Nevertheless, while the act of 1950 contributed a new understanding of budgeting as a management tool, it still failed to design features for program assessment.

In 1965, President Johnson attempted to address the shortcomings of previous efforts with the Planning, Programming Budgeting System (PPBS) (see Radin, chapter 6 in this volume, for a discussion of this initiative). PPBS advocated a new approach that included developing multiple budget alternatives, establishing program objectives, and pursuing multiyear planning to improve the quality of budgeting decisions. Three key functions of PPBS were: strategic planning in setting objectives and evaluating alternative scenarios; management control of goals, objectives, projects, and activities; and operational control involving budget execution and auditing. While previous notions of budgeting focused on control and management, PPBS merged these approaches into one framework.

PPBS, which was mandated throughout the federal government, was founded on several key assumptions. It assumed that different levels of program performance could be quantified through policy analysis and that would help leaders make the best decisions, an assumption that tended to minimize the political nature of budgeting. Agency objectives were linked to measured outputs, which provided a picture of the benefits and costs of various ways of achieving those outputs, which in turn assumed a causal link between those outputs and desired results. Additionally, multiyear planning was based on agency need, "program structure," activities planned, and national resources. Together, the methodology of PPBS added up to a colossal amount of analysis, which slowed down agencies and provided limited meaningful information for decision-makers to use during budget deliberations.

In 1973, President Nixon advanced the Management by Objectives (MBO) model, which sought to better link agency objectives to budget proposals. MBO attempted to make managers responsible for achieving agency outputs and outcomes, which were rated through agreed-upon processes. In theory, managers were accountable for achieving objectives determined by supervisors while agency heads responded to presidential objectives of national priority. More importantly, MBO was the first significant effort to articulate a model for measuring and achieving outcomes rather than outputs.

Similarly, in 1976, President Jimmy Carter promoted the Zero Based Budgeting (ZBB) system, which advocated for a reevaluation of all expenditures annually. Like several other proposals, ZBB had its origins in state government. Its champion, President Carter, believed that ZBB had been a successful technique for improving performance in the State of Georgia when he served as governor there. Essentially, ZBB requires that every year, policymakers assume nothing about the budget and start from an evaluation of all programs. To make budget decisions, ZBB was based on discrete packages, each of which included detailed proposals describing what could be achieved with discrete increments of funding. Accordingly, agencies would advance discrete packages prioritized for different levels of spending for a specific program. Although this approach appeared useful in theory, the process proved to be too time consuming and expensive to execute, and eventually lost political support. Although Carter later modified this policy to start the evaluation process at a specified percentage of department funding, it was still difficult to compare the same increments across different agencies. ZBB sought to create a clear link between budgetary resources, decisions, and results but its approach failed to recognize the practical limits of agencies' ability to manage large amounts of performance information and the ultimately political nature of budgetary processes. President Ronald Reagan rescinded ZBB in 1981. Under the Reagan administration, David Stockman, OMB director, required agencies to conduct economic analyses as part of the budget process. Critics suggest that this was ineffective because analyses lacked objectivity.

Immediately upon taking office, President Bill Clinton proposed the implementation of a National Performance Review (NPR) (see Radin, chapter 6, and Curristine, chapter 15, in this volume, for analyses of this initiative). President Clinton described his platform as a call for "reinventing government," a proposal modeled after similar reforms he had championed as governor of the state of Arkansas and similar to approaches used in the Texas Performance Review. Initially, NPR, under the direction of Vice President Al Gore, focused on administrative initiatives such as reducing red tape by streamlining processes and eliminating unnecessary regulatory overkill, improving customer service by creating more market-like dynamics, decentralizing decision-making processes to empower employees, and other measures. Numerous revisions made during the following several years as a result of congressional legislation continued to build on the policy themes originally advanced through NPR.

The Government Performance and Results Act (GPRA) of 1993 was Congress's first contribution to performance management and complemented initiatives of the Clinton administration (Posner and Fantone, in chapter 5 of this volume, provide an extensive review of this legislation). GPRA was similarly modeled after one particularly successful local government experience in the city of Sunnyvale, California. GPRA also drew from some of the features of the Budget and Accounting Procedures Act of 1950 and is perhaps the most significant federal effort directed at improving government accountability to date, if only because it engages Congress in the process. GPRA requires federal agencies to identify both annual and long-term goals, to collect and report performance data, and to implement strategies to improve. For the first time, each federal program was required to explicitly identify measures and goals for judging its performance and to collect information on an annual basis in order to determine whether it was meeting those goals. Acknowledging that GPRA provided valuable performance management tools, the Clinton administration incorporated these congressional mandates under NPR. Agencies have spent substantial effort developing strategic plans and performance measures and reporting these to satisfy GPRA requirements, in the process creating an infrastructure of goals and measures that laid an informational foundation for the Bush administration's BPI and PART.

Throughout the twentieth century, state and local governments were similarly experimenting with various performance-based management models (Rivenbark summarizes these in chapter 7).[3] In fact, changing citizen expectations during this period challenged state and local jurisdictions to adopt new measures for improving government performance. Most notably, taxpayers' rage over rising taxes and perceived wastefulness in California led to the well-known "tax revolt" embodied in the tax and expenditure limitation called Proposition 13. This critical public mood compelled state and local governments throughout the country to experiment widely with innovative solutions to ensure greater government performance. In 1988, David Osborne published *Laboratories of Democracy,* highlighting the efforts of many governors across the country to improve public services in innovative ways. In 1992, Osborne and Ted Gaebler described innovative state and local efforts to become more efficient and effective in *Reinventing Government.* Both books launched a tidal wave of performance management activity across states and local governments.

It is often forgotten that municipalities have always been at the forefront of performance management. In 1907, the New York Bureau of Municipal Research was created to link resource allocation to program goals. In 1906, the Government Finance Officers Association (GFOA) was formed to promote good budgeting practices in cities. In the 1930s, the International City Managers' Association (ICMA) was formed, in part to establish measurement standards for cities. The accomplishments go on and on.

States also have a long history of budget and management improvements. Following the publication of Osborne's books in the late 1980s, the Council of Governors' Policy Advisors (CGPA)—a sister organization of the National Governors' Association (NGA)—established a special unit to transfer knowledge about performance widely across state governors' offices. The unit—the Alliance for Redesigning Government—then moved to NAPA to work at all levels of government. NGA operates the Center for Best Practices to offer technical assistance to governors and transfer lessons learned in performance management and budgeting.

The same pressures at work in the United States have similarly influenced national governments abroad to adopt performance-based mechanisms. The Organization for Economic Cooperation and Development (OECD) has found evidence for widespread use of performance measures and evaluations in budget processes throughout OECD countries. In 2005, twenty-six of twenty-eight countries reported that they were currently using measures and evaluations to assess performance (see Curristine, chapter 12 of this volume, for detailed results from the OECD survey). Moreover, during the last fifteen years, the majority of OECD governments have shifted their emphasis away from measuring input units toward a focus on social results and outcomes. The OECD Senior Budget Officers (SBO) working group, developed in 1980, has for years promoted performance management and budgeting through member countries.

Scandinavian nations have a strong record of innovative performance-based approaches. Sweden established over 200 small performance-based agencies with clear measurable goals and indicators, and agency managers were held professionally accountable for their success. Meanwhile, New Zealand employed "a series of comprehensive reforms of the economy and public sector, rooted in a combination of institutional economics, principal/agent, transaction cost, and public choice theory" (Fosler and Lipitz 2000). Later, the United Kingdom and other European countries followed with similar endeavors (see Curristine, chapter 12, for a discussion of OECD countries).

Zaltsman's research on monitoring and evaluation (M&E) mechanisms in Latin America shines light on the experiences of a handful of developing countries, including Argentina, Chile, Colombia, Costa Rica, and Uruguay (see chapter 13). These cases highlight the common trends shared by governments around the world, such as fiscal constraints and citizen dissatisfaction with rising government costs. More importantly, they illustrate the existence, and value, of numerous approaches to performance-based management, and their successes and limitations in addressing all the needs of citizens, lessons that can help point us toward further possibilities for building management strategies in the public sector.

Multilateral aid organizations have placed performance management and budgeting at the top of their respective agendas. These organizations hold themselves accountable for achieving results. They invest a lot of resources in evaluating their operations and programs, they catalog and share vast amounts of performance information, they have sophisticated knowledge of management functions, they engage in continuing training efforts to maintain and develop capacity, and managers are held accountable for results. But they also hold aid recipient countries accountable for results. Grants and loans are administered in performance-based contracts, so countries must develop extensive capacity to manage aid and their own finances. And aid is often reduced, redirected, or expanded based on results obtained. The United Nations Development Programme (UNDP), for example, launched a local government performance budgeting project in Armenia in 2005. UNDP extensively documented this effort, and the lessons learned are being widely disseminated in developing countries (UNDP 2004).

Performance management and budgeting in the past few years has intersected with theories of public administration leadership. The predominant model is the New Public Management (NPM), which argues that public managers should run public programs like businesses.[4] This comports with the various performance movements that seek accountability and results. Syfert and Eagle, in chapter 8 of this volume, lay out the NPM model and establish its linkages to performance management and budgeting.

Issues in This Volume

The editors recruited authors who not only were ready and able to address the "big issues" swirling around performance management and budgeting (PMB), but who also had a lot of experience actually working in the field. Questions touched on in the volume include:

1. *Strategic Planning*—How does PMB relate to strategic planning processes in programs and agencies? Specifically, how do goals and objectives—in the context of mission, vision, values, and legal authority—interface with PMB?
2. *Performance Assessment*—How will performance be assessed in PMB? What indicators or metrics will be used, what is the quality of data gathered or available, how much does information cost to produce, what are the IT system issues under PMB, and is objectivity in the process possible?
3. *Results and Budgets*—How is performance assessment information linked to budgets?
4. *Results, Budgets, and Decision Making*—Are results data used by decision-makers to decide how to allocate resources?

Figure 1.1   **Annual Strategic Planning Cycle and Its Integration with Budgeting**

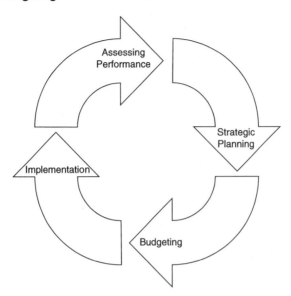

5. *Results and Management*—Are results used by managers to improve or alter operations—that is, in implementation?

6. *Stakeholder Input and Buy-In*—Who (executives, legislators, citizens) has input into different aspects of the budget process? More specifically, who are the stakeholders in the process, are their views taken seriously, have they bought into the process, and what happens if buy-in is not obtained?[5]

Figure 1.1 illustrates how these elements of a performance management and budgeting process can be fitted into an integrated periodic review, strategic planning, and budgeting cycle.

All contributors to the book are sensitive to the realities of PMB processes, not just the theory. Most note the pervasiveness of PMB, but acknowledge that there is a gap between the rhetoric and reality. Most see the performance movement as progressing through time, although much remains to be done; even so, there certainly will never be consensus on the perfect system. Most are concerned with the sustainability of any given PMB system. And most note the extent to which governments have learned from one another: GPRA, a federal effort, was informed by the initiatives of public officials in Sunnyvale, California; advances in some Latin American countries are exemplars for some developed countries; programs dedicated to making loans to college students provide methods for programs making loans to homeowners and businesses. So, all governments, agencies, and programs face similar issues. Most agree that regardless of their opinion about PMB generally, there have been numerous successes. Astonishingly, most agree that there is little agreement on what performance management and budgeting is, what it does, and how it is done. Everyone agrees that much more is yet to come in the field.

Organization of the Book

We asked the Honorable David M. Walker, Comptroller General of the United States, to prepare the foreword to this volume. He cogently lays out major issues—natural disasters, federal deficit, and aging populations, to name a few—facing the United States in the future, carefully tying these into performance management and budgeting.

We have arranged the chapters on performance management and budgeting in four parts—the PART as the latest in a long tradition of reform efforts at the federal level; state- and local-level efforts in the performance arena, along with intergovernmental issues under federalism; international approaches in developed and developing countries, as well as in foreign assistance agencies that transfer funding from developed to developing countries; and state-of-the-art tools—including performance measurement and program evaluation, and a presidential agenda for promoting effective financial and budget management.

PART, PMA, BPI and the Quest for Results

The editors have selected four chapters that represent the latest and best thinking on the Bush administration's long-term effort to improve federal government performance through the PART, PMA, and BPI. John Gilmour, in chapter 2, leads off with the results of a study detailing how agencies adopted PART and PMA in their operations. The study, based on interviews with managers in numerous agencies, including OMB and GAO, explains why some agencies succeeded and others were not as effective. Gilmour lays out a strategy not only for succeeding on the PART, but also one that would apply to any performance management and budgeting approach in the design and implementation phases.

Philip Joyce, in chapter 3, presents a framework showing how federal managers can work within the budget process to accomplish agency goals and promote performance, and in the process further their careers. Joyce argues that lack of evidence for the use of performance information in budgeting occurs because observers have only considered looking in the budget office or legislative committees, rather than deeper within agencies.

Lloyd Blanchard, in chapter 4, answers an important question about PART and PMA: were programs assessments used by decision-makers in budget allocation decisions? Many believe that PART is merely a compliance exercise, not to be taken seriously. Blanchard finds, however, that PART does have an effect on budget outcomes. This is a critical demonstration of the power of these techniques to move budget resources to more productive uses.

In chapter 5, Paul Posner and Denise Fantone, after carefully examining GPRA and PART in a broad context, offer a strategy to make the approaches fit better with realities of the federal budget process so that these might be sustainable over time.

The tenor of most of the chapters in this volume is positive about performance management and budgeting under the Bush administration, especially in the context of PART and PMA. However, Beryl Radin, in chapter 6, argues that PART has some critical flaws that may be impeding effective performance assessment, rather than promoting it. She goes on to argue that these flaws were recognizable in PART's predecessors, PPBS and NPR.

State and Local Government and Intergovernmental Contexts

William Rivenbark, in chapter 7, looks at the history of performance budgeting in municipal government, reminding readers that performance budgeting has a long tradition in local government, as it does at the federal level. Rivenbark reviews social science literature on the extent to which cities have adopted performance budgeting. He offers case studies illustrating successful performance budgeting efforts at the local level.

In chapter 8, Pamela Syfert and Kim Eagle detail the efforts of the city of Charlotte, North Carolina, in successfully incorporating the principles of the New Public Management (NPM) in the city's daily operations, to great effect. In so doing, they also link NPM principles in the public administration literature to Charlotte's performance management agenda. Of particular note is their recounting of how the balanced scorecard methodology was adopted as the management tool of choice in promoting strategic planning and performance.

Cities, states, and federal governments, of course, manage performance in their own spheres of influence. But, the three levels of government also are part of a federal system, wherein the activities of one level can very much affect the others. Richard Nathan, in chapter 9, argues that the federalism dimension in performance has been too often ignored, especially from the federal government perspective. Nathan illustrates his point by reviewing federal initiatives that fund programs in states and cities, including the prominent No Child Left Behind program. Nathan offers an agenda that would make performance management more effective in a federalism context.

Richard Keevey, in chapter 10, looks at block grants offered by the federal government to state and local governments, a major federalism issue. Keevey looks first at GPRA, PART, and other federal performance mandates, then at several programs—for example, Weed and Seed and Temporary Assistance for Needy Families block grants—as cases in point. He then goes on to propose solutions to problems in the intergovernmental context.

In chapter 11, Terry Buss focuses on the Community Development Block Grant (CDBG) program, reporting on the problems and solutions encountered in trying to design a performance system that could accommodate federal, state, and local government needs in documenting results. In spite of what appeared to many to be insurmountable problems, Buss points out that a working group of stakeholders in CDBG—including the Department of Housing and Urban Development, OMB, and associations—were able to overcome many intergovernmental issues to yield a viable performance measurement system. Buss discusses performance issues that ought to be addressed when working in the intergovernmental arena.

International Approaches

Performance management and budgeting is becoming increasingly sophisticated not only in developed countries, but in developing ones as well. Teresa Curristine, in chapter 12, presents the results of a survey of thirty member countries in the OECD that are operating performance-based management systems. She reveals the extent to which developed countries are moving increasingly toward performance, but also suggests that many have a long road to travel before their systems meet all of the challenges in the field.

Ariel Zaltsman, in chapter 13, provides detailed case studies of five Latin American countries—Argentina, Chile, Colombia, Costa Rica, and Uruguay—that have developed highly sophisticated performance systems, some that rival the efforts of many developed countries. Zaltsman provides interesting commentary on why and how the systems developed, how they are used, and what modifications might make them better. His analysis will appeal to any country developing and implementing a performance management system.

Buss, in chapter 14, presents a case study of the Millennium Challenge Corporation (MCC), a new federal program designed to produce results in allocating foreign assistance to developing countries. Buss shows how MCC was designed to eliminate problems in other foreign assistance agencies, notably the U.S. Agency for International Development (USAID). MCC grants funding only to countries that can demonstrate their capacity to manage aid funding and achieve results. But MCC also is designed to be a high-performance organization, not in the mold of more traditional federal programs. Although it has been in operation for only three years, MCC has made some important contributions in understanding how to achieve results in the international arena.

In chapter 15, Curristine compares, retrospectively, GPRA and NPR in the United States with similar efforts in the United Kingdom under the Next Steps Agencies program. The highway administrations of both countries serve as a focal point. Curristine offers insights into what common factors make programs accountable in the context of performance management and budgeting.

Tools for Performance Management and Budgeting

Chapters 16 to 18 look more generally at performance management and budgeting in governments, agencies, and programs. This section looks closely at some of the tools available to policymakers and managers in seeking results.

Harry Hatry, in chapter 16, lays out a comprehensive framework for understanding and crafting performance measurements to achieve results as part of the budget process. As the field has progressed at astonishing speed, performance measurement has become fraught with imprecise concepts, principles, and methods. Hatry clears away this underbrush, laying out a clear conceptual framework laced with examples, along with some guiding principles on how to use measures generally.

Jon Baron, in chapter 17, performs a similar service as Hatry but in the field of program evaluation. Baron argues that for performance assessment to be effective, it must employ rigorous social science program evaluation methods, rigorous enough to document convincingly the results programs achieve. Baron details how effective evaluations have been undertaken in a wide variety of programs, showing in the process that many government programs could benefit from similar scrutiny.

Redburn and Joyce, in chapter 18, opine that in addition to well-designed performance systems in the federal government, the president must also have authority to manage executive agencies to attain performance goals for the administration. The authors propose a set of sweeping reforms in budgeting and financial management that would give the president the tools needed to better manage the federal system's finances as it learns from experience.

Notes

1. BPI is one of many related performance management and budgeting initiatives. They are detailed at the Office of Management and Budget website: www.whitehouse.gov/omb/, accessed February 9, 2007 and analyzed at the Government Accountability Office website: http://searching.gao.gov/query.html?qt=+PART&charset=iso-8859–1&ql=&x=12&y=8, accessed February 9, 2007.

2. The PART is an ever-evolving assessment effort that is under continuous improvement. Those interested in learning about the latest developments and current PART data are encouraged to visit the PART website at www.whitehouse.gov/omb/, accessed February 9, 2007 under the "management" icon.

3. One of the most extensive efforts to track state and local government performance management activities was conducted by the Maxwell School at Syracuse University in its Government Performance Project, funded by the Pew Foundation from 1996 to 2002. Available at www.maxwell.syr.edu/gpp/about/index.asp, accessed February 9, 2007.

4. In a companion book in the M.E. Sharpe series, *Transforming Public Leadership in the 21st Century* (2007), Ricardo Morse and Terry F. Buss (eds.) present a collection of articles on public leadership, its evolution, shortcomings, advances, and future directions.

5. In a companion book in the M.E. Sharpe series, *Modernizing Democracy* (2006), Terry Buss, Steve Redburn, and Kristina Guo (eds.) address issues of citizen participation, especially in the era of the Internet.

References

Fosler, Scott R., and Roger C. Lipitz. 2000. "Performance-Based Governance: Review and Perspective." Prepared for the International Conference on Governance Challenges for the 21st Century: Sustainable Development, Environmental Conditions, and Public

Management in the United States, Japan, and Other Pacific Rim Nations. Tokyo, Japan, July 26–28, 2000.

Grifel, Stuart S. 1993. "Performance Measurement and Budgetary Decision Making." *Public Productivity and Management Review* 16(4) (Summer): 403–7.

Osborne, David and Ted Gaebler. 1992. *Reinventing Government.* New York: Plume.

Osborne, David. 1990. *Laboratories of Democracy.* Cambridge: Harvard Business School Press (revised edition).

UN Development Programme (UNDP). 2004. *Performance Budgeting: Armenia.* New York: UNDP.

Part 1

PART, PMA, BPI, and the Quest for Results

2

Implementing OMB's Program Assessment Rating Tool

Meeting the Challenges of Performance-Based Budgeting

JOHN B. GILMOUR

The federal government has been on a decade-long journey to improve its performance and accountability by measuring how well its programs work, and to link performance measures to allocation of budgetary resources (Joyce 1999). For example, the goal of the Government Performance and Results Act of 1993 (GPRA) was to refocus government agency efforts on results as opposed to inputs and standard operating procedures. After the first decade, the Government Accountability Office (GAO) found that it was clear that GPRA created a steady supply of performance information, but its assessment found no strong demand for this information by policymakers or program managers.

Shortly after taking office in 2001, President George W. Bush committed to an ambitious agenda to improve government management, a key element of which was to make government more results oriented by expanding use of performance budgeting. He directed the Office of Management and Budget (OMB) to work with agencies to recast their budgets to include performance information. In 2003, he expanded this effort by committing to a program-by-program assessment. At the time, there were about 1,000 major programs that might be assessed. The president directed OMB to lead this assessment effort as well. OMB developed an assessment framework, with the assistance of agencies and outside experts, which it named the Program Assessment Rating Tool (PART). PART has become a vital component of the President's Management Agenda (PMA) and the Budget and Performance Integration initiative (BPI).

PART is designed to build upon performance information developed by agencies in response to GPRA; OMB FY2005 PART guidance states: "The PART is a vehicle for achieving the goals of GPRA." PART appears to put "teeth" in GPRA, especially since OMB develops the president's budget, and its budget decisions are to be influenced to some extent by PART.

In the FY2004 budget, released in early 2003, the Bush administration numeri-

Figure 2.1 **The PART Scoring Mechanism**

OMB devised twenty-five to thirty questions grouped into four categories to assess the performance of agency programs. Each of the categories contains a series of questions, the answers to which are given a weighted score for relative significance:

1. Program Purpose and Design (weight = 20 percent): to assess whether the program design and purpose are clear and defensible.
2. Strategic Planning (weight = 10 percent): to assess whether the agency sets valid annual and long-term goals for the program.
3. Program Management (weight = 20 percent): to rate agency management of the program, including financial oversight and program improvement efforts.
4. Program Results (weight = 50 percent): to rate program performance on goals reviewed in the strategic planning section and through other evaluations.

Source: OMB.

cally rated the quality of management in 234, or about 20 percent, of major federal programs. In each of the three succeeding budgets approximately 200 additional programs were assessed, for a total of about 800 as of 2006. It is based on twenty-five to thirty questions, grouped into four categories, resulting in a total weighted numerical rating ranging from 0 to 100 (see Figure 2.1).

Based on the numerical scores, OMB assigns a management and performance rating to programs, ranging from the highest rating of *effective,* to *moderately effective,* to *adequate,* to a lowest score of *ineffective.* In addition, there is another rating, *results not demonstrated* (RND), which means that the measures the program's managers had developed were not adequate to determine its effectiveness.

The approximately 1,000 programs are assessed and reassessed on a five-year schedule. Program managers whose programs have been assessed but who are dissatisfied with their score, or who have instituted improvements, can request they be reassessed sooner.

This chapter—based on interviews with staff representing twenty-five programs and OMB officials—examines OMB's PART initiative from a very practical standpoint: how have federal agencies dealt with the requirements of PART? What strategies have they have employed to be successful? What challenges do they face?

Four challenges confront both agencies and OMB as they assess all 1,000 programs. The *first* challenge is to manage the PART assessment process. There are great differences among departments and agencies in the scores given by OMB to their programs, and it is almost certain that these are due to the nature of the departmental and agency responses. The *second* is using the PART questionnaire as a means of communicating accomplishments and successes to OMB and to other interested stakeholders. Without careful, hard work at mastering the PART, even well-run programs with good results are not guaranteed a good rating. The *third* is developing suitable measures. This is a challenge, since managers are under pressure from OMB to develop measures of outcomes, and a challenge for OMB also in that the success of PART as an assessment tool depends on appropriate measures. The *fourth* is interpreting program performance measures and their associated results to understand the extent to which program managers can be held accountable for performance.

Much has been written about performance measures and performance budgeting, but there has been little published so far about PART. For example, Hatry (1999, 2001) has written about different measures that can be used, and Melkers and Willoughby have explored adoption of state performance budgeting requirements (1998) and how they are used (2001, 2004). Joyce (2003) has written about linking performance and budgeting. GAO has examined the extent to which PART has influenced allocations in the president's budget, as have Gilmour and Lewis (2006). The focus here is different, looking instead at how programs have responded to PART, and the experiences of program- and bureau-level staff in dealing with its demands.

PART and Performance Budgeting

PART is a key element in President Bush's broader push to expand performance budgeting. Performance budgeting is not just a federal challenge. It is not easy to do at any level of government, but it holds promise for solving the fundamental challenge of budgeting—knowing where to direct scarce resources for maximum public benefit.

A deep frustration in legislatures, executive offices, and budget offices is that it is difficult or impossible to know which programs are doing good work and which are wasting money. Consequently, ineffective programs can continue to receive funding year after year, when that money could generate greater public benefit if directed to programs that produce results. Lack of reliable information about program effectiveness leads to adoption of strategies of incrementalism—small increases or reductions at the margin of program budgets—as a way of dealing with the uncertainty about where to allocate resources for maximum benefit.

The aspiration of performance budgeting is immense—to provide decision-makers with information needed to better allocate scarce resources in a way that will yield the greatest benefit. Even modest success in identifying effective and ineffective programs and facilitating some movement of money away from the ineffective and toward the effective, will be valuable.

A second, and perhaps equally important, aspiration is to induce organizational change—to encourage agencies to find better ways of achieving goals and to improve results. Allen Schick (2001) points out that behind all performance measurement is "the notion that an organization can be transformed by measuring its performance." He is pessimistic about this logic, but there are many optimists, and the jury is still out on the question of whether and to what extent measurement can induce change. Optimists contend that if agencies cannot document that they are producing results, they will be compelled to change.

Some observers believe that PART will help induce change by introducing transparency. For example, Clay Johnson, deputy director of OMB, stated recently that "transparency leads to accountability, which leads to results. Without transparency, you don't have accountability." In February 2006 OMB unveiled a new website that makes available the assessments of about 800 programs that had been subjected to the PART at www.ExpectMore.gov. With this website, the federal government has taken a giant and unprecedented step to make available to its citizens assessments of individual government activities. By exposing programs that are not performing, OMB hopes to compel them to improve, and to give their constituents and stakeholders arguments to demand improvements. In 2005, PART was awarded a Ford Foundation Innovations in American Government prize.

This recognition is remarkable, given that the U.S. states, not the federal government, have led the way in adopting performance budgeting. Performance budgeting has been widely adopted abroad (Schick 1990), and, as of a 1998 report, forty-seven out of fifty states had adopted some form of performance budgeting (Melkers and Willoughby 1998).

Although the federal government has been slow in adopting performance budgeting, its current approach is comprehensive and impressive. For example, the care taken in devising the PART tool to be objective, and the analysis and documents that support it, both reflect careful thinking about the challenges of assessing performance across a wide spectrum of programs.

The PART Process

The PART process begins with the annual release of the list of programs to be assessed that year. The definition of what constitutes a "program" is developed jointly between an agency and OMB. The program officials then begin their task of formulating their suggested answers to the questions, along with explanations and evidence. The PART document is now completed online. The budget examiner for the program reviews program submissions and decides what answers to give for each of the questions. Needless to say, program managers give themselves more "yeses" than examiners give them. Program officials who do not agree with the assessment can appeal up the chain of command in OMB. There are appeals each year, and a few are successful.

Programs are given scores, based on the proportion of "yes" answers a program is awarded in each of the four sections. Although OMB never reports an overall score for programs, one can easily calculate summary scores using the official weights for each section. Then, based on overall scores, OMB assigns grades to programs: *ineffective, adequate, moderately effective,* or *effective.* Figure 2.2 reports the overall scores needed to be awarded the different grades. If a program lacks adequate measures, OMB rates it as *results not demonstrated.* Programs given grades of *results not demonstrated* have overall scores ranging from a low of 11 to a high of 83. The lowest-scoring program, with an 11, is the Tribal Courts pro-

Figure 2.2   **Converting Scores to Grades**

Numerical Score	Grade
85–100	Effective
70–84	Moderately Effective
50–69	Adequate
0–49	Ineffective

gram in the Interior Department, the highest score—a 97—is held by the Inspector General Oversight of Federal Health Benefits (FEHBP) program in the Office of Personnel Management.

Scores and grades are not just for show: An important goal is to link budget decisions with assessments of outcomes and overall program quality, although OMB is also clear that these assessments are not the only factor in budget decisions. A high rating will not necessarily be rewarded with a budget increase, and low-rating programs may receive increases because they may have been too underfunded to be effective.

PART emphasizes outcomes rather than outputs. GPRA also required outcome measures, but PART takes this to a new level. Scholarship on performance budgeting has discussed different measures at length, distinguishing between outcomes and outputs (Hatry 1999, 2001). PART guidance is clear—"Measures should reflect desired outcomes. . . . Outcome measures are informative, because these are the ultimate results of a program that benefit the public. Programs must try to translate existing measures that focus on outputs into outcome measures by focusing on the ultimate goal of the program. . . ." OMB examiners who do the PART evaluations insist that programs find true outcome measures whenever possible. An exception is research and development programs, for which OMB guidance acknowledges that outcome measures may be inappropriate because a result cannot be predicted in advance of the research.

OMB examiners have been successful in prodding programs to adopt better measures. Adopting measures is not new, since they have been required since 1993 under GPRA, but less was at stake. With PART, there is far more emphasis on adopting end outcome measures, and there is a link between assessments and budget decisions. Further, the threat that a program will be labeled *results not demonstrated* is an important incentive to program managers. Departments with too high a proportion of programs rated *results not demonstrated* cannot get a green on the performance section of the PMA scorecard. In one department, OMB examiners informally told officials that if they did not reduce programs rated *results not demonstrated,* OMB would consider reducing its administrative budget. GAO, which has examined PART, contends that in some departments a rating of *ineffective* is preferred to *results not demonstrated,* because of the PMA scorecard impacts.

Individual programs have made significant progress. Initially a very large pro-

Figure 2.3   **Comparison of FY2004 and FY2007 Program Grades**

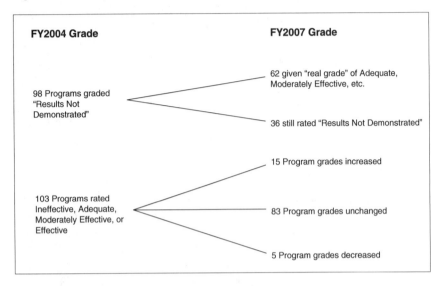

Source: Author's tabulation from OMB documents.

Note: 34 of the FY2004 cohort of programs could not be compared with FY2007 grades because they were either merged into other programs or otherwise changed such that they could not be paired with a program in the FY2007 budget. These have not been included in this figure.

portion of programs were graded *results not demonstrated.* In subsequent years many programs have been able to earn "real" grades by adopting suitable measures. Figure 2.3 compares grades assigned to the initial cohort of programs assessed in the FY2004 budget with those in FY2007. These programs have had several years to respond to OMB. Most programs initially graded RND have been able to get a real grade. Programs initially assigned a "real" grade of either *ineffective, adequate, moderately effective,* or *effective* have had success in getting higher grades. Of 103 programs with real grades, fifteen were raised; five were lowered.

In addition to assessing outcomes, the strength of PART is the inherent reasonableness of the assessment questions. It is hard to argue with an assessment that asks programs to have a clear statement of program purpose, good planning, strong financial management practices, and so on.

Based on my research, PART is taken very seriously at the program and bureau levels. Management systems imposed from above always meet a certain amount of skepticism and resistance. But attitudes about PART have changed as managers have seen the determination and persistence of OMB. Agency officials who might have thought that PART was a passing fancy now know that it is here to stay, at least under the Bush administration.

Challenge 1: Organizing for Success

There are differences between departments in PART ratings. Is this due to the inherent nature of the programs, or is it related to something else? The departments of State, Treasury, and Defense have been successful, receiving a large proportion of high ratings. The seriousness with which a department takes PART has an effect on their scores. State has been particularly successful. It has a high proportion of *effective* and *moderately effective* ratings, no *ineffective* ratings, and few *results not demonstrated*. Only 16 percent of all programs assessed across government had earned a rating of *effective* by the release of the FY2007 budget, but 34 percent of programs at State had. Treasury and Defense also had large proportions of programs earning *effective* ratings. Labor had only one program with an *effective* rating, while Veterans Affairs and the Environmental Protection Agency had none. Fifty-five percent of programs assessed in the Education Department were rated *results not demonstrated* (RND).

Table 2.1 ranks departments by their relative success with PART; it shows the percentages of programs that have been rated either *effective* or *RND*. A useful summary of department success is to subtract the percentage of programs with *RND* ratings from the percentage of those rated *effective*. Departments with a positive score are doing reasonably well. Those in negative territory are having problems. State comes out on top because it has a lot of programs in the *effective* category and few in *RND*. Education comes in last because it has hardly any rated *effective,* and most rated *RND*. The stark differences in Table 2.1 must be due to more than the inherent differences in departmental missions.

State has succeeded in getting initial ratings raised. Program officials dissatisfied with the rating first assigned can ask to be reassessed before the normal five-year period ends. Of the 234 programs first assessed in the FY2004 budget, seventy-seven had raised their score by the release of the FY2007 budget. Of those, sixty-two replaced a rating of *RND* with a real rating, meaning they had gotten approval for their measures of results. Of the fifteen instances in which a program was initially assigned a real rating and then got it raised, five were in State and four in Energy. Outside those two departments, improving a rating is unusual.

There are two important characteristics of State's approach to PART. First, top leaders took PART seriously. Second, the Resource Management Bureau plays a central role in organizing the bureau-level responses to PART. Success at State is a product of two nonexclusive factors. Part of the success stems from the programs' being generally well run. Second, State figured out how to work the system. They work hard at complying with PART.

While State offers a number of explanations as to why it has done well, it uniformly stresses one—that Secretary of State Colin Powell took PART seriously. Interviews with officials at the State Department made it clear that they understood that PART was considered important at the very highest levels and, consequently, at lower levels as well.

Table 2.1

Percentage of Programs Rated *Effective* and *Results Not Demonstrated*, by Department, FY2007 Budget

	Percent *Effective*	Percent *RND*	*Effective* Minus *RND*
State	38	7	31
Treasury	44	16	28
Defense	34	13	21
Transportation	20	0	20
Energy	22	8	14
Commerce	18	18	0
Labor	4	11	−7
Justice	11	19	−8
Environmental Protection Agency	0	13	−13
Health & Human Services	11	27	−16
Agriculture	6	27	−21
Homeland Security	16	38	−22
Housing & Urban Development	4	32	−28
Interior	8	37	−29
Veterans Affairs	0	33	−33
Education	3	55	−52

Source: Author's calculations from OMB-provided data.

State is also notable for the extent to which it seeks to have low-rated programs reassessed. If a program gets a rating below *effective,* the next year they seek a program reassessment. State appears relentless in seeking new assessments; some programs have been assessed three times. At State, anything less than an *effective* rating is unacceptable, so they keep going back until they get an *effective* rating. This stands in marked contrast to other departments, which have not sought to change ratings once assigned, except to get rid of the dreaded *RND.*

What State has done probably does not seem unusual or extraordinary, but some other departments appear to follow a far more relaxed procedure. Bureau-level staff in other departments said that the department served mostly as a conduit and passed along papers from OMB. The bureaus were on their own in responding to PART. Even in departments with a reputation for taking PMA seriously, bureaus work on their own.

No doubt other departments have adopted approaches similar to states. In one bureau at Energy that has done very well on PART, the bureau director has each of the programs self-assess with the PART instrument each year. He holds them accountable for the extent to which their self-assigned answers match those handed down by OMB.

The second factor is that bureau personnel are not left to their own devices on PART. Instead, the Bureau of Resource Management (RM) leads in organizing bureau-level responses. RM's experience is important because they have worked with numerous programs and have a sense of the kinds of measures OMB likes, and they can help programs in devising acceptable measures. Finally, when PART evaluations come out, RM convenes "after action" reviews.

Education also stands out, but for having very low assessments. More than half its programs are rated *RND,* and only two out of seventy-four programs are rated *effective.* State sought to get the highest possible ratings for its programs, but Education took a different approach, not using PART to validate its successes, but to create motivation for transformation. According to OMB's Robert Shea, low ratings do not reflect lack of interest in performance. Rather, leadership at Education believes the department is burdened with many ill-conceived, poorly designed programs. They use PART as a means of shining a light on those deficiencies. They think a low baseline is a fine place to be, if that is what it takes to get programs redesigned.

Challenge 2: Communicating Accomplishments

The biggest question for staff charged with working on a PART is always, "What can I do to get a better rating?" The most important prerequisite to getting a good score is having a strong, well-managed program. PART is not a perfect yardstick, but it is implausible that a weak program will be able to get one of the higher ratings. Good programs have, however, gotten bad ratings. It takes hard, careful work to get a score that reflects a program's true merit. As an Energy budget official explained, success on PART is a matter of both "achievement and articulation." For program managers, a challenge is to learn how to use PART to communicate what they do, why it is important, and what they have accomplished.

A useful strategy for learning about agencies' success with PART, and the impact of PART, is to look at programs that have managed to raise their ratings. Of the 234 programs assessed in the initial PART ratings released in 2003, sixty-two were able to convert a *results not demonstrated* score to a real score by 2006. Of the programs that got a real grade, fifteen were able to raise their grade by 2006. Were the raised grades evidence of improved results? Better program management? That only fifteen programs got higher grades suggests that PART is not yet causing large-scale management innovation or change. The key factor mentioned by officials in programs that got increased grades was that they learned how to better use PART.

Officials from several of the programs that raised their ratings explained their success with almost identical language. "We learned how to take the test," they said. They learned better how to use PART as a device to communicate their accomplishments to their examiner. Questions are clear, but can be interpreted in different ways. There can be disagreements about the appropriate evidence to document claims. Over time program staff can learn better how OMB is viewing the questions, and learn to write better—or more acceptable—answers. Equally important, they learned how to devise acceptable outcome measures.

Officials did not attribute their success to program changes. None of the officials interviewed claimed that they had introduced significant management improvements or changed program design to raise their rating. This is disappointing: an important goal of performance measurement is program improvement. Yet it should not be surprising. PART has been in place since 2002, not enough time to turn around a weak program. In the short run, at least, the best strategy for getting a better score is to become better at "taking the test"—to better communicate.

Over time, however, if program managers find that efforts to communicate more effectively do not result in higher ratings, they may change program management. In one case where the PART rating for a Labor program was increased because major changes had been made in its management, the change was in response not to PART but to GPRA.

This study examined only a fraction of all PARTed programs, and it is possible that in other programs there is more evidence of management change in response to PART. Improving program management is an important goal, one that will come only as the result of perseverance over more time than has yet elapsed under PART. An overall assessment of PART and its contribution to the quality of federal program management must wait.

Challenge 3: Overcoming Measurement Challenges

For OMB and the programs assessed through PART, an important challenge is developing good outcome measures. OMB has taken a strong stance in favor of outcome measures. But because they have maintained a high standard for approving measures, a large number of programs have been lumped in the RND category. The problem for OMB is that, without measures of outcomes, it is difficult to engage in performance budgeting.

Given the tremendous diversity of federal programs, simple prescriptions for measuring accomplishments are likely to fail to assess the real merits of some. The PART guidance recognizes program differences by dividing them into direct federal, research and development (R&D), block grant, and so on, providing questions designed to assess each. However, PART imposes a near-uniform standard on all programs, an insistence on finding end outcome measures. Guidance makes one exception and does not require R&D programs to devise outcome measures, acknowledging that this would be infeasible. Because federal programs are so varied in design and aspiration, devising good outcome measures requires ingenuity and flexibility, as well as some accommodation from OMB. In practice, OMB recognizes this.

Because PART is intended to assess results, its success depends on programs' ability to identify suitable measures of outcomes or results. This has been a weakness, as well as the broader efforts promoting performance budgeting, because good outcomes measures can be hard to come by. In the first several years of PART about half of programs assessed received a rating of *RND*. Paradoxically, the large number of programs labeled *RND* is evidence that OMB is holding agencies to a high standard, and not accepting whatever measures the programs propose. In subsequent years, some of those labeled *RND* have been able to have their measures approved and accordingly received a real rating. By the fourth year of PART, released with the FY2007 budget, the proportion of *RND* ratings had dropped to about a quarter.

OMB has come down squarely in favor of "end outcome" measures, rather than output measures. OMB offers important guidance. Measures should as much as possible be of "outcomes" rather than "outputs." Outputs are seen as easier to measure, but outcomes are the preferred measure because good outcome measures should encourage the agency to expend its efforts in solving problems and having real impact. An "efficiency" measure is required.

When programs are asked to develop outcome measures, there is a predictable pushback. A typical response is, "what we do can't be measured." There is some truth to this claim, as there really are accomplishments of programs that defy measurement. But programs that are accomplishing results must leave some mark on the world, and the challenge for program administrators is to think creatively about ways of measuring it. After initial resistance and prodding from OMB, many programs devised inventive, useful measures of their results.

Reading the PART guidance issued by OMB, one would get the impression that OMB is unyielding in its insistence on end outcome measures. But an examination of programs that have gotten high ratings indicates that OMB examiners are flexible, and open to persuasion that in the case of particular programs outcome measures are either impossible or inappropriate. This section surveys difficulties some programs have had in assessing outcomes, the solutions they found, and OMB's response.

Measuring Success in Programs with "Lumpy" Outcomes

Some program outcomes have an either/or quality that makes it difficult to use outcome measures for tracking progress. The Secure Transport Asset program at Energy has the goal "to safely and securely transport nuclear weapons, weapon components, and special nuclear materials." Consequently it might choose for an outcome measure "thefts of nuclear bombs or fuel." Though a good measure, this would be misleading, since there has never been a theft of nuclear material. There might be no thefts in a given year, even if security is poor. This program requires a measurement of "security," an output, not an outcome. Measures include:

1. Annual average scheduled overtime hours per federal agent.
2. Annual percentage of mission hours reduced by shipment optimization.
3. Cumulative number of safeguards transporters in operation.
4. Cumulative number of federal agents at the end of each year.

These are all output measures, but they may be the best way to assess "security." These measures have been approved, and the program is rated *moderately effective*.

Another Energy program, the Elimination of Weapons-Grade Plutonium Production, has a similar problem. Its mission is building new fossil fuel power plants in Russia to replace the energy supplied to two cities by plutonium processing plants. The desired outcome is the removal of these sources of fissionable plutonium. It will take about ten years to complete construction of the new plants, at which point the plutonium processing plants can be shut down and decommissioned. The goal is to close to the plants, but using that outcome as a measure would produce a weird and misleading reporting—nine straight years of not achieving the outcome, and then, in the tenth year, 100 percent attainment of the outcome. Instead, the program measures progress toward the goal of completing the new plants, and also the tons of plutonium produced in the former Soviet Union:

1. Percent of construction completed on fossil fuel plant in Seversk that will facilitate the shutdown of two weapons-grade plutonium producing reactors.
2. Percent of construction completed on fossil fuel plant in Zheleznogorsk that will facilitate the shutdown of one weapons-grade plutonium producing reactor.
3. Metric tons of weapons-grade plutonium produced per year in the Russian Federation.

The first two are process or output measures, but the third would seem to be an outcome measure. OMB has not approved the measures.

Measuring Results of Enforcement Programs

Enforcement programs have a problem with outcome measures because there is often a dynamic relationship between effectiveness of enforcement and incidents that the enforcers are trying to stop. The Border Security Program (BSP) in State has this problem. Its goal is to maintain secure borders. The program at one point had considered using as its outcome measure the number of prohibited persons stopped from entering the country. The problem with this measure, they realized, was that if they did a great job of increasing security at the nation's borders, prohibited persons would themselves choose not to seek entry, meaning that there would be few apprehensions at the border. In order to score well on this measure, the bureau might be forced to encourage known terrorists to enter the country, just so they could be stopped. Of course BSP would never do such a thing, but a measure that suggests that an agency is not doing its job when it is actually doing a great job is seriously flawed. BSP solved this problem by carefully crafting its statement of program purpose. According to PART, "the purpose of the Border

Security Program (BSP) is to protect American citizens both here and abroad and safeguard US borders *through improvements in consular programs, processes, and systems.*" By saying that the purpose is to introduce improvements, the statement of purpose invites assessment of outputs—the improvements introduced. Their measures are clearly process and output oriented:

1. Development of a biometric visa program for the United States.
2. Number of Consular Management Assessment Team (CMAT) assessments.
3. Number of days between receipt of routine passport application by Passport Services and issuance of a passport.
4. Percentage of passport applications processed to issuance within a certain number of days after receipt.

OMB approved the measures and gave the program an *effective* rating.

Measuring the Results of Data Collection Organizations

Programs that have data-generating missions have trouble measuring outcomes, as is the case with agencies like the Bureau of Labor Statistics (BLS). As they began PART, they asked, "what is the intended goal of our statistics?" The answer they came to was "better informed business decisions," a difficult concept to measure. So, instead of trying to measure the quality of business decisions, they measured outputs—the timeliness with which they release the twenty-four separate studies they conduct each year. They measure the extent to which they release studies on schedule, a nontrivial accomplishment but not a true outcome measure. As a surrogate for an outcome measure, they assess customer satisfaction.

1. Percent of scheduled releases issued on time.
2. Customer satisfaction with BLS data and assistance.
3. Number of months elapsing between collection and publication of detailed employee-benefits data, with no increase in production spending.

OMB has accepted these, and the program has earned an *effective* rating.

The U.S. Geological Survey (USGS) is a scientific agency that produces a great deal of data. The Geological Hazards Assessments Program provides earth science data to reduce loss of life and property from volcanoes, landslides, and other geological hazards. If the Geological Hazards program is doing its job well, the end outcome should be a safer country, since people will better understand risks of earthquakes and other dangers, and be able to stay out of their way or prepare for surviving them. Measuring the actual impact of this data will be nearly impossible, however, putting the Geological Hazards program in much the same position as BLS. But because the program is classified as research and development, it need not employ outcome measures (BLS is classified as direct federal). Rather than attempting to measure actual outcomes, the USGS measures progress toward data collection goals, the usability of its data, and customer satisfaction. These are measurable steps likely to lead to the desired but unmeasurable outcome:

1. Percentage of potentially active volcanoes monitored.
2. Number of urban areas for which detailed seismic hazard maps are completed.
3. The number of counties, or comparable jurisdictions, that have adopted improved building codes, land-use plans, emergency response plans, or other hazard mitigation measures based on USGS geological hazard information.

The third of these is the most interesting: the program attempts to assess the actual use that customers have made of its data. OMB has given the program a *moderately effective* rating.

Producers of statistics have a difficult time documenting their actual results, and so do agencies that make grants to support scientific research. Energy's Office of Science administers a program called Basic Energy Sciences. It provides grants to support energy research, the goal of which is to "expand the scientific foundations for new and improved energy technologies." Documenting that the research they fund is actually accomplishing its goal is difficult, since the impacts of research projects undertaken today may not be seen for years, and may not be predicted in advance. OMB's "Research & Development Investment Criteria" explicitly acknowledge the difficulties. The criteria require programs to demonstrate relevance, quality, and performance, but not outcomes. The Basic Energy Sciences examiner for OMB urged them to adopt Committees of Visitors (COVs), groups of distinguished scientists who are knowledgeable in the field and who come to the agency and review the funding decisions, an idea borrowed from the National Science Foundation. COVs review the proposals and assesses whether proper procedures have been followed in awarding grants; they ensure that the proposals being funded meet recognized standards of good research. They cannot assess the outcome of the research that is funded, but they can assure that the research meets high standards. The presumption is that if the correct procedure is followed in distributing grants, good science will result, and the aims of the program will be advanced. COVs are universally thought at the Office of Science to be a good tool. Associate directors have found COV feedback very helpful, and COVs have recommended changes that have been adopted. They have made criticisms that have been taken seriously.

Measures That Are Outputs for One Program, Yet Outcomes for Another

With some programs, there is no outcome that can be distinguished from an output. In the Overseas Buildings Operations Bureau (OBO) at State, the Capital Security Program is rebuilding more than 100 U.S. embassies. Many of the older U.S. embassies are located in urban areas where there is insufficient space to provide for adequate security. Thus the embassies are being relocated outside of city centers. In a sense, the desired outcome is enhanced security, which might be measured in terms of attacks against embassies, injuries to personnel, or damage to facilities. Instead the program has chosen to measure its success in the timeliness and cost-effectiveness of building new embassies. These are output measures, but important ones that are closely associated with the desired outcome of enhanced security.

1. Percent of capital security construction projects completed within the approved construction budget.
2. Percent of capital security construction projects completed within the schedule authorized in the construction contracts.
3. Number of new capital security construction projects awarded.

One can even argue that in a case like this, simply building new embassies that satisfy security requirements is the outcome desired. OMB has approved these measures and the program is rated *effective.*

Programs with Statutory Limitations on Measures

In nearly everything they do, public programs are limited by their authorizing statutes. Some programs are set up in a way that deliberately prevents them from focusing on end outcomes, and requires them instead to emphasize compliance with procedures. In a sense, such limitations can constitute serious design flaws because they prevent a program from accomplishing as much as it might, or accomplishing goals in efficient ways. But Congress often has reasons for designing programs as it does, and programs may make good political sense, even if from a rational policy standpoint they are less than optimal. Congress can be aware of these weaknesses but be uninterested in revising them, because the perceived flawed program design may address a particular political need. Should programs be held accountable to an end outcome measure if Congress has withheld the powers needed to accomplish the outcome? This is a difficult question. The position OMB has taken is that all programs must produce results. Design flaws are no excuse. This is a good position to take, since low program ratings can highlight design flaws and stimulate Congress to correct them. But it can be discouraging when a manager is held accountable for performance failures beyond her or his control.

The Federal Perkins Loans program is an example of a program that received a weak PART assessment (*ineffective*) because of design flaws. The Perkins Loans program provides loans to college students based on need. The design flaw is that its money is distributed through the intermediary of the school, and the aid formula gives more money to schools that have been in the program longer. Those colleges and universities obviously like this arrangement, but it does not allocate money to the students most in need. The critique in the PART report is serious:

> The program's institutional allocation formula (i.e., how much program funding is given to each school to offer Perkins aid) is designed to heavily benefit post-secondary institutions that have participated in Campus-Based programs for a long time, at the expense of more recent entrants or new applicants. Since these longstanding institutions do not have a higher proportion of needy students, this allocation formula tends to limit the program's ability to target resources to the neediest beneficiaries.

The obvious preference of OMB and Education is to eliminate the program, and shift its resources to other, better-targeted student loan programs. Congress, however, still funds the program. The Bush administration has asked for legislative changes to the program, but Congress has so far declined.

Medicare is another instance of a program that was graded down for having "design flaws." Medicare may have flaws, depending on how one sees its mission. Is its goal to provide quality health care to beneficiaries, or efficiently and fairly to administer a law as passed by Congress? If the former, Medicare has significant flaws; if the latter, it does not. PART for Medicare gives it a *no* on question 1.4, which asks whether a program is free of major design flaws. The discussion in PART describes the flaw that OMB sees in the program:

> Several features of the Medicare program reflect its outdated statutory design. For example, unlike most private health insurance, Medicare does not protect beneficiaries against high out-of-pocket costs—i.e., it does not provide cata-strophic protection. . . . Updating the statutory design will allow Medicare to better serve beneficiaries.

The design flaw stems from the original creation of Medicare as an entitlement program providing "social insurance." In the social insurance concept, beneficiaries "earn" their benefits by paying for them with "contributions," and consequently there is no means test. Because of this design feature, Medicare provides health insurance for many individuals who need no help buying insurance. And because all beneficiaries receive an equal benefit without any means testing, Medicare provides a fairly limited benefit, conspicuously omitting coverage for catastrophic illnesses, which in turn limits its ability to affect outcomes.

These are legitimate criticisms of Medicare, but the lack of catastrophic cover-age is not an oversight. In the 1980s Congress created a program to pay the cost of catastrophic illnesses, and then quickly killed it in the face of determined opposi-tion by the wealthier retirees who paid for the program. Good arguments can be made for restructuring Medicare. For example, an alternative program design that allocated more resources to the neediest beneficiaries could do more to improve health outcomes within existing budgetary constraints. But at present there is little interest either in Congress or in the administration to initiate a major redesign of

Medicare. Given that Medicare is stuck for the foreseeable future with its "flawed" design, it probably makes more sense to assess how well CMS implements the program as devised by Congress. In fact, the program performance measures for Medicare reflect the statutory limitations, and consequently assess intermediate rather than end outcomes:

1. Percent of Medicare beneficiaries receiving influenza vaccination; pneumococcal vaccination.
2. Percent of women who receive a biennial mammogram.
3. Percent of diabetic beneficiaries who receive diabetic eye exams.

In addition, the program has measures to assess efficiency and some outputs, but none to assess health insurance or overall health of beneficiaries. OMB has approved the measures and given the Medicare program a rating of *moderately effective*. If not for two "no's" on questions attributed to statutory problems, Medicare would have earned a grade of *effective*.

Some programs at the Environmental Protection Agency (EPA) have similar problems with design. Ideally, environmental programs should have goals that can be expressed as end outcomes, such as cleaner air or water. One can easily see the advantage of holding EPA accountable for end outcomes—for a program that has the goal of cleaning the nation's waters, it makes sense to assess how well they are doing by measuring water quality. Yet EPA points out the problems with holding them accountable for end outcomes. Many EPA programs have statutory designs that limit their authority to achieve their mission. Consequently, there are important sources of pollution that they cannot regulate. For example, EPA has no authority over local zoning and land use decisions, even though local decisions have an important impact on water pollution. These are limitations created by Congress, and unlikely to change.

End outcome measures are very useful, but they are not possible to devise or appropriate to use in all circumstances. In many cases OMB has exhibited more flexibility in approving measures than the PART guidance would suggest.

While there can be certain advantages in having flexibility in adopting measures, this comes at the cost of sacrificing the considerable advantages of outcome measures. Robert Shea, the OMB manager of the PART initiative, contends that this flexibility is actually a weakness in the implementation of PART. In the future he would like to see those programs that still have output measures push harder to find suitable outcome measures. This tension remains a considerable challenge for OMB and PART.

Challenge 4: Linking Performance to Outcomes

Once suitable outcome measures have been adopted, a challenge remains in knowing how to use them. One cannot attribute all blame and responsibility for changes in outcome measures to a program, as a recent story from the corporate world makes clear. On January 30, 2006, ExxonMobil announced that its annual profit for the prior year had been $36 billion, a record for U.S. companies, beating its own previous record by more than $10 billion. Judging by its end outcome measure of profitability, ExxonMobil was doing a wonderful job. However, informed observers of the oil business recognized that Exxon's immense profits did not necessarily reflect excellent performance by the company and its executives, since the profit was due mostly to causes beyond the control of company executives: high international oil prices and supply interruptions from Hurricane Katrina.

Outcome goals are considered better than output goals because they reward a program for producing results, not for just producing. But using outcome measures as an accountability tool may not be appropriate, because we cannot always attribute changes in outcome measures to the actions of a program. Outcomes are often a step or two removed from the outputs of the program, and have causes other than the program. Thus we do not always know whether movement in a measure, good or bad, is due to actions of the program or to external causes. This is the "attribution problem," knowing how much of a change in an outcome indicator can be attributed to actions of the program, and knowing how much control over an outcome it is reasonable to expect of a program. It cuts to the heart of performance measurement and performance budgeting. An important challenge in using outcome measures is being able to *hold programs accountable in the right degree* for their attainment of outcome measures.

A program at State that chose pure outcome measures highlights both the promise and the limits of using end outcome measures. Programs in the international affairs field often have extremely lofty goals that are difficult to influence or measure directly. Nonetheless, it still makes sense to try to assess impacts on outcomes, although the measures must be treated with caution. The SEED/ACE program in the European and Eurasian Bureau at State makes hundreds of grants in the countries of the former Soviet Union and Eastern bloc with the purpose of promoting democracy and increasing market orientation in the economies of the target countries. Developing measures of the success of the program was difficult because it makes literally hundreds of grants—grants dissimilar in nature, which cannot be assessed by any common benchmark. Staff explained that the first time they completed PART, they received a low rating. After that they went back and completely redid their measures, and adopted new measures that were audacious in the extent to which they assessed true end outcomes. To measure "democratization," they adopted the independent Freedom House's "freedom scores" for countries in which they gave grants. To measure market orientation they adopted other measures that were similarly ambitious—actual measures of market orientation in the economy. In adopting these measures they took real risks because these are variables over which they have some—but far from complete—control. Yet they did exactly what they should have and selected measures that assess the outcome the program is supposed to influence.

At the same time, the outcome measures are coupled with measures of outputs, organizational structure, effective coordination, and efficiency. The overall set of measures adopted seek to assess a balanced array of features of the program, from some over which the program has a great deal of control to others over which it has only loose control. This seems to be a sensible approach to assessing a program with such an immense aspiration.

With the outcome measures there is a problem of attribution—knowing how much of the change in the selected measures can actually be attributed to the work done by recipients of the program's grants. If the countries that receive grants become more democratic, is that because the grants are doing what they should, or is it because other forces were driving democratization in Eastern Europe? There is no way of telling, because there are no direct measures of the actual impact of the individual grants, and no measures of other causes of democratization. The same is true of the measure of economic change.

The OMB examiner who approved these measures understood that there would be problems of attribution. Not only could the program be given credit for improvements that they were not responsible for, the program could also be blamed for reverses of democratization that they could not have prevented. She asked the staff members of the program whether they were willing to be held accountable to those measures; they said they were. What is good about having such outcome-oriented measures is that they give the program all the right incentives. They have every reason to make grants that will really have an impact on the desired outcomes, and they will have an incentive to remove funding from programs that are not accomplishing anything useful.

But what if there are military coups that remove democratically elected governments from power, or if governments reverse market-oriented reforms? The examiner for the program indicated that if forces clearly beyond the control of the program had caused a decline in measures, it would not be reasonable to hold the program responsible. These measures must be interpreted within the context of other available information. This is an imperfect process, however, and it is possible that the program will be credited with successes it did not cause, or blamed for failures it could not prevent. Still, the use of end outcome measures keeps attention focused on the purposes the program was created to serve.

The Migration and Refugee Assistance—Protection program in the Bureau of Population, Refugees and Migration (PRM) at State has chosen as an outcome measure reductions in the number of refugees displaced across national borders in the world: "Percent reduction of long-standing global refugee population due to achievement of durable solutions." Their goal is to reduce the number of refugees by 25 percent by 2009. That is an end outcome measure in the purest sense, coupled with an ambitious target. This outcome measure is combined with a variety of measures of outputs and intermediate outcome measures. As outcome measures should, this will tend to keep the program focused on achieving desired results.

Activities of PRM programs tend to reduce the number of refugees, but many other causes contribute to the number of refugees. It would be unreasonable to conclude that PRM was failing in its mission if another war were to break out in the Balkans, increasing the number of refugees. But if the bureau cannot be held accountable for such increases in the number of refugees, it can be similarly difficult to know when it should be given credit for declines in the number of refugees. In the case of this program, as with the SEED program, examiners must evaluate evidence of results in the context of factors that might impact the outcome indicator.

Challenge 5: Interpretation Challenges of Attributing Program Performance to Outcomes

An important challenge for OMB examiners is knowing how to interpret and use outcome data. Performance budgeting has an appeal in that it appears to provide the information needed to make budget decisions. But on closer examination it is clear that outcome data, while important, are only part of the picture. Because outcomes are often several steps removed from the actual actions of a program, there is some question about the extent to which changes in outcome indicators are due to the program or to other causes. Following are examples of how attributing outcomes to program performance can be problematic:

Sorting Out Multiple Causes of Outcomes

Many outcomes sought by programs are subject to many separate causes. A program to reduce premature births might be doing a good job, but the results of a separate cause beyond its control, such as an epidemic of crack cocaine, might erase all of the program's accomplishments. If the program were not working, outcome indicators might look even worse. Program activities are but one factor moving the outcome indicator. Alternatively, causes apart from program activities might be improving the outcome, which might improperly credit the program with accomplishments it did not generate.

Accounting for Time Lags between Performance and Results

Some programs have measurable outcome goals but even when the program is doing what it should, there may be a long time lag between program activities and observable impacts. Research activities may produce benefits that are not seen for many years. The Superfund program of EPA cleans up toxic waste sites, and an important goal of this remediation process is to reduce groundwater pollution. But it may take years for groundwater quality to improve.

Having Limited Authority to Act

In some cases programs have, by law, too little authority to have a major impact on outcomes, or they labor under statutory design flaws. EPA is supposed to clean up the nation's water bodies, and while it has authority over certain kinds of contaminants and pollutants, it lacks the power to control others. For example, residential development has a major impact on water quality of the Chesapeake Bay, but EPA has no control over local zoning decisions. EPA actions stop some pollutants from entering the bay, but still overall water quality may decline (although not as fast as it would without EPA regulations in place).

When completing PART and devising measures to satisfy PART, program officials need to think hard and exercise creativity in devising the most outcome-oriented measures they can, but at the same time they need to be alert to the possibility that they can persuade their examiner that other kinds of measures are more appropriate.

In some cases it may be more straightforward to hold programs accountable for intermediate outcomes than for end outcomes. Intermediate outcomes are helpful because they (1) have a close relationship to the actual goal of a program and (2) are more readily under the control of a program. This is not to say that a quest for end outcome measures should be abandoned. They are important since they show whether a program is contributing to the solution of the problem it is intended to mitigate.

Interpretation of outcome measures will always require some judgment. Robert Shea of OMB says "there is no on-off switch" whereby a program either is or is not responsible for observed outcomes. "You can never make decisions solely on the basis of measures," he explains. "This is a framework for having a discussion about finding ways to make programs perform better." His is a sensible approach in dealing with end outcome measures. But this attitude undermines the goal of PART: to make budget decisions more results based.

Conclusions

OMB has succeeded in implementing an intelligent and effective system of performance budgeting, producing 800 assessments in four years, and will complete all federal programs in 2007. The preeminent strength of PART is the reasonableness of the questions. OMB has worked diligently to produce a set of questions that direct public managers to think carefully about important issues. Numerous observers have said that they found the questions to be good and sensible, and to focus attention on important aspects of public management. Answering the questions causes program managers to think in useful ways about how their program is designed and run, and produces results.

Further, there is reason to think that the program ratings are objective, and are able to be used to distinguish between effective and ineffective programs. A danger in any system of program assessment is that differences in the scores will not manifest true differences in program management and program quality, but instead will reflect differences in the skill of individuals in filling out the form or other similar irrelevant factors. It is difficult to assess the validity of PART scores—that is, whether they are measuring something real—because there is no other available external gauge that is known to be a reliable measure of program quality. In this sense, PART is a pioneering effort. However, this author's research and interviews indicate that PART ratings, even if not a perfect measure of program quality, measure real differences in programs. Senior career officials who had participated on the program side in multiple assessments generally believed that the programs that got the higher scores were in fact the better programs. Within bureaus, at least, assessments are ranking programs correctly, but that does not tell us whether comparisons across bureaus and across departments are also valid. Further, the analysts and programs managers interviewed by the author—virtually all careerists—almost uniformly believed that the exercise of completing PART was good for programs.

PART is notable for the emphasis it places on results and outcomes rather than on processes and outputs. However, it appears that some of the programs that have received effective scores do not have true outcome measures; instead, budget examiners for these programs have approved measures of outputs or processes. The decisions of the examiners in these cases seem reasonable, given the difficulty or inappropriateness of measuring outcomes in those particular cases. Just as people in state and local government often criticize the federal government's insistence on "one-size-fits-all solutions," a rigid insistence on the use of only outcome measures fails to take cognizance of the tremendous diversity of federal programs. Whenever possible, budget examiners should insist that programs develop outcome measures, but they should also recognize that for certain programs other measures are most appropriate. It appears likely, however, that OMB will continue prodding programs that do not yet have outcome measures to identify some.

Programs face an important choice in adopting measures. OMB has a strong preference for end outcome measures, and insofar as a program can identify measures that are acceptable to OMB, that can lead to a better score. If OMB signs off on the measures there is an immediate reward in that the program will escape the dreaded *results not demonstrated* category. Initially, OMB has required only that the measures have been identified and adopted, not that there necessarily be any data to plug into them. That comes later. The downside to adopting true outcome measures is that the program will be held accountable based on those measures; and if it cannot meet targets or demonstrate improvements in the measures, OMB may deem the program ineffective. The strategic dilemma is this: (1) By adopting a true outcome measure they can get a better score right now; but they must then be held accountable to that measure down the road. (2) Adopting a true outcome measure is a good idea if events are moving in the right direction, because then they may be credited with successes they did not cause. (3) If it is clear that failure to achieve an outcome goal is due to circumstances the program cannot possibly control, they may escape being held accountable. (4) Thus it is possible that a program can take credit for improvements it does not cause, but avoid blame for problems it cannot control. This is an ideal situation for the programs, but it does not promote transparency and accountability.

Like GPRA, PART focuses attention on outcomes and results, but it has not yet succeeded in bringing about significant changes in program management.

Improvements in ratings have come predominantly from learning better how to use the PART tool, not from introducing important changes in program design or management. Performance budgeting is intended to improve resource allocation by devoting budget increases to programs that perform well, but, by emphasizing results rather than process, performance budgeting is also intended to encourage programs to improve management and change the means by which they accomplish their goals. If managers find that existing processes do not allow them to achieve the desired results, they may rethink how the program operates. The officials interviewed for this report did not report that the improved ratings for their programs came from management changes.

The absence of major management changes should not be surprising at this point. PART has been in place for only a few years, and the kinds of management innovations that PART should ideally bring about will take years to emerge. Change will occur when programs find they cannot get good scores without changing. Further, the author mostly spoke with individuals in programs that got good scores, and these are the programs that have the least need to change. Assessing the success of PART as an incubator of management reform will take time and patience. This is difficult for OMB officials because they are understandably in a hurry to demonstrate that their efforts have generated successes. But producing useful assessments of 1,000 federal programs in five years will itself be a tremendous accomplishment.

Lessons Learned and Recommendations

The insights of this initial assessment of the OMB PART initiative can be summarized in a set of lessons learned and recommendations for both agency personnel who prepare the materials used by OMB in conducting their assessments and ratings, as well as for OMB itself.

Lessons for Departments and Agencies

1. Don't Give PART to the Intern

Answering the questions well and persuasively requires extensive knowledge of the program. Experienced staff need to be deeply involved in preparing the PART. There are cases of programs' giving the PART questionnaire to a low-ranking or new employee, or in one case of giving it to a consultant who was not deeply familiar with the program. Less certain is the question of who should do the PART in the department. In most cases it appears that the primary responsibility is given to an individual in a planning or budget office at the bureau level. In many programs that have been successful with PART, a fairly senior official has responsibility for PART. Typically they work closely with a more junior person. But whoever runs the PART, they need to be in close touch with people who know the program very well. In science-based programs, the scientists are typically involved in answering the questions. In addition, make sure the people doing the PART are good writers. PART is not a writing test, but a good writer can answer questions artfully and make a program look its best, and a bad writer can fail to communicate the performance of a good program.

2. Get Professional Help, If Needed

Staff at one program that received a weak rating on the PART recognized that they faced a major challenge in devising measures of results. They were convinced that the program was well run and well designed, but that documenting the accomplishments would be difficult. To solve this problem, the program rehired a former staffer of the program with extensive program evaluation experience, providing them with an individual with a unique and valuable combination of skills. Experts in program evaluation may be able to help a program explain what it does, and help devise measures OMB will approve.

3. Work with Your OMB Examiner

Individuals whose programs have raised their PART rating repeatedly emphasized the importance of working with their OMB examiner. In some cases the examiner came to the agency and spent the day with program personnel working on their performance measures. Involving examiners in the process of devising measures may increase their "buy-in" of the measures, and may also increase their understanding of why certain measures were adopted. Make friends with your budget examiner. Program officials with good ratings often praise their OMB examiner. They spend a lot of time educating their examiner, and the examiner can in turn help program staff with the task of articulating accomplishments.

4. Link PART to Your Strategic Plan

PART does not take place in a vacuum, detached from planning. Programs with strong strategic planning already in place have a better experience with PART. Strategic planning under GPRA prepares programs to answer the PART questions, and encourages program staff to think clearly about means-ends relationships. Individuals who have worked on successful PARTs stress the seamless connection between their strategic planning and PART efforts. PART is not a replacement for GPRA; PART is a natural extension of the planning process put in place by GPRA.

5. Read OMB's Guidance Carefully

OMB supplies detailed "guidance" for examiners that lays out the criteria a program must meet to get a "yes" answer to each question. Program officials need to pay very close attention to those criteria and address them exactly as they supply answers to the questions. Program officials should read the explanation supplied for each "no" answer and make sure that the examiner has justified it precisely in terms of the guidance. Some program officials have noticed that examiners have strayed from the guidance in justifying "no" answers, holding programs to higher standards. Make sure the examiner is holding a program to the exact criteria in the guidance, not another standard.

6. Provide Ample Documentation

OMB wants evidence to document answers, so programs should provide ample evidence. Programs that have successfully negotiated PART emphasize the importance of providing complete, voluminous documentation for all claims. That means thousands of pages of evidence to back up every claim made on the PART questionnaire. The point is not to inundate or intimidate an examiner with an ominously large stack of paper, but to anticipate questions the examiner might have. Examiners may not have time to read all of the documentation provided, but it is important that, if they look for something, they can find it. Thus it also makes sense that the documentation should be carefully organized and easy to navigate.

7. Measure What You Can

There is a lot of pressure for programs to adopt outcome measures, but it has been possible in some circumstances to gain approval for measures of outputs. PART guidance makes an exception for research and development programs. But other kinds of programs have been able to persuade an examiner that outcome measurement is impossible or inappropriate in their case. To see if this is possible, look at programs that have had output measures approved to see if their circumstance applies to you.

8. Understand OMB's Perspective

Individuals at the program level who are answering the PART questions should make sure that they are interpreting the questions the same way that OMB and their examiner are. Staff at one program that managed to raise their rating said they found that the examiner looked very differently at some of the questions than they did. The second time around they were better able to anticipate what the examiner wanted. If the OMB examiner does not like the measures a program proposes, it can be useful to look at other, similar programs elsewhere in the federal government that have had their measures approved. Perhaps it is possible to emulate or devise analogues to successful measures. In State, the Bureau of Resource Management serves as a central clearinghouse and helps program staff identify the kinds of measures that have been approved elsewhere at State. Figure out the kinds of measures that they like and emulate successful measures. Get to know your examiner. Spend time with your examiner. Get them to discuss measures in advance—get them to buy in.

9. Renegotiate the Definition of the Program

Many of the program definitions or demarcations are idiosyncratic at best. Defining programs in terms of budget accounts does not work in all cases. The Bureau of Population, Refugees and Migration initially defined programs in terms of international organizations to which they made contributions for refugee assistance—the UN High Commissioner for Refugees or the Red Cross. They have since decided to redefine the programs in terms of functions performed, such as "protection." In Interior, the Land and Water Conservation Fund—Land Acquisition Program got a bad score, at least in part because it is not a program but an "activity." In the first year of PART a large number of small programs in Health and Human Services were assessed; by the second year, many had disappeared, apparently merged with other programs that were assessed.

10. Express Measures in Nontechnical Language

An important goal of PART is transparency, but technically worded measures are opaque. Some examiners have technical backgrounds, but most do not. Nor do most members of Congress. Measures that ordinary people can understand are likely to meet a better reception at OMB and in Congress. It is important for government programs to document their accomplishments in ways that the people who pay for them—the taxpayers and legislators—can readily understand and appreciate.

Recommendations to OMB

1. Formally Introduce Appropriate Flexibility about What Constitutes Acceptable Measures

It is laudable that OMB has pressed diligently for outcome measures whenever possible. It is equally laudable that examiners have exercised discretion and allowed some programs to substitute other kinds of measures when appropriate. The PART guidance is not as clear as it should be, however, about the circumstances under which something other than outcome measures are acceptable. The guidance indicates that "Programs that cannot define a quantifiable outcome measure—such as programs that focus on process-oriented activities (e.g., data collection, administrative duties or survey work)—may adopt a "proxy" outcome measure." But in fact other kinds of programs have had output or intermediate outcome measures approved. It would be helpful to program-level staff and OMB examiners alike if they had clearer indications about when alternatives to end outcome measures are acceptable.

2. Provide Multiple Response Categories for Answers to PART Questions

While the questions are sensible, it is a problem that they must be answered with either a "yes" or a "no." Since the phenomena being assessed with the questions tend to be continuous variables, forcing the answers into two categories necessarily introduces error. The real answers to the question about clarity of program purpose must reside along a continuum stretching from, say, one to ten. Suppose OMB decides that scores of eight and above get a "yes," and those below get a "no." Such a system gives the same score to programs with a one and a seven, even though they are very different, and gives very different scores to programs with a seven and an eight, even though they are very close. The scores will not reflect reality as well as they might. Examiners report that they often have difficulty deciding how to answer a question, which means that there are a lot of close calls, and thus a lot of error. The solution is a simple one of allowing more response categories. Some of the questions in Section 4 permit a response of a "large extent" rather than just "yes" or "no." Permitting intermediate responses to all questions would yield more accurate assessments.

3. Distinguish between Design and Management Failures

There is no shortage of programs that fail because Congress has saddled them with a design that makes political sense, but that inhibits the ability of managers to produce good results. With PART, OMB is standing up to Congress and pointing out design problems, and insisting that all programs produce results. As OMB sees it, congressionally mandated bad design is no excuse. But it can be discouraging to agency program managers if their programs are designated *ineffective* or *results not demonstrated* because of a program design that Congress has foisted on them and that they cannot control. It would be useful if PART ratings made a distinction between (a) failures that are caused by a congressionally mandated program design, and (b) failures caused by poor program management. One could also add a third category—failures caused by unpredictable circumstances beyond the control of program managers, such as natural disasters, wars, or inadequate resources. The solutions to these problems are completely different. A manager who is doing a good job of running a flawed program needs recognition for his or her achievements, just as Congress needs to be continually reminded of the importance of eliminating statutory impediments to program effectiveness.

Note

This chapter, in much longer form, was originally released as a report in 2006 by the IBM Center for the Business of Government, which has granted us permission to revise and publish it.

References

Hatry, Harry. 1999. *Performance Measurement: Getting Results.* Washington, DC: Urban Institute Press.

———. 2001. "What Types of Performance Information Should be Tracked?" In *Quicker, Better, Cheaper,* ed. Dall Forsythe. Albany, NY: Rockefeller Institute Press.

Gilmour, John B., and David E. Lewis. 2006. "Assessing Performance Budgeting at OMB: The Influence of Politics, Performance, and Program Size." *Journal of Public Administration Research and Theory* 16: 169–86.

Government Accountability Office (GAO). 2004. *Performance Budgeting: Observations on the Use of OMB's Program Assessment Rating Tool for the Fiscal Year 2004 Budget.* Washington, DC: GAO, GAO-04-174.

Joyce, Philip G. 1999. In *Performance-Based Budgeting. Handbook of Government Budgeting,* ed. Roy T. Meyers. San Francisco: Jossey-Bass.

———. 2003. *Linking Performance and Government: Opportunities in the Federal Budget Process.* Washington, DC: IBM Center for the Business of Government.

Kettl, Donald. 2005. *The Global Public Management Revolution.* 2nd ed. Washington, DC: Brookings Institution.

Melkers, Julia E., and Katherine G. Willoughby. 1998. "State of the States." *Public Administration Review* 58: 66–73.

———. 2001. "Budgeters' View of State Performance-Budgeting Systems: Distinctions across Branches." *Public Administration Review* 61: 54–64.

———. 2004. *Staying the Course: The Use of Performance Measurement in State Governments.* Washington, DC: IBM Center for the Business of Government.

Romero, Simon, and Edmund L. Andrews. 2006. "At ExxonMobil, A Record Profit but No Fanfare." *New York Times,* January 31.

Schick, Allen. 2001. "Getting Performance Measures to Measure Up." In *Quicker, Better, Cheaper,* ed. Dall Forsythe. Albany, NY: Rockefeller Institute Press.

———. 1990. *The Capacity to Budget.* Washington: Urban Institute.

3

Linking Performance and Budgeting

Opportunities for Federal Executives

PHILIP G. JOYCE

Government reformers have been trying to increase the use of performance information in budget processes for more than fifty years. Why does this recurring reform have such currency? In short, because budget processes allocate scarce resources among competing purposes. Since taxpayer dollar resources are limited, understanding the effects of resources on the objectives of government action is important. In fact, the more scarce the resources, the more important it is that they be allocated wisely. In such an environment, it becomes even more vital that resource allocation decisions be focused primarily on the effectiveness of spending and tax policies.

Reporting of performance information in government budgets is nothing new. Governments have consistently reported performance information as a part of budget documents for many years. Unquestionably, the supply of performance information, at all levels of government, has increased over the past twenty years. There is less evidence of the *use* of performance information by these governments—that is, of performance information having widespread influence on government funding decisions. Increasing the influence of information on the results of government is a key duty of appointed and elected officials, who should be focused on achieving results.

In part, this chapter argues that lack of evidence of the use of performance information for budgeting occurs because observers have not looked in the right places. That is, the implicit assumption is that resource allocation is something that occurs only (or at least mostly) in the central budget office or in the legislature. This chapter shows leaders and managers how acting in accord with a more comprehensive definition of performance-informed budgeting can help them make a greater impact on decision making at all stages of the process—in the agency, in the Office of Management and Budget (OMB), and in Congress. Further, quality performance measurement can be the key to how appointed and career managers effectively achieve improved program results.

A Comprehensive Framework for Linking Performance and Budgeting

Past and current reforms have one thing in common: their attempt to more explicitly bring together performance information, on the one hand, and the budget process (and program management), on the other. Understanding what that really means, however, has been less than straightforward. Scholars, practitioners, and successive administrations have used many different terms to describe this desired linkage, including *performance budgeting, performance-based budgeting, results-based budgeting, performance funding,* and *budgeting for results* (Joyce and Tompkins 2002). Each of these has in common some desired linkage between the budget and performance, and the rejection of a budget process that focuses primarily on the use of inputs, the marginal change in inputs purchased (so-called "incremental budgeting"), or exclusively on the purchase of outputs. If the budget process is to become more effectively centered on the achievement of results, such a transformation from traditional budgeting involves simultaneously considering two factors in order to make budgeting more results focused. The first is the availability of appropriate information on strategic direction, results, and costs. The second is the actual use of that information to make decisions at each stage of the budgeting cycle.

How, given this situation, does a leader (of an agency or program) clearly articulate a strategy to incorporate better performance information into the budget process? First, we should recognize that the budget process does have clear (if not always smoothly functioning) stages (see Table 3.1).

If we recognize that traditional discussions of "performance-based budgeting" involve discussions of a portion of the first stage (decisions by OMB and the president) and the second stage (decisions by the Congress) a further articulation of the process permits us, at a minimum, to recognize that there is ample opportunity for asking questions about the availability and use of performance information at each of these stages, as follows:

1. To what extent are performance and cost information available for budget preparation and negotiations?

This itself implies three separate activities. First, public entities need to know what they are supposed to accomplish. That is, in order for any organization to evaluate either its performance or its use of resources in pursuit of that performance, it must first know what it intends to do. This is not an academic exercise; strategic planning establishes the context in which program leaders and managers can best use performance and cost information. Second, valid measures of performance need to exist. It is often hard to convince agency staff to be held accountable for outcomes; people find it much more comfortable to focus on outputs that are largely within their control. The challenge of a new leader is to get past that kind of thinking by defining outcomes in the context of all the factors that influence them, since the

Table 3.1

Stages of the Federal Budget Process

Stage of Budget Process	Key Actors Involved	Description of Activities	End Product
Budget Preparation—Agency	Agency budget offices; agency subunits, views of program managers	Agency prepares budget for submission to Office of Management and Budget	Budget request
Budget Preparation—OMB	Agency head, agency budget office, Office of Management and Budget, White House, president	Analysis of agency budget request on behalf of the president; negotiation with agencies and White House staff on budget allocation levels	President's budget
Budget Approval—Congress	Agencies, congressional committees, congressional leadership	Congress makes overall fiscal policy, authorizes programs, and appropriates funds	Budget resolution; authorization bills; appropriation bills
Budget Approval—President	President, agencies, Office of Management and Budget	Action on congressional legislation affecting budget	Negotiation, signature, or veto
Budget Execution	Agencies, Office of Management and Budget	Implementation of programs by federal agencies, and allocation of dollars by agency subunit	Administration of programs
Audit and Evaluation	Agency managers and evaluators (internal and external), OMB, GAO, and auditors (internal and external)	Review of tax and budget actions after the fact; recommendations for changes	Audits and evaluations; guidance for program redesign and improvement

goal is to achieve important results with scarce resources. Third, accurate measures of cost need to be developed. Connecting resources with results implies knowing how much it costs to deliver a given level of outcome. When a leader or manager discovers that his or her organization cannot accurately measure cost, it is crucial to develop better cost-measurement systems, or it will not be possible to know whether programs are successful or cost effective.

2. To what extent are performance and cost information actually used to make decisions about the allocation, management, or monitoring of resources at this stage of the process?

The message here is simple. Every agency leader and every agency manager could use performance and cost information to manage their programs, even if they did not receive those resources through a performance-informed process. If agency managers have timely and accurate data on cost and performance, they can use that information to direct and redirect resources and hold responsible staff accountable to achieving results.

There is no simple decision rule for relating cost and performance in the public sector, at least at a macro level. A simple, but incorrect, approach (allegedly embraced by some members of Congress) would be to take money from those who fail to meet performance targets, and give more money to those who meet targets. In fact, there are a great many reasons why programs may not meet their goals, including poor management, poor program design, or insufficient funds. When performance expectations are not met, it is important to ask why. If the program design is flawed and program management is bad, no amount of money will successfully solve these problems. If the program is conceptually strong with good management, then it may be that a mismatch between resources and expectations is the issue. In addition, budget decisions are appropriately influenced by other (non-performance) concerns, such as relative priorities, unmet needs, and equity concerns, to name three.

Beyond the conceptual underpinnings of the relationship, however, participants in the budget process must have incentives to use performance information. Good managers and leaders work to create these incentives, again by asking why agency employees are not using performance information to manage, and why policymakers are not using the information to allocate resources. In fact, the incentive question is probably the most important one to focus on in determining the possibility that performance information will actually be used as an input in the various stages of budget decision making.

The crucial leap in a more robust understanding of the role of performance information in the budget process involves looking at the whole process, from start to finish. The preoccupation with OMB and the Congress fails, however, to acknowledge the formal and informal use of discretion by program managers—which is also policymaking—that occurs in federal agencies. There are many possible decision points at which performance information can be incorporated by managers and agency leaders into the budget process. For example, agencies might make substantial use of performance information in building the budget (an effort that can pay dividends for resource management in budget execution), even if other actors (OMB and the Congress) make little or no use of that information at subsequent stages. Conversely, the absence of performance concerns in preparation and approval would not prevent a given agency from using its discretion to execute its budget by considering the effects of different execution strategies on its goals and objectives (i.e., applying outcome measures).

Potential Uses of Performance-Informed Budgeting in the Federal Budget Process

Budget Preparation

The budget preparation stage of the budget process is itself divided into two phases—the development of the request from the agency to OMB and the analysis of the request by OMB and the decision processes involved prior to transmittal of the budget by the president to the Congress. Performance information can be used during both of these portions of the process, either to maximize the effects of funding on performance, or to better justify the budget request as it goes forward to OMB or from the president to the Congress.

Developing the Agency Budget Request

As noted above, the budget preparation stage begins with the initial planning by the agency, which can start a year or more prior to the submission of the budget request to OMB. For large agencies, this process can entail a time-consuming internal process within the agency. Any cabinet department, for example, contains a great many subunits or bureaus. For federal agencies, the budget preparation stage is constrained by many factors, including political constraints imposed by interest groups and the Congress. Within those limitations, the budget request itself, and the information required to be included in the requests, is dictated by OMB Circular A-11, and particularly part 2 of that circular, entitled *Preparation and Submission of Budget Estimates.* Circular A-11 is a crucial agenda-setting tool for making the agency budget request focused on performance. While managers and leaders do not read A-11, they must tap the knowledge of their budget experts at the department, bureau, or other level.[1]

Making budget development more focused on performance requires that the agency budget office, through frequent interaction with agency leaders and program managers, develop some framework for budget requests that clarifies the relationship between costs and performance. Such a budget request made to the agency budget office would include the following characteristics:

1. A Strategic and Performance Context—At least since GPRA became fully effective, departments and bureaus are expected by law to have publicly articulated some strategic vision. This means that budget requests should be presented in the context of their effects on the strategic priorities of the agency, normally established in the strategic plans developed in light of the laws governing agency programs and administration direction.
2. Performance Information—Agencies should have output and outcome measures related to programs that are related to the larger strategic vision of the agency. They should have indicators of its success in meeting its objectives. These measures may be at several levels (output, intermediate outcome, final outcome) but ideally the agency, at all levels, could show a logical relationship between its various types of measures and its strategic objectives.
3. Cost Information—The budget request should identify the true cost of providing services, with costs charged to the appropriate bureau or program. This will not be possible without some relatively sophisticated means of allocating overhead or indirect costs. Administrative costs are now often accounted for separately, and not allocated to individual programs.

How can this information be used? First and foremost, it can be used to justify budget requests. Managers could ask a number of specific questions at this level:

- How well are my programs working to achieve their goals and objectives?
- How productive is my staff (productivity normally defined as the relationship of inputs to outputs), compared to past productivity or perhaps benchmarked against staff in some other agency or organization?
- What opportunities exist to contract out or competitively source particular services, in order to save money while maintaining or improving performance, understanding that contracting does not relieve the manager of ultimate responsibility for results?
- Does my organization have the right mix of skills (from staff or contractors) at the right place at the right time in order to maximize the achievement of performance goals?
- What are the effects of different levels of funding on the performance of the bureau, given key performance measures?

It is hard to overstate the importance of agency budget preparation to the overall effort to make the budget process more informed by performance. If the agency budget request, at all levels of the agency, has not laid the groundwork for relating funding to performance, it is highly unlikely that, as changes are made at higher levels (in OMB and the Congress, for example) the agency will be able to understand the performance implications of those changes. If these relationships are not well understood, agency managers and line employees may later find themselves managing "pots of money" without any clear understanding of how their actions can contribute to—or detract from—the overall performance of the agency. In the end, having appropriate performance and cost information can enable the agency head (and the agency budget office on behalf of the agency head) to analyze budget requests in the context of their performance implications, make tradeoffs in a way that maximizes performance, and build a better-justified budget request to OMB.

OMB Analysis of the Agency Budget Request

Once the agency submits the budget request to OMB, the president's budget office begins the difficult job of attempting to fit too many expenditure requests into too few revenues. That is, invariably the sum of agency requests far exceeds the total amount that can (or at least will) be included in the president's budget. This means that the process of arriving at a recommendation for each agency will involve, in most cases, attempts by OMB to reduce the agency's budget request to a number that will fit within the overall budget constraint.

The same performance, cost, and strategic planning information that is necessary at the agency level is also necessary for OMB's evaluation of the budget request, with one addition. Frequently only a limited number of resources are actually "in play" in a given budget. That is, those expenditures that are relatively "uncontrollable" (interest on the debt and most entitlement expenses) account for approximately 65 percent of the current federal budget. Most entitlement costs for current recipients are not a focus of the annual budget process, although presidents routinely propose, and Congress routinely enacts, changes that affect entitlement programs for future recipients. In addition, many benefits are provided through the tax code, by providing tax credits and other preferential treatment to encourage particular activities. Even for the remaining 35 percent of the budget, representing discretionary (appropriated) accounts, the process is not "zero-based;" that is, decisions are almost always being made "at the margin" (how much more and how much less will the agency receive compared to last year?). It is the decisions concerning how these marginal dollars are to be allocated that are most likely to be informed by performance considerations. Simply building a baseline budget that continues past programs without paying attention to the performance effects (past, present, and future) of funding runs the risk of freezing current priorities and policies in place, rather than continually evaluating expenditures to determine which mixture of policies will best achieve the president's aims.

Perhaps the greatest payoff to the use of better performance and cost information during this stage will come in the "conversation" between the agency and the OMB budget examiner(s). To the extent that cost and performance information are available, and brought together, the debate between the parties can truly focus on whether the level of funding requested is justified by the results that will be achieved, as opposed to being driven by anecdotal evidence. This may prove advantageous to agencies that can build a strong case for the performance effects of their programs. It may prove advantageous to OMB in cases where programs or agencies have continually received funding despite a general lack of evidence for the success of their programs.[2]

At higher levels, the president or the White House staff may make decisions concerning funding based on performance considerations, or based on other factors. Obviously, presidents have priorities, and presidential decisions take into account the policies and preferences of the administration. A program with excellent data on results and unmet need may not receive more resources and may even have its budget reduced if its purpose is not a high priority for the administration, if senior officers prefer a different approach, or if those resources are needed for another purpose. Conversely, a program with data showing poor results may nonetheless be important to the administration and need to be funded, hopefully with actions to improve it.

The Bush administration, building on the progress made in the Clinton administration in developing more performance information, has stressed the use of that information for decision making. This has manifested itself in the Program Assessment Rating Tool (PART) exercise and (perhaps most importantly) in the efforts made by federal agencies to negotiate performance budgets with the Congress. This represents the logical next step in performance-informed budgeting, and should continue with future administrations.

Budget Approval

Once the president's budget is transmitted to Congress, the budget approval stage begins. Budget approval is largely the province of the Congress, as it approves legislation that affects both taxes and spending. It does involve the president in the sense that he must approve the bills that are passed by the Congress prior to their becoming law, and the administration is heavily involved in negotiations with the Congress on legislation as it is being considered. How might the Congress make better use of performance information? In order to answer this question, one must focus on the various parts of the congressional process—the development of the budget resolution, the authorization process, and the appropriations process.

The Budget Resolution

The budget resolution lays out the "big picture" of fiscal and budget policy, and creates the overall framework for specific decisions on taxes and spending that must be made by congressional committees as the process goes forward. The budget resolution does not deal with the details of the budget, but rather creates a framework within which decisions on those details can be made by congressional committees. Budget resolutions, nonetheless, set the context for decisions at the agency or program level that occur in the authorization and appropriation processes.

The Authorization Process

The authorization process creates and extends programs, creates the terms and conditions under which they operate, and may create performance expectations for programs and agencies. This can include creating or making changes in *mandatory spending* programs—such as Social Security and Medicare (where funding is provided in continuing law), or making changes to laws governing the collection of revenues. Authorization bills often include direction concerning performance expectations, but frequently do not include any specific performance targets. In this context it might be very useful for federal agencies and programs if performance expectations were made clearer in authorizing legislation. This would assist agencies in developing priorities, since authorizing legislation involves reaching consensus between the Congress and the president. It would necessitate more frequent authorizations for some programs than has historically been the case, since meaningful performance expectations must be consistent with the views of the current Congress and the current president. The important point is that the authorization process is crucial to developing expectations about the performance of programs, and it is therefore the most logical place for performance information to gain a foothold into the congressional budget process. Program managers can influence congressional authorization action by working to incorporate performance goals in administration bills, making performance expectations part of the normal negotiations with Congress, and focusing the conversation on performance expectations in hearings and meetings with congressional staff.

The Appropriations Process

Those agencies and programs funded from discretionary appropriations have no legal authority to spend money without the appropriation of those funds. Thus, the appropriations process is an important (in many years, THE important) annual budgeting ritual. Critics of the appropriations process usually cite the following as among the limitations of this process, each of which is a criticism that some make of the executive branch process as well:

- the process is usually focused only on marginal decisions, rather than on the comprehensive effects of spending;
- there is little evidence that appropriations committees consider performance information in any systematic way when making decisions on allocations, relying instead on anecdotal information on program and agency performance; and
- members of Congress use the appropriations process, in part, as a vehicle to dole out money for "member priorities" (frequently referred to as "pork barrel projects"), sometimes at the expense of program or agency performance.

In addition, many appropriation accounts are not connected to programs or specific activities of the agency. Frequently the accounts are aggregate "salary and expense" items, which commingle several programs or activities into one relatively large account. This can make it difficult to tie the costs to specific programs, let alone to performance of particular programs.

How could performance and cost information be used in the appropriations process? First, accounts could be reorganized so that they tie more specifically to agency missions or programs. A reform of account structures might allow for a more transparent illumination of costs that are associated with programs, and could lay the groundwork for relating program costs to program performance. Changes in account structures are already being advocated by executive branch agencies, which have had some success in convincing the Congress to allow them to restructure accounts. For example, the U.S. Marshals Service completely restructured its accounts in the context of its fiscal year 2004 budget request (OMB 2003). Restructuring accounts, however, often requires managers and agency budget offices to engage in difficult negotiations with Congress.

Second, the appropriations committees could demand, and make better use of, performance information as a part of the appropriation process. To the extent that many members of Congress attempt to focus on pork barrel spending or on anecdotal information when making budget decisions, they may be less likely to demand information on the effects of overall spending. If such information became a normal part of the congressional debate, however, it is more likely that the effects of appropriation decisions on performance would become more transparent.

Third, the appropriations committees could consider agency budgets more comprehensively, reducing the number of cases where they are focused on changes at the margin. That is, they could relate program performance to cost at different funding levels, including the baseline level, as well as at levels that deviate from the baseline level (either positively or negatively). This would allow members of Congress to have a better idea of the performance tradeoffs inherent in providing different levels of funding to different agencies and programs.

What can federal executives do to make the congressional process more focused on performance? First, when authorization bills are considered, they can propose legislative language that makes clear the performance expectations associated with various programs. Further, they can get agreement on performance measures that will be used to gauge progress toward authorization goals. In the appropriations process, they can ensure that budget justifications focus not just on dollars, but on the performance that is being purchased for those dollars. By helping to put performance on the congressional agenda, executive branch leaders can enable clearer performance signals to be sent and can assist the Congress in making performance-informed choices.

Budget Execution

Without question, there are important potential applications of performance information in each of the preceding stages of the budget process. Even if none of these preceding applications have occurred, however, there are myriad ways in which federal agencies can use performance information for budget execution—that is, for implementing the budget after it has become law. Put simply, agencies have discretion. Agencies and their management need to "fill in the details" during the implementation (or budget execution) stage of the process (see Table 3.2). There are many specific ways in which performance information can be brought to bear on managing resources, including:

Understanding the Specific Implications of the Approved Budget for Performance

Once the budget is received, agency leaders and program managers can evaluate how all of the factors that affect results—such as funding, legislative factors, environmental or economic conditions, or regulations—would be expected to affect performance. Having done such an analysis, the agency can communicate the expected performance from the approved budget to agency staff and other interested parties. If the approved budget is different than the proposed budget, these expectations might be revised based on the budget as approved. As noted above, it is most likely that the performance expectations associated with the approved budget will be transparent if the performance implications of the budget were made clear at earlier stages, beginning with the development of the budget request from the lowest levels of the agency.

Using the Agency's Discretion to Allocate Funds within the Agency

The approved budget from the Congress normally leaves a significant amount of discretion in the hands of the agency to allocate resources. For many, this means allocating dollars toward different agency programs, or regional subunits, or both. In either of these cases, the agency can use information on the relationship between dollars and performance to attempt to maximize the level of performance that may be leveraged from a given budget. Several examples will illustrate this:

- The Food and Drug Administration restructured staff assignments in order to enable it to complete reviews of generic drugs in a more timely fashion.
- The Internal Revenue Service allocated training resources between its toll-free customer service centers based on needs as indicated by the error rates across the different centers.
- The Administration for Children and Families (ACF) often allocates Training and Technical Assistance funds and salaries and expense dollars to its different programs "based on program performance and needs."
- The Department of Agriculture's Animal and Plant Health Inspection Service's Fruit Fly Exclusion and Detection program uses outcome data to "allocate field personnel, vehicles, supplies, and other resources to . . . problem area(s)."

Table 3.2

Performance-Informed Budgeting in Budget Execution

Potential Information Sources	Potential Uses	Could Be Used By
• Agency- and government-wide strategic plans	• Understanding legislative and other constraints and their effects on the achievement of agency performance goals	Agency head: Allocating funds to agency subunits; communicates performance expectations
• Levels of funding (through apportionments and allotments)	• Allocating funds between agency missions, subunits, or regions/local offices	Program managers: Using flexibility to spend money in line with strategic priorities; communicates performance expectations
• Performance (outcome) measures	• Allocating funds to third parties	Individual employees: Managing funds/ spending money consistent with their contributions to strategic objectives
• Output (activity) measures	• Monitoring cost and performance during budget execution	Grant recipients: Purchasing goods and services with an eye toward overarching program goals
• Cost information		

- The Department of Housing and Urban Development uses outcome information, in part, to prioritize its use of resources for its Public and Indian Housing program, to prioritize site visits based on outcome information, and to use information on physical conditions of buildings to prioritize capital spending.
- In the Veterans Health Administration (VHA) funds are allocated to its twenty-two health care networks (or VISNs) based on the number of veterans being served, but performance information plays an important role in the allocation of resources to different hospitals, clinics, and offices within each VISN. VISN directors are held accountable for the achievement of outcome goals within their network, giving them incentives for maximizing performance partially by using their discretion to allocate dollars where they are most needed. GAO reviewed budget execution practices at two VISNs and found that "(i)ntegrating performance information into resource allocation decisions is apparent" in these networks (GAO 2002, 3).

This is by no means a comprehensive listing of performance-informed budget execution strategies by federal agencies. It has not examined in detail budget allocation practices at the lowest managerial levels of the organization—in an individual veterans hospital, or in a national park, or in a local immigration office. Clearly, the payoff for performance-informed budgeting also occurs at these lower levels as well. A hospital administrator can allocate staff between missions or between shifts based on the implications for veterans' health, or a national park superintendent can use resources in a way that best assists the National Park Service in achieving its customer service, conservation, and maintenance objectives.

Allocating Funds to Third Parties

Many third parties, including state and local governments (for example, in Medicaid) and private contractors (for example, defense contractors) play important and necessary roles in managing federal programs. Clearly performance information may be used by these agencies to attempt to allocate resources to these external parties in a way that can best leverage performance. Two specific uses are allocating and reducing funds to grant recipients, and deciding whether to contract or provide a service in-house, as well as monitoring the performance of contractors.

1. Allocating Funds to Grant Recipients. An inherent challenge of managing grant programs is that agencies with the grant funds do not directly control the behavior of the grant recipients. In the case of formula grants, performance considerations do not influence budget allocations during budget execution, but can influence the design of the program and the formula itself. For discretionary awards (so-called "project grants"), however, it is crucial that granting agencies are attentive to the performance implications of grants before the fact. A recent evaluation of three programs in the Department of Education unearthed a number of examples of this phenomenon; for example the Adult Education and Literacy Program used outcome data to determine which states would receive monetary incentive awards. State performance on adult education outcomes partially determines the amount of money each state receives.

Further, the Administration for Children and Families (ACF) uses an instrument, called the Grant Application and Budget Review Instrument (GABI) along with other information in order to assist them in identifying applicants that have unusually high administrative costs, teacher/classroom ratios, etc. This assists ACF in both monitoring existing grants and deciding on future grant funding.

2. Outsourcing Decisions and Contract Management. Federal agencies have contracted out a great many services since the beginning of the republic, and this outsourcing has increased in recent years (Light 1999). Among the services most frequently contracted out are information technology, maintenance services, weapons development, research and development, evaluation, food service, and specialized technical services (for example, legal services). Performance and cost information can be used in order to inform contracting decisions. Sometimes the stated justification for outsourcing is that outside vendors will be able to provide a service at a lower cost. These cost comparisons themselves can be difficult to make, given the state of many federal and private-sector accounting systems. Even if this problem can be overcome, however, a reasonable comparison of in-house versus contractual production of a good or service requires a good understanding of the performance implications of both options. Spending less money for worse performance is not necessarily a good deal; spending less money for the same or better performance, on the other hand, is a clear improvement.

Performance considerations also come into play in the contract management process. The initial contract can specify performance targets and milestones for the agency. Contract management around results (as opposed to technical contract compliance traditionally done by procurement offices) is one of the weaker aspects of federal management. New leaders should examine closely the skills of their contract managers and move quickly to upgrade or replace those who lack sufficient skills, lest resources be wasted and results not achieved.

Monitoring the Budget and Performance during Budget Execution

It is not only important for initial allocation decisions to be informed by performance. It is also crucial that personnel in the agency engage in constant communication about the relationship between resources and performance during the budget execution phase. Priorities change, as do factors that influence performance, during the budget year. The cost of items important to service delivery may change, as may environmental factors. The GAO highlights the importance of performance monitoring during budget execution so that "management has credible, up-to-date information for monitoring and decision making. Such monitoring should form the basis for decisions that address performance gaps by looking for root causes and, if necessary, adjusting funding allocations to rectify performance problems" (GAO 2002, 20).

Tracking costs during the fiscal year can itself have important implications for performance. If the costs of a given activity or program run substantially over or under projections, this can clearly affect performance. Further, for many programs productivity or cost measures are a significant component of performance measurement. GAO notes that the ability to account for direct and indirect costs necessitates an information system that permits total costs (direct and indirect) to be associated with program goals (GAO 2002, 23).

Audit and Evaluation

Finally, performance information can be used in important ways in the audit and evaluation stages of the process, during which federal programs will be reviewed to determine compliance with laws, management practices, and program performance. Theoretically, the results of the audit and evaluation stage should feed into the formulation of the budget during some subsequent fiscal year. This frequently occurs with a significant time lag, since by the time audit results are known from one fiscal year, the budget preparation phase may be under way for a fiscal year two (or more) years after the year to which the audit information applied. The Bush administration's initiatives share this focus, perhaps particularly manifested in the Program Assessment Rating Tool, which requires after-the-fact knowledge of performance and inputs in order to succeed.

What specific ways, then, can the audit and evaluation process be supportive of performance-informed budgeting?

- *Appropriate Estimations of Cost*—As noted above, understanding the connection between resources and results requires the appropriate measurement of each. Audits can assist by providing information on the status of cost accounting, and by making recommendations on further developments.
- *Reporting on Performance*—The performance reports that are required under GPRA are clearly themselves exemplary of a performance-informed audit and evaluation process. These reports, to the extent that they highlight gaps between expected and actual performance, can themselves be useful tools for future planning. Managers need to know that while OMB has exerted extreme pressure on agencies to have timely and accurate cost information, no such pressure has been exerted on agencies regarding performance information. Managers whose programs have not already done this on their own need to take the initiative here, lest their tenure be marked by inability to manage and report accurately on program performance.
- *Developing "Logic Models" Concerning the Relationship between Resources*

and Results—Understanding costs and understanding performance levels is not enough. A mature performance-informed budgeting system must be able to make connections between the two. Making connections between dollars and performance requires that we understand how the former affects the latter, meaning that the causal relationships between resources and results must be clearly understood. Since there are many other factors (besides the level of funding) that can affect performance, this is potentially a complex undertaking.

- *Highlighting Data Limitations and Problems*—Finally, audits and evaluations can present information that enables users of data to understand the limitations and problems associated with data that would be necessary to develop a mature performance-informed budgeting system. This can include problems with data reliability, timeliness of collection, timeliness of reporting, or failure to understand causal relationships.

In the end, any sophisticated performance-informed budgeting system requires the ability not only to specify performance before the fact, and use performance information in allocating resources at all stages of the process, but the ability to evaluate performance after the fact and make adjustments for the future accordingly. This necessitates an investment in evaluation capacity that has been lacking recently in federal agencies (Newcomer and Scheirer 2001). It also requires that these auditors and evaluators ask the right questions (see above) and that information included in these audits be provided to agency staff and leadership, OMB, and the Congress in a timely fashion.

Conclusions

The preceding discussion has illustrated that there are many potential uses of performance information in the federal budget process, and that there are numerous examples, particularly at the agency level, where such information is already being used. There are also significant gaps in our understanding of performance-informed budgeting, and filling these knowledge gaps can contribute to making the budget process, in all stages, more informed by performance. Substantial progress has been made in the federal government over the past decade in making performance information more widely available. The next step is to move toward the use of performance information at all stages of the budget process.

For federal managers, this means that there needs to be an understanding of the decisions that are made on a daily basis that affect agency performance, and how those decisions can be better informed by performance. Specifically, federal executives can link budgets and performance by:

- Ensuring that the budget preparation process at the agency level is focused on allocating future resources in the agency based on performance considerations;
- Helping to set the agenda for OMB and the Congress by providing performance

information as a part of the budget request to OMB, the authorization process, and budget justifications to congressional appropriations committees;

- Focusing on performance in all aspects of budget execution, including resource management, contracting, and performance monitoring; and
- Evaluating the extent to which programs are working to meet their stated objectives.

Notes

This chapter is a revision of a much longer report on the same topic prepared for the IBM Center for the Business of Government. The author wishes to thank the IBM Center, and particularly Mark Abramson, Jonathan Bruel, and John Kamensky, for support and previous comments. That paper, and therefore this chapter, also benefited from comments from Paul Posner, Barry White, and Rita Hilton. The full report, entitled *Linking Performance and Budgeting: Opportunities in the Federal Budget Process,* is available on the IBM Center's website, www.businessofgovernment.org/pdfs/Joyce_Report.pdf, accessed September 24, 2007.

1. For example, the FY2004 circular included requests for the following types of data: Information related to progress in implementing the President's Management Agenda, including the section focusing on budget and performance integration; evaluation of selected programs using the PART; the integration of the budget request with the annual GPRA performance plan, including the performance targets outlined in that plan (part 6 of the circular deals in its entirety with preparation of GPRA strategic plans, performance plans, and performance reports); a requirement that programs with similar goals report common performance measures that have been articulated by OMB; information indicating the unit cost of delivering various agency programs, reflecting "the full cost of producing a result including overhead and other indirect costs"; consistency with guidelines for performance-based investments, including those included in the Clinger-Cohen Act and the OMB *Capital Programming Guide* (which is included as part 7 of the circular); and a program evaluation schedule, including the issues to be addressed and the methodology to be employed. Further, the budget request should be informed by the "judgment of the agency head regarding the scope, content, performance and quality of programs and activities proposed to meet the agency's missions, goals and objectives."

2. The preceding discussion, of course, demonstrates an important point, which is that the introduction of more performance information into the budget process is not neutral. Clearly, there are also cases where agencies and OMB would prefer that the performance effects of funding are not known. In fact, there are probably relatively few places where both OMB and the agency would be equally enthusiastic about having more performance information brought into the budget process. To the extent that performance information is available and used uniformly, however, it is less likely to become simply a political tool.

References

General Accounting Office (GAO). 2002. *Managing for Results: Efforts to Strengthen the Link between Resources and Results at the Veterans Health Administration.* Washington, DC: GAO, GAO-03–10, December.

Joyce, Philip G., and Susan Tompkins. 2002. "Using Performance Information for Budgeting: Clarifying the Framework and Investigating Recent State Experience." In *Meeting the Challenges of Performance-Oriented Government,* eds. K. Newcomer, E. Jennings, C. Broom, and A. Lomax. Washington, DC: American Society for Public Administration.

Light, Paul C. 1999. *The True Size of Government.* Washington, DC: Brookings Institution.

Newcomer, Kathryn E., and Mary Ann Scheirer. 2001. *Using Evaluation to Support Performance Management: A Guide for Federal Executives.* Washington, DC: PriceWaterhouseCoopers, Endowment for the Business of Government, January.

Office of Management and Budget (OMB). 2003. "Budget and Performance Integration." *Budget of the United States Government, Analytical Perspectives, Fiscal Year 2004,* Chapter 1. Washington, DC: U.S. Government Printing Office.

4

PART and Performance Budgeting Effectiveness

LLOYD A. BLANCHARD

V.O. Key (1940) once asked, "on what basis shall we decide to allocate X funds for program A instead of program B?" If this question were presented to the average American, she might suggest that policy and program performance should direct budget allocations. She would realize that political power has its place, but she might prefer that it not dominate the budget process. If it were presented to the average federal employee, he might advocate incremental funding, with each program receiving a small increase or decrease each fiscal year depending on the policy and political exigencies of the day. Reasonable people can disagree about the bases on which to allocate public resources, but few would argue that performance be the sole basis for such allocation. In practice, budget decisions must to some degree consider both politics and performance. Therefore, this chapter asks, to what extent does performance serve as a basis for resource allocation in the federal government?

Most modern presidents, and Congress, accept the proposition that program performance should be considered in the budget process, without adhering to the fantasy of it replacing policy or political power as a dominant factor. It is now standard practice for newly elected presidents to initiate a management reform program to address what many describe as "waste, fraud, and abuse" in the federal government. Vice President Al Gore initiated the National Performance Review (NPR) for the Clinton administration, and the deputy director for management at the Office of Management and Budget (OMB), Clay Johnson, leads the President's Management Agenda (PMA) for the Bush administration. A cursory review of these two agendas reveals similarities in the focus of reform, suggesting a bipartisan consensus on the key management challenges facing the federal government.[1] A common theme—influenced most by Osborne and Gaebler's *Reinventing Government* (1992)—is to create federal agencies that run more like businesses, enhancing efficiency and effectiveness in program service delivery.

The PMA's Budget and Performance Integration (BPI) initiative highlights the Bush administration's effort to install performance as a rational basis for resource allocation, under the assumption that this would create incentives that lead to greater efficiency and effectiveness. The Performance Assessment Rating Tool (PART)—another administration innovation—is an assessment instrument used to establish whether agencies engage in the "best practices" of performance management, and serve as the fulcrum of the BPI effort. Thus, it is natural to ask whether the PART rating process has managed to facilitate this integration of performance and budgeting in the federal government. This chapter will examine this question, as well as others related to PART's effectiveness in promoting the consideration of performance in budgeting and—in a very preliminary way—in guiding steps to improve program performance.

Congress demonstrated its interest in performance budgeting with the passage of the landmark 1993 legislation, the Government Performance and Results Act (GPRA). This law formalized the requirements for agency strategic planning, which included the development of performance measures, performance plans, and accountability reporting. Although it did not require that budget proposals be linked to the performance measures being newly mandated, among the act's six stated purposes was to improve congressional decision making by providing more objective information on achieving statutory objectives, and on the relative effectiveness and efficiency of federal programs and spending. This statement clearly points to Congress's desire to use cost-based performance information for purposes of decision making. Moreover, GPRA explicitly authorized the director of OMB to designate "not less than five agencies as pilot projects for performance budgeting."[2]

Most observers agree that GPRA has created a wealth of performance information in the federal government, but question the extent to which such information is used meaningfully (Joyce 2005; Kamensky, Morales, and Abramson 2005; U.S. GAO 2005). According to U.S. GAO (2005), federal managers reported in three government-wide surveys (1997, 2001, and 2003) that although the government had "significantly more" performance information, the use of this information for program management had not changed significantly from 1997 to 2003. U.S. GAO (2005) suggests that two uses of performance information are to "develop strategy and allocate resources" and "recognize and reward performance." However, Hatry et al. (2003) find four obstacles that prevent federal managers from using performance information meaningfully: (1) lack of authority or interest in change; (2) limited understanding in using outcome data; (3) outcome data problems; and (4) fear of "rocking the boat." Thus, the adoption of performance budgeting faces both technical (2 and 3) and cultural (1 and 4) obstacles.

Despite its leadership in promoting performance budgeting by passing the GPRA, Congress may not follow President Bush's efforts to implement it government-wide. The most obvious reason is the need to direct resources to support national imperatives of war and homeland security that have dominated policy deliberations since September 11, 2001. According to the Congressional Budget Office (CBO 2006), the amount appropriated for these activities through FY2006 was $432 billion. Another reason is the growing deficit, which the CBO reported as having gone from a $128.2 billion surplus in FY2001 to a $412.1 billion deficit in FY2004, before coming down to $260 billion in FY2006. Finally, evidence shows that Congress has reached record levels in its infamous practice of doling out "pork." According to Citizens Against Government Waste (CAGW), a nonprofit organization that tracks such spending, Congress increased the number of pork projects included in the thirteen appropriations bills from 6,325 in FY2001 to 9,362 in FY2003 (a 48 percent increase), concomitantly increasing the costs from $18.4 to $22.5 billion (a 22 percent increase). In FY2006, CAGW counted 9,963 such projects costing $29 billion. It is certainly difficult to imagine performance-based appropriations being made in this budgetary environment.

Gruber (2003) reports that a senior staff assistant on an appropriations committee claimed at a summer 2003 conference that he had never heard of, let alone used, PART program assessments in his deliberations and that he had rarely heard fellow staffers discuss the tool. The staffer reportedly indicated that appropriators "ultimately rely on traditional tools" such as "thousands of pages of budget justifications" to make decisions. He suggested that OMB keep congressional appropriators "more informed about the assessments." Soon thereafter, the newly appointed government-wide leader on performance budgeting reform, and coeditor of this volume, Robert Shea, began an initiative to do just that. This chapter will examine whether or to what extent congressional appropriators have gotten the message and now use PART performance information to appropriate budget resources.

Studies to date on the budgetary impact of PART suggest that higher-scoring federal programs are being rewarded with larger budgetary increases (Gilmour and Lewis 2006; Olsen and Levy 2004; U.S. GAO 2004). This chapter reviews the evidence and seeks to determine the extent to which it is true for both budget proposals made by the president and the ultimate appropriations passed by Congress. This chapter updates these analyses, which only covered the first two PART cycles, by examining the budget proposal impacts in the four fiscal years since PART's creation (FY2004 to 2007), and by examining program appropriations impacts in three of these years (FY2004 to 2006). Finally, this chapter answers a broad set of questions related to PART's effectiveness in influencing program planning, management, results, and accountability.

Findings to be presented below are consistent with the conclusion that PART performance ratings have a statistically significant impact on budget outcomes. The evidence shows that, on average, higher-performing programs have been rewarded with larger approved funding increases by OMB and Congress alike, and that programs that do not demonstrate results have been punished for it. For example, in the president's budget submission for FY2007, OMB was estimated to have increased funding by an average of 5 percent—relative to the previous year's appropriation—for programs rated at least *moderately effective* relative to lower-rated programs. Moreover, in its FY2006 appropriations, Congress increased funding by 4 percent relative to the previous year for programs rated *moderately effective* relative to lower-rated programs. Finally, OMB and Congress are both found to hold programs accountable for not demonstrating results by reducing approved funding for that group by an average of 3.4 percent and 5 percent, respectively.

First, this chapter briefly describes PART and how PART helps integrate budgeting and performance. Second, it discusses the goals of performance budgeting, how GPRA contributed to its evolution, and the evidence on PART's contributions. Finally, it describes the data and methodology used in this study, followed by a presentation of the analytic results used to answer the following five questions:

1. How has PART influenced budget proposals and appropriations?
2. Does PART lead to program improvement, redesign, and reform?
3. Do strategic plans and use of performance information influence the management and performance of federal government programs?
4. Does performance budgeting enhance government accountability for results?
5. What has PART brought to the party?

Answers do not provide definitive proof of the effectiveness of PART, because they will derive from the analysis of very limited data. Ideally, an analyst would have measurements for the myriad political influences on the budget process, but this is quite a tall order. Nevertheless, the key results of this analysis are consistent with existing studies on PART's budgetary impact, and improve our understanding of how PART is being used and its prospects for improving performance management and budgeting in the federal government.

What Is PART?

OMB constructed PART as a straightforward questionnaire requiring only "yes" or "no" answers in order to create objective performance scores in four areas—Program Purpose and Design, Strategic Planning, Management, and Results. The questions—answered by OMB career examiners based on evidence supplied by the agencies—elicit whether program managers are engaging in certain "best practices" in the four areas above. According to OMB:

> PART is designed to provide a consistent approach to assessing and rating programs across the Federal government. . . . Responses must be evidence based and not rely on impressions or generalities. A Yes answer must be definite and reflect a high standard of performance.

First, with a 20 percent weight, the Program Purpose and Design component rates whether the program's purpose and design are "clear and sound" (U.S. OMB 2006, 11). Second, with a 10 percent weight, the Strategic Planning component rates whether the program has "valid long-term and annual measures and targets" (11). Third is the Management component of PART, weighted at 20 percent, which rates "program's management, including financial oversight and program improvement efforts" (12). Finally, with a 50 percent weight, the Results score rates program performance on "measures and targets reviewed in the strategic planning section and through other evaluations" (12). An accumulation of "yes" answers to the questions in each of these four sections results in a quantitative score from 0 to 100, and one can multiply these scores by the associated weight and take the sum of the weighted scores for the total (weighted) PART score.

PART scores have been given qualitative interpretations. An *effective* rating is awarded to programs with a total weighted score between 85 and 100 percent; a *moderately effective* rating is associated with a total score between 70 and 84 percent; an *adequate* rating is given for a score between 50 and 69 percent; and an *ineffective* rating is linked to scores of 49 percent and lower. A *results not demonstrated* rating is given to programs when they "do not have acceptable performance measures or lack baselines and performance data" (U.S. OMB 2006, 11).

Several versions of the PART exist to accommodate different programs:

1. Direct federal programs are where services are provided primarily by employees of the federal government.
2. Competitive grant programs provide funds to state, local, and tribal governments, organizations, and so on through a competitive process.
3. Block/formula grant programs provide funds to state, local, and tribal governments and others by formula or block grant.
4. Regulatory-based programs engage largely in rule making that implements, interprets, or prescribes law or policy, or describes procedure or practice requirements.
5. Capital assets and service acquisition programs develop and acquire capital assets (e.g., land, structures, equipment, and intellectual property) or purchase of services (e.g. maintenance, and information technology).
6. Credit programs provide support through loans, loan guarantees, and direct credit.
7. Research and development programs focus on knowledge creation or its application to the creation of systems, methods, materials, or technologies.

OMB incorporates PART assessments into the federal budget formulation process, and publishes them prominently on its website. Since the initiative was first rolled out with the FY2004 budget, OMB has produced four presidential budgets that feature PART performance assessments (FY2004 to FY2007), and Congress has passed appropriations for three years (FY2004 to FY2006). After reviewing the goals of performance budgeting, this chapter will turn to an analysis of PART's influence on program budget changes in the president's budget and appropriations by Congress in these years.

The Goal of Performance Budgeting

The goal of performance budgeting is to inject into a highly political process a more objective, rational, and economic basis for budgetary decision making (Rubin 1997). The concept of performance budgeting in the federal government first emerged with President Harry S. Truman's 1947 Commission on Organization of the Executive Branch of the Government, commonly referred to as the Hoover Commission. It was the first to recommend that budgets shift the focus away from the inputs of agency operations to their "functions, activities, costs, and accomplishments" (U.S. GAO 2005). While outcome-based performance measures and "managing for results" are associated with performance management and the real accomplishments of government programs, performance budgeting focuses on the link between the performance of government programs (whether measured by outputs or outcomes) and the resources they receive through the budget process. This focus on "costs" and "accomplishments" is not unique; it lies at the foundation of federal cost accounting principles.

If the primary budget strategy of public organizations is to enhance (if not maximize) their budgets, as Niskanen (1971) posited, then a mechanism is necessary to apply a counterbalancing downward pressure on the overall budget.[3] Moreover, because budget resource allocation may occur largely on an incremental basis, then it may be reasonable to target the annual budget change as the object of performance budgeting reform efforts.[4] Linking incremental budget rewards to performance has been thought to be a reasonable approach to counteract the bureaucratic behavior Niskanen identified.

The idea is that because there is no natural incentive to promote efficiency and effectiveness in government program service delivery, an incentive can be created by rewarding better-performing programs with larger increases in their budgets, and punishing poorer performers with smaller increases or decreases in budgetary allocations. This is a simple example; one can easily imagine variations on this basic incentive structure, like making the rewards contingent on the size of the program's budget or a particular aspect of performance such as program efficiency. Endowed with an unambiguous profit motive in the midst of competition, private-sector firms possess such a natural incentive, and seek to shed costs and innovate whenever feasible. On the other hand, democratic public organizations must respond to a multitude of demands from their executive leadership, congressional authorizing, appropriations, and oversight committees, and the various public constituencies and stakeholders they serve (Rainey 2003). Thus, motivation for public organizational action may be multifaceted, even contradictory, and will certainly lead to inefficiency in public service delivery, if not goal displacement (Gross and Etzioni 1985).

The Federal Accounting Standards Advisory Board (FASAB) effectively set performance-based managerial cost accounting standards for the federal government with paragraph 35 of its Statement #4, "Managerial Cost Accounting Concepts and Standards for the Federal Government," as follows:

> Measuring costs is an integral part of measuring performance in terms of efficiency and cost-effectiveness. Efficiency is measured by relating outputs to inputs. It is often expressed by the cost per unit of output. While effectiveness

in itself is measured by the outcome or the degree to which a predetermined objective is met, it is commonly combined with cost information to show "cost-effectiveness." Thus, the service efforts and accomplishments of a government entity can be evaluated with the following measures: (1) Measures of service efforts which include the costs of resources used to provide the services and non-financial measures; (2) Measures of accomplishments which are outputs (the quantity of services provided) and outcomes (the results of those services); and (3) Measures that relate efforts to accomplishments, such as cost per unit of output or cost-effectiveness.

While this statement does not speak to performance *budgeting* standards per se, its does speak to the managerial importance of linking costs and accomplishments, and includes as a primary goal congressional use of such information for allocating budget resources. It is in cost terms that budgeting takes place, and budget choices that would be informed by an ideal performance budgeting process would have considered strongly the relative efficiency and cost-effectiveness of government programs. However, this assumes that the outputs, outcomes, and costs are properly measured; and this lies at the heart of the technical challenges identified by Hatry et al. (2003) and listed above. These technical challenges have also plagued the effectiveness of GPRA in promoting performance budgeting.

GPRA and Performance Budgeting

The most significant law in the United States related to performance budgeting is GPRA, which established federal requirements for strategic planning and performance accountability reporting. While GPRA mandated including performance indicators in budget requests, and despite its intent to use such program performance information to inform budgetary and policy deliberations, it fell short of requiring programs to demonstrate how varying levels of budget resources would accomplish varying levels of performance (U.S. GAO 2000). In its first status report on GPRA, U.S. GAO (1999) found that thirty of the thirty-five agencies whose performance plans were reviewed provided some discussion of the relationship between program activities and performance goals. However, only fourteen agencies translated this relationship into budgetary terms, showing how funding would be used to achieve performance goals. By 2002, twenty-three of the thirty-two agencies reviewed were able to translate links between program activities and performance into budgetary terms (U.S. GAO 2002, 10). However, according to GAO, the nature of the linkages between performance and the requests varied considerably.

A large literature addresses the merits of this legislation, with much of it skeptical that GPRA's goals will be fully realized in the crucible of the U.S. political system.[5] McNab and Melese (2003) offer three criteria by which one might consider GPRA successful. The first is to institutionalize a framework to build consensus on objectives. The second is that resources are linked to results. The third is to change the traditional system of budgeting. Radin's (2000) critique expands on the consensus-building obstacles by suggesting that GPRA's underlying assumptions do not fit with the three key attributes of the federal decision-making process, which are: (1) the institutional structure of fragmented decision making; (2) the imperatives of conflicting functions of budgeting; and (3) political dynamics. To Radin, GPRA's assumptions are too narrow or simple to adequately represent the complexity of decision making within a U.S.-style democratic system of governance, leading her to conclude that "GPRA has failed to significantly influence substantive policy and budgetary processes." To the extent that GPRA influenced the creation of PART, however, this judgment may have been premature.

PART: The Next Generation

Three studies examine the influence of the PART performance measures on the budget proposals submitted by the president. U.S. GAO (2004) examined 196 discretionary programs (of a total of 204 that were "PARTed" for FY2004), and found that eight of the ten programs rated *effective* received budget allocation increases from FY2003. Seventy-five percent of the forty-four programs rated *moderately effective* received budget increases, while 55 percent of the twenty-nine programs rated *adequate* and eight of the twelve programs rated *ineffective* received budget decreases. While these results would suggest that performance budgeting is at work, 54 percent of the programs rated *results not demonstrated* also received budget increases, undermining the apparent reward structure just posited. After accounting for program size, GAO found that the positive total PART score impact on budget changes for small programs ($93 million and less) was three times the impact for medium-sized programs ($93 million to $600 million), and six times the impact for large programs (those of more than $600 million). However, GAO did not control for other agency, program, policy, and political factors that might explain the proposed budget increases.

Olsen and Levy (2004) exclude mandatory programs and outlier programs with large budget changes in a similar analysis of one-year and two-year changes (FY2003 to 2004 and FY2003 to 2005) and find similar evidence. In general, they find positive—2.4 and 4.3 percentage point—impacts on funding associated with each 1 percent increase in the total quantitative PART scores for one- and two-year changes, respectively. They also find a positive—8.2 percentage point—one-year impact for small programs (same criteria as GAO above), and a positive—1.1 percentage point—impact for large programs. However, Olsen and Levy control only for program type and agency, making no attempt to control for policy or political influences.

Gilmour and Lewis (forthcoming) model the budget proposal changes from FY2003 to FY2004 to be a function of historical, performance, and political factors. To measure history, they rely on the well-known incremental theory of budgeting that says that the best predictor of next year's budget is this year's budget. They use the total quantitative PART score to measure performance; and for politics, they use variables distinguishing whether agencies are favored by Democrats or Republicans based on the policy focus of each over the past ten years. After also controlling for program type and department fixed effects, they find that a 10 percentage point higher PART score is associated with an extra 1.2 percentage point budget change relative to the previous year.

Perhaps not surprisingly, they found politics to have the most dominant influence, with programs "housed in Democratic departments" receiving an average 12 percentage point lower proposed funding level compared to other programs. However, when they analyze the data under the assumption that OMB might impose some political influence by making performance and budgeting decisions simultaneously, they find that the performance-funding link disappears. This analysis is performed using a well-known two-stage method that models budget changes as a function of PART scores in one equation, and models PART scores as a function of budget changes in a second equation.[6] This procedure requires separate instrumental variables correlated with the PART scores but not correlated with budget changes. Gilmour and Lewis argue (with due caveats) that programs administered by political appointees, commissions, and managers with fixed terms serve as acceptable instrumental variables. However, while they claim that these variables have no significant bivariate relationship with budget changes, the two-stage results are not convincing without the instruments' having a closer conceptual relation with program performance and formal specification tests having been performed.[7]

While each successive study builds on the previous one by controlling for more potential alternative explanations for the observed PART performance–budget proposal link, none (other than the unconvincing two-stage results) are able to explain away the statistically significant impact of the PART indicators. Moreover, neither of these studies examines the performance-appropriation link. Now that four budgets have been proposed and three have been passed since PART implementation, we have more data with which to study its impact. This chapter turns next to the task of examining how PART performance information impacts the key budgetary outcomes, both on the executive side during budget formulation and on the legislative side during budget approval.

Estimating the Impact of PART

This study uses publicly available PART data available from OMB's website to examine whether PART has a funding impact. Two difficulties exist in performing such an analysis, both related to the challenges of properly specifying the estimation model. First, the analyst must adequately control for alternative explanations of the observed changes in funding. While he might find a simple correlation between PART scores and funding, this correlation could result if PART were correlated with some other factor, like congressional advocacy savvy in the budget process, and this factor was not accounted for in the estimation model. The second difficulty is properly modeling the budget process itself.

The first challenge is addressed by following the previous studies, particularly Gilmour and Lewis, and controlling for the size of the program, previous fiscal year's funding change, program type, home department, and political factors, while limiting this sample of programs to those with funding changes less than 50 percent. The analysis below adds to the set of alternative explanatory variables a policy variable to capture budget changes associated with the fight against terrorism. It employs the sample limiting strategy as a control for policy choices, as funding changes larger than 50 percent likely point to "big," that is, non-incremental, policy decisions about the program, not as likely to be performance based. While decisions about programs receiving changes smaller than 50 percent also may be driven by factors other than performance, this sampling strategy balances a focus on smaller and therefore more normal decisions against the need to sustain a healthy sample of programs. The second challenge is addressed by formally testing whether the assumption of simultaneity between performance and funding in the budget formulation process is warranted.

U.S. GAO (2004) and Olsen and Levy (2004) exclude mandatory programs from their samples, but here they are included. It becomes increasingly difficult to accurately identify these programs among the growing list of PARTed programs, now up to 800 or so. The original rationale behind this selection procedure was that performance incentives would only be directed to discretionary programs, with non-discretionary program funding presumably determined only by formula. However, for some non-discretionary programs aggregate targets are set in a discretionary fashion, with the formula used only for the distribution of funding among program recipients. Performance enhancements can be implemented by linking awards to the aggregate budget amount and avoid being included in the formula. Moreover, policy choices made annually about whether to propose statutory changes in mandatory programs can be based on PART scores and other performance considerations and thus affect estimated future funding.

This selection procedure brings the sample of FY2004 programs to 177, 76 percent of the programs PARTed for that year's budget; 255 programs, or 64 percent of the programs PARTed for FY2005; 390 programs, or 64 percent of the programs PARTed for FY2006; and 680 programs, or 85 percent of those PARTed for FY2007. The dependent variable is the percent change in programs' budgets—whether through budget proposal by OMB or congressional appropriation—from the previous fiscal year's appropriation. The performance variables that are the focus of this analysis include three versions of the PART performance scores: (1) the quantitative Results score; (2) the qualitative *moderately effective* rating, which is based on the total weighted PART score; and (3) the qualitative *effective* rating, which is also based on the total weighted PART score. While other studies focused on the total quantitative PART score, program performance is most closely measured by the Results component of PART, and the two qualitative versions above adequately capture aspects of the total quantitative score. Secondary analyses using less-rigorous methods will examine relationships among

Table 4.1

Summary of Data

Fiscal year	2004	2005	2006	2007
Number of programs	146	255	390	680
Dependent variables				
% budget proposal change	4.5	0.97	−0.09	−0.01
% appropriation change	10.5	8.7	2.4	−2.0
Performance variables				
Results score	44.7	48.1	47.7	49.5
% rated at least moderately effective	32.2	40.8	43.1	47.6
% rated effective	6.2	12.9	15.6	16.6
Program type				
% Block programs	15.7	15.3	14.9	14.8
% Competitive programs	12.3	11.8	14.4	14.3
% Credit programs	1.4	2.0	2.8	3.4
% Regulatory programs	6.2	9.0	7.2	8.4
% Capital programs	18.5	10.6	10.0	9.1
% Research & development programs	8.2	11.0	11.0	8.8
Home Department				
% in Commerce Dept.	5.5	5.1	4.3	3.8
% in Education Dept.	7.5	7.5	7.9	7.2
% in Energy Dept.	13.0	10.2	7.4	6.0
% in HHS	11.0	11.8	12.3	11.0
% in HUD	2.7	2.7	2.8	2.8
% in Labor	4.1	5.1	4.6	3.7
% in Interior	7.5	9.4	9.0	9.0
% in Treasury	3.4	4.7	4.4	4.0
% in Transportation	2.7	2.7	3.3	3.2
Size, policy, and political variables				
% said to be favored by Democrats	31.5	32.2	33.8	30.7
% in major fight against terrorism	19.2	16.9	17.7	21.2
% with budgets below $100 million	24.0	28.2	36.2	40.4
% with budgets above $1 billion	33.0	27.1	23.6	21.0
% in Commerce-Justice-State appropriations committee	10.3	11.0	10.0	10.5
% in Energy-Water appropriations committee	15.1	12.2	10.3	8.5
% in Transportation, Treasury, etc. appropriations committee	12.3	14.1	13.6	13.1

other PART components, Program Purpose and Design, Strategic Planning, and Management, as well as Results.

As mentioned above, the models below include controls for program type, size, policy, and politics. To control for the possibility that different program types systematically face more or less funding changes from year to year, the models below include indicators for whether a program was a credit program, mixed, or a regulatory program.[8] To control for the fixed impacts of home departments, the models above include indicators for nine of the cabinet departments (shown in Table 4.1).

Small programs are designated as those with budgets below $100 million, and large programs are those with budgets totaling $1 billion or more. The key policy control is a program indicator for being in a department instrumental in fighting the war on terrorism. These include the PARTed programs within the Departments of Defense, State, Homeland Security, Justice, and Transportation. The "Democratic department" political variable used here is defined slightly differently than in Gilmour and Lewis. The associated variable in this analysis excludes Energy programs, so this variable indicates PARTed programs in Housing and Urban Development, Education, Labor, Health and Human Services, and the Environmental Protection Agency. Finally, the models below further attempt to control for political influences by including indicators for programs based on selected appropriations subcommittees from which their funding is authorized. They include the Commerce-Justice-State, Energy-Water, and Transportation-Treasury-Judiciary appropriations subcommittees.[9]

Table 4.1 presents the summary statistics for these variables. The data reveal an average 4.5 percent increase in program appropriations from FY2003 to 2004, and a 1 percent increase from FY2004 to FY2005. The FY2006 and FY2007 proposals essentially remained flat on average. Table 4.1 also shows that while average program performance scores increased from 45 to 50 percent over three years, the proportion of programs rated *moderately effective* or better increased by half, from 32 to 48 percent. Although the data comprise programs from a fairly balanced mix of home departments, nearly one-half of the sampled programs are capital programs (19 percent), block grant programs (16 percent), or competitive grant programs (12 percent). About one-third are indicated as being in a "Democratic department," and around one-fifth are associated with fighting the war on terrorism. The small programs become better represented in later years; therefore larger programs become a smaller proportion. Programs that received funding from the three selected appropriations subcommittees make up about one-third of the programs included.

Has PART Been Effective?

This section presents analytic results for the associated questions serving as subheadings. Table 4.2 presents preliminary results for the main question about performance budgeting. Tables 4.3 and 4.4 present results from the regression analyses of budget proposals and appropriations, respectively, on PART performance measures. Figures 4.1 through 4.3 are designed to show the relationships relevant to questions about program design, planning, and management. Table 4.5 presents the results used to answer the questions related to PART's impact on accountability.

How Has PART Influenced Budget Proposals and Appropriations?

Table 4.2 presents preliminary evidence on the relationship between program performance and funding. PART Results scores are divided into four groups delineating

Table 4.2

Relationship between Results and Budget Proposals and Appropriations

Fiscal year	2004		2005		2006		2007	
Number of programs	146		255		390		680	
Percent change in budget proposals								
Results in 1st quartile	−0.4	(36)	−1.3	(58)	−2.7	(94)	−3.1	(174)
Results in 2nd quartile	2.9	(34)	−.47	(68)	−1.6	(114)	−0.05	(168)
Results in 3rd quartile	7.5	(52)	5.1	(67)	3.6	(89)	0.19	(167)
Results in 4th quartile	6.2	(24)	0.18	(62)	0.9	(93)	3.0	(171)
Percent change in appropriations								
Results in 1st quartile	4.0	(38)	−1.4	(66)	−2.6	(99)	—	
Results in 2nd quartile	4.4	(38)	6.5	(53)	1.0	(72)	—	
Results in 3rd quartile	2.8	(48)	6.7	(57)	5.6	(65)	—	
Results in 4th quartile	5.0	(131)	0.48	(188)	2.0	(338)	—	

Note: For each performance group and fiscal year, reported are the mean percent changes in budget proposals and appropriations, with the number of programs in parentheses.

low to high performance, and average program budget proposals (top panel) and average program appropriations (bottom panel) are shown for each group. Programs with the lowest performance scores (in the first quartile) averaged budget reductions from OMB in each of the four fiscal years of PART's existence. This pattern is also found with the other programs performing at below-average levels (in the second quartile), except in the initial year of the PART initiative. Programs scoring just above average performance (in the third quartile) faced average increases up to 6 percent in their approved budget proposals. This suggests that OMB is allocating budget resources at least partially based on program performance.

The bottom panel of Table 4.2 suggests that Congress is easing its way into performance-based funding using the PART performance regime. For FY2004, there is no evidence that Congress engaged in such, as the lowest-performing programs (in the first and second quartiles) averaged almost as great an increase in appropriations as the highest-performing ones (in the fourth quartile). Those programs performing just above the average (in the third quartile) appear to receive the smallest budget increases. For FY2005 and FY2006, the lowest performers received an average reduction in appropriations, with the others receiving average increases. By FY2006, the largest increases (5.6 percent) accrued to programs performing just above average, with those performing just below average and at the highest levels receiving 1 and 2 percent increases, respectively.

These preliminary results certainly support the hypothesis that OMB is rewarding high-performing programs and punishing low performers through the budget process. Congress appears at first glance slower to do so. Nevertheless, many other factors may explain these outcomes. Change in policy and the political environment

Table 4.3

Estimated Results Effect on Percent Change in Budget Proposal

Fiscal year	2004	2005	2006	2007
Number of programs	146	255	389	680
Model 1: Results effect	0.09*	0.6	0.08***	0.08***
(with no controls)	(0.05)	(0.04)	(0.03)	(0.02)
	1.6	0.6	1.5	2.3
Model 2: Results effect	0.10*	0.07*	0.09***	0.09***
(with full controls)	(0.05)	(0.04)	(0.03)	(0.02)
	5.1	7.9	11.4	6.3
Model 3: Effect from being rated at least	3.5	4.1**	4.2***	4.9***
moderately effective (with full controls)	(2.8)	(2.2)	(1.8)	(1.1)
	3.7	8.0	11.0	7.0
Model 4: Effect from being rated	−1.2	1.6	0.80	3.3**
effective (with full controls)	(5.3)	(3.1)	(2.4)	(1.5)
	2.4	6.7	9.7	4.9

Note: For each model and fiscal year, reported are the performance effect estimate, standard error (in parentheses), and the adjusted R-square statistic indicating the proportion of the variation in funding change explained by the model.

*** denotes statistical significance at 1 percent level (i.e., 1 percent chance that estimate is due to chance or error);

** at 5 percent level;

* at 10 percent level.

are the most obvious. Thus, a set of regression analyses is performed to control for these and other factors that might explain observed changes in budget proposals and appropriations. Table 4.3 presents these results for the president's budget proposals from FY2004 to FY2007, and Table 4.4 presents them for program appropriations from FY2004 to FY2006.

The first row of Table 4.3 presents the estimates from baseline regressions (with no additional controls) of budget proposal changes on PART Results scores. The dependent variable for FY2004 is the percent change from FY2003 appropriations to FY2004 budget proposals; for FY2005, it is the percent change from FY2004 appropriations to FY2005 budget proposals; and so on. The estimates from Model 1 suggest that for FY2004, 2006, and 2007, there was a statistically significant performance effect on the president's budget proposals, although the FY2004 results are significant only at the 10 percent level. The 0.08 estimates for FY2006 and 2007 suggest that a 1 percentage point change in the PART Results score leads to a 0.08 percentage point change in the budget proposal (from the last appropriation). In other words, a 10 percentage point change in performance is estimated to lead to just less than a 1 percentage point increase in OMB-approved funding. Moreover, performance appears to explain about 1.5 to 2.3 percent of the variation in funding changes.

Table 4.4

Estimated Results Effect on Percent Change in Program Appropriation

Fiscal year	2004	2005	2006	2007
Number of observations	151	249	418	
Model 1: Results effect (no controls)	−0.003	0.03	0.10***	
	(0.05)	(0.03)	(0.02)	—
	0.0	0.0	4.4	
Model 2: Results effect (full controls)	−0.004	0.002	0.11***	
	(0.05)	(0.4)	(0.03)	—
	6.5	3.9	7.1	
Model 3: Effect from being rated at least	−0.55	−0.54	4.2***	
moderately effective (full controls)	(2.7)	(2.0)	(1.3)	—
	6.5	3.9	5.5	
Model 4: Effect from being rated effective	2.3	−4.4	3.0*	
(full controls)	(4.9)	(3.0)	(1.8)	—
	6.6	4.8	3.9	

Note: For each model and fiscal year, reported are the performance effect estimate, standard error (in parentheses), and the adjusted R-square statistic indicating the proportion of the variation in funding change explained by the model.

*** denotes statistical significance at 1 percent level (i.e., 1 percent chance that estimate is due to chance or error);

** at 5 percent level;

* at 10 percent level.

The estimates from Model 2 show that this conclusion is not altered even after accounting for last year's budget change, program type, budget size, selected home departments, whether the home department has a substantial role in the fight against terrorism, and the political variables. About 5 to 11 percent of the variation in funding changes could be explained by Model 2, and this suggests our limited ability to fully model a political policy process for quantitative analysis of budgetary changes. Nevertheless, this modest explanatory power is expected.[10]

The previous two models use the quantitative PART Results score to predict the budget outcome. While the strength of the relationship has been demonstrated, it is not likely that OMB analysts consistently use performance-based algorithms—whether implicitly or explicitly—to guide their recommendations. They are more likely to look at gross qualitative distinctions as indicated by the associated PART ratings to distinguish high- from low-performing programs. Thus, Model 3 examines the effect of being rated at least *moderately effective* (which is based on the total PART score, not just the Results component) on budget proposal changes. With the additional controls (from Model 2), Model 3's estimates show that OMB has been rewarding programs rated at this level, with increases that start from an average 4.1 percent in FY2005 to 5 percent in FY2007. Model 4 estimates show that OMB rewarded programs rated *effective* in the FY2007 budget with a 3.3 percent increase relative to programs rated at other levels. This evidence further suggests that OMB has followed through on its commitment to link budgets to performance, rewarding higher-performing programs relative to others.

Table 4.4 presents estimates of the PART impact on congressional appropriations, with the first row presenting the baseline results (with no additional controls). The dependent variable is the change in program appropriations for the last three fiscal years for which data are available. The estimates from Model 1 suggest that only in FY2006 did Congress begin linking funding to the PART Results scores, with the magnitude of the effect being very close to the OMB proposal effect. In other words, a 10 percentage point change in performance is estimated to lead to a 1 percentage point increase in congressionally approved funding. Also, about 4.4 percent of the variation in appropriation changes can be attributed to differences in performance.

The estimates from Model 2, which include the additional controls, suggest that this conclusion is robust after accounting for alternative explanations. When we consider those programs being rated at least *moderately effective* in Model 3, Congress is found to increase program appropriations by an average of 4.2 percentage points relative to lower-performing programs. Those rated *effective* are estimated to receive a 3 percentage point increase relative to lower performers, but this result is only statistically significant at the 10 percent level. Given that no significant effect was found in FY2004 or FY2005, these findings suggest that Congress got off to a slow start in using PART ratings but eventually caught on.

Estimates in Tables 4.3 and 4.4 show that performance budgeting is being practiced both by OMB and by Congress in similar ways. An additional set of analyses was performed to investigate the claim by U.S. GAO (2004) and others that performance budgeting allocations seem to be targeted to smaller programs. To accomplish this, Models 2 and 3 were run on small and large programs separately. Estimates are not shown for brevity, but key results are reported.

For programs with budgets of less than $100 million, a 10 percentage point change in performance leads to a 1.5 and 1.2 percentage point change in budget proposals for FY2006 and FY2007, respectively. This performance effect is twice the magnitude for large programs, with budgets totaling $1 billion or more in budget resources, although the latter result is statistically significant at the 10 percent level. Smaller programs rated at least *moderately effective* in FY2007 were found to receive a 7.8 percent increase relative to larger programs. This estimate is almost 3 percentage points higher than for all programs, suggesting that performance budgeting practices may well be targeted to small programs.

For congressional appropriations in FY2006, a similar differential effect is found between small and large programs. While small programs receive on average 1.5 percentage points more in appropriations, relative to other programs, for a 10 percentage point higher performance score, large programs were not found to receive any performance awards. Moreover, small programs are found to receive 7.2 percentage point increases, on average, in appropriations for rating at *moderately effective* or higher. These results confirm those from previous studies that perfor-

Figure 4.1   **Program Design Trend by Performance Quartile**

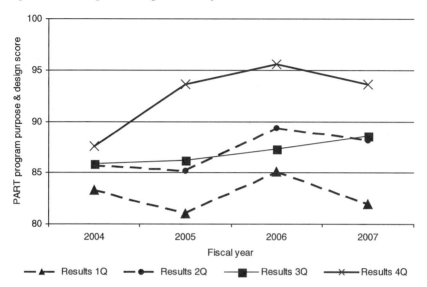

mance budgeting allocations may be contingent on the size of the budget, with both OMB and Congress showing reluctance to pad the budgets of large programs even if they do perform well.

Does PART Lead to Program Improvement, Redesign, and Reform?

Rather than simply reducing funding, another possible administration or appropriator response to poor performance would be to sustain funding while proposing program reforms to strengthen performance. While there is no way with limited data to carefully evaluate whether the implementation of PART led to programmatic reform, the PART score's Program Purpose and Design component may have changed since implementation, and the extent of this change may vary by performance. Figure 4.1 summarizes this trend, with each line representing programs in a performance quartile. The dotted lines represent the two low-performance quartiles, and the solid lines represent the two high-performance quartiles. The relationship between performance and programmatic reform is represented by the extent to which the lines are separated from one another vertically.

Figure 4.1 shows first that Program Purpose and Design scores did not change much over this interval except for the highest-performing programs. The highest-performing programs increased substantially in the second and third years after PART implementation, before slipping in FY2007. The two lower-performing program groups exhibited an up-and-down pattern in design score, while the second-highest-performing group increased its scores on average, slightly and steadily.

Figure 4.2   **Management Trend by Planning Quartile**

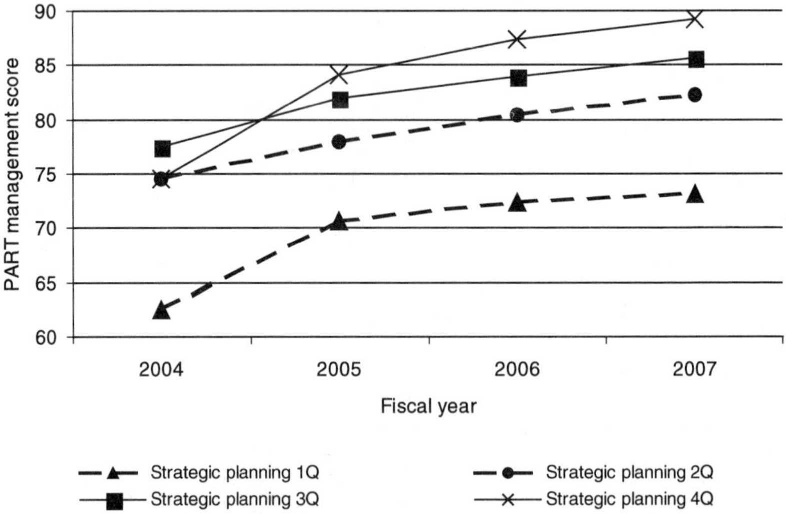

While there are plenty of alternative explanations that go unexplored here, the pattern of results in Figure 4.1 shows that higher-performing programs appear to engage in successful program design changes more than lower-performing ones do, suggesting a correlation between program design and performance. However, the downturn in three of the four performance groups suggests that program design improvements may have hit a natural ceiling in FY2006. Thus, the relationship between program design and performance scores appears to be one where the highest-performing programs seem to improve program design more effectively.

Does Strategic Planning Influence the Management and Performance of Government Programs?

This is also an area where the data are not up to the task of offering a convincing explanation. Nevertheless, the influence of planning on management and results is a question that points directly to the effectiveness of GPRA in laying a performance budgeting foundation. Figure 4.2 shows how the PART Management scores changed by planning quartile, while Figure 4.3 shows how PART Results changed by planning quartiles.

Figure 4.2 shows a relatively stark relationship between planning and management. While programs at all levels of planning show reasonably steady increases in management proficiency in the years following PART implementation, programs in the lowest planning quartile have far lower management scores than the other low-

Figure 4.3   **Performance Trend by Planning Quartile**

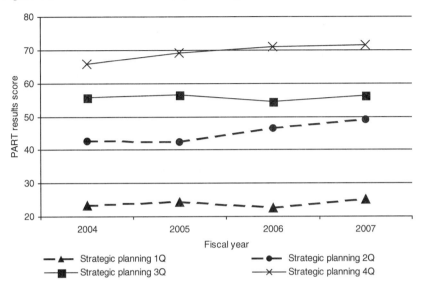

performing program group. Programs in the lowest planning quartile score from 7 to 9 percentage points lower than the next-lowest group, suggesting a low planning threshold before management improves significantly. That is, the relatively tight grouping of the top three quartiles being separated from the bottom one suggests that management improvements may be linked to planning proficiency only at the most basic levels of planning. Any bit of planning seems to raise management proficiency considerably. Thus, planning improvements may not require extraordinary efforts and resources to reap benefits in management improvements.

Figure 4.3 shows a similar pattern in the relationship between planning and performance, but more pronounced and linear (lines are more evenly separated vertically) than between planning and management. Programs at every level of planning do not display strong increases in performance over time, but the best planning programs outperform the second best by 10 to 15 points, and outperform the worst planners by 40 to 45 points. Programs in the lowest planning quartile are found to suffer in performance even relative to programs in the other below-average performance group; with the first quartile group scoring 20 to 25 points lower than programs in the second quartile group. Similar to the relationship between planning and management, these patterns suggest that there is some threshold of planning proficiency (again around the 25th percentile) below which performance really suffers. However, beyond this threshold, performance gains appear to grow substantially with each successive jump in planning quality. Thus, Congress may have gotten it right with GPRA and its emphasis on strategic planning being an important component to enhancing government performance.

These simple illustrations of the relationship between planning and management and between planning and performance are not nearly conclusive in what they suggest. However, the suggestion that improved quality of planning leads to improved management and results is an intuitive one and precisely the theory behind the intent of GPRA. What these illustrations begin to show is the particular nature of these relationships. While management improvements after PART implementation have grown steadily, only planning improvements for the worst planners reap substantial gains in management. Planning improvements for all other levels of planning proficiency reap small gains in management. On the other hand, while performance improvements appear hard to come by over time, substantial performance gains appear to come with improved planning at all levels. These patterns suggest a clear relationship between planning and management on the one hand, and planning and performance on the other. Further research is required on this question to draw a definitive link. Nevertheless, the intent of GPRA is supported by this preliminary evidence.

Does Performance Budgeting Enhance Government Accountability for Results?

To answer this question, we must first define what we mean by "accountability," as it could mean different things to different people. For some, it simply means providing transparency on government activities so the citizens can hold its elected officials accountable (positively or negatively) at election time. "Being held accountable" could mean losing one's job, or being put on notice, but most people seem to use it (rightly or wrongly) to refer to some consequence for falling short of expectations.

As the GAO recently changed its name to have the "A" stand for "Accountability" instead of "Accounting," we might glean this meaning from U.S. Comptroller General David Walker's 2004 published statement entitled, "GAO Answers the Question: What's in a Name?"[11] Walker uses the word *accountability* or *accountable* in three different contexts. First, it is linked to ensuring "truth and transparency in government operations" in referring to the "accountability failures" à la WorldCom and Enron. In its second use it is linked to results, in the sense of holding both GAO itself and the rest of government accountable. In explaining how it will lead by example in holding itself accountable, Walker explicitly linked GAO's performance with the resources it had been given, arguing that GAO had produced a "$78 return on every dollar invested." In the third context, similar to the second, he states that the first priority of his agency is "to improve the performance of the federal government and ensure its accountability to Congress and the American people." Whatever accountability means, the government's chief accountability officer clearly places it within the context of performance and the associated resources expended.

What happens when adequate performance and cost measures are not available? How is a program or manager held accountable in this situation? The evidence

Table 4.5

Estimated Accountability Effects for Not Demonstrating Results

Fiscal year	2004	2005	2006	2007
Number of programs	146	255	390	680
Model 1: Budget proposal effect of not	−3.2	−4.9***	−3.9**	−3.2***
demonstrating results (no controls)	(2.4)	(2.1)	(1.9)	(1.3)
	0.6	1.9	0.9	0.8
Model 2: Budget proposal effect of not	−3.6	−4.7**	−3.4**	−3.4***
demonstrating results (full controls)	(2.8)	(2.2)	(1.9)	(1.3)
	3.7	8.4	10.4	5.2
Model 3: Appropriation effect of not	0.28	−2.0	−4.6***	
demonstrating results (no controls)	(2.4)	(1.9)	(1.4)	—
	0.0	0.1	2.5	
Model 4: Appropriation effect of not	1.0	−0.72	−5.1***	
demonstrating results (full controls)	(2.7)	(2.1)	(1.5)	—
	6.7	4.0	6.0	

Note: For each model and fiscal year, reported are the performance effect estimate, standard error (in parentheses), and the adjusted R-square statistic indicating the proportion of the variation in funding change explained by the model.

*** denotes statistical significance at 1 percent level (i.e., 1 percent chance that estimate is due to chance or error);

** at 5 percent level;

* at 10 percent level.

presented thus far makes a reasonably strong case that OMB and Congress reward high PART performance with larger funding increases. This can be considered the positive side of an accountability regime that attempts to use "carrots and sticks" to create a performance incentive. Evidence of the "stick," or the negative side of accountability, is also revealed in this analysis. Table 4.5 presents estimates of the budgetary effect from programs' being rated *results not demonstrated*. It shows that even with the additional controls for alternative explanatory factors, OMB and Congress punish programs that cannot demonstrate results by reducing their approved funding levels.

In the FY2005 budget, OMB punished such programs with an average 5 percent reduction, and including full controls does little to diminish this apparent "stick" effect. The estimates for FY2006 and FY2007 show that, holding other factors constant, OMB reduces such budgets by 3.4 percentage points. For FY2006, Congress was tougher, punishing programs not demonstrating results with an average 5 percentage point reduction in appropriations, controlling for other factors. If accountability for results means to link that which is most important to agencies, funding, to performance to create an incentive for improvement, PART appears to do just that on the negative and positive side of accountability, using both stick and carrot.

What Has PART Brought to the Party?

In McMurtry's (2005) review of the recent performance budgeting developments, she pointed to Robert Shea's statement imploring agencies to communicate more closely with congressional staffers, particularly appropriators, showing how the PART process can be beneficial to them. She concluded with the following statement: "Such guidance to the agencies from OMB arguably may lead to increased congressional awareness of the potential utility of performance information in budget deliberations." The evidence presented in this chapter suggests that she is right. It shows that OMB began practicing performance budgeting in earnest by the FY2005 budget, which was in its formulation stage in the summer and fall of 2003, when Gruber (2003) reports appropriator ignorance of the PART. The administration responded by issuing the guidance referenced above; and by FY2006, we observe a statistically significant link between PART performance indicators and congressional appropriations. This suggests indeed that Congress "got on board" with the president in performance budgeting.

This evidence strongly suggests that PART has reinvigorated the movement toward performance budgeting. The vast amount of performance information mandated by GPRA is certainly useful to congressional staffers in understanding how programs are performing, but it provides little basis for comparing the disparate performance measures across government programs for budget allocation decision making. What is needed is a performance regime that maintains a consistent basis of measurement for the purposes of comparing many government programs. For example, a performance score of 75 percent has to mean the same thing for NASA's Space Shuttle program, SBA's business loan program, and the AmeriCorp community service program alike. PART provides such a consistent performance measurement regime and the results from this analysis show that it has a significant impact on budget allocation decisions in the executive and legislative branches of government.

Conclusion

This chapter has examined the influence of the PART performance scores and ratings on budget outcomes, and found reasonably strong evidence that performance budgeting is being practiced in the ways intended. That is, the evidence shows that higher-performing programs are being rewarded with larger approved funding increases by OMB and Congress alike; and that programs that do not demonstrate results are being punished for it. In the president's budget proposals for FY2007, OMB is found to increase funding by nearly 1 percentage point for each 10 percentage point increase in the PART Results score. Moreover, programs rated at least *moderately effective* received a 5 percentage point bump in funding, holding other factors constant. In its FY2006 appropriations, Congress also increased funding by nearly 1 percentage point for every 10 percentage point increase in the PART

Results score. Congress rewarded programs rated at least *moderately effective* with a 4.2 percentage point bump in funding. Moreover, both OMB and Congress are found to hold programs accountable for not demonstrating results by reducing approved funding by 3.4 and 5.1 percent, respectively.

These findings clearly suggest that Congress is responding to the Bush administration's initiative to link budget outcomes to performance via the PART performance indicators. The initial concern among agency officials with respect to PART was that OMB would use it to justify its own decisions regarding budget outcomes. This would require OMB to make budget allocations prior to or simultaneous with setting PART performance scores. A final analysis tests this hypothesis, and no evidence is found to support it.[12]

It took the failure of GPRA to provide a consistent means of measuring performance to chart the path for PART to follow. PART's simple and consistent design, with all its warts and critics, seems to have become a useful means to compare government programs in two branches of government. We might expect to find this use in the executive branch, where OMB has long looked for ways to install a more rational basis for decision making. Congress's following suit suggests either that they are being loyal to their leader and approving requests with few changes, or that they find PART performance information useful and are acting on its evaluations in the ways we might expect, or both.

This simple tool seems to pack a more powerful punch than many expected. The consistently observed relationship between performance and funding suggests the utility of PART as a performance budgeting tool. OMB and Congress may well have been practicing performance budgeting all along. We just didn't have the consistent performance measurement regime to tell that before PART.

Federal agencies now have an answer to the question often issued in hushed tones: "why should we give OMB the rope they will use to hang us?" Based on the above analysis, the answer is "because OMB and Congress will hang you if you don't." Performance budgeting is alive and well in the federal government, and PART helped make it happen. It is not dominating decision making by any means; but clear, statistically significant patterns consistent with performance budgeting can be found in the data. The larger question now is whether such performance allocations can lead to improved effectiveness and efficiency in government operations across the board.

Notes

The author is grateful to Jessica Lee and Jesse Olczak for their research assistance.

1. The five PMA initiatives are: Strategic Management of Human Capital, Competitive Sourcing, Improved Financial Management, Expanded Electronic Government, and Budget and Performance Integration.

2. The implementation of the mandated performance budgeting pilots was delayed by OMB director Franklin Raines, and there is little evidence that they were taken up in the "pilot" form. Congressional testimony by Paul Posner, GAO director of budget issues, on July 1, 1999, reveals the challenges and reasons behind this delay. These challenges and the

spirit of the mandated pilots were addressed in the standards set by the PMA's BPI initiative and with the implementation of PART.

3. Blais and Dion's (1990) review of the empirical evidence provides qualified support for the Niskanen hypothesis, qualified largely on the basis that the evidence shows budget "enhancing" not "maximizing" behavior.

4. For empirical evidence in support of the hypothesis, see Davis, Dempster, and Wildavsky (1966). See also Reddick (2002), who found support for this hypothesis only at aggregate spending levels for the United States, Canada, and England. See Berry (1990) for a critique of the "incrementalism" literature.

5. While most of this literature was produced by the GAO and the Congressional Research Service, GPRA-focused studies by scholars include McNab and Melese (2003), Radin (2000), and Joyce (2005).

6. This method is two-stage least squares (2SLS) with PART scores being treated as endogenous to budget changes (i.e., they occur simultaneously). If this condition exists, then estimates of the PART effect will be biased using traditional multivariate analytic methods like ordinary least squares (OLS).

7. The analysis formally tests the hypothesis of simultaneity, and supports the conclusion that none existed in the data. Thus, Gilmour and Lewis's significant OLS estimates showing that a 10 percentage point increase in the total PART score leads to an extra 1.2 percent budget increase may well be their best ones.

8. Most indicators are "dummy" variables with a value of one indicating the presence of the factor, and a value of zero indicating the absence.

9. There is no conceptual reason for selecting these three subcommittees. The effort is simply to control variations in funding that result from fixed differences between these powerful subcommittees relative to the others.

10. U.S. GAO's (2004) analysis of PART score effects produced similarly small R-squares, from 3 to 15 percent. Gilmour and Lewis' (forthcoming) analysis produced R-squares up to 27 percent, but both these analyses focus only on FY2004, with only 196 or so programs.

11. This statement was published in *Roll Call* on July 19, 2004. The new name became effective on July 7, 2004.

12. This analysis uses the well-known Hausman specification test to test the null hypothesis that the OLS and 2SLS procedures would produce estimates with no systematic differences. This essentially tests the simultaneity assumption, with it being rejected if the Hausman test statistic cannot reject the null hypothesis. In each fiscal year, the null hypothesis could not be rejected, leading to the conclusion that the PART performance scores for each fiscal year are indeed exogenous and determined before funding. This means that OLS is an appropriate method for estimating the PART performance effects.

References

Berry, William D. 1990. "The Confusing Case of Budgetary Incrementalism: Too Many Meanings for a Single Concept." *Journal of Politics* 52: 167–96.

Blais, Andre, and Stephane Dion. 1990. "Are Bureaucrats Budget Maximizers? The Niskanen Model & Its Critics." *Polity* 22(4): 655–74.

Congressional Budget Office. 2006. *The President's Budget Proposals for FY2007.* Washington: Congressional Budget Office.

Davis, Otto A., M.A. Dempster, and A. Wildavsky. 1966. "A Theory of the Budgetary Process." *American Political Science Review* 60: 529–47.

Gilmour, John B., and David E. Lewis. 2006. "Does Performance Budgeting Work? An Examination of OMB's PART Scores." *Public Administration Review* 66(5): 742–52.

Gross, Edward, and Amitai Etzioni. 1985. *Organizations in Society.* Englewood Cliffs, NJ: Prentice-Hall.

Gruber, Amelia. 2003. "OMB to Brief Appropriators about Program Ratings." *Government Executive Magazine,* July 2.

Hatry, Harry, Elaine Morley, Shelli Rossman, and Joseph Wholey. 2003. "How Federal Programs Use Outcome Information: Opportunities for Federal Managers." In *Managing for Results,* eds. John M. Kamensky and Albert Morales. Washington, DC: IBM Center for the Business of Government.

Joyce, Philip G. 2005. "Linking Performance and Budgeting: Opportunities in the Federal Budget Process." In *Managing for Results,* eds. John M. Kamensky and Albert Morales. Washington, DC: IBM Center for the Business of Government.

Kamensky, John M., Albert Morales, and Mark Abramson. 2005. "Useful Measures to Measures Used." In *Managing for Results,* eds. John M. Kamensky and Albert Morales. Washington, DC: IBM Center for the Business of Government.

Key, V. O. 1940. "The Lack of a Budgetary Theory." *The American Political Science Review* 34(6): 1137–44.

McMurtry, Virginia. 2005. *Performance Management and Budgeting in the Federal Government.* Washington, DC: Congressional Research Service.

McNab, Robert M., and Francois Melese. 2003. "Implementing the GPRA: Examining the Prospects for Performance Budgeting in the Federal Government." *Public Budgeting and Finance* (Summer): 73–95.

Niskanen, William A. 1971. *Bureaucracy and Representative Government.* New York: Rand-McNally.

Norcross, Eileen C. 2005. "An Analysis of the Office of Management and Budget's Program Assessment Rating Tool (PART)." Working paper, Accountability Project, Mercatus Center, George Mason University.

Olsen, Robert, and Dan Levy. 2004. "Program Performance and the President's Budget: Do OMB's PART Scores Really Matter?" Working paper presented at the Annual Meeting of the Association for Public Policy Analysis and Management, October.

Osborne, David, and Theodore Gaebler. 1992. *Reinventing Government.* New York: Addison-Wesley.

Radin, Beryl A. 2000. "The Government Performance and Results Act and the Tradition of Federal Management Reform: Square Pegs in Round Holes?" *Journal of Public Administration Research and Theory* 10(1): 111–35.

Rainey, Hal G. 2003. *Understanding and Managing Public Organizations.* 3rd ed. San Francisco: Jossey-Bass.

Reddick, Christopher G. 2002. "Testing Rival Decision-Making Theories on Budget Outputs: Theories and Comparative Evidence." *Public Budgeting and Finance* 22(3): 1–25.

Rubin, Irene. 1997. *The Politics of Public Budgeting: Getting and Spending, Borrowing and Balancing.* Chatham, NJ: Chatham House.

U.S. Government Accountability Office (GAO). 1999. *Performance Budgeting: Initial Experiences under the Results Act in Linking Plans with Budgets.* GAO/AIMD/GGD-99–67.

———. 2000. *Managing for Results. Using GPRA to Help Congressional Decision Making and Strengthen Oversight.* GAO/T-GGD-00–95 (March).

———. 2002. *Managing for Results: Agency Progress in Linking Performance Plans with Budgets and Financial Statements.* GAO-02–236 (January).

———. 2004. *Performance Budgeting: Observations on the Use of OMB's Program Assessment Rating Tool for Fiscal Year 2004 Budget.* GAO-04–174 (January).

———. 2005. *Managing for Results: Enhancing Agency Use of Performance Information for Management Decision Making.* GAO-05–927 (September).

U.S. Office of Management and Budget (OMB). 1995. "Statement of Federal Financial Accounting Standards, Number 4."

———. 2006. "Guidance for Completing the Program Assessment Rating Tool (PART)."

5

Performance Budgeting

Prospects for Sustainability

PAUL L. POSNER AND DENISE M. FANTONE

Public managers throughout the world have sought to strengthen public decision making and performance by establishing strategic goals and performance measures as the touchstone for accountability. The shift to a results-oriented framework promises to improve program and organizational effectiveness by systematically linking administrative activities to the performance outcomes that matter most for the organization and its publics.

Performance-based reforms have in fact had a long history in the United States. Public administrators at all levels have become gripped by waves of performance reforms intended to improve performance and enhance public confidence in government. Ushered in with great expectations, reforms such as Planning, Programming and Budgeting System (PPBS), Zero Based Budgeting, and Management by Objectives (MBO) achieved significant improvements but are widely acknowledged to have fallen well short of their mark in institutionalizing a *sustainable* focus on performance within government over the longer term.

Many factors accounted for the checkered history of performance reforms in U.S. government, from the complex and burdensome implementation requirements to the failure to gain buy-in on performance goals from legislators and key interest groups. One lesson learned from these past initiatives is that the ultimate success of performance reforms will be predicated on their integration with the most important process engaged in by public managers every year—the budget process (GAO 1997). The introduction of performance goals and metrics into the budget process gained the moniker of "performance budgeting" and this has become a fundamental feature of current performance reforms at federal, state, and local levels of government, as well as in most Organization for Economic Cooperation and Development (OECD) nations.

The impetus for performance budgeting also stems from wide dissatisfaction with the incremental nature of budgeting. Public budgeting was institutionalized in the early 1900s as a process with a primary focus on ensuring appropriate controls of expenditures to ensure that public laws were implemented faithfully by bureaucracies. This emphasis led to a focus on inputs, reflected in many budgets today, which are structured around object classes of expenditures such as salaries, construction, and equipment. Public sector reformers have long harbored hopes that public budgeting could be transformed into a process for more systematically reviewing the performance of the public sector by institutionalizing a more rigorous process of tradeoffs among competing claims. To do this, they have sought to shift the orientation of public budget structures from inputs to outputs and, ultimately, outcomes. The introduction of program budgeting in the 1960s was a step in this direction, leading many states and localities to restructure budgets based on programs and outputs.

In this chapter, we argue that the performance movement in general, and performance budgeting in particular, has achieved a level of continuity and sustainability at the federal level that is at once both surprising and tenuous. The institutionalization of performance reforms in agencies' management and in the executive budget process itself is working to usher in new challenges to the performance movement. Building off the relative success of the past decade, reformers are pressing for a more central role for performance in determining the allocation of scarce resources and rewards, both in the budget process and in the human resource management process. While such initiatives do indeed promise significant benefits, they are also fraught with risks. As performance budgeting evolves, we argue that its future sustainability can be promoted only if the advocates reexamine premises that do not fit the realities of our contemporary policy process at the federal level. Important questions need to be addressed for the movement to make significant progress that can be sustained.

GPRA: First Steps toward Performance Budgeting

Notwithstanding the mixed results of past reforms, the performance movement has attained greater success and sustainability in recent years than could have been imagined when these reforms were introduced. The Government Performance and Results Act (GPRA), passed in 1993, has ushered in a period where performance information and justifications have become widely accepted in federal agencies, in Office of Management and Budget (OMB) reviews, and even sporadically in certain committees of Congress itself. Notably, the reform has not only survived through two administrations of different parties, but became a vital part of the management reform strategies of both the Clinton and Bush administrations.

How did a reform whose passage late at night was little noticed, and discounted by many savvy observers as yet another reform destined for the dustbin of history, overcome some of the obstacles that bedeviled its predecessors? Part of the explanation may lie in the growing importance of federal programs in the social and economic fabric of the nation. As the federal role has grown in such areas as health care, education, and environmental protection, the relative success of those programs in achieving their often ambitious programmatic objectives has taken on greater importance in national debates. Lawrence Brown (1981) argued many years ago that as the federal policy expansions from the New Deal and Great Society were completed, policymakers would increasingly become preoccupied by what he calls "rationalizing policy"—that is, revisions and reforms to the major initiatives of the past. While members may not get as much political credit for rationalizing policies, in fact government programs create their own political and policy momentum by becoming more central to the social and economic well-being of the nation. Accordingly, policymakers become beset with demands to modify, revise, revisit, "fix," and fill gaps in such critical programs as social security, Medicare, and education. As Wildavsky argued, policy was "its own cause" as the "evils that worry us now spring directly from the good things we tried to do before" (Wildavsky 1979, 63).

Allen Schick (1966) foretold this over thirty years ago when he commented on the evolution of the focus of budgeting from control to management and to planning. The story of the persistence of performance reforms in fact has its parallels in other OECD nations as well. An OECD report notes that most advanced nations have retained performance budgeting systems for over ten years, but that many have made substantial changes in those systems to adapt to changing political and administrative realities (OECD 2005; see also Curristine, chapter 12 of this volume).

While the evolving political and policy agenda no doubt has whetted the appetites of public officials for performance information, at least a portion of the sustained implementation of performance management in federal agencies can be attributed to the design of the GPRA itself and subsequent initiatives that have served to help reinforce the importance of performance information for agencies and the policy process. GPRA was premised on careful study of the lessons learned from the past. First, the reform was anchored in an act of Congress, as reformers realized that past initiatives undertaken without the support of Congress had failed to transcend the terms of their executive political champions. Those who conceive of management reforms as executive affairs come to learn what it means to work in a system with a legislative branch that is the strongest in the world. Congress views itself as a comanager of executive agencies, a perspective that is exercised through appropriations, oversight, nominations, organizations, authorizations, and so on. Agencies in turn take cues from their congressional committees, led by officials and staff who will typically be around longer than presidents and White House staffs.

The second important lesson learned from the failures of the past is that performance reforms need to be linked to the budget for agencies to take them seriously. Previous reforms were either implemented outside the budget process itself or attempted to create wholly separate budgetary regimes, such as PPBS, which never became integrated with the mainstream budget process (GAO 1997). The rationale for budget linkage and integration is sound and compelling. After all, the budget is the one annual process where priorities are determined and scarce resources are allocated. If performance metrics become relevant to this process, the theory is that it would elevate their significance in the eyes of agency managers.

Placing GPRA in the Continuum of Performance Budgeting

While the linkage of performance plans and metrics with budgeting was viewed as critical to the success of performance management, few really examined what this meant. Indeed, most simply treated performance budgeting as a proverbial "on-off switch"—you either did it or you did not. As will be discussed below, performance budgeting in fact is a dimmer switch, with many different kinds of models to choose from.

While performance budgeting is still evolving worldwide, a continuum can be defined, ranging from least to most ambitious and demanding. All of these systems inform budget decisions through performance goals and data. They vary based on how tightly this linkage is defined. Approaches range from presentational strategies that attempt to blend performance information into traditional budget structures to more demanding strategies where attempts are made to link budgetary allocations with desired levels of performance.

The following strategies have been deployed in federal, state, and local governments as well as OECD nations:

- *Presentations*—Budgeting and planning remain separate activities with separate structures and reporting but they are linked by relational approaches. The goal is to present the performance consequences of budget decisions. The presentations can be linked both at the individual account level in the budget and at the aggregate performance plan goal level. Crosswalks are often presented that translate budget figures into performance goal frameworks.
- *Budget Restructuring*—Given the critical role played by budget accounts in structuring tradeoffs in budgeting, reformers often seek a restructuring of budget account structures along the lines of performance goals. The theory is that budgetary choices can more easily and transparently be made among competing performance levels and goals when budgets are structured to organize costs based on these goals.
- *Performance Reviews and Assessments*—Some jurisdictions have established formal assessment processes to build off performance management and budget processes. These processes evaluate how well programs and operations are meeting performance goals and outcomes. Assessments can potentially carry performance measures a step further by specifying the impact of government activities on outcomes through detailed evaluation studies. Such a process is particularly helpful if it assesses the comparative performance of related programs and entities in achieving common goals.
- *Performance Targets*—Agencies have targets that are set in either outcome or output terms for performance for the coming year. Agencies pledge to take action to achieve targeted changes in levels of outcomes or outputs, with *ex post facto* reporting to ascertain whether these targets were achieved and the reason for any slippage. In some systems, targets are explicitly linked to funding levels

authorized in the budget. In the United Kingdom, for instance, a set of Public Service Agreements (PSA) that specify performance targets in both outcome and output terms are negotiated with each agency by the Ministry of Treasury. These PSA targets then become linked to the budget as they form an important basis for budget requests and decisions by agencies and the Treasury. However, a recent survey of OECD budget officers found that few nations, if any, eliminate programs as a result of performance budget targets. In fact, nearly all nations indicated that performance against targets rarely determines budget allocations (OECD 2005; see also Curristine, chapter 12).

- *Performance Linked Funding*—This approach is what many advocates of performance budgeting envision, but is typically the most difficult to implement. Some advocates harbor hopes that budgeting can become a formulaic exercise where resource allocation decisions are driven in some mechanical way by performance levels and comparisons. In concept, funding is provided based on the units of outputs delivered by the agency based on a set price per unit of output produced. The prices can be determined based either on actual practice or on what the most efficient provider would experience. Agencies achieving greater efficiencies by producing at higher levels get higher payments, while those falling short experience budgetary reductions.
- *Outcome Based Budget Formulation*—Several jurisdictions have sought to go beyond the confines of traditional agency-centered models of budget formulation to establish outcomes as the new unit of analysis for the budget process. The outcome based reformers contend that even when accounts are restructured, agency-centered budgets can limit the potential of performance budgeting by containing tradeoffs to the boundaries of agencies themselves, notwithstanding the fact that many programs across agencies often are relevant to achieving broader performance goals. The state of Washington notably was among the first to initiate this reform, with the help of David Osborne and others (Osborne and Hutchinson 2004).

The GPRA strategy of linkage fits well within the presentational and budget accounting models. The planning and metrics would come first, with the last event in the train being the budget linkage. Very sensibly, the authors of the act felt that the budget linkage required a supply of credible information before it would be taken seriously by budget officials. Accordingly, the authors conceived of a phased implementation process. First, a series of pilots would test out the concepts and lead to midcourse corrections. Then agencies would develop strategic plans, followed by annual performance plans and reports to develop a credible "supply side" of goals, measures, and data to build a solid foundation for performance management. Only then did the act call for performance budgeting pilots to test the more ambitious model of Performance Linked Funding, where changes in budget levels would be linked with changes in performance levels in test programs and agencies. In their report to Congress on the results, OMB concluded that this more ambitious model was not realistic for most programs, partly because the link between budgetary inputs and programmatic outcomes was too tenuous.

The GPRA model in fact was reasonable and provided both a vision and the flexibility to accommodate other important values served by budgeting. While information is never costless, the linkage contemplated by GPRA left discretion in the hands of agencies, as reviewed by OMB, to perfect these linkages. GPRA was essentially a planning and agency-driven tool. The strategic and performance plans were drivers of this reform, with the metrics and linkage to the budget to follow. Agencies had primary responsibility for constructing these plans, with input from stakeholders, including the Congress as one among many stakeholders.

GAO found in its ten-year retrospective on GPRA that the act has provided a solid foundation. Federal managers surveyed reported having significantly more types of performance measures and that the GPRA reporting process had also begun to facilitate better linkage between performance information and planning and budget decision making, although more remained to be done to promote the use of this information, particularly for resource allocation (GAO 2004a).

With regard to budgeting, the agencies have taken the coverage issue seriously, as all found some way to find a bridge between the traditional appropriations structures and the newer performance planning models. Most retained traditional appropriations account structures and program activities and developed displays crosswalking these accounts to performance goals; several went further to recast their account structures in performance terms. The GAO reports on these initiatives concluded that these crosswalks constituted a useful form of performance budgeting, which assured Congress that traditional budget structures would be maintained while also showing the budgetary implications of agencies' performance plans (GAO 1999). As such, these initial agency efforts could be said to reflect an evolutionary approach to performance budgeting—the introduction of a new way of understanding and accounting for budgetary inputs might at some future time become compelling enough to become a basis for decisions and possibly for a restructuring of budget accounting structures themselves.

The Bush administration built on the GPRA infrastructure to carry performance budgeting initiatives further along the continuum. These proposals used existing GPRA frameworks and information to more actively pursue a central management agenda developed by OMB, which was viewed by appropriators and some agency managers as laying down the proverbial gauntlet by challenging traditional information, oversight, and program management routines (GAO 2005a). The administration's Program Assessment Rating Tool (PART) extended the definition of accountability under GPRA by adding an assessment component that built on the infrastructure of plans, metrics, and data that agencies developed under GPRA. Reportedly, the PART reviews have further stimulated agencies' interests in enhancing their evaluation capability and information systems, if for no other reason than to ward off the public embarrassment of receiving less than *effective* PART scores (GAO 2006).

Reaching a New Plateau: The Dilemmas of Success

Since the 1990s agencies have made progress in developing the "supply side" of performance management—agencies have developed strategic goals, metrics, and data sources that over the years have been tested and refined. Logic models are in the process of being developed to link agency outputs with ultimate outcomes. In turn, agencies are also engaged in validating data and using this information to defend resource requests. Make no mistake, this is a long-term enterprise and not all agencies have reached this level—this is not surprising since civilian agencies had generally not been required to develop strategic plans prior to GPRA.

Developing a credible supply of information on performance and costs remains an important predicate to promoting sustainable demand by public officials and publics throughout a jurisdiction. It is only when such information is perceived to be fair, balanced, comprehensive, and accurate that it will be taken seriously as a new input to an inherently political process.

Now that we have made progress on supply, the demand for the information has appeared to be less robust and predictable. It is widely believed, for instance, that Congress has largely remained uninterested in performance reports and plans. Senator Fred Thompson summed up the frustration of reformers well when he said in 2002: "We are at the point after all these years of implementing the Results Act where we need to start using performance information to make decisions or we might as well give up on the Act" (Thompson 2002).

In fairness, the demand for performance information has not been as empty as it is often portrayed. Although appropriators have shown active resistance to the administration's performance budgets and PART analyses, other committees have reportedly used agency performance information for oversight and authorization purposes. A Congressional Research Service (CRS) report found that mentions of performance information by congressional authorization committees grew to the point where seventy-six public laws from the 106th Congress (1999–2000) contained statutory or committee report language relating to GPRA and performance measurement (McMurtry 2001). Oversight committees have held hearings at times and, in the 1990s, the House majority leader issued "report cards" grading the quality of agencies' GPRA plans. As noted earlier, OMB under both the Clinton and Bush administrations has been an active user of performance information generated in this process.

While evidence of interest exists, the demand for performance information is probably episodic at best. This is to be expected in a complex democracy where analytic information vies with other bases of policy and political legitimation. One recent model suggests that there are four "pathways to power" that compete for primacy in governing how our policy process frames issues and makes decisions across various policy arenas. The four pathways—interest group, partisan, symbolic, and expert—vary in their ascendancy over time in individual issue areas. Thus, for instance, in tax policy, the 1996 farm reform overturning conventional subsidies, according to these authors, represented a triumph of the influence of experts in the policy process, which was followed in short order by the 2002 Farm Bill, which reflected the recapture of farm policy by interest groups who succeeded in restoring and even enhancing federal subsidies for agriculture. We conclude that expert-based forms of legitimation, such as performance information, will compete with other deeply rooted forces for policy influence and control (Beam, Conlan and Posner 2002).

Many might agree that this perspective captures the empirical realities of our policy process, but nonetheless would argue from a normative perspective that more should be done to institutionalize more predictable and routine demand for performance information. Placing performance more centrally in the budget process is viewed as the primary strategy to achieve this objective. Some fear that agencies may eventually lose interest in generating the supply of information if the supply is unrequited by the demand for and actual use of the information.

Moving Along the Performance Budgeting Continuum: Risks and Rewards

It is understandable that we would look to the budget process to stimulate and incentivize the demand side of the performance management equation. Clearly, making performance more relevant for the budget cycle offers the promise of gaining greater prominence for this information in the decision-making process that matters most each year. Given the great investment made by federal agencies over the past decade, it is understandable that many would search for new opportunities to make this information more relevant and important.

The tendency to use the budget as leverage has become taken for granted as the single most efficacious strategy to gain traction for management reforms at the federal level. Whether it is capital planning, human capital reforms, or financial management and accounting, reforms that have succeeding in gaining a place in the budget process are perceived to have improved their chances to be taken seriously. In fact, a common pool problem began to emerge in the 1990s, with the budget commons increasingly encumbered and congested with a host of management initiatives competing for the hearts and minds of budgeters. Certainly, those reforms that have succeeded in institutionalizing themselves in the budget process do improve their prospects for gaining agencies' attention, at least in the short term. However, in the race for short-term recognition, we need to give more thought to the implications of budget integration for the priorities, direction, and sponsorship of management reforms.

As the performance movement has become institutionalized at the federal level, pressures are mounting to "use" the information in the decision-making process. This is to be expected—considerable investments have been made and a performance infrastructure has been established within the bureaucracy with a healthy interest in strengthening the demand side of the equation discussed earlier. This has manifested itself in rising expectations to tie performance data more directly to budgetary allocations, as well as efforts to link the pay of civil servants to their performance in achieving goals and objectives. For example, actors in the budgetary process have begun to clamor for the direct use of PART scores to prioritize funding claims in the budget process. While the administration has studiously avoided promising to mechanically link budget allocations to PART scores, they nonetheless articulate a reasonable goal that, over time, such information will influence the debate and thereby help reallocate federal budgetary resources away from poorly performing programs to those that are most effective over time (OMB 2006). PART has inspired some in Congress and elsewhere, however, to expect more direct and formulaic ties between PART scores and budgetary decisions. John Mercer (2003), the principal staff member responsible for the development of GPRA in the Senate, argues,

> A true Performance Budget is not simply an Object Class budget with some program goals attached. It tells you much more than just that for a given level of funding a certain level of result is expected. A real Performance Budget gives a meaningful indication of how the dollars are expected to turn into results. Certainly not with scientific precision, but at least in an approximate sense, by outlining a general chain of cause and effect. The most effective governmental Performance Budget does this by showing, for each program area, how dollars fund day-to-day tasks and activities, how these activities are expected to generate certain outputs, and what outcomes should then be the result.

This push to more directly tie funding and other high-stakes decisions to performance marks a new chapter for the performance movement at the federal level. Referring to the continuum of performance budgeting discussed above, it reflects a desire to move toward more direct linkages between performance and funding decisions. If this shift does in fact come about, this would constitute a distinct change in emphasis for the performance movement itself by moving from what we will call a "strategic" orientation to a more "instrumental" focus.

To date, the performance movement could be characterized as focused on what we will call "strategic accountability," where the emphasis has been on developing strategic goals, gaining agreement, developing metrics and data to support the process, and engaging a community of practice within agencies and across the stakeholders in their issue environments. In this context, the primary "use" of performance plans and information has been to promote internal management direction and oversight and to help reframe questions for budgeting and oversight by OMB and to some extent the Congress itself, largely as a valuable supplement to ongoing accountability frameworks. Given the relative immaturity of many performance systems in the early years of the performance management life cycle, it would have been premature for the goals and data to become the primary driver for high-stakes budgetary allocations or more detailed budgetary accountability regimes.

Articulating performance plans and developing data systems is a long-term enterprise, and it may take many years for such information to become a compelling dimension for decision making. Political obstacles must be overcome—each programmatic area involves multiple stakeholders and decision makers who must buy in and take ownership of performance goals and metrics that are often highly contentious and contestable. Moreover, considerable technical obstacles need to be overcome in defining logic models linking complex implementation chains between often modest federal inputs and ultimate programmatic outcomes. When compared to other governmental systems, such as New Zealand and local government where performance reforms originated, the tie between the inputs of federal resources and the performance outcomes in our federal system of government can be quite tenuous. Even as these technical issues are worked out, it would be ill advised to expect these systems to have tightly coupled models relating inputs to outcomes. Programs typically have multiple outcomes, some of which are inherently difficult to measure, involving decisions to weigh their relative importance that are inherently political. Given these uncertainties, performance can play a role that is nonexclusive, supplemental to other forms of accountability, and only loosely coupled to resource decisions.

The pressures are now building to turn the movement toward what we call an "instrumental accountability" focus, where performance information is given a central role in allocating scarce resources and making other high-stakes decisions. The more performance is used to judge, reward, and sanction, the more the information will certainly gain greater attention and visibility. However in our eagerness to "rationalize" an inherently political process using performance metrics, there are significant risks to both the budget process and the performance movement that may be easy to overlook.

For the budget process itself, an instrumental approach to performance budgeting is likely to accentuate political conflict, rather than obviating it through compelling rational frameworks. When the focus of the debate shifts from incremental shifts in inputs and outputs, such as dollars expended or number of workload units to be achieved, to outcomes, such as numbers of lives saved or improved, we can expect the perceived stakes of budgetary combat to grow exponentially. Imagine a process where the bargaining between the Bush administration and Democrats in Congress shifts from dollars to be expended to numbers of lives saved and envision the political gridlock that could ensue. Now, economists will say we always make these decisions anyway given limited resources, but performance-linked budgeting would make these issues more explicit. Stable democracies sometimes depend on the "comfort of ambiguity" to resolve vexing political conflicts (OECD 1999). In some cases, suboptimizing economically is the key to optimizing politically.

Moreover, there are many other legitimate factors that must be weighed in budget allocations besides performance in making tradeoffs among competing claims—relative priorities, equity considerations, and the need for poorly performing programs to obtain greater resources in the near term to deal with problems, among others. Thus, for instance, it is not at all obvious that the response to a spike in the number of drug abusers would be to penalize the drug programs and their administrators with a loss of funds, but that is the rather unsophisticated result of the instrumental approach.

There are risks for the performance movement as well from the instrumental approach. First, there are potential threats to the analytic integrity of the models and metrics that are the basis for the performance management systems. As the stakes grow, so does the temptation to frame and even distort analytic findings for political purposes. As David Beam notes in his commentary on the use of policy research by policymakers, rather than depoliticizing policymaking, the close exposure to government has tended to politicize and degrade major segments of the research enterprise (Beam 1996). In the high-stakes setting of budgetary conflict, will agencies be able to be truly neutral in defining performance metrics and data when doing so may jeopardize their budgetary resources? Donald Moynihan (2004) has reminded us that there is no such thing as neutral and objective interpretation of performance results in such a high-stakes arena as budgeting. A single performance indicator, whether it is trends in drug abuse, serious crimes, or welfare caseloads, is subject to multiple interpretations about what the performance data mean and how they should be used in making decisions. As performance information becomes more central to budget decisions, models of competitive advocacy will better capture the behavior to be expected than the model of the omniscient mandarin.

PART scores produced by OMB illustrate these issues. While OMB is engaged in a systematic process to rate the relative performance of every program in the budget, the scores themselves were either taken seriously or seriously discounted based on such analytic issues as different weighting of the multiple performance goals that each program attempts to address and the relative balance between measurable goals and those more qualitative objectives that elude measurement. Of course, these analytic differences themselves were rooted in differential political vantage points occupied by the actors in the budgetary debate. The GAO assessment of PART concluded that the experiences with the rating tool illustrate "the inherent limitations of any tool to provide a single performance answer or judgment on complex federal programs with multiple goals" (GAO 2004b).

When performance metrics are used to ground political decisions, their gaps and analytic controversies become more important. While it is often difficult to measure all important values we care about, these gaps cannot be ignored when metrics are used instrumentally to reward or punish. In these cases, the well-known tendency of systems to manage to measures can induce significant behavioral and policy distortions. Beryl Radin argues that those programs whose goals are more amenable to measurement can gain significant advantages in tightly linked systems, independent of their relative merits, when compared to those programs with less observable and quantifiable dimensions (2006; see also Radin, chapter 6 of this volume).

Moreover, there are tensions between performance planning and budgeting that have not been sufficiently examined by the performance community (Schick 1966). Often grounded in scans of the future environment facing organizations and programs, strategic and performance planning is broad, inclusive, and longer term in nature. The focus is on gaining buy-in by stakeholders throughout the political environment and attempting to ensure a broad base of support. The unit of analysis is broader based—what difference does the agency and its programs intend to make for outcomes that matter to the various publics in a democratic society? Budgeting, on the other hand, has a very different focus. The budget is built from narrowly defined programs, defined as budget accounts and activities. While budgetary allocations can certainly be grounded in broader plans and priority statements, the focus of budget decision making is on the margin—what changes are being proposed to add or subtract resources from some baseline, most often last year's budget? When it comes to the discretionary appropriations portion of the budget—one third of federal spending but the only portion that is annually determined through the appropriations process—the focus is on obligations and outlays for a single year, the "budget year" in federal parlance, rather than the longer-term outlook. Most importantly, in contrast to planning, budgeting is a closed process—at the federal level, OMB deliberations and agency inputs to those deliberations are considered "predecisional" and not available for public disclosure or debate. This is true not only for the budgetary figures and decisions themselves, but also for performance plans and PART scores that affected the president's budget under both the Clinton and the Bush administrations.

What are the implications of this for performance budgeting? There is a contest for the soul of the movement—will the ethos and unit of analysis of the budget or the planning/performance perspective govern the process? The closer that performance gets to directly influencing budgetary decisions, the more likely it is that the ethos of budgeting will gain the upper hand. This is entirely understandable—if the goal is to influence budgetary decisions, to some extent one has to take the budget process as they find it. However, there is a tradeoff—while performance data may gain greater influence in budgeting, this may come at the expense of the breadth and openness that characterize strategic planning processes. The GAO made this point in their observations on the PART. While commending OMB for stimulating greater interest in performance evaluations and metrics among federal agencies, the agency noted that the unit of analysis used by OMB was that of the budget itself—the relatively narrow budget accounts and activities for the most part. The agency also noted that this contrasted with the broader planning and goal orientation of the GRPA planning process. The agency called on OMB to broaden their focus by retaining PART reviews, with a focus on broader goals and objectives cutting across many programs and agencies (GAO 2004b).

Do these concerns spell a need to rethink the entire effort to integrate performance into the budget process? We do not think so—the benefits of the relationship for both performance and budgeting are important. However, the significance of these concerns is a function of how far we choose to go down the performance budgeting continuum. In particular, the push from strategic to instrumental models of performance budgeting is fraught with risks that may lessen both the performance and the budgeting enterprises.

Allen Schick (2006) has made a similar point when he distinguishes between the use of performance as an analytic tool in the budget and its use as a decision rule. Schick argues that performance results are not a sufficient guide in themselves for budget decisions. Poor results may compel government to spend more or less, depending on context, relative priorities, and other important factors. Politically, officials in a democracy need to have the flexibility to make these judgments based on the values and interests of their coalitions. Analytically, Schick argues that there are rarely sufficient linear connections between budgetary inputs and outcomes to guide the decision-making process in a formulaic or mechanical fashion. Moreover, he argues that it is beyond the capacity of most governments to map how marginal changes in resources—which is after all the focus of budget decisions every year—link to marginal changes in outcomes. Our logic models are not very well defined, particularly at the federal level, which is so far removed from the ultimate point of impact of its programs. While this is well known to the performance community, the implications for the decision rules that should link performance results to budgeting have not been as clearly thought through.

Reconceptualizing the Role of Performance Budgeting

How can we define a role for performance in budgeting that is sustainable in our political system? And how can the integration of performance in budgeting be defined to support the performance movement itself as well as strengthen the budget process? As the foregoing suggests, this is no simple task.

In addressing this challenge, we first need to look at the assumptions behind the performance movement that we believe have given rise to unrealistic and unreasonable expectations for the linkage between "resources and results." Many of these premises were inherited from the performance management and budgeting experiences of other systems of government and the private sector that are far more cohesive and centralized than our federal system. While performance budgeting is never easy, it is arguably less challenging when there is more political cohesion and agreement on goals and objectives. Whether it be strong Westminster-style parliamentary systems like in New Zealand; strong city manager governments such as in Sunnyvale, California; or business firms with clear bottom lines, there is likely to be greater consensus on goals and stronger authority accorded to a single actor to define budget decisions and the weight given to performance.

By contrast, our federal environment is characterized by separated institutions sharing powers, and multiple, diverse, and pluralistic interests vying for control of goals and objectives as well as resources. In this environment, agreement on goals is less likely, the meaning of performance metrics is more contestable, and the implications of performance data for budget decisions are more debatable. Notwithstanding these differences, many in the performance movement have held views about the institutionalization of performance in government and budgeting that arguably reflect these other systems more than ours.

We are concerned that these expectations could, if unchecked, prompt unnecessary disillusionment and premature burial of this cycle of performance budgeting. As an alternative, we should learn from the experience of our system and others like it with performance budgeting, and develop alternative assumptions and models that are better suited for our complex, pluralistic policymaking and implementation process.

The following comprise the key questions that we believe need to be addressed to enable performance budgeting to move forward and become more sustainable in our system. For each of these issues, we discuss the premises of the performance movement and present alternative approaches to guide expectations and implementation of performance budgeting systems.

1. How Closely Do Budget Decisions Need to Link to Results to Be Useful?

Many advocates base their accountability models for performance on a naive rationalism that rests on what we call the "mechanical model." If performance goes up, the agency or staff get rewarded with increased resources; if it goes down, they get penalized. This expectation stems partly from the notion that performance will, in fact, eliminate political judgment and conflict, enabling decisions to be entirely based on measured results. In the debate over GPRA, members of Congress argued that the act would enable Congress to put the federal budget on automatic pilot—programs that improved in their performance would be increased while programs with lower performance would experience budget cuts.

Budgeting is an inherently political process. The integration of performance information cannot, and should not, be expected to "take politics out of budgeting" or to supplant the judgment of performance evaluators and analysts for elected officials. V.O. Key's fundamental question over sixty years ago has no analytic answer: "On what basis will it be decided to provide X dollars to activity A rather than activity B?" (Key 1940). Even if we agree on the costs and outcomes of competing programs, the answer to this question depends on values.

Political leaders must necessarily weigh other important criteria beyond performance that properly belong in budgetary debates, including judgments about equity, needs, and the relative priorities given to competing claims. Moreover, the link between budget amounts and performance goals is often too tenuous to permit this kind of mechanical, pseudoscientific model to be taken seriously. The presence of performance problems often prompts decision makers, rather than cutting funding for poorly performing programs, to increase funding in the hopes that this will at least partly address the problem in the future. Eventually, should a program be characterized by sustained performance shortfalls, decision makers might well decide to change or eliminate the program, but the decision outcome is anything but straightforward. Moreover, this view, what we will call the "mechanical model," creates an impossibly high bar for performance budgeting to cross, laying the ground for disillusionment and the ultimate death of yet another well-meaning performance-based reform (Schick 2006).[1]

In our view, a more appropriate model to guide expectations for the linkage of budget decisions with results is what we would call the "agenda model." The goal of performance budgeting from this perspective should be to inform the debate, to place performance on the agenda for budget formulation alongside other important dimensions. In this respect, performance budgeting should not be expected to provide the *answers* to inherently political choices in the budget process but could be expected to provide a new set of *questions*. The shift in the agenda for the budget process could be expected to bear fruit in a more informed debate that adds performance goals and results to the other important issues addressed in annual resource allocation debates.

2. Is Consensus Necessary for Performance Budgeting?

There is a presumption that performance information and interpretations of that information can attain consensus sufficient to rise above political conflict. While the authors of GPRA recognized that a process of consensus building would be necessary to gain stakeholder buy-in, there is nonetheless the expectation that eventually consensus on goals and the meaning of performance information can, in fact, be attained. Indeed, there may be areas where this is the case. For instance, the leading economic indicators began as a research enterprise by the National Bureau of Economic Research (NBER) and matured to the point where most political actors accept these indicators as the foundation for debates about the state of the economy. However, even here, torrid debates break out about the validity of the consumer price index, the unemployment rate, the poverty rate, and many other statistical series, based in no small part on the differing political perspectives of the critics.

In our system, it is at least equally likely that information will be contested. Our system has many contending political interests vying for influence over important programs, coupled with a highly fragmented policymaking process anchored in our separation of powers and federal systems. Even when they are controlled by the same party, our system guarantees a certain amount of healthy debate and conflict between Congress and the executive, not to mention between federal bureaucrats and states. In recent years, a larger and more diverse range of interests have gained organizational representation, further fueling political conflict over information and goals. Political agreement on goals may very well be achieved, but to expect it as the norm would be naive and unrealistic.

Given the contested political setting through which policymaking and implementation takes place in our system, performance reformers need a more sophisticated understanding of the role that data and metrics can play. Rather than expecting agreement, it may be more realistic to expect that political debates should be conducted, at least at times, in performance terms. Rather than wringing our collective hands when political interests "politicize" data, we might come to celebrate this outcome as a tribute to the importance of performance information in a highly diverse, pluralistic political system.

Many years ago, Charles Lindblom (1968) advised that policy analysis would influence policymaking, but not through the sheer authority of ideas that policy analysts hoped for. Rather, he argued that ideas would have an impact to the extent that they became useful to various advocates in the politics of policymaking. In what he called the "partisan mutual adjustment model," performance metrics and data can influence debates, not through consensus or agreement with the bottom line of a single actor in our system, but rather through the results of healthy political competition.

3. Should the Success of Performance Budgeting Rest on Its Use in Budget Formulation and Appropriations Decision Making?

As noted previously, many management reforms test their mettle by whether their reforms play a central role in resource allocation, both in the executive branch and in the Congress through the appropriations process. This is not unreasonable, for decisions to prioritize scarce resources are among the most important that any system makes every year. As worthy a goal as this may be, there are good reasons for expanding our definition of success to include budget execution activities that support program implementation post appropriations. Not only because the resource allocation decision process continues as agencies respond to statutory requirements, congressional guidance, and administration priorities, but because it provides a natural nexus for considering tradeoffs in performance. We potentially overlook opportunities to view performance budgeting in real time, for it is in the agencies during budget execution/program implementation that resources expended for agreed-upon goals and objectives, directed to the best and most efficient uses, and accounted for through measurable results plays out. As Phil Joyce argues, at each stage of the budget process performance information can be useful and the value it brings is independent of what is done in other phases. He concludes that "budgeting is not a narrow enterprise that happens only in discrete places at discrete times, the opportunities for integrating budgeting and performance information are also not narrow and limited" (Joyce 2003, 17).

Many of the attributes of the environment of budget execution better fit with the assumptions of the movement. Unlike budget formulation, budget execution has the advantage of occurring after both congressional and executive branch actors weigh in. Although this does not obviate political choice or imply agreement, questions of program priorities are clearer and a focus on "how much performance for what level of funding" is less abstract. Budget execution in fact entails its own decision-making process and conflicts. However, this takes place within top-line decisions that provide a more stable environment for performance management.

The demands of program implementation involve more than the budget process, so that the hammer of budgeting becomes one of several tools that can be used to motivate desirable performance. Various incentives, such as scorecards, public disclosure in the media, pay for performance, and other reward schemes (for example, gain sharing) build on the competition that actors face in a pluralistic system such as ours. The competition for resources is always there, but the need to maximize the resources that a program manager has, coupled with incentives, can be powerfully motivating. The possibility is that we have reached the point of less reliance on the budget process to give weight to performance information—that performance should carry valence because program managers and agencies see this as serving their best interests. This is also not limited to individual agencies and programs. This administration's President's Management Agenda (PMA) and OMB's PART are two recent examples of how central agencies can capture the high ground by pushing performance through multiple strategies and not just by proposals that cut or increase funding.

4. Can Performance Budgeting Meet the Needs of Both the Executive and the Congress?

Given Congress's prominent role in budgeting and appropriations, congressional buy-in and support have been viewed as critical to sustain management and budgeting reforms. In a system where the legislature and the executive vie for control of agencies, prospects for sustaining reforms improve when both branches are either supportive of initiatives or at least not actively hostile.

For many years, research has shown that the legislatures, at both the federal and the state levels, have largely been uninterested in performance reforms. This research shows that legislatures use performance information more as an exception than a rule, preferring politically derived decision rules to analytically grounded ones. Some have concluded that legislatures constitute a barrier to reform. For instance, it has been noted that legislatures can create three obstacles to performance budgeting: (1) promulgate unclear or ambiguous policy objectives that complicate strategic goal setting, (2) rely on input and anecdotal information rather than comprehensive performance data in making budget decisions, and (3) devote insufficient attention to oversight of program performance (Joyce 2005).

While Congress may indeed have weak incentives to systematically "use" performance information generated by the executive branch, Congress nonetheless has a considerable interest in performance in the more generic sense. While members of Congress must always be focused on representing their districts and promoting their own reelection, members are also driven by the desire to create good policy (Fenno 1978). Recent work has discovered that Congress, at times, goes to extraordinary lengths to promote general benefits, even delegating its power to extra legislative commissions and the executive in specific cases (Becker 2005). Research on congressional behavior suggests that while strongly motivated by the "electoral connection," Congress has incentives to use information to reduce the uncertainties associated with legislature proposals, making members interested in the connections between their policy position and actual policy outcomes. Indeed, it is possible that legislators will feel vulnerable if they are associated with legislation that proves either ineffectual, or even worse, wasteful or harmful in some important ways

(Krehbiel 1992). The considerable uncertainty that surrounds any major legislative proposal constitutes a source of political risk to members of Congress interested in good policy and a powerful incentive for members to search for information on policy results that may include performance data (Esterling 2004).

Staff agencies supporting the legislature played a substantial role in promoting and validating performance information for legislative use at both federal and state levels. David Whiteman's study of congressional information search shows that policy analyses and information produced by support agencies such as the Congressional Budget Office (CBO) and GAO played a surprisingly central role in the substantive development of legislative policy proposals and in policy augmentation (Whiteman 1995). A study of state performance budgeting also found that performance information has influenced state legislative deliberations on such issues as assessing prospective impacts of proposed policy changes, exploring ways of reducing costs, and considering approaches to improving effectiveness (GAO 2005b).

Moreover, recent research suggests that Congress has played an important role in the performance movement, even if it does not actively use the information in a consistent way in decision making. In areas ranging from performance management to financial management, information technology, and acquisition reform, Congress passed wide-ranging reforms institutionalizing the development of new information and reporting in federal agencies for these critical areas. Although relatively unheralded, these congressional statutes have had a formative and sustained influence in improving the analytic base of information developed and maintained by federal agencies on their programs and operations. The enactment of these statutes illustrates a form of congressional influence and oversight that has been called "fire alarm oversight" by political scientists Matthew McCubbins and Thomas Schwartz. In contrast to "police patrol oversight," where Congress actively uses information to highlight problems and change programs, in the fire alarm model, Congress establishes the infrastructure of information that it can use when and if it decides to examine particular programs and operations in the future (McCubbins and Schwartz 1984).

The foregoing suggests that, at the very least, there may be mixed incentives in the Congress regarding performance information. Generalizations can be hazardous when discussing a pluralistic institution like the Congress. There are times when oversight and reviews are done and done well and times when there is little interest in these issues. Many usefully have called for reforms to enhance congressional use of information. Such process reforms include more regular schedules for oversight, improved transparency, and augmented legislative capacity. The GAO has suggested that Congress consider developing a more centralized and cohesive strategy for targeting its oversight and for reviewing the relative contribution of individual programs to broader performance goals (GAO 2004b). Should Congress be interested, such reforms may very well improve prospects for the use of information.

However, several cautions are in order. While process reforms may very well be useful, such processes will change and be actively used only when political leaders see that oversight and performance reviews benefit their political careers and programmatic interests. The oversight that has occurred has blossomed when it serves such political incentives as credit claiming, blame assignment, and competition with the executive and other political actors. We need to be far more savvy in working within our democratic political system rather than wishing for a system we do not, and perhaps should not, have.

When seeking congressional support and interest, we must also recognize that the congressional needs and use of performance information will be different than those of executive agencies. One size does not fit all. For instance, performance reformers often have advised Congress to replace input controls and appropriations accounts with outcome-oriented structures. Reformers have, further, sought to justify these proposals as a way to eliminate congressional "micromanagement" of the agencies. Although such bromides may be appropriate to a Westminster-style parliamentary system where the legislature plays a relatively weak role in the budget formulation and oversight process, they are not well suited for a separation of powers regime such as ours. Under our system, the challenge is how to build performance as a compelling basis for oversight to complement, not replace, existing oversight processes and criteria.

At times, the switch from input to outcome orientations is argued as a way to enhance legislative oversight and control—agencies gain more discretion over managing while legislatures gain more control over outcomes. However, from the vantage point of principal agent theory, such a tradeoff is in fact asymmetrical. Agencies gain the benefits of increased discretion immediately while the prospects for holding agencies accountable for failing to reach performance outcome targets is far more contestable and challenging. Legislatures may be left grasping for someone to blame for performance shortfalls that are caused by various social, economic, or demographic forces having little to do with the actions of executive agencies. By contrast, oversight of inputs is far more straightforward and more directly connected to legislative actions and appropriations. By this, we are not suggesting that these reforms are not worth doing, only that they may have consequences for the power stakes of legislatures that must be recognized if legislatures are to gain an interest in these reforms.

As the foregoing suggests, our system thrives on multiple forms of accountability, reflecting the multiple players empowered to play a role in governance. Different kinds of information will be appropriate for different actors and settings. Dall Forsythe notes, for instance, that higher-level outcome systems such as Oregon's Benchmarks are useful for strategic planning but not for oversight and control of government agencies. On the other hand, "real time" performance management systems such as CitiStat and other data management systems are useful for day-to-day control but not for overarching goal setting (Forsythe 2001, 522). The balanced scorecard movement reflects the needs of managers and decision makers alike for a portfolio of information addressing different but equally legitimate needs and interests. Rather than a single performance regime, a "menu approach" to performance management makes far more sense of our system of government.

Accordingly, any reforms to introduce performance into budgeting can be expected to be additive, supplementing rather than replacing traditional information and controls. While performance can and should be encouraged to be added as an important perspective for budgeting, other perspectives are equally important to political actors in our budget process. Indeed, the federal budget itself retains multiple displays through which the same information can be presented. While the basic budget is presented by account, the information can be displayed using a number of different orientations and perspectives, including programmatic; object class; "character class," reflecting the economic purpose of the program; and functional, reflecting the broader mission to which the budgetary item contributes.

Conclusions

Performance budgeting promises to improve how we think about tradeoffs in the budget process. The performance perspective is a valuable addition to the current budget process, and one that will arguably become more important as the nation confronts new challenges and fiscal realities in the coming decades. The nation has grown to expect more from government at all levels, and it is likely that the pressures on public officials will intensify over the years. Performance budgeting offers a key tool that will enable public officials to help sort out competing claims and justify their choices to increasingly restive publics.

In this chapter, we have argued that, contrary to initial expectations, progress has indeed been made at the federal level. As the "supply side" of the performance movement has strengthened, questions remain over how to incentivize demand for the information. More demanding forms of performance budgeting that entail a shift from strategic to instrumental models, in our view, involve considerable risks for budgeting and the performance movement alike. Further progress on performance budgeting can and should be made, but we are concerned that the performance movement can potentially stall if we don't adapt our expectations and models of performance budgeting to the realities of our system of governance.

Under our model, we would counsel a form of performance budgeting that would have the following attributes:

- Strategic rather than instrumental approach—performance should inform the questions, but not be expected to directly drive the budgetary answers in a political process.
- A competitive rather than a consensus approach to the use of information— each actor should be encouraged to marshal performance data to support their interests in the budgetary "marketplace of ideas."
- Accountability by addition not subtraction—performance budgeting should recognize the needs for different kinds of information to support multiple actors, environments, and purposes.

- A search for opportunities to influence budget decisions selectively rather than systematically—performance can be expected to have influence when policy "windows of opportunity" open when decision makers are most receptive.
- Focus of more attention on agencies' success in using performance information in budget execution and program implementation rather than solely on budget formulation and appropriations.
- Looking to non-budgetary incentives to promote and sustain the use of performance information rather than sole reliance on the budget process—a full range of incentives including scorecards and public disclosure as well as nonmonetary tools can promote interest in performance.
- A continuation of finding ways to engage various congressional actors in formulating their own performance agenda, rather than only seeking buy-in and support for executive proposals.

Notes

The views in this chapter represent the author's own views and do not necessarily reflect the views of the U.S. Government Accountability Office (GAO).

1. Schick argues that the model articulated is a version of what he calls "commercial budgeting." Most large businesses have variable budgets—spending varies based on how much the unit produces. See Allen Schick, "Performance Budgeting and Accrual Budgeting: Decision Rules or Analytic Tools?" (2006).

References

Beam, David R. 1996. "If Public Ideas Are So Important Now, Why Are Policy Analysts So Depressed?" *Journal of Policy Analysis and Management* 15(3): 430–37.
Beam, David R., Timothy J. Conlan, and Paul L. Posner. 2002. "The Politics that Pathways Make: A Framework for Analysis of Contemporary Federal Policy Making." Paper presented at the Annual Meeting of the American Political Science Association, Boston, MA, September 20.
Becker, Lawrence, 2005. *Doing the Right Thing: Collective Action and Procedural Choice in the New Legislative Process.* Columbus, OH: Ohio State University Press.
Brown, Lawrence. 1981. *New Policies, New Politics.* Washington, DC: Brookings Institution.
Esterling, Kevin M. 2004. *The Political Economy of Expertise: Information and Efficiency in American National Politics.* Ann Arbor: University of Michigan.
Fenno, Richard E., Jr. 1978. *Home Style: House Members in Their Districts.* Boston: Little Brown.
Forsythe, Dall. 2001. "Pitfalls in Designing and Implementing Performance Management Systems." In *Quicker Better Cheaper?: Managing Performance in American Government,* ed. Dall Forsythe. Albany, NY: Rockefeller Institute Press.
General Accounting Office (GAO). 1997. *Performance Budgeting: Past Initiatives Offer Insights for GPRA Implementation.* Washington, DC: GAO.
———. 1999. *Performance Budgeting: Initial Experiences under the Results Act in Linking Plans with Budgets.* Washington, DC: GAO/AIMD/GGD-99–67.
———. 2004a. *Results-Oriented Government: GPRA Has Established a Solid Foundation for Achieving Greater Results.* Washington, DC: GAO-04–38.

———. 2004b. *Performance Budgeting: Observations on the Use of OMB's Program Assessment Rating Tool for the FY 2004 Budget*. Washington, DC: GAO-04–174.

Government Accountability Office (GAO). 2005a. *Performance Budgeting: Efforts to Restructure Budgets to Better Align Resources with Performance*. Washington, DC: GAO-05–117SP.

———. 2005b. *Performance Budgeting: States' Experiences Can Inform Federal Efforts*. Washington, DC: GAO-05–215.

———. 2006. *Performance Budgeting: PART Focuses Attention on Program Performance, but More Can Be Done to Engage Congress*. Washington, DC: GAO-06–26.

Joyce, Philip C. 2003. *Linking Performance and Budgeting: Opportunities in the Federal Budget Process*. Washington DC: IBM Center for the Business of Government, October.

———. 2005. "Linking Performance and Budgeting under the Separation of Powers: The Three Greatest Obstacles Created by Independent Legislatures." Paper presented at the International Monetary Fund seminar on performance budgeting, December 5.

Key, V.O. 1940. "The Lack of a Budgetary Theory." *American Political Science Review* 34(6): 1137–40.

Krehbiel, Keith. 1992. *Information and Legislative Organization*. Ann Arbor: University of Michigan Press.

Lindblom, Charles E. 1968. *The Policy-Making Process*. Englewood-Cliffs, NJ: Prentice Hall.

McCubbins, Matthew, and Thomas Schwartz. 1984. "Congressional Oversight Overlooked: Police Patrols and Fire Alarms." *American Journal of Political Science* 28 (February): 165–79.

McMurtry, Virginia A. 2001. *Government Performance and Results Act: Overview of Associated Provisions in the 106th Congress*. Washington, DC: Congressional Research Service.

Mercer, John. 2003. *Cascade Performance Budgeting*. http://www.john-mercer.com/library/cascade_pb.pdf, accessed January 25, 2007.

Moynihan, Donald P. 2004. "What Do We Talk about When We Talk about Performance? Different Approaches to Understanding Performance Budgeting." Paper prepared for the Annual Meeting of the American Political Science Association, September 2–5.

Office of Management and Budget (OMB). 2006. *Analytical Perspectives: Budget of the U.S. Government, FY 2007*. Washington, DC: OMB.

Organization for Economic Cooperation and Development (OECD). 1999. *Performance Management and Financial Management—How to Integrate Them?* Paris: OECD.

———. 2005. *Performance Information in the Budget Process: Results of the OECD 2005 Questionnaire*. Paris: OECD.

Osborne, David, and Peter Hutchinson. 2004. *The Price of Government*. New York: Basic Books.

Radin, Beryl A. 2006. *Challenging the Performance Movement*. Washington: Georgetown University Press.

Schick, Allen. 1966. "The Road to PPB: The Stages of Budget Reform." *Public Administration Review* 26 (December): 243–58.

———. 2006. "Performance Budgeting and Accrual Budgeting: Decision Rules or Analytic Tools?" Paper presented at the Annual Meeting of the OECD-Asian Senior Budget Officers Network, Bangkok, Thailand, December 14–15.

Thompson, Fred. 2002. "Linking Program Funding to Performance Results." Statement for the Record before a joint hearing of the House Government Reform Committee and the Subcommittee on Legislative and Budget Process of the House Rules Committee, 107th Congress, 2nd Session, September 19.

Whiteman, David. 1995. *Communication in Congress: Members, Staff, and the Search for Information*. Lawrence: University of Kansas.

Wildavsky, Aaron B. 1979. "Policy as Its Own Cause." In *Speaking Truth to Power: The Art and Craft of Policy Analysis*, ed. Aaron B. Wildavsky. Boston: Little Brown.

6

The Legacy of Federal Management Change

PART Repeats Familiar Problems

BERYL A. RADIN

There are many ways to approach public management issues. Two, however, explain why the field is characterized by strong differences in views and approaches. The first focuses on tasks of administration, best described by Luther Gulick, one of the founders of the public administration field: All executives perform similar functions, whether they are in the United States, in other countries, or in the private sector. He called those functions POSDCORB, a term that is made up of the initials of a range of activities that take place inside an organization. In addition, this approach tends to concentrate on a top-down administrative approach. The functions are planning, organizing, staffing, directing, coordinating, reporting, and budgeting.

The second approach to public management/administration emphasizes the public side of the term. It looks beyond internal aspects and functions of organizations and emphasizes how institutions and decision processes play a role in defining the public sector. While this approach also is concerned about internal functions of organizations, it emphasizes the impact of context and actors outside of the organization on those functions. Among those factors are the fragmented and shared power structure of the U.S. system, the impact of federalism, diversity of the U.S. population, and the assumption that decisions are made through bargaining and negotiation. This route was viewed by Aaron Wildavsky as a bottom-up process that produced incremental change (Wildavsky 1974).

Much of the controversy that surrounds the discussion about performance measurement and its impact on budget process can be explained by focusing on this dichotomy. What some have termed "unanticipated consequences" of the Program Assessment Rating Tool (PART) and other performance management activity actually stem from the different assumptions that proponents of each approach bring to the table. Indeed, some have argued that the decision to take the first of these approaches has led to "the perverse effects of performance measurement" (de Bruijn 2003, 21).

My argument here (see also Radin 2006) is that use of the first approach without serious attention to the second has led to practices that do not always produce the results anticipated nor may not be appropriate in all situations. Because accountability and attention to performance of public programs and agencies is important, it does not make sense to move along a pathway that cannot deliver on the promises of increased accountability. While the linking of budgeting and performance measurement has achieved some benefits in some situations, in others, it has decreased performance and, instead, has increased cynicism and skepticism within the public sector.

Two Approaches

The first approach (I'll call it the internal management approach) tends to emphasize technical aspects of budgeting. It is the approach budget staffs usually take, assuming that budgets are largely based on clear and neutral data or information and that good analysis is what drives the process and leads to clearly defined goals and objectives. Actors with this set of assumptions are attracted to a single, consistent approach—what one might call the one best way. It also assumes that decisions within the organization are made by those at the top. This emphasizes the role of the White House and the Office of Management and Budget (OMB) in the federal government decision process. It rarely focuses on the motivations of those involved in the analytical process; rather it accentuates the data used to support a position and highlights the achievement of efficiency goals.

By contrast, the second approach emphasizes the politics of budgeting. It assumes that the U.S. structure and system do not give the executive branch control over the budget process. Rather, it focuses on the development of decision-making venues where various actors (both those with formal authority and those with influence or interest in a program or policy) have the ability to bargain over the allocation of resources, as well as the substantive requirements attached to the program or policy. This bargaining process often leads to budgets and policies that reflect multiple perspectives on an issue, rather than clear definition of goals and objectives. The imperative in this process is to achieve the required votes to pass the budget or program. As such, decisions emerge as a result of the trade-off between competing values and the likely involvement of players with very different sets of motivations and values.

The writer C.P. Snow has provided us with a framework to describe the conflict between two very different cultures illustrated by these two approaches. While Snow wrote about the conflict between literary intellectuals and physical scientists, his description of the gulf between these two worlds is applicable to the conflict between the world of technical budgeting and the world of politics. Snow wrote: "Between the two a gulf of mutual comprehension—sometimes (particularly among the young) hostility and dislike, but most of all lack of understanding. They have a curious distorted image of each other. Their attitudes are so different that, even on the level of emotion, they can't find much common ground" (Snow 1963, 4).

A similar dichotomy is found in the public administration literature on the conflict between politics and administration. Administration is viewed as a concrete set of activities frequently organized around efficiency goals. By contrast, what we call politics is a much less precise set of activities. Politics take many different forms. At the most basic level, it is important to remember, as Deborah Stone reminds us, that policy analysis is political argument and that policy conflicts are produced by political conflicts. Yet, as she writes: "Inspired by a vague sense that reason is clean and politics is dirty, Americans yearn to replace politics with rational decision making. . . . [P]olicy is potentially a sphere of rational analysis, objectivity, allegiance to truth, and pursuit of the well-being of society as a whole. Politics is the sphere of emotion and passion, irrationality, self-interest, shortsightedness, and raw power" (Stone 1997, 373). Stone argues that while most social scientists and proponents of policy analysis try to develop a middle ground between these two spheres, that approach is not appropriate. *"Reasoned analysis is necessarily political.* It involves choices to include some things and exclude others and to view the world in a particular way when other visions are possible" (Snow 1963, 4).

Many of the performance measurement advocates would eliminate politics from the public sector and create a decision-making system that rests on technical grounds. Still others want to use the performance agenda to accomplish their political agenda. It is difficult to disentangle the motivations for concern about performance since individuals often use the same vocabulary to express their agenda. I have seen at least three agendas at play.

- *A Negative Agenda:* This agenda seeks to eliminate programs and tends to blame those running the programs for problems. In the public sector it blames the bureaucrat for problems and seeks to cut back on responsibilities of government. This is a political agenda.
- *A Neutral Agenda:* This focuses on a concern about change. Individuals who work from this agenda argue that what worked in the past does not always make sense in the current or future environment. This appears to be both a political and a technical agenda.
- *A Positive Agenda:* Advocates of this approach want to get value for taxes and expenditures and emphasize efforts to assure accountability. This appears to be a technical agenda.

This Volume Relies on the First Approach

Most of the contributions to this book come from those who are most comfortable with the first approach. A number of the contributors are budgeting professionals whose training and experience pushes them to search for a way to avoid or minimize the toss and turn of politics. They are attracted to the dimensions of budgeting that flow from the internal management approach, including a reliance on the technical skills of the budget staff, a belief in a rational resource allocation model, a belief that information is neutral and can be determined to be true or false, a search for apolitical or at least bipartisan approaches, an emphasis on efficiency norms, a tendency to use the private or business sector as a model, and a strong reliance on the executive branch of government.

These dimensions are not new. Indeed, they clearly follow the tradition of past reform efforts within the federal government. This tradition, according to the Government Accountability Office (GAO), failed in large part because its proponents created performance budgeting systems that ignored the political questions found in congressional processes. These past efforts included the Planning, Programming and Budgeting System (PPBS), the Management by Objectives approach (MBO), and Zero Based Budgeting (ZBB) (GAO 1997, 7).

Despite this inheritance, much of this book rests on a belief that the contemporary performance movement has qualities that were not found in the past world of federal management reform. Excitement that has accompanied much of the performance measurement activity often surrounds these perceived qualities, including at least six elements. The first is a focus on outcomes rather than an emphasis on inputs, processes, or even outputs. The second is a sense that the U.S. activity is a part of a global movement that is frequently associated with what is called New Public Management (NPM) (see also Syfert and Eagle, chapter 8 of this volume). The third is an acknowledgment that changes in federal government management must be linked to a third-party environment; that government activity in the twenty-first century is dependent on actions of both public-sector and private-sector actors outside of the federal government. The fourth is a recognition that federal activity has followed reforms that have taken place in state or local governments. The fifth is a broad reach that argues that performance information can be used as a single source of data for multiple players ranging from political actors, to top level career officials, to middle managers, to program managers. And the sixth is the link between performance activity and various other elements in what has been termed the President's Management Agenda (PMA).

These six elements do suggest that today's performance activities are variations on the past theme. In some ways they depart from a long history of federal management reform activities in the United States. But in other ways they support the mind-set of the past reform efforts because they continue the assumptions found in the internal management approach. As I argue elsewhere, they do not fit easily into the institutional structures, functions, and political realities of the U.S. system (Radin 2000a).

Despite the array of management reform efforts over the years, couched in different guises and forms, few attempts to deal with management have resulted in any significant change. "The time and energy that have been expended in this process have created significant opportunity costs within the federal government. . . . Too often these reforms have evoked a compliance mentality and cynicism among the individuals in the bureaucracy who are expected to change" (Radin 2000b, 112).

The Experience of PPBS and NPR

For the purposes of this discussion, I emphasize two past efforts: PPBS in the 1960s and National Performance Review (NPR) in the 1990s. Both management reforms illustrate some of the same problems found in the performance measurement initiatives discussed in other chapters in this volume but often glazed over or at least minimized.

PPBS

In the post–World War II period, social scientists began to play a role in the decision-making process. The imperatives of war had stimulated new analytic techniques—among them systems analysis and operations research—that sought to apply principles of rationality to strategic decision making. Although still in an embryonic form, the computer technology of that period did allow individuals to manipulate what were then considered large data files in ways that had been unthinkable in the past (Radin 2000a).

In a sense, techniques that were available in the late 1950s cried out for new forms of use. Yehezkel Dror, one of the earliest advocates for the creation of policy analysis as a new profession, described the early phases of this search for new expressions as "an invasion of public decision-making by economics" (Dror 1971, 226). Further, he wrote, "Going far beyond the domain of economic policymaking, the economic approach to decision making views every decision as an allocation of resources between alternatives, that is, as an economic problem" (Dror 1971, 226).

Hugh Heclo also noted that the analytic and conceptual sophistication of the economic approach "is far in advance of any other approach in policy studies, with the result that a mood is created in which the analysis of rational program choice is taken as the one legitimate arbiter of policy analysis. In this mood, policy studies are politically deodorized—politics is taken out of policy-making" (Heclo 1972, 131).

All of this took form in components of PPBS, a decision allocation process established in the Department of Defense (DoD) in 1961 and eventually extended by President Lyndon Johnson to other parts of the federal government. The analytic approach would always be closely associated with the style and interests of President John Kennedy's secretary of defense, Robert McNamara. A graduate of the Harvard Business School and former president of the Ford Motor Company, McNamara had great confidence in analytic skills and the rational framework that would produce data.

The process itself required an analyst to identify the objectives of the agency, to relate costs and budgetary decisions to these objectives, and to assess the cost effectiveness of current and proposed programs. This analytic planning process was linked to the budget process (former RAND staffer Charles Hitch was named as comptroller of DoD with responsibility for the budget), providing a way to translate what might have been academic exercises to the actual allocation of resources. It represented the first serious effort to link strategic management processes to the budget.

The PPBS system that was put into place had at least three different goals. First, it sought to create opportunities for control by top agency officials over fragmented and diffuse organizational and program units. Despite the organizational chart, the DoD was clearly a federal department that operated more like a feudal system than a tight bureaucratic hierarchy. The separate services—Army, Navy, and Air Force—were distinct and separate units with their own programs, cultures, and constituencies. The secretary of defense had limited ways of reining in the services to operate as a single department. The PPBS system sought to look at the DoD as a unit and to provide advice to the secretary; it represented a way for the secretary to establish control over hitherto decentralized operations. Analytical categories used provided a way for the secretary to identify cross-cutting programs and issues within the highly fragmented department.

Second, the PPBS system was an attempt to improve efficiency in the way that resources were allocated and implemented. Looking at DoD from a centralized vantage point and defining functional categories across the department, it was obvious that there were overlaps and redundancies found within the multiple units, particularly in the procurement process. For example, economic efficiencies were not served by processes that could not define areas of economies of scale.

Third, the PPBS process rested on a belief that increased use of knowledge and information would produce better decisions. The experience of World War II was a heady one; advances in the availability and production of information gave the PPBS proponents the sense that it was possible to differentiate the false from the true and that the conceptual models that they relied on would produce accurate and appropriate information.

The office that was established in DoD to carry out McNamara's analytical agenda became the model for future analytic activity throughout the federal government. As the office developed, its goal of providing systematic, rational, and science-based counsel to decision makers included what has become the classic policy analysis litany: problem identification, development of options or alternatives, delineation of objectives and criteria, evaluation of impacts of these options, estimate of future effects, and—of course—recommendations for action. These recommendations were not only substantive directives but also recommendations for budget allocations.

In many ways, the establishment of this office represented a top-level strategy to avoid what were viewed as the pitfalls of traditional bureaucratic behavior. Rather than move through a complex chain of command, the analysts in this office— regardless of their rank—had direct access to the top DoD officials. Their loyalty was to the secretary, the individual at the top of the organization who sought control and efficiencies in running the huge department. In addition to the PPBS system, they introduced a range of analytic methods to the federal government, including cost-benefit analysis, operations and systems research, and linear programming.

This office was viewed as an autonomous unit, made up of individuals with well-hewn skills who were not likely to have detailed knowledge of the substance of the policy assignments given them. Their specializations were in the techniques of analysis, not in the details of their application. While these staff members thought of themselves as specialists, their specializations were not a part of the areas of expertise found within the traditional bureaucracy. Sometimes called the "Whiz Kids," this staff was highly visible; both in PPBS as well as when its general expertise came to the attention of President Lyndon Johnson. In October 1965, the Bureau of the Budget (later OMB) issued a directive to all federal departments and agencies, calling on them to establish central analytic offices that would apply PPBS to all of their budget submissions. Staff were sent to various educational institutions to learn about the PPBS demands.

According to a report in the *New York Times,* Johnson met with the cabinet and instructed them "to immediately begin to introduce a very new and very revolutionary system of planning and programming and budgeting through the vast Federal government, so that through the tools of modern management the full promise of a finer life can be brought to each American at the lowest possible cost" (as quoted in Williams 1998, 61). Johnson argued that the use of "the most modern methods of program analysis" would "insure a much sounder judgment through more accurate information, pinpointing those things that we ought to do more, spotlighting those things that we ought to do less" (Ibid).

Even during these days, however, there were those who were skeptical about the fit between the PPBS demands and the developing field of policy analysis. In what has become a classic article, Wildavsky published an argument in 1969 in the *Public Administration Review* that argued that PPBS had done damage to the prospects of encouraging policy analysis in U.S. national government (Wildavsky 1969). While the secretary of defense and the White House pushed the new system, Congress was uncomfortable with it. The budget for DoD was actually presented in two forms: the PPBS form inside the executive branch and the traditional line item budget form for Congress.

NPR

NPR was the federal management reform effort of the Clinton administration. Like its predecessors, the initiative sought a panacea solution that would rid the administrative system of politics. Drawing on private-sector values, the models for change met the growing global anti-bureaucracy mood and the belief that it was increasingly difficult to justify reasons for the public-sector point of view (Radin 1997).

Much of the NPR activity was grounded in the book by Osborne and Gaebler *Reinventing Government.* It emphasized the ways that analogies can be drawn between the public sector and the private sector, using the concept of markets as the basis for its agenda. Contracting out of government, viewing citizens as "customers," and encouragement of entrepreneurial spirit within the public administrative sector were key issues.

These values helped to define the administrative reform effort of the Clinton administration. NPR was located in the White House and launched by Vice President Al Gore. It utilized direct communication with citizens, face-to-face exchanges with career bureaucrats, and a series of teams of experienced federal employees that examined agencies and cross-cutting decision issues. Teams were composed of individuals drawn from agencies but assigned to assess areas other than those of their home organizations. The approach that was used emphasized a generic, government-wide agenda that reflected broad issues such as procurement reform, flattening organizations, minimizing mid-level controls, and changing personnel practices. A parallel set of activities took place in each of the federal departments and agencies. The first report issued by the NPR (*Creating a Government that Works Better and Costs Less*) came out in September 1993, just a little over six months into the Clinton administration.

Executive branch departments and agencies were given implementation responsibilities for the specific agency recommendations included in the NPR report as well as cross-cutting agendas. From the beginning of the process, NPR focused only on the executive branch and both analytically and politically avoided dealing with the Congress.

The focus of the effort was broad and established goals that were not always compatible with one another. They included budget reductions, policy change, reorganization, empowering line managers, improving customer service, and changing decision systems. The predominant values found in these efforts were driven largely by efficiency concerns and the philosophy articulated by Osborne and Gaebler and the private-sector gurus whose work informed the efforts. Many organizations confronted widespread cynicism among the career staff as they embarked on their activities. Some careerists believed that NPR was one more in a series of management reforms that had been unsuccessfully advanced by political figures over the years. Others were skeptical about the linkage within NPR between budget and personnel cuts and the other aspects of management change. In those cases where NPR produced change, it appeared to occur because some federal agencies modified the government-wide effort to meet their own needs.

When the White House pointed to savings of an estimated $63 billion from NPR activities, others disputed this, noting that many of the NPR recommendations could not be achieved without congressional support and there was little evidence of such support from Capitol Hill. The focus on efficiency values in the recommendations tended to drive out issues of equity and redistribution. Budget cutting and downsizing of the federal workforce drove a number of the recommendations. Institutions involved in NPR were focused on the White House, especially the vice president's office. Departmental activity did not involve agency or program staff. Congress was effectively avoided (Foreman 1995).

Table 6.1

A Comparison of GPRA and PART

Issue	GPRA	PART
Focus	Focuses on offices and organizational units	Focuses on programs
Branch of government involved	Both the Congress and the executive branch	Only in executive branch, centered in OMB
Organizational approach	Bottom up, begins with program units	Top down, OMB must approve measures
Requirements	Multiple; strategic plan, performance plan, performance report	Performance measures
Approach to measures	Multiple types but highlights outcomes	Focus on efficiency outcomes

The PART Experience

Most presidential administrations seem to want to put their own imprint on management reform efforts.[1] In this respect, the George W. Bush administration is no different from many that preceded it. Although some believed that the passage of the Government Performance and Results Act (GPRA) in 1993 established an approach to management reform that involved both Congress and the White House and was bipartisan in nature, the Bush administration created its own approach to performance management within the executive branch. This approach is implemented by OMB alongside the GPRA requirements.

This effort, PART, is viewed as a part of the Bush PMA—the effort to integrate the budget and performance assessments (OMB 2004). While PART shares some perspectives with GPRA, it does differ from the earlier effort in a number of ways. Its focus is different (GPRA focuses on the organizational unit while PART focuses on specific programs), it is located only in the executive branch, it has more of a top-down than a bottom-up approach, it does not attempt to include all programs every year, it focuses only on performance measures, and it emphasizes efficiency approaches (see Table 6.1).

PART started as a small-scale effort and reported information on sixty-seven programs as a part of the FY2003 presidential budget. Following that, it expanded the process to include 20 percent of all federal programs within the FY2004 budget document (231 programs). The process further expanded to include 20 percent more federal programs for the FY2005 budget. Some changes were made in the requirements but the general format remained fairly consistent. Unlike GPRA, which focuses on agencies and departments, the PART analysis focuses on specific programs. The OMB budget program examiner plays the major role in assessments.

Each of the programs included in a special volume of the budget documents was rated along four dimensions: Program Purpose and Design (weight 20 percent); Strategic Planning (weight 10 percent); Program Management (weight 20 percent); and Program Results (weight 50 percent). Questionnaires were available to agencies (but completed by the OMB budget examiners) that were theoretically fine-tuned to respond to the program type; thus different questionnaires were given for competitive grant programs, block/formula grant programs, regulatory-based programs, capital assets and service acquisition programs, credit programs, direct federal programs, and research and development programs. Five categories of ratings were used: *effective, moderately effective, adequate, results not demonstrated,* and *ineffective.* Of the programs included in the FY2004 budget document, fourteen were rated as *effective,* fifty-four *moderately effective,* thirty-four *adequate,* eleven *ineffective,* and 118 *results not demonstrated* (OMB 2004). In the FY2005 budget document, 11 percent of the programs were rated *effective,* 26 percent *moderately effective,* 21 percent *adequate,* 5 percent *ineffective,* and 37 percent *results not demonstrated* (OMB 2004).

Although both PPBS and the NPR highlighted the role of information and analysis, the rhetoric around the PART effort emphasized the availability and use of neutral information. OMB characterized itself as an unbiased evaluator of results and performance and through the availability of PART information on the OMB website sought to give the impression that the president's budget was data driven.

At the same time, despite this rhetoric, it is not easy to determine how an annual presidential budget was created. One analysis emphasized the disparity between PART assessments and program budget proposals. It noted that of the eighty-five programs receiving top PART scores in 2006, the president proposed cutting the budgets of more than 38 percent of them. Conversely, some programs that received the lowest possible rating of *ineffective* received either no reduction in funding (the Substance Abuse Prevention Block Grant) or substantial funding increases (Earned Income Tax Credit Compliance Program) (Hughes 2006).

In addition, there are two other reasons why it is difficult to ascertain a pattern of rating programs. The first involves variability among OMB budget examiners (this is a staff that prides itself on its autonomy and discretion). This variability was pointed out by GAO in its assessment of the process. In addition, the political and policy agenda of the administration plays some role. Of the programs rated *ineffective* in the 2006 budget that were targeted for elimination, more than 78 percent came from the Department of Housing and Urban Development or from the Department of Education. Congressional reaction to PART was variable during the last Congress controlled by the Republicans. Some members of the House introduced legislation that, although it was not passed, would make PART a statutory obligation. Called the Program Assessment and Results Act, the proposed legislation, according to its sponsor, would call on OMB to review and assess each federal program at least once every five years (Congressional Record 2005). By contrast, however, the House of Representatives Appropriations Subcommittee, with authority for the OMB budget, put a limitation on OMB's authority and approach to PART. It required OMB to provide a detailed description of programs, methodology, data, and responsible agencies' involvement. The committee report stipulated that if the committee did not agree with OMB's plans for PART, it would prohibit OMB from using information from PART in its budget requests. Republican Mike Hettiner, staff director for the House Government Reform Subcommittee on Government Management, told a conference he did not approve of using PART as a budget tool because the numerical scores can be subjective. "Some of the political judgments of the administration don't match the political judgments of the Congress" (as quoted in Mandel 2006).

There are a range of problems that have been identified with PART. Five issues are relevant for this discussion: (1) conflict between the PART assessment and congressional requirements; (2) use of an overly simplistic model; (3) variations in the structures of programs; (4) differences between research and development programs and other efforts; and (5) competing requirements.

The Conflict between the PART Assessment and Congressional Requirements

A number of the stated reasons for scoring programs negatively reflected OMB's disagreement with the way Congress designed a program or with priorities established in annual appropriations. In these cases, OMB scores a program negatively and imposes reduced budget requests because the agency is following the law. OMB justifies its decision using the rhetoric of results rather than a direct statement of its disagreement with Congress. The Consumer Product Safety Commission, the Occupational Safety and Health Administration, and the Mine Safety and Health Administration were criticized for failing to use economic analysis in their rule-making process even though Congress and the Supreme Court forbid that analytic approach.

The Use of an Overly Simplistic Mode

The federal legislative process, the necessity of crafting coalitions to pass legislation, and the shifts in congressional representation often lead Congress to create (and later amend) programs with multiple and conflicting goals. PART is not robust enough to capture this complexity. It ignores the multiple and diverging reasons why a program succeeds or fails. A program may be struggling to achieve its mission because it is underfunded, not because it is doing the wrong things. In some cases, there is significant disagreement within the policy or program area about what is needed to accomplish progress. PART measures ignore this complexity. In the case of elementary and secondary education, for example, the definition of "highly qualified" teachers within the No Child Left Behind program avoids dealing with the acknowledged disagreement within the teaching profession about what makes an effective teacher.

Table 6.2

Block/Formula Grant Program Ratings, FY2005

Rating	All 399 programs	Block/formula grant programs	Block grant programs only
Effective	11%	less than 3%	0%
Moderately effective	26%	27%	14%
Adequate	21%	20%	14%
Ineffective	5%	10%	43%
Results not demonstrated	37%	40%	28%

Social problems are complex and diverse and one should expect federal programs to attempt a number of approaches and address a wide range of needs. PART's design—its assumption that all that can be meaningfully known about programs is quantifiable—can lead to a short-sighted, narrow, and simplistic view of the role of government.

Variations in the Structures of Programs

Grant programs, whether competitive grants or block grants, are rated lower on average than other programs are. In fact, this was the case for the block/formula grant programs that were included in the PART analysis for the fiscal year 2005 budget. PART, during that budget year, included 399 programs, seventy of which were designed as block/formula grant programs and seven of which were designated as block grant programs. Table 6.2 compares the distribution of ratings for the block/formula grant programs with the broader pattern for the 399 program efforts.

Fewer programs in the block/formula grant category were rated as *effective* and twice as many programs were rated as *ineffective*. This is true even though there are different types of grants; some have a history of more active federal presence while others have a clear agenda for more autonomy for the grantees. When one looks only at the seven block grants, the pattern is even more divergent. No program was rated *effective* and three of them were rated *ineffective*. The block grant program that was rated as *adequate* was the Community Mental Health Services Block Grant. Yet its sister block grant, the Substance Abuse Block Grant, was rated as *ineffective.* Both programs could be viewed as efforts designed with fiscal objectives that sought to operate within a broader funding stream, and supported diverse activities, but PART did not provide a way to acknowledge those realities and observers believed that the differences in rating were attributable to differences between OMB budget examiners.

It is important to remember that many of the grant programs involved policy areas that have been criticized by the Bush administration. These programs were faced with performance review efforts that highlight the federal government's oversight role, while the premise of block grants is that funds are sent to the states with various degrees of freedom from complex federal oversight requirements. Many states and local governments have their own performance and accountability review processes; overlaying federal PART reviews has the effect of overriding state and local government self-management, contrary to the intent of block grant projects (see Buss, chapter 11 of this volume, on the Community Development Block Grant program). This set of problems is likely to continue unless OMB acknowledges that the federal role is passive, not active, in some program areas.

Variations between Research and Development Programs and Other Program Types

Although the general OMB instructions regarding PART did specify that research and development programs would be treated differently from other forms, the detailed requirements did not allow such a different treatment. Research and development programs often involve multiyear grants, support of uncertain scientific procedures, ability of grantees to determine the details of expenditure of funds, and the use of peer review processes to determine which grantees will be funded. The nature of scientific inquiry means that research can yield as much from surprises and negative findings as from achievement of hypothesized findings. But even though OMB seemed to move to differentiate between program types, these questions suggest that there was a strong tendency to think about research programs as efforts to meet specific annual goals and to avoid acknowledging the uncertainties involved in scientific endeavors. Questions used in this process for research and development programs included: Does the program demonstrate proposed relevance to presidential priorities, agency mission, relevant field of science, and other "customer" needs? Is a research program the most effective way to support the federal policy goals compared to other policy alternatives such as legislation or regulation? Does the program have a limited number of specific, ambitious long-term performance goals that focus on outcomes and meaningfully reflect the purpose of the program? Does the program track and report relevant program inputs annually? Does the program have annual performance goals and outcome and output measures that they will use to demonstrate progress toward achieving the long-term goals? Does the program (including its partners) achieve its annual performance goals? Were program goals achieved within budgeted costs and established schedules?

Research programs, by design, are intended to close gaps in our knowledge rather than lead to immediately measurable outcomes (such as reduced incidence of cancer or decreases in lifetime fatality risk from exposure to toxic substances). The federal government has invested in these types of programs not because they lead to other measurable consequences but because they are valuable in themselves. PART's bias for short-term impacts rather than long-term effects has been criticized by a number of observers. A member of EPA's Science Advisory Board testified that "it appears that the weighting formula in the PART favors programs with near-term benefits at the expense of programs with long-term benefits. Since research inevitably involves more long-term benefits and fewer short-term benefits, PART ratings serve to bias the decision-making process against programs such as STAR ecosystem research, global climate change research, and other important subjects" (Matanoski 2004)

Competing Requirements

PART sometimes conflicts with or at least complicates other government-wide reform initiatives. Collecting new data within agencies to comply with the PART rating system is often constrained by the Paperwork Reduction Act, which requires agencies to reduce the number of data elements collected from the citizenry. In addition, agency data collection cannot occur until the agency obtains OMB approval before collecting any information that asks the same questions of ten or more people. Data collection efforts that satisfy PART requirements can be expensive but there is no way for an agency to satisfy different parts of OMB and obtain such funding.

OMB Watch, a nonprofit monitoring PART, commented on the overall process (see also Gilmour, chapter 2, and Blanchard, chapter 4, of this volume for an analysis of the PART results):

> In his recent efforts to further promote a "good-government" approach, the president often referred to a list of 154 programs slated for deep cuts or elimination in his FY 06 budget because those programs were "not getting results." OMB Watch has analyzed this list and other sections of the FY2006 budget and compared program funding requests to the ratings received under the PART. This analysis has yielded some interesting and puzzling results. Out of the list of 154 programs to be cut or eliminated, supposedly for lack of results, more than two-thirds have never even been reviewed by the PART. It is unclear what kinds of determinations, if any, the president used to identify these failing programs when the White House budget staff has yet to assess them.
>
> A quick review of programs rated under PART since its inception finds no logical or consistent connections with budget requests. Of the 85 programs receiving a top PART score this year, the president proposed cutting the budgets of more than 38%, including a land management program run by the Tennessee Valley Authority and the National Center for Education Statistics. . . .
>
> However, this is not the only illogical aspect of the PART. Another puzzling situation is how the PART relates to and is integrated with the Government Performance and Results Act (GPRA) of 1993. GPRA, which was fully implemented in 1997, set out to establish a system for measuring each agency's performance—both on the whole and for specific programs—that could be tied to the congressional appropriations process. . . .
>
> OMB Watch's current analyses of the PART have produced more questions than answers about its value and purpose. It is unclear how the PART scores impact budgeting decisions within OMB as there are no consistent patterns to follow. It is hard to determine whether the PART is measuring programs accurately, consistently and in a value-neutral way. Even if it achieves these, there has been little attention paid to the question of what the PART is measuring.

A Reform Legacy

This relatively short description of PPBS, the NPR, and PART indicates that all three attempts to tie program information to the budgetary process have not yielded the results that their proponents have promised. There are significant similarities between these three efforts in terms of the definition of the context of decision making, defining the task of government, dealing with technical versus political approaches, and assumptions about the role of information in the process (see Table 6.3). All three focused almost exclusively on executive branch authority and ignored or attempted to bypass the Congress. All three tied reform to the budget process. All three created a government-wide strategy for change despite the great variety of programs within the federal portfolio. All three relied on the technical approach to policy issues that avoids politics and minimizes the complexity of policy and program design. And all three of the efforts were constructed on a belief in an ability to produce neutral information.

What's the Alternative?

I am not arguing against a serious concern about performance in the public sector. We know that there are many examples of programs that are not achieving all that we hoped that we would accomplish. Yet the approach that has been taken through the PART process (and its predecessors) has generated many perverse consequences, many of which stem from faulty assumptions about the process. Like its predecessors, PART suffers from its attempt to ignore the political or public-sector approach to change. It seeks to operate within a private-sector mind-set, and ignores the fragmented and shared power structure of the U.S. system, federalism, and the diversity of the U.S. population. It seeks to replace politics within a technocratic approach (see Table 6.4).

There are some alternatives to that approach. I offer them as ten lessons that can be drawn from the PART and past experience.

1. Remember that performance measurement usually takes place in a society that is diverse, with multiple populations who have differing values.
2. It is useful to think about a repertoire of performance measures, not a narrow set of measures.
3. Provide opportunities for trade-offs between multiple actors and conflicting values.
4. Don't forget that the political system provides the best approach in a democracy to achieve the trade-offs.
5. Modesty does become you; don't ignore constantly changing environments.
6. Involve a range of actors in the definition of goals.
7. Try to predict negative responses to the requirements.
8. Be skeptical about data systems.

Table 6.3

Similarities between PPBS, NPR, and PART

	PPBS	NPR	PART
Context of decision making	Executive branch White House control Top of department Exclude Congress Avoid bureaucratic SOPS	Executive branch Exclude Congress Private-sector model Avoid SOPS and bureaucratic norms	Executive branch OMB Exclude Congress Avoid SOPS traditional bureaucratic and interest group approaches
Task of government	Efficient allocation of resources Built on private sector Control	Be more like private sector Markets, customers, entrepreneurship Budget cutbacks Changes	Budget allocation Efficiency Outcomes
Technical vs. political approaches	Technical override political Parallel budgets for Congress	Technical used to cut budget, staff Government wide	Technical definitions Good government Government wide One size fits all
Information assumptions	Produces better decisions Information accurate, appropriate Determine what is true and what is false	Generic information produced by generalists Separate fact and value	Neutral information Establish cause/effect relationships

Table 6.4

Alternative Assumptions

Issue	Assumptions in performance movement	Alternative assumptions
Context of decision making	Actors share strategies, needs	Different actors have different strategies
	Executive and legislative branches on the same wavelength	Conflict between executive and legislative branches
	Legislative committees have common approaches	Appropriation/authorizing differences
	Federal government pays, thus can define performance	Devolution of authority to states, localities
Task of government	Efficiency values predominant	Multiple values, goals
	Laws lead to literal action	Symbolic action
Technical vs. political approaches	Can remove political overlay, make decisions based on "technical" grounds	Always conflict between technical and political
Information	Available	Not always available
	Affordable	Costly
	Neutral	Value laden
	Know what we are measuring	Conflict over measures
	Cause-effect relationships	Not clear about cause-effect relationships

9. Be skeptical about panacea solutions.
10. Develop allies in your response to performance measurement requirements.

Note

1. This section is drawn from Radin (2006, chapter 6).

References

Committee Report, House of Representatives Committee Report, H RPT 109–153, June 24, 2005.

Congressional Record. January 4, 2005 (Extensions). "The Introduction of the Program Assessment and Results Act." Page E15 from the Congressional Record Online via GPO Access, wais.access.gpo.gov (DOCID:cr04ja05–55).

de Bruijn, Hans. 2003. *Managing Performance in the Public Sector.* New York: Routledge.

Dror, Yehezkel. 1971. *Ventures in Policy Sciences.* New York: Elsevier.

Foreman, Christopher H., Jr. 1995. "Reinventing Politics? The NPR Meets Congress." In *Inside the Reinvention Machine: Appraising Governmental Reform,* eds. Donald F. Kettl and John J. DiIulio, Jr., 152–68. Washington, DC: Brookings Institution.

Government Accountability Office (GAO). 1997. *Performance Budgeting: Past Initiatives Offer Insights for GPRA Implementation.* Washington, DC: GAO, AIMD 97–46, March.

———. 2004. *Performance Budgeting: Observations on the Use of OMB's Program Assessment Rating Tool for the Fiscal Year 2004 Budget.* Washington, DC: GAO, GAO-04–174.

Heclo, Hugh. 1972. "Modes and Moods of Policy Analysis." *British Journal of Political Science* 2(1) (January): 131.

Hughes, Adam. 2006. Director of Federal Fiscal Policy, OMB Watch, "Testimony to the Senate Homeland Security and Government Affairs Subcommittee on Federal Financial Management, Government Information, and International Security," June 13.

Mandel, Jenny. 2006. "OMB Program Assessments Viewed as Flawed Budget Tool." *GovExec.com,* April 4.

Matonoski, Genevieve. 2004. EPA Science Advisory Board, testimony at Hearing before the Subcommittee on Environment, Technology and Standards of the House Committee on Science, 108th Congress (2004) WL 506081 (FDCH).

Office of Management and Budget (OMB). 2002. "OMB Program Assessment Rating Tool (PART), Research and Development Programs," Draft, FY 2002 Spring Review.

———. 2004. PART Frequently Asked Questions, http://www.whitehouse.gov/omb/part/2004_faq.html, accessed September 24, 2007, Question 27.

———. 2004 "Performance and Management Assessments." *Budget of the United States Government,* Fiscal Year 2004.

Osborne, David and Ted Gaebler. 1992. *Reinventing Government.* New York: Plume.

Radin, Beryl A. 1997. "Balancing Policy and Administrative Change." In *The White House and the Blue House*, eds. Yong Hyo Cho and H. George Frederickson, 15–25. Lanham, MD: University Press of America.

———. 2000a. *Beyond Machiavelli: Policy Analysis Comes of Age.* Washington, DC: Georgetown University Press.

———. 2000b. "The Government Performance and Results Act and the Tradition of Federal Management Reform: Square Pegs in Round Holes?" *J-PART* 10(1):111–35.

———. 2006. *Challenging the Performance Movement: Accountability, Complexity and Democratic Values.* Washington, DC: Georgetown University Press.

Snow, C.P. 1963. *The Two Cultures and a Second Look.* Cambridge, MA: Cambridge University Press.

Stone, Deborah. 1997. *Policy Paradox: The Art of Political Decision Making.* New York: W.W. Norton.

Wildavsky, Aaron. 1969. "Rescuing Policy Analysis from PPBS." *Public Administration Review* 29: 189–202.

———. 1974. *The Politics of the Budgetary Process.* New York: Little, Brown.

Williams, Walter. 1998. *Honest Numbers and Democracy.* Washington, DC: Georgetown University Press.

Part 2

State and Local Government and Intergovernmental Contexts

7

Performance Budgeting in Local Government

WILLIAM C. RIVENBARK

The appeal is simple. Rather than making incremental adjustments to the current year's budget when preparing and adopting a balanced budget for the coming fiscal year, local officials use a budget process that incorporates information on service performance when making allocation decisions. This approach to budget development—commonly referred to as performance budgeting—has made progress in local government since the push for productivity improvement emerged in the 1970s. *Progress* for this discussion is being defined as the percentage of local governments that have expanded their budget processes to accommodate performance, allowing allocation decisions to be informed by the efficiency and effectiveness of service delivery. It is not being defined as budget outcomes, where performance accountability trumps political and financial accountability (Rivenbark and Kelly 2006).

The notion that performance budgeting represents a determinate budgeting system is exactly what has hindered its success in local government from the time it was introduced in the early 1900s by the New York Bureau of Municipal Research. Performance accountability, which is derived from performance measurement systems, requires departments and programs to monitor their outputs, outcomes, and efficiencies within the context of stated goals and objectives. The performance data generated from these systems are then used to monitor and evaluate service performance and used to justify budget requests. But once performance becomes part of the budget process, it must compete with political mandates and fiscal constraints for example. An outcome-based definition of performance budgeting is simply not practical for federal, state, or local governments. Elected officials make budget decisions based on their own perceptions and on the needs of their constituents, and these decisions may or may not be supported by the performance of service delivery. A decision not based on performance does not equate to failure for performance budgeting when defined as a process; it reflects the reality of operating in a democratic environment.

Another reason that performance budgeting has struggled in local government from a historical perspective is because it is often implemented as a budget initiative rather than an organizational initiative (Kelly and Rivenbark 2003). Performance budgeting does not begin and end in the budget office. It begins with well-managed performance measurement systems in departments and programs. In other words, there is not a "chicken-or-egg" problem in this case. Performance measurement comes first, with department heads and program managers using performance data to manage and evaluate their operations for continuous improvement. The use of performance data for informing daily management decisions is known as performance management. When department heads and program managers use performance data for supporting budget requests, they have embraced performance budgeting.

This chapter begins with a brief overview of the lineage of performance budgeting in local government, beginning with the work of the New York Bureau of Municipal Research. It then presents the current status of performance budgeting in local government based on survey research. There is a caveat, however, when using survey research to explore the utility of any management tool. Different research approaches and different definitions can yield a wide range of estimates (Poister and Streib 1999). This observation is especially important when gathering information on the status of performance budgeting in local government, given the problem of actually knowing when an organization has made the paradigm shift to a performance-based budget (Joyce 1996). Two cases are presented in the following section on how municipal and county governments—Concord, North Carolina, and Davidson County, North Carolina—have been successful with performance budgeting when defined as a process to accommodate the service performance and to inform budget decisions. This chapter concludes with a discussion on the organizational capacity needed to evolve from an incremental-dominated budget to one that promotes the performance of service delivery.

Historical Overview

Budget reform represents a major theme in public administration literature, but most of the budget reform information focuses on state and federal government, for two possible reasons: (1) documenting budget reform in a limited number of governments (fifty state governments and one federal government) is more manageable than in the thousands of local governments that exist in the United States, and (2) reform often originates in larger organizations and moves downward over time. Fortunately, historical information on budget reform in local government is available.

Recent research on performance measurement by Daniel Williams provides valuable insight on how performance budgeting was conceived in local government. The New York Bureau of Municipal Research, incorporated in 1907, played a major role in developing the functional budget of separating expenditures by activity and promoting measurement of government in regard to outputs, outcomes, and efficiencies (Williams 2003). One of its goals was to link resources to intended governmental objectives (Williams 2004). However, lack of professionalism in local government stymied reform movements during the early 1900s.

Another push for budget reform came in the 1930s from the International City

Managers' Association, which is now the International City/County Management Association (ICMA). Based in part on the work of the New York Bureau of Municipal Research, the ICMA was primarily focused on measurement standards in city administration (Ridley and Simon 1937b). The research of the ICMA also included a budget reform component, which would allow department heads to defend their budget requests with information on the performance of service delivery (Ridley and Simon 1937a). While immediate reform did not result from the early work of the ICMA, many of the modern approaches to performance measurement can be traced back to the work of Clarence E. Ridley and Herbert A. Simon.

A.E. Buck suggested during a 1948 address before the Municipal Finance Officers Association—now the Government Finance Officers Association (GFOA)—that the need for proper budgeting in local government has been recognized for over forty years (Buck 1948). In describing some of the best practices in local government budgeting, he explained that a budget is a work program in terms of results to be accomplished and that monthly reports on departmental performance would be used as signals for executive action reports. He also explained that most local officials approach the budget from a dollar perspective, while very few think of it in terms of efficiency and effectiveness.

An emphasis then emerged during the 1950s and 1960s on an organization's ability to calculate and track efficiency measures, which included a professional push for the adoption of cost accounting in local government (Rivenbark 2005). Similar to the earlier research on performance standards by the ICMA, this expanded interest in cost control included budget reform. But while the desire to incorporate performance in terms of efficiency during the budget process made some progress, there is a plausible reason for its never becoming a widespread professional practice in local government during this period of time.

The need to establish professional standards on financial management and reporting in local government was paramount over budget reform. After the GFOA was created in 1906, one of its primary goals was the dissemination of uniform governmental accounting and financial reporting standards in local government. However, the leadership of the GFOA felt that a membership-based organization could not be truly independent in the promulgation of generally accepted accounting principles (GAAP) and pushed for an independent standard-setting body. This eventually resulted in the creation of the Governmental Accounting Standards Board (GASB) in 1984, which establishes GAAP for the public sector (Rivenbark and Allison 2003).

Another performance agenda emerged during the 1970s that set the stage for the current advancement of performance budgeting in local government. Individuals like Harry Hatry, who also was a member of the ICMA's Committee on the Quality of Municipal Services, overcame the "chicken-or-egg" problem and initiated the advancement of performance measurement systems in local government on the premise of productivity improvement (Hatry 1973). This more structural approach, along with professional organizations like the ICMA, the GFOA, and the

American Society for Public Administration (ASPA) advocating for its use (Kelly and Rivenbark 2002), has allowed performance measurement to make significant progress toward becoming a professional standard in local government. GFOA, for example, promotes the management tool as part of its Distinguished Budget Presentation Awards Program and as part of its recommended practices for local government (GFOA 2001).

The percentage of local governments that have adopted performance measurement provides evidence of its acceptance as standard practice for tracking the efficiency and effectiveness of service delivery (Poister and Streib 1999; Rivenbark and Kelly 2003). Local officials are drawn toward the utility of performance measurement for its support of numerous management functions—accountability, planning and budgeting, operational improvement, program evaluation and Management by Objectives, and contract monitoring (Ammons 2001). Accountability has been especially important to the adoption of performance measurement. Financial accountability has always been acknowledged by local officials. Performance accountability is now gaining ground in becoming an equal partner. GASB even encourages citizen engagement in performance measurement, which allows citizens to assess governmental performance and community conditions (Fountain et al. 2003).

The reinventing government movement of the early 1990s placed additional awareness on the need for local governments to start steering the boat with outcomes in addition to rowing it with inputs (Osborne and Gaebler 1992). Local officials are now encouraged to establish mission statements, service delivery goals, quantifiable objectives, and performance measures (outputs, outcomes, and efficiencies) at the program level to monitor the performance of service delivery. While a well-managed performance measurement system provides continuous feedback for monitoring and improving service delivery, it also establishes the foundation for performance budgeting (Kelly and Rivenbark 2003).

Current Status of Performance Budgeting

Research documenting the current status of performance budgeting in local government was selected on the criterion of using performance indicators to inform the budget process rather than to impact budget outcomes. Again, a determinate budgeting system in local government is simply not practical. In exploring the usefulness of performance indicators during the budget process, Cope (1987) surveyed 1,000 local governments with populations of 10,000 and above during the summer and fall of 1985. Surveys were received from 358 local governments, for a response rate of 36 percent. A critical finding of this research was that 60 percent of the respondents reported that they collected performance indicators as part of the budget process, which provides the capacity for performance budgeting. Another question was then used to explore the usefulness of performance indicators for defining future budget needs. Cope (1987) found that 33 percent of the respondents collected performance measures during the budget process and found them very useful when defining future budget needs.

Another study conducted during the same time period produced findings on the status of performance budgeting in local government similar to those of Cope (1987). O'Toole and Stipak (1988) surveyed 750 local governments during 1985–1986 with populations ranging from below 25,000 to above 1 million. Surveys were received from 526 local governments, for a response rate of slightly over 70 percent. O'Toole and Stipak (1988) reported that 84 percent of the respondents used workload measures, 81 percent used efficiency measures, and 87 percent used effectiveness measures. When asked whether or not these different types of measures influenced fiscal allocation decisions, 45 percent and 47 percent reported that workload and effectiveness measures, respectively, played an important role during the budget process. The percentage dropped to 29 percent when asked specifically about efficiency measures. The drop in efficiency measures is not surprising given the lack of cost accounting systems in local government that track direct, indirect, and capital costs. In other words, simply dividing outputs by a program's budget or direct cost is a crude methodology for calculating service efficiency.

More recent research provides additional insight on the status of performance budgeting in local government. Wang (2000) mailed a survey in late 1998 to 856 counties with populations of 50,000 and above to explore the relationship between performance measurement and budgeting. Based on the 311 counties that did respond to the survey and a random sample phone survey of the counties that did not respond to the survey, Wang (2000) reported that 75.6 percent of counties with populations of 50,000 and above used performance measurement in at least one stage of the budget cycle (executive preparation, legislative review and evaluation, or execution and evaluation). Notice that Wang (2000) defines the budget process beyond preparation and adoption, a definition mirroring the work of the National Advisory Council on State and Local Budgeting (1998), where the budget process consists of development, implementation, and evaluation.

Based on the percentage of counties that used performance measurement during the budget process, Wang (2000) reported that 77.7 percent used performance indicators for preparing departmental requests, 57.6 percent for analyzing funding levels, and 62.9 percent for identifying service problems and solutions. One explanation for these large percentages is the size of jurisdictions that were used to explore the status of performance budgeting in county government. More specifically, there is a correlation between jurisdictional size and management innovation in local government, where larger organizations are more likely to adopt new management tools because of awareness and capacity.

Rivenbark and Kelly (2006) explored the status of performance budgeting in municipal government with a survey mailed in the fall of 2002 to a stratified random sample of 1,143 municipalities with populations of 2,500 and above. The methodology produced 346 usable responses for a response rate of slightly over 30 percent. The authors found that 28 percent of municipalities with populations of 2,500 and above were engaged in performance budgeting when defined as a process rather than a budget outcome, which is slightly below the percentage reported by Cope (1987). However, Rivenbark and Kelly's (2006) finding was based on populations of above 2,500 and Cope's (1987) on populations of 10,000 and above.

While survey research has produced mixed results on the status of performance budgeting in local government given the methodology variations used to collect and report the findings, there is one conclusion that can be made. Performance budgeting, when defined as a process, is currently being used in local government to some degree. This is especially true for larger jurisdictions. But how do local governments actually use performance indicators for informing budget decisions? Because gathering information on the actual use of management tools through survey instruments is extremely difficult (Frank and D'Souza 2004), we must turn to descriptive research of individual local governments on how performance budgeting works.

Cases of Performance Budgeting

While evidence exists that local officials are using performance data to inform budget decisions, what's missing is a reservoir of information on how local officials are actually using performance data to support management decisions, which would include resource allocation. Cases are presented in this section on how the city of Concord, North Carolina, and Davidson County, North Carolina, have used performance data to help make the paradigm shift to a performance-based budget as noted by Joyce (1996). These local governments were chosen given the author's knowledge of them and the ability to provide hard evidence that performance data have been used to support management decisions.

Concord, North Carolina

Concord's commitment to performance budgeting begins with a well-managed performance measurement system. Each program of service delivery contains a mission statement, ongoing service delivery goals and quantifiable objectives, and a collection of performance measures that focus on the higher-order measures of efficiency and effectiveness. The focus on higher-order measures is especially important given that recent research has revealed that local officials are more likely to use performance data for making decisions when they reflect the efficiency and effectiveness of service delivery (Ammons and Rivenbark 2006). In other words, a performance measurement system dominated by workload or output measures provides minimal inspiration for service improvement.

The success of Concord's performance measurement system goes beyond proper structure. The leadership promotes performance measurement from an organizational learning and improvement perspective, including the desire to create a more data-driven decision-making environment. Another key factor is the investment in training. Concord has developed internal capacity to provide ongoing technical assistance with performance measurement and to provide annual training on the management tool. In fact, the annual budget process begins with training on budget data entry and on the ongoing development of meaningful goals and objectives.

Figure 7.1 provides partial information on fleet services in the *FY 2006–07 Approved Operating Budget for Concord,* which includes the goal of providing high-quality and timely vehicle maintenance for city departments to achieve low downtime and high-quality customer satisfaction. Quantifiable objectives and benchmark targets are provided in the performance summary table to define parameters in which to measure progress toward accomplishing the goal. The program then uses one efficiency measure and three effectiveness measures to track the performance results of fleet services (maintenance). The efficiency measure of hours billed as a percentage of billable hours reflects fleet services accounted for in an internal service fund. The effectiveness measure of customer satisfaction rating is a new measure, responding to the best practice of obtaining ongoing feedback from customers of service delivery.

A key aspect of the budget process in Concord, which operates on a fiscal year beginning July 1 and ending June 30, is how information is collected. After the budget packets are distributed, departments are required to submit their updated goals and objectives in February. Actual budget requests are not due until March. This sequence of information represents an important step in successfully implementing performance budgeting. Expanding on the reinventing government movement (Osborne and Gaebler 1992), budget requests (rowing the boat) are made after the desired levels of performance (steering the boat) have been established in regard to service efficiency and effectiveness.

Concord also participates in the North Carolina Benchmarking Project, which is a consortium of municipalities that uses the benchmarking methodology of comparison of performance statistics as benchmarks (Ammons 2000). This allows Concord not only to track the performance of selected services over time but to compare its performance against other service providers. After publication of the *Final Report on City Services for FY 2001–2002* (Rivenbark and Dutton 2003), which is the annual publication of the consortium, Concord noticed that hours billed as a percentage of billable hours (53 percent) was much lower than the municipal average and that the percentage of work orders requiring repeat repair within thirty days (1.1 percent) was notably higher. After an analysis of fleet services was conducted, multiple strategies were implemented to improve the overall productivity of the program. As shown in Figure 7.1, hours billed as a percentage of billable hours improved to 76 percent, and the percentage of work orders requiring repeat repair within thirty days decreased to 0.4 percent.

Another strategy from the analysis was the elimination of a management position in fleet services that resulted in an annual cost savings of approximately $45,000 (Rivenbark, Ammons and Roenigk 2005). This decreased the total number of authorized positions in fleet services from fourteen in FY2002–2003 to thirteen

Figure 7.1 **Fleet Services in Concord**

Mission:
Fleet Services will provide city departments with the most timely and cost-effective vehicle/equipment maintenance, repair, and fueling services. Our focus is to maintain a competitive advantage by providing the best value to our customers, which will in turn allow a greater level of service to city of Concord citizens.

Performance Goal:	
Major Service Area:	Maintenance
Goal:	To provide high-quality and timely vehicle maintenance for city departments in order to achieve low downtime and high customer satisfaction.

Performance Summary:

Major Service	Performance Indicator	Measure Type	FY04 Actual	FY05 Actual	FY06 Obj.	FY06 Actual	FY07 Obj.	Benchmark Target
Maintenance	Hours billed as % of billable hours	Efficiency	70%	72%	75%	76%	85%	85%
Maintenance	% of work orders completed within 24 hours	Effectiveness	94%	95%	95%	97%	96%	98%
Maintenance	% of work orders that require repeat repairs within 30 days	Effectiveness	0.4%	0.7%	0.4%	0.4%	0.4%	0.4%
Maintenance	% of customers rating overall service as "Excellent" or "Good"	Effectiveness	N/A	N/A	N/A	N/A	85%	N/A

Budget Summary:
Cost Center #: 4240

	2003–2004 Actual Expenses	2004–2005 Actual Expenses	2005–2006 Council Approved*	2005–2006 Actual Expenses**	2006–2007 Manager Recommended	2006–2007 Council Approved
Personnel Services	$633,495	$713,523	$850,796	$854,947	$722,036	$722,036
Operations	$831,990	$932,820	$932,463	$1,166,004	$1,477,880	$1,477,880
Capital Outlay	$5,795	$115,845	$23,454	$19,432	$25,000	$25,000
Debt Service	$36,677	$3,056	$—	$—	$—	$—
Cost Allocations	$(1,507,957)	$(1,765,244)	$(1,806,713)	$(2,040,384)	$(2,224,916)	$(2,224,916)
Total Expenses	$0	$0	$0	$0	$0	$0
% budget change	14%	17%	2%	16%	9%	9%
Authorized FTE	13.00	13.00	14.00	14.00	14.00	14.00

*As amended.
**Unaudited.

Source: Concord, North Carolina, FY 2006–07 Approved Operating Budget. For more information, see www.ci.concord.nc.us [accessed 8-9-07]

in FY2003–2004. Figure 7.1 shows the approval of a new position request in FY2005–2006, which returned the total number of authorized positions in fleet services back to fourteen. This new position allowed fleet services to discontinue outsourcing tire services and to bring the function in-house, with the desire of making additional progress toward the overall goal of providing high-quality and timely vehicle maintenance.

The utility of this example from Concord goes beyond providing the details of how performance budgeting works in practice. It demonstrates that performance budgeting does not begin in the budget office. It begins in programs with managers who are committed to using performance data when making decisions. Simply collecting performance measures as part of the budget process does not qualify as performance budgeting. Informing decisions during the budget process with performance data, like the elimination of a management position and the approval of a technician position for fleet services, does qualify as performance budgeting. Moreover, these decisions were being made over multiple budget cycles and were being driven, at least in part, by the goals and objectives of the program.

Davidson County, North Carolina

Program managers often approach performance measurement and performance budgeting with skepticism, fearing that budget reduction is the goal of measuring the efficiency and effectiveness of service delivery. Davidson County acknowledged this skepticism by rewarding accountability with flexibility (Rivenbark and Ammons 2005). Davidson had been collecting basic workload measures and reporting them in the budget process for some time. However, the measures were of minimal use beyond making the budget document look more professional.

The county manager, after building interest among the county commissioners and starting with seven volunteer departments, contracted for training on adopting and implementing a performance measurement system that focused on service efficiency and effectiveness. The purpose was to create quantifiable objectives from service delivery goals, which would establish what each department desired to accomplish in measurable and achievable terms. For example, emergency communications established a 96 percent accuracy rate for relaying location and patient information to responding units; the job training and employment center established a 79 percent employment rate for adults exiting the job training program; and tax administration established a 97 percent collection rate for property taxes. The quantifiable aspects (percentage) of these objectives are reviewed and adjusted during the annual budget process as a means of informing allocation decisions. Figure 7.2 contains the flexibility given in return to the volunteer departments for establishing and tracking operational accountability.

The purpose of Davidson's performance budgeting model goes beyond informing the budget process with performance. It is designed to promote performance management during the fiscal year of operations and to overcome the spend-it-or-

Figure 7.2   **Departmental Flexibility in Davidson County**

- Shift budget amounts within the line items of the personnel, operating, and capital categories of a given program.
- Transfer as much as $20,000 from the personnel and operating categories to the capital category.
- Use available funds in the personnel category to hire part-time and temporary employees.
- Fill vacant positions without filing for additional authorization.
- Reclassify positions as long as the reclassifications do not increase the total number of approved positions and do not create a current or recurring liability.
- Carry over budgetary savings within prescribed limits from one fiscal year to the next, subject to meeting performance expectations.

Source: Rivenbark, William C., and David N. Ammons. 2005. "Rewarding Greater Accountability with Increased Managerial Flexibility in Davidson County." *Popular Government* 70: 12–19.

lose-it mentality that governmental agencies often have at fiscal year end. Davidson allows departments to carry over a percentage of budgetary savings from one fiscal year to the next as long as they meet or exceed their performance expectations as established by the quantifiable objectives (see Figure 7.2). This key element of flexibility encourages departments to make decisions based on outcomes and promotes employee buy-in by rewarding success. Budgetary savings can be used for capital purchases and employee bonuses (non-reoccurring obligations).

Since performance budgeting was implemented in Davidson in FY2002–2003, additional departments have volunteered to establish and track their objectives in return for departmental flexibility. However, the broadening interest in performance budgeting is no longer being driven by the manager's office. It is coming from the original volunteer departments that have experienced the advantages of making decisions within the context of service performance. As noted by one of the department heads, accountability in return for flexibility has created an environment where employees want to experiment with strategies for continuous process improvement. However, building the capacity necessary for performance budgeting requires ongoing leadership and meaningful performance measurement systems.

Organizational Capacity for Performance Budgeting

Rivenbark and Roenigk (2006) created the mission, assessment, and performance (MAP) approach for analyzing the organizational capacity of performance management in local government (see Figure 7.3). A well-managed performance measurement system, which creates an environment for performance management, precedes performance budgeting. Therefore, the focus of this section is on building organizational capacity for performance management, which establishes the foundation for performance budgeting.

Figure 7.3 **Capacity for Performance Management**

Categories	Best Practices
Mission	
Leadership	You are personally committed to performance management for service improvement as good management and as an ethical obligation because you are spending public resources.
	Performance management language (objectives, outcomes, strategies, improvement) is part of your daily conversation.
	Periodic training is required in regard to performance measurement.
	Experience in performance management is part of job announcements for supervisory positions and part of the interview process.
Goals and Objectives	Service delivery goals and quantifiable objectives are established for major programs and service areas.
	Employees are provided opportunities to participate or provide feedback on departmental goals and objectives.
Customers	You know who your customers are and understand what they want.
	Feedback on customer needs and satisfaction is obtained on a periodic basis.
Assessment	
Performance Measures	Your measures are reflective of the program's goals and objectives.
	You collect a broad array of measures, including outputs, but concentrate on measures of efficiency and effectiveness for service improvement.
	Your measures provide you with information to support management decisions.
Comparative Statistics	You use comparative information (trends, objectives, targets, professional standards, or benchmarks) to assess performance.
Logistics	You have standard processes for data collection.
	Data are audited or reviewed on a periodic basis for accuracy and reliability.
Performance	
Reporting and Evaluation	You report performance information on a semiannual or annual basis for accountability (citizen and council review and budget preparation).
	You report performance information on a monthly or quarterly basis for operations and feedback to employees.
	You or staff members have the necessary skills for data analysis.
	You evaluate your performance (program evaluation, continuous process improvement, etc.) on a periodic basis.
Change	Performance information is being used in your program to support and drive change for improvement.
	Employees understand and are part of change management.
Rewarding Success	You acknowledge individuals or groups in regard to performance success (awards, recognition, bonuses, etc.).
	The role of performance management is part of personnel evaluations for supervisors.

Source: Rivenbark, William C., and Dale J. Roenigk. 2006. "A 'MAP' Approach to Performance Management in Local Government." *Government Finance Review* 22: 28–34.

Mission includes the categories of leadership, goals and objectives, and customers. One could make the argument that leadership represents the most important element. While there has never been an agreed-upon definition of leadership, it includes a personal commitment to performance management by department heads and program managers and to ongoing training on the multiple dimensions of performance measurement. Service delivery programs must have well-defined goals and objectives, including periodic feedback from customers.

Assessment represents the categories of performance measures, comparative statistics, and logistics. Performance measures are meaningful performance indicators that are identified from the goals and objectives of the program. Comparative statistics are targets or benchmarks that provide feedback on performance gaps. The logistics category represents standard data collection processes and periodic review of the data collected for accuracy and reliability. However, the need for leadership is evident with assessment as well. Simply adopting a performance measurement system will not provide meaningful performance indicators for supporting decision-making processes. The system must be managed on an ongoing basis similar to financial management systems in order to produce usable information.

Performance contains the dimensions of organizational capacity for performance management to actually take place. The category of reporting and evaluation includes the staff capacity to analyze the performance data and to evaluate operational routines. When evaluation is driven by performance measures, the likelihood that they will be used for informing decision-making processes dramatically increases. It also sets the stage for performance budgeting. The category of change is where performance information is driving service improvement, which includes budgetary implications as provided in the example for Concord, North Carolina. The final category of rewarding success is an often overlooked dimension of organizational capacity in local government. However, it can be accomplished, as illustrated in the methodology presented for Davidson County, North Carolina. Again, the need for ongoing leadership becomes apparent when presenting the categories of performance. In taking leadership to a new level regarding performance management, Brown and Stilwell (2005) make the case that performance management represents ethical management for public leaders.

Summary

Performance budgeting was introduced to local officials as a management tool in the early 1900s. However, it struggled to become an accepted professional norm due in part to its being implemented as a budget initiative rather than an organizational initiative. The performance movement that emerged during the 1970s helped to alleviate this problem by pushing for the implementation of well-managed performance measurement systems for productivity improvement. Performance data produced from these systems are used to augment budget processes by informing allocation decisions. Survey research has shown that performance budgeting is present in local government, especially among the larger jurisdictions. Case studies also have provided the details of how some local governments have been successful in making the paradigm shift from incrementally driven budgets to performance-based budgets.

While performance budgeting is making progress in becoming a professional norm in local government, more information is needed on the organizational capacity to make this happen. This chapter provides a modest overview of the various dimensions of organizational capacity in regard to performance management. However, the study and practice of public administration need to address these dimensions in more detail on how they relate to the successful adoption and implementation of performance measurement systems in local government (De Lancer and Holzer 2001), which is required before performance budgeting can occur. We need to document more success stories to further the momentum of performance budgeting, created in part by the reinventing government movement.

References

Ammons, David N. 2000. "Benchmarking as a Performance Management Tool: Experiences among Municipalities in North Carolina." *Journal of Public Budgeting, Accounting & Financial Management* 12: 106–24.

———. 2001. *Municipal Benchmarks.* 2nd ed. Thousand Oaks, CA: Sage Publications.

Ammons, David N., and William C. Rivenbark. 2006. "Factors Influencing the Use of Performance Data to Improve Municipal Services." *Public Administration Review,* forthcoming.

Brown, Michael F., and Jason Stilwell. 2005. "The Ethical Foundation of Performance Measurement and Management." *Public Management* 87: 22–25.

Buck, A.E. 1948. "Techniques of Budget Execution." *Municipal Finance* 21: 8–11.

Cope, Glen Hahn. 1987. "Local Government Budgeting and Productivity: Friends or Foes?" *Public Productivity Review* 10: 45–57.

De Lancer, Julnes, and Marc Holzer. 2001. "Promoting the Utilization of Performance Measures in Public Organizations: An Empirical Study of Factors Affecting Adoption and Implementation." *Public Administration Review* 61: 693–717.

Fountain, James, Wilson Campbell, Terry Patten, Paul Epstein, and Mandi Cohn. 2003. *Reporting Performance Information: Suggested Criteria for Effective Communication.* Norwalk, CT: Governmental Accounting Standards Board.

Frank, Howard A., and Jayesh D'Souza. 2004. "Twelve Years in the Performance Measurement Revolution: Where We Need to Go in Implementation Research." *International Journal of Public Administration* 27: 701–18.

Government Finance Officers Association (GFOA). 2001. *Recommended Practices for State and Local Governments.* Chicago, IL: GFOA.

Hatry, Harry P. 1973. "Applications of Productivity Measurement in Local Government." *Governmental Finance* 2: 6–11.

Joyce, Philip G. 1996. "Appraising Budget Appraisal: Can You Take Politics out of Budgeting?" *Public Budgeting & Finance* 16: 21–25.

Kelly, Janet M., and William C. Rivenbark. 2002. "Reconciling the Research: Municipal Finance Officers on the Role of Performance Data in the Budget Process." *Public Administration Quarterly* 26: 218–33.

———. 2003. *Performance Budgeting for State and Local Government.* Armonk, NY: M.E. Sharpe.

National Advisory Council on State and Local Budgeting. 1998. *Recommended Budget Practices.* Chicago, IL: Government Finance Officers Association.

Osborne, David, and Ted Gaebler. 1992. *Reinventing Government.* New York: Penguin Group.

O'Toole, Daniel E., and Brian Stipak. 1988. "Budgeting and Productivity Revisited: The Local Government Picture." *Public Productivity Review* 12: 1–12.

Poister, Theodore H., and Gregory Streib. 1999. "Performance Measurement in Municipal Government: Assessing the State of the Practice." *Public Administration Review* 59: 325–35.

Ridley, Clarence E., and Herbert A. Simon. 1937a. "Development of Measurement Standards." *Public Management* 19: 84–88.

———. 1937b. "Technique of Appraising Standards." *Public Management* 19: 46–49.

Rivenbark, William C. 2005. "A Historical Overview of Cost Accounting in Local Government." *State and Local Government Review* 37: 217–27.

Rivenbark, William C., and Gregory S. Allison. 2003. "The GFOA and Professionalism in Local Government." *Journal of Public Budgeting, Accounting & Financial Management* 15: 228–38.

Rivenbark, William C., and David N. Ammons. 2005. "Rewarding Greater Accountability with Increased Managerial Flexibility in Davidson County." *Popular Government* 70: 12–19.

Rivenbark, William C., David N. Ammons, and Dale J. Roenigk. 2005. *Benchmarking for Results.* Chapel Hill: School of Government, University of North Carolina.

Rivenbark, William C., and Matthew H. Dutton. 2003. *Final Report on City Services for Fiscal Year 2001–2002.* Chapel Hill: School of Government, University of North Carolina.

Rivenbark, William C., and Janet M. Kelly. 2003. "Management Innovation in Smaller Municipal Government." *State and Local Government Review* 35: 196–205.

———. 2006. "Performance Budgeting in Municipal Government." *Public Performance & Management Review* 30: 31–42.

Rivenbark, William C., and Dale J. Roenigk. 2006. "A 'MAP' Approach to Performance Management in Local Government." *Government Finance Review* 22: 28–34.

Wang, Xiaohu. 2000. "Performance Measurement in Budgeting: A Study of County Governments." *Public Budgeting & Finance* 20: 102–18.

Williams, Daniel W. 2003. "Measuring Government in the Early Twentieth Century." *Public Administration Review* 63: 643–59.

———. 2004. "Evolution of Performance Measurement until 1930." *Administration & Society* 36: 131–65.

8

The Context and Implications of Administrative Reform

The Charlotte Experience

PAMELA A. SYFERT AND KIM S. EAGLE

Whether performance measurement can make governments more accountable to their citizens and more democratic is a key question for academics and practitioners alike. This chapter discusses the theory that undergirds performance measurement activities today and offers a case study illustrating how one local government's practices can be placed in a theoretical context and show how government can learn from experience. We discuss the City of Charlotte's New Public Management (NPM) approach, including use of the Balanced Scorecard performance measurement tool to operationalize accountability and democratic governance (see also Rivenbark, chapter 7 of this volume, on other North Carolina cities).

The new context of performance measurement is based on the tenets of NPM, also known as the market model. [Editors' note: The debate over public management and governance is the focus of a book in this series, *Transforming Public Leadership for the 21st Century,* published by M.E. Sharpe, 2007.] Whether or not performance measurement can help make governments more accountable and more democratic cannot be addressed adequately without acknowledgment of this new context. Traditional public administration is based on legal or political standards with an emphasis on the role of the administrators as one of a policy implementer focused on limited politically defined objectives, bound by the law, and concerned with developing programs and providing services through the traditional agencies of government. Accountability is achieved through limited administrative discretion and reliance on neutral expertise to implement policies.

NPM is based on economic or market standards emphasizing entrepreneurial management, customer satisfaction, performance measurement, and competition. John Kamensky, an author of Vice President Al Gore's National Performance Review (NPR), commented that NPM is tied to the public choice movement, specifically as it relates to self-interest (Gore 1995). Accountability is achieved through choices that government offers its customers and responses to individual preferences for services (Lynn 1998; Osborne and Gaebler 1992; Osborne and Plastrik 1997).

Overview of New Public Management

The NPM context raises questions about the market context in the current wave of administrative reform. Although interest in performance measurement has intensified over the last decade, it dates back as far as Frederick Taylor's scientific management and the measurement of worker efficiency and productivity. NPM argues that government should be run like a business and that entrepreneurial-based techniques should be utilized in an effort to enhance government performance (Hughes 2003; Adams 2000; Barzelay 1992; Osborne and Gaebler 1992). Some scholars are critical, contending that such techniques conflict with the traditional role of government and democratic principles (Terry 1998; Cohen and Eimicke 1997; Clay 1994). Transfer of governmental responsibilities to market-based approaches—performance management and managed competition—are at the forefront of reform.

NPM purports to "fix the problems of government," such as low public confidence in bureaucracy, waste, poor program design, and performance deficiencies (Pollitt 2003; Hood 1991). Due to our nation's strong commitment to individual liberty and freedom, ongoing doubts concerning government power are not surprising. King and Stivers's (1998, 9) statement "anger at, and discontent with, government is also related to people's perceptions of the ineffectiveness and inefficiency of government policies and services" helps us understand how NPM techniques and principles have taken hold. Stivers, King, and Nank (1998, 25) contend,

> in response to this legitimation crisis and to charges that government—especially the federal government—is inefficient and wasteful, recent years have witnessed a turn toward making government functions and services more business like, further strengthening connections between business and government and disconnects between government and its citizens.

Although the label is new, NPM has roots in the long line of U.S. administrative reform efforts, including the Brownlow and Hoover Commissions; Planning, Programming and Budgeting System; Zero Based Budgeting; Managing by Objectives; Total Quality Management; and reinvention (see chapter 1 of this volume for an overview). Globalism and worldwide competition, coupled with the current public perception of government as inefficient and wasteful, are reasons to apply business principles to governmental entities. Reinvention argues that one of the five strategies for "banishing bureaucracy" and reinventing government is creation of an entrepreneurial culture (Osborne and Plastrik 1997).

The public sector is characterized as rule following, staying out of trouble, doing just enough ("good enough for government work") and never making a mistake (Osborne and Plastrik 1997). The perception that government is exercising illegitimate power and the suggestion that using "proven" business approaches can solve this problem is at the heart of many peoples' desire to apply the market model, including two central tenets: (1) the market, not the government, is the best allocator of resources; and (2) individuals are the best judges of their own welfare (Hughes 2003).

NPM's Critics

NPM's goal of embedding economic values of business and the market into the activities of government is often challenged. Critics argue that real entrepreneurs cannot be created in government, market incentives cannot be substituted for law, and reinventers undermine public management capacity by eliminating management layers trying to empower lower levels of public employees (Moe and Gilmour 1995; Schachter 1995).

Terry (1998) made the field aware of the potential threat of ignoring the constitutional regime values that should guide governance when turning to a business orientation. In his work on neo-managerialism, Terry discusses the issues and concerns that NPM brings to the practice of public administration under democracy. A negative view of human nature, in the context of neo-managerialism, embodies the entrepreneurial management movement. Terry sees a direct conflict with the promotion and protection of democratic theory in the context of an entrepreneurial tone of government that is market driven and competitively motivated. Moreover, the public choice–oriented character of neo-managerialism, as the foundation of entrepreneurialism, brings forth the opportunistic, self-interested, self-serving, and deceitful manager (Terry 1998).

The impact of NPM is of particular concern, as summarized by Eikenberry and Kluver (2004, 132),

> Central to their argument is a concern that the market-based model of public management, with its emphasis on entrepreneurialism and satisfying individual clients' self-interest, is incompatible with democratic accountability, citizenship, and an emphasis on collective action for the public interest. Furthermore, the market model places little or no value on democratic ideals such as fairness and justice.

That public organizations exist to administer the law and that an organization's structure, staffing, budget, and purpose are the products of legal authority is pertinent (Eikenberry and Kluver 2004). Moreover, public administrators are bound by public law and the Constitution—and act within the discretion allowed by the law and ethical constructs.

Frederickson (1997) argues that business and government have different goals and therefore private-sector entrepreneurship techniques are seldom appropriate and result in unethical behavior. Unethical behavior in government is increasing due to the growing emphasis on managing government organizations like private businesses. Moe and Gilmour (1995) argue that the market element of NPM is inappropriate because the two sectors, public and private, are derived from and based upon completely different legal doctrines.

Williams (2000) contends that NPM makes contradictory prescriptions in the call for a more businesslike government, while lacking a complete and historically accurate understanding of public administration (also see Russell and Waste 1998; Coe 1997; Wolf 1997; Fox 1996; Kobrak 1996; Nathan 1995; Goodsell 1992). Williams also argues that NPM provides conflicting, ambiguous advice and states that if NPM were merely inconsistent and inaccurate, we could simply ignore it. However, NPM dispenses advice that is counter to effective and democratic government and espouses information so misleading that it is deceptive. Thus, he argues, we cannot ignore it.

Pollitt (2003) takes this further, elaborating on the alternative logics posed by NPM and arguing that a contradictory message is being presented to public managers. When concerns over accountability and the primacy of politics, which restrict the manager, intersect with the NPM call for letting managers manage through the liberation motive, the message becomes mixed. Demands for increased performance evaluation and stakeholder participation complicate the message even more as the public entrepreneur is creative and responsive, transparent and measured or audited, while not making any decisions affecting groups without involving them in the process.

Critics assert that the market approach fails to capture the political considerations prevalent in local government (Denhardt and Denhardt 2003; Stark 2002; Box 1999; Kaboolian 1998; Kelly 1998; Moore 1995; O'Looney 1993). The movement has limited value and negative implications for democracy, because it neglects issues such as accountability, the issue of separating politics and administration, the difficulty in attaining social equilibrium among citizens/consumers, and some of the contradictions in trying to run government like a business (Terry 1998; Clay 1994). Despite heated debate, study of the impact on practice is not as prevalent.

Overview of the City of Charlotte

Established December 11, 1762, the City of Charlotte is approximately 527 square miles with 1,138.5 people per square mile. Charlotte is 67.2 percent white, 28.6 percent black, and 4.2 percent other. Charlotte is the largest city in a fifteen-county bistate region.

Now the twenty-fifth-largest city in the country, Charlotte has grown from a population of 395,000 in 1990 to approximately 623,000 in 2007. Charlotte's 20 percent growth rate is exceeded only by Phoenix and Las Vegas among cities with a population of a half million or more. Much of Charlotte's recent population growth is due to successive annexations. City limits expand an average of 6.7 square miles each year, adding an average of 45 miles of streets each year. Charlotte local government employs over 6,000 employees in fourteen key business units.

The political environment in Charlotte is strongly influenced by business. There are 292 Fortune 500 companies with offices in the city. Charlotte is headquarters for Bank of America, Wachovia Corporation, Duke Energy, Nucor Steel, B.F. Goodrich,

Figure 8.1 **Overview of Charlotte's Focus Areas**

Community Safety. In 1994, the city council adopted a five-year community safety plan. That plan has been expanded and combined with housing and neighborhood development initiatives and the implementation of community problem-oriented policing. Therefore, the city considers community safety from the perspective of the livability, stability, and economic viability of a neighborhood—not just the lack or presence of criminal activity.

Housing and Neighborhood Development. This is the city's comprehensive approach to meeting the economic development and quality of life issues in the neighborhoods and business districts. This includes efforts such as providing adequate code enforcement; developing strategies for affordable housing; and requiring neighborhoods and business districts to take an active role in problem identification and solution development.

Environment. This initiative was added in 2006 to acknowledge that environmental stewardship is fundamentally important to our quality of life and to a strong economy, both now and in the future. Protecting and improving the environment is a necessary element of the city's mission to enhance the quality of life for its citizens.

Transportation. This initiative is broadly defined as addressing all issues related to transportation opportunities and challenges, including maximizing public transit; implementing and maintaining roads; adopting and implementing land-use policies to support growth and transit goals; and ensuring adequate pedestrian and bicycle connections while meeting stringent federal air quality standards.

Economic Development. This initiative involves sustaining the prosperity and assuring the opportunity for participation by all residents. It also involves a focus on keeping jobs and the tax base in Charlotte by building and maintaining infrastructure, as well as building a skilled and competitive workforce to encourage businesses to locate and remain in Charlotte.

and Coltec, and is a hub city for USAirways. The Charlotte-Douglas International Airport is the seventeenth busiest in the country. The large concentration of banks and financial institutions makes Charlotte the second-largest banking and financial center in the United States.

Governance Structure—Council-Manager Form of Government

Charlotte operates under the council-manager form of government, with an annual operating and capital budget of approximately $1.4 billion. The city manager serves at the direction of the part-time mayor and city council. Since it adopted the council-manager structure in 1929, Charlotte has had only ten city managers. The last four city managers have had an average tenure of 12.5 years, somewhat unusual for large cities in the United States.

The mayor and council have led several initiatives over the last decade that connected government and business in an effort to foster economic development. These ties, according to city staff and publications, are witnessed in the culture of city government. The chamber of commerce, and the private sector in general, are viewed as supporting the city in operating as a business, favoring such practices as managed competition, performance measurement, use of corporate nomenclature for departments, and offering of gain-sharing pay incentives for employees. Implementation of both rightsizing and managed competition were guided by citizen advisory committees led by prominent business leaders.

Charlotte and New Public Management

In the early 1990s, the national recession and limited prospects for future annexation led to a forecast of flat or decreasing tax revenues. Continued population growth translated into increasing service demands and costs. The mayor and council at that time expressed strong support for NPM, especially for cost reduction, market-driven choices in service delivery, innovation, and reducing hierarchy. After Osborne and Gaebler's book *Reinventing Government* came out in 1992, Charlotte's mayor encouraged the business community to host a speech by Gaebler, much to the city manager's consternation. However, that event prompted the city manager to propose a plan for organizational change designed to meet increased service demands of a growing urban area with flat revenue growth and no options for increased revenues: (1) cultural change to focus on strategic thinking and planning; (2) empowering and holding key business executives accountable through enhanced and formalized performance measurement; and (3) realignment of human resources, through reorganization and rightsizing to better accomplish council goals.

In the early 1990s, Charlotte implemented an extensive "rightsizing process" with the goals of efficiency, reducing the cost of government, and aligning the priorities with resources. Also in the early 1990s, Charlotte embraced managed competition to address cost reduction and greater efficiency in services—water and sewer plant operations, meter reading, and garbage collection. Managed competition is an NPM-based activity, representing a significant departure for Charlotte from the more traditional public administration approach. Instead of focus on quality and community needs, the competitive service delivery model was driven by cost.

In the mid 1990s, Charlotte adopted the Balanced Scorecard (BSC) performance measurement tool in a continuing effort to address government performance, efficiency, effectiveness, and strategic planning. BSC is a tool first developed for the private sector to align mission and strategy into tangible objectives, and to balance measures of organizational performance between financial results and other critical success factors. This tool has been adopted by a number of local governments, Charlotte being one of the first. Both rightsizing and managed competition were implemented by the city manager, who was directed by the mayor and council to adopt NPM ideas about running government like a business by reducing layers of management, privatizing services, and focusing on the citizen as customer. BSC was identified, selected, and implemented by the city manager as a more traditionally focused means for strategically emphasizing community needs and not merely the "bottom line."

Organizational Change and Transformation

Reorganization

In the early 1990s, Charlotte rode the first wave of the reinventing government movement. Facilitated by the fiscal crisis facing the State of North Carolina, increasing expenditure demands for public-safety resources, and elected officials' desire to not raise property taxes, significant change characterized city government in the early 1990s. Specifically, in 1991, North Carolina withheld $4.5 million in budgeted revenues from Charlotte. The revenue situation persisted into 1992, when the city was forced to accommodate another $9.4 million decrease in revenues from the state. Decreases in state funding and slowdowns in other revenues prompted several steps, including a hiring freeze; offering all general fund employees time to take unpaid leave or five unpaid holidays; freezing operating expenses (no out-of-town travel, reduced subscriptions and membership fees); and reducing services, including garbage pick-up and transit schedules. The council then decided to hire 100 additional police officers, with no increase in funding.

At this same time, the city restructured in an effort to become more customer focused, results oriented, decentralized, competitive, and innovative. Charlotte reduced management layers and trimmed city departments from twenty-six, reporting to assistant city managers, to fourteen, reporting directly to the city manager. These newly formed departments were renamed "key businesses." Ten of the key businesses provide services directly to citizens; the remaining four provide internal support services to the ten service units. Although the reorganization effort was significant, more action was needed to address the fiscal constraints by rightsizing of staff levels.

Rightsizing

Charlotte took advantage of its strong connection with the corporate community and "borrowed" business executives and consultants to help with the rightsizing effort. According to "The Charlotte Story Public Service is Our Business" (City of Charlotte 2000), a *Charlotte Observer* editorial stated that "though 'rightsizing' may be an ominously annoying bureaucratic term, the City of Charlotte is making it an effective strategy to keep taxes in line and run city government more efficiently. Sluggish revenues have forced the City to find ways to streamline its operations."

Rightsizing successfully reallocated resources based on transferring positions and resources from lower-priority to higher-priority areas instead of merely making organization-wide cuts. As a result of the rightsizing effort, from 1992 to 2005 the number of police and fire employees increased from 52 percent to 63 percent. The percent of general fund, non-public-safety employees decreased from 48 percent to 37 percent in the same time period. Although a success, the rightsizing lessened the importance of traditional government concerns such as program development, citizen participation, and planning in the deliberations of council and administration in the early years of the 1990s.

Managed Competition

Managed competition is the establishment of competitive bidding for service provision between internal (government) providers and external (private) contractors.

Charlotte has been active in managed competition and privatization for over a decade. The managed competition policy requires adherence to three service delivery goals: first, providing the best-quality service at the lowest cost; second, a greater focus on performance outcomes; and third, an increased attention to accountability.

The competition philosophy in Charlotte is simple—best service, lowest cost. The managed competition mission statement for Charlotte reads:

> In evaluating the most efficient way to provide public services, the City shall use a competitive process in which private service providers are encouraged to compete with City departments to provide such services, and in which the option of delivering services through public employees and departments must be justified through the competitive bidding process. The City shall encourage the provision of public services through contracts with private service providers, wherever this offers the lowest cost, most effective method of service delivery consistent with service level standards and other adopted City policies.

Since 1994, fifty-eight services, with an annual value of $44.2 million, have faced competition with the private sector. The city has won forty-eight competition projects and lost ten. In addition, sixty-seven services, with an annual value of $27.3 million, have been outsourced to private businesses through the privatization program, seven optimization projects—using lessons from competition to optimize similar areas—with a total annual value of $36.5 million have been held and thirty-three benchmarking projects have been conducted since 1994 with an annual value of $9.5 million.

Strategic Thinking and Planning

Charlotte has developed both vision and mission statements that are used to guide the efforts of the organization. The vision statement stresses the desire to be a model of excellence and a platform for economic activity in order to give the city a competitive edge in the marketplace. The mission statement continues this theme by stating a desire to ensure the delivery of quality public services that promote safety, health, and quality of life for all citizens.

Vision

The City of Charlotte will be a model of excellence that puts citizens first. Skilled, motivated employees will be known for providing quality and value in all areas of service. We will be a platform for vital economic activity that gives Charlotte a competitive edge in the marketplace. We will partner with citizens and businesses to make this a community of choice for living, working, and leisure activities.

Mission

The mission of the City of Charlotte is to ensure the delivery of quality public services that promote the safety, health, and quality of life of its citizens. We will identify and respond to community needs and focus on the customer by creating and maintaining effective partnerships, attracting and retaining skilled, motivated employees, and using strategic business planning. **Public Service is Our Business**

In 1990, council participated in a strategic visioning exercise to establish consensus on the strategic themes that would guide goal setting, performance measurement, and resource allocation. After a series of follow-up workshops, council settled on five "focus areas:" (1) community safety, (2) housing and neighborhood development, (3) government restructuring, (4) transportation, and (5) economic development. Focus areas are the first or top layer of city strategy. Council also outlined objectives for each focus area. Focus areas have remained virtually unchanged since 1990 with the exception of government restructuring being replaced with the environment in 2006.

Council went a step further by creating institutional mechanisms to ensure that the objectives for each focus area would be met. Council committees are structured around the focus areas. At the staff level, focus area cabinets were established to ensure that council's priorities were being implemented. Comprising senior managers whose units directly affect one of the focus areas, the cabinets meet at least once a month to discuss progress toward strategic outcomes. The work of the focus area cabinets has created positive changes in organizational culture. City business units now think more strategically, and their activities are better aligned with the priorities of council. The cabinets play an active role in the policy process; they are responsible not only for developing a strategic plan for their focus area, but also for drafting or reviewing policy items before they are presented to council for consideration.

Since 1990, when it first identified five focus areas, council has held an annual priority-setting retreat. Prior to the retreat, a professional facilitator interviews the members of the council and lists their goals and concerns. From this list, the city council identifies top priorities for the next budget year, organized by focus area. Focus area cabinets develop initiatives and performance measures under direction from council. These measures are then consolidated into a strategic focus area plan approved by the city council.

Impact on Citizens

The focus area approach has had significant impact by providing a structure for meeting goals. A concerted, coordinated focus on policy implementation within the specific focus areas was made possible by the approach. All employees can see how their work contributes to council's priorities and understand how those priorities help respond to community needs. Focus areas have become a part of the community language, enabling the city to be more responsive to citizens' needs. The way Charlotte serves the community has evolved since 1994.

The City Within a City (CWAC) initiative is one example of how the focus area approach has worked to facilitate a more responsive local government, particularly in poorer areas. CWAC is an area in the older core of Charlotte, roughly within four miles of downtown. It contains about one-quarter of the population, living in seventy-three neighborhoods that include the poorest as well as some of the most affluent. The CWAC initiative had a twofold mission—to sustain economic development and to promote a high quality of life in Charlotte's urban neighborhoods and business areas. Providing leadership and resources to make individuals and families self-reliant and strengthening deteriorated neighborhoods were key objectives of the initial focus area plan for the city. Several principles made up the CWAC philosophy, which concentrated on neighborhoods, empowerment, capacity building, sustainability, partnerships, collaborative service delivery, and neighborhood accountability. The CWAC focus area success was also dependent on the success and strategies of other focus areas, such as transportation and economic development.

Measuring Success

Quality of Life Study

For over a decade, Charlotte has monitored neighborhood-level quality of life and taken proactive actions to protect and improve these basic building blocks of the city. Starting with the CWAC Neighborhood Assessment in 1993, city leaders and policymakers have had a document, based on citizen input, that enabled them to take a detailed look at the issues that need to be addressed in order to maintain and improve neighborhood vitality.

In 1997, the Neighborhood Assessment was followed by the CWAC Neighborhood Quality of Life Index. This study evaluated the quality of life in the seventy-three inner-city neighborhoods through an analysis of a wide-ranging set of variables. In turn, these variables were aggregated into social, physical, crime, and economic dimensions that were combined to create a quality of life index or score for each neighborhood. Planners and social scientists have long noted that neighborhoods evolve and change—socially and physically—as they move from initial development and occupancy to a mature state. Charlotte developed a strategic process and policy framework to monitor neighborhood change, and, as necessary, to take actions to guard against the negative effects that can accompany neighborhood maturation and change.

The Neighborhood Quality of Life Index measures the multifaceted impacts of neighborhood change. The community elements used in the analysis are structured around quantitative measures that can be directly or indirectly influenced by local government actions or policies. In this way, the study is focused on examining neighborhood change that is affected by deliberate public intervention, rather than change processes beyond public impact.

Results

From 2002 to 2006, of the 173 neighborhoods in Charlotte, eighty-six were classified as "trending up," seventy-four were in a "no change" group, and thirteen were labeled as "trending down." Geographically, the neighborhoods with improving quality of life rankings are found throughout the city. This is a positive finding, affirming the citywide scope of efforts to guard against neighborhood deterioration. A majority of the inner-city CWAC neighborhoods were in the "trending up" category. Success on the CWAC focus area plan objectives over the years prompted the city council to broaden the scope of the focus area in 2003 and change the name and emphasis from CWAC to Housing and Neighborhood Development.

The intrinsic constitutive value of administration can be weakened when the focus on values, participation, and relationships is reduced in favor of the "bottom line." This recognition helps to uncover the intrinsic value inherent in administration as it draws attention to formative or constitutive activities such as participation, value building, equity maintenance, and relationship development. Public administration is not merely an instrumental tool, as it serves to facilitate and shape norms and values through daily service to society (Cook 1996). The constitutive nature of public administration is illustrated in the example of the CWAC focus area. By focusing on what the communities wanted and needed, in the context of a business-oriented strategy, Charlotte addressed problem areas in a way that enhanced democratic governance and accountability. The next level of strategy is BSC.

Charlotte's Balanced Scorecard Experience

Background

Responding to public calls for greater accountability and efficiency, governments at all levels are now using performance measurement in one form or another. However, establishing an effective priority-setting system, allocating scarce resources based on those priorities, and measuring outcomes are ongoing challenges for most governments, including Charlotte. The evolution of Charlotte's strategy and performance measurement, with an emphasis on the lessons learned from over ten years of using BSC, characterizes the city's management framework. Operating within the NPM context, Charlotte has used BSC to translate mission and strategy into tangible objectives and measures that provide a comprehensive view into performance as it relates to strategic priorities.

Developed for the private sector in an effort to balance measures of organizational performance between financial results and other critical success factors, BSC has been adapted for the public sector by local governments. From implementing the scorecard to the most recent challenge of linking strategy to resource allocation, efforts are characterized by a focus on continuous improvement.

Implementation

In 1996 Charlotte formally adopted BSC. Although BSC was designed for business and industry, Charlotte modified the approach to fit the public sector and was the first municipality to implement the scorecard. Unlike the way in which the city adopted rightsizing and managed competition (through advocacy and direction of council), the city manager researched and advocated to council the adoption of BSC. The manager believed that this tool had the potential to meet the government's needs for accountability and performance measurement, and to focus the efforts of council and city management on broader community needs and priorities than just efficiency of services. BSC linked the five focus areas to program development strategies (such as Housing, Neighborhood Development, and Community Policing) and provided the framework for emphasizing the priority of managed competition for service delivery. BSC also focused on training and development of the public employee, to achieve goals of staying competitive—that is, acquiring job-based skills valued in the private sector for service delivery, and promoting public-service ethics and values such as openness, responsiveness, and accountability. The city hired a consultant and organized a leadership team to guide BSC implementation. Led by staff from the Budget and Evaluation unit, the team used the city's strategic plan as the foundation for what became known as the corporate scorecard. The city then piloted the new performance measurement system in four business units, each of which developed its own scorecards.

Focus areas are validated at the annual council retreat, and are used to guide the development of initiatives and objectives, which in turn direct the work of council committees and focus area cabinets throughout the year. The corporate scorecard includes sixteen objectives that connect the focus areas, council priorities, and individual key business unit scorecards. Comprehensive Citizen Service is the strategic umbrella, which is why it is shown above the focus areas. Performance measures are used to gauge progress toward achieving the sixteen objectives. Examples of corporate measures include service delivery ratings, the quality of life index, crime rates, and transit ridership. The corporate scorecard has proven a useful tool for setting strategic targets and fostering the organizational collaboration necessary to accomplish strategic initiatives (see Figure 8.2).

Early in Charlotte's implementation of NPM practices, the concept of citizen

Figure 8.2   **Charlotte's Balanced Scorecard Template**

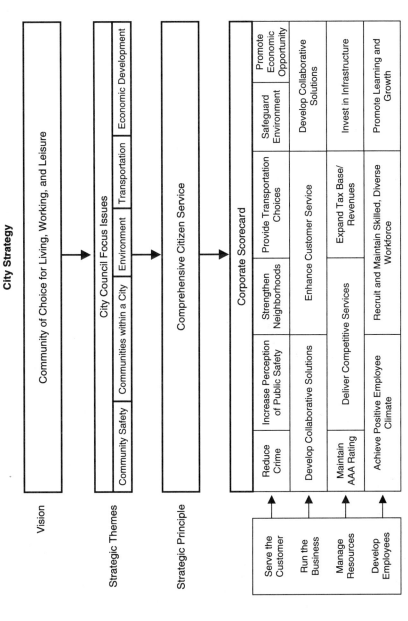

Source: City of Charlotte. Used by permission.

as customer engendered vigorous debate. The idea of *customer* did not resonate with employees responsible for development of regulation, long-range planning, fire prevention, police patrol, or general administration. These employees viewed their work as supporting the overall health, safety, and welfare of the community and its citizens, not specific customers.

For the garbage collector, water billing clerk, meter reader, or airport shuttle driver, the focus on *customer* did make sense because their key business unit or division was organized around a specific customer base. What has evolved in Charlotte is a flexible idea of *customer,* which includes both the customer of a well-defined service delivery system—garbage collection, transit, and water and sewer—and the citizen who lives within the geographic boundary of the city and wants participation in government decisions, equity, and access. BSC includes goals for the citizen such as strategies to strengthen neighborhoods, increase safety, provide transportation choices, and protect the environment.

Charlotte has integrated BSC into all levels of the organization. Each business unit develops a BSC outlining how they plan to address focus areas, council priorities, and corporate scorecard objectives. Business units determine the corporate objectives on which they have a direct impact and develop measures to track their progress in contributing to the achievement of those objectives. In developing their scorecards, business units answer a number of important questions, organized around the four perspectives:

- *Serve the Customer.* In order to meet the needs of our *customers/citizens,* what are our objectives? How can these objectives be achieved? How is success best measured?
- *Manage Resources.* In order to succeed *financially,* what are our objectives? How can these objectives be achieved? How is success best measured?
- *Run the Business.* In order to meet our objectives, what *internal processes* are required? How can these processes be established? How is success best measured?
- *Develop Employees.* In order to succeed, what *skills and resources* do we need? How can we obtain and maintain these skills and resources? How is success best measured?

Business units identify key objectives in the scorecards that link their individual goals to organizational goals and strategy.

Use of Performance Measure Information in Budget Decisions

High political stakes involved in budgeting decisions make the development and effective use of outcome measures difficult at best. Charlotte's budget deliberation process draws directly from BSC measures. Outcome measures related to the key issues debated during the FY2007 budget process included street condition ratings, housing and nuisance code compliance, private funds leveraged from public investment in affordable housing, fire response times, adoptable animal euthanization rate, and quality of life study ratings. Prior to the implementation of BSC, outcome-focused performance information was not being generated that could be used for decision making.

Use of Performance Information—Necessary Conditions for Success

Charlotte has learned a lot about strategic planning over the last decade. Experience with BSC suggests that there are two primary keys to making this approach work in a government setting. First, strategy must be supported. Consistent support of senior management is particularly critical, but there must be support for the effort at all levels of the organization. Second, strategy must be operationalized. The best strategy benefits no one unless it is put into action. The implementation of the managed competition program is one example of a tool used by the city to operationalize strategy.

Organizational support for strategy development and implementation is fundamental to success. This support must reach from the governing body and the chief executive through the entire organization. Strategy can and should become institutionalized within the culture of the organization to the point that it becomes part and parcel of how the organization operates, as opposed to an add-on that most people expect will eventually go away. For this to happen, the organization must invest in people, technology, and research. Finally, to ensure that strategy remains a visible priority for the organization as a whole and a meaningful exercise for all levels of the organization, staff at all levels should be recruited to champion the effort and to make the most of the scorecard tool.

For organizational strategy to reach the operations level, where it gets translated into tangible results, employees need to be able to see—"line of sight"—how their daily activities contribute to the accomplishment of overall strategy. One method Charlotte is using to strengthen this relationship is to link employee performance evaluations and compensation to the achievement of business unit scorecard goals. The framework connects the city's focus areas and corporate objectives to each of the key business units.

Strategy, in Charlotte's BSC, is a continuous and accountable process that must be communicated so everyone can understand it and see how they contribute to its organizational achievement. Implementing strategy is not easy, but is one of the most important factors in shaping how an organization can and will respond to community needs.

Quantifiable Benefits

Prior to BSC implementation, the Management by Objectives audit tool provided output-oriented data less strategic in nature and function. Benefits derived from implementing the scorecard tool to measure success are numerous. Some quantifiable examples include: Documented savings from the city's managed competition program are connected to the Balanced Scorecard initiative Deliver Competitive Services. The city has saved over $10 million since 1995 as a result of the managed competition initiative. Citizen survey results, measuring how safe citizens feel in their neighborhoods, improved from 71 percent in 2001 to 74 percent in 2006. This measure is linked to the objective Perception of Safety. Transit ridership, representative of the objective to Provide Transportation Choices, increased 62 percent in eight years, increasing from 11.82 million riders annually in 1998 to 19 million in 2006. Finally, the objective Strengthen Neighborhoods demonstrated results related to nuisance code compliances. From 2001 to 2006 nuisance code compliances increased from 26,000 to over 38,000, annually.

Impact on Practitioners

The transition to a market-based mind-set, including an emphasis on strategy development in the context of BSC, challenged city staff. Establishment of an economic context for decision making and accountability brought forward the need for mid-level and upper-level managers to reconcile traditional approaches to service delivery with the themes of NPM while maintaining an adequate focus on accountability and democratic governance. BSC fosters accountability in numerous ways, from the city manager's performance evaluation to council discussions on performance results, key business executive performance evaluations, incentive payment programs, and public access to information.

Charlotte recognized the significance and importance of democratic governance and the constitutive role of administration while also adopting a market orientation to managing service delivery and performance measurement. A distinction between public administration and business management must be acknowledged. As discussed previously, Terry (1998) attempted to make the field aware of the internal danger of ignoring the constitutional regime values that should guide governance when it turns to a business orientation. If public administration is a calling, attention should be given to the evaluation of the relationship between reform practices and service delivery approaches. It is imperative that leaders do not forget their role in governance and the public-service ethic that keeps them true to their calling to serve.

Conclusion

This chapter summarized Charlotte's experience, framed in a theoretical context. In the early 1990s, Charlotte embraced NPM for local government management. Experience has shown the importance of viewing the citizen as someone with a stake in government, from the democratic governance and accountability perspectives, as well as an individual customer to be served. Democratic governance and accountability are fundamental issues in public administration debate and discourse. Grounding our practical experiences in theory is the first step to answering the question, does performance measurement make governments more accountable to their citizens and more democratic? NPM demonstrates that use of performance measurement tools can provide a level of operational transparency and customer responsiveness toward reaching the goal of democratic governance and accountability. However, additional study is required to establish whether performance measurement tools are the answer to both governments' and citizens' goals of democratic governance and accountability.

Looking back at the Charlotte experience over sixteen years leads to several observations and general conclusions.

1. The early adoption of practices such as managed competition and right-sizing were responses to the fiscal challenges, as well as the advocacy of elected officials for NPM.
2. In early years, efforts for cost reduction, organizational change, and performance measurement lacked a strategic framework linking those efforts to the needs and desires of the community. Without the framework, the community can begin to view government merely as a "vending machine" for services.
3. BSC has been a useful and effective tool to align community goals with finding solutions to make government more accountable, efficient, and responsive.
4. Although unintentional, the consequences of managed competition and other cost-reduction efforts are that public employees are treated only as costs to be managed. BSC requires public managers to think about public employees as crucial in achieving organizational vision and mission.
5. BSC drove performance achievement and balanced NPM with democratic governance.

References

Abels, Michael. 2004. "The Middle Manager, Leadership, and the Public Interest." *Public Administration Times,* March: 4.

Adams, Guy. 2000. "Uncovering the Political Philosophy of the New Public Management." *Administrative Theory & Praxis* 22(3): 498–99.

Aucoin, Peter. 1990. "Administrative Reform in Public Management: Paradigms, Principles, Paradoxes and Pendulums." *Governance* 3: 115–37.

Barzelay, Michael. 1992. *Breaking through Bureaucracy.* Sacramento: University of California Press.

Behn, Robert. 2001. *Rethinking Democratic Accountability.* Washington, DC: Brookings Institution Press.

Blair, Robert. 2000. "Policy Implementation Networks: The Impact of Economic Development on New Public Management." *International Journal of Economic Development* 2(4): 511–36.

Blais, A., and S. Dion, eds. 1992. *The Budget-Maximizing Bureaucrat.* Pittsburgh, PA: University of Pittsburgh Press.

Blanchard, Lloyd, Charles Hinnant, and Wilson Wong. 1998. "Market-Based Reforms in Government: Toward a Social Subcontract?" *Administration and Society* 30(56): 483–512.

Box, Richard C.. 1998. *Citizen Governance: Leading American Communities into the 21st Century.* Thousand Oaks, CA: Sage Publications.

———. 1999. "Running Government like a Business: Implications for Public Administration Theory and Practice." *American Review of Public Administration* 29(1): 19–43.

Boyne, George. 1998. "Bureaucratic Theory Meets Reality: Public Choice and Service Contracting in U.S. Local Governments." *Public Administration Review* 58(6): 474–93.

City of Charlotte. 2000. *The Charlotte Story: Public Service is Our Business.*

———. 2001. *Managed Competition Best Practices.*

———. 2002. *Competition Overview.*

———. 2003. *FY2006 Corporate Balanced Scorecard Report.*

———. 2006a. *Five-Year Competition Plan.*

———. 2006b. *Strategic Focus Area Plan.*

Clay, Joy. 1994. "Public-Institutional Processes: Beyond Conventional Wisdom about Management Processes." *Administration & Society* 26(2): 236–52.

Coe, Barbara A. 1997. "How Structural Conflicts Stymie Reinvention." *Public Administration Review* 57(2): 168–73.

Cohen, Steven, and William Eimicke. 1995. "Ethics and the Public Administrator." *The Annals of the American Academy of Political and Social Science* 537(1): 96–108.

———. 1997. "Is Public Entrepreneurship Ethical? A Second Look at Theory and Practice." Presented at the 1997 Annual Meeting of the American Political Science Association, Washington, DC.

———. 2002. *The Effective Public Manager.* 3rd ed. San Francisco, CA: Jossey Bass.

Connolly, M., and N. Jones. 2003. "Constructing Management Practice in the New Public Management: The Case of Mental Health Managers." *Health Services Management Research* 16(3): 203–11.

Considine, Mark, and Jenny Lewis. 1999. "Governance at Ground Level: The Frontline Bureaucrat in the Age of Markets and Networks." *Public Administration Review* 59(6): 467–87.

Cook, Brian J. 1996. *Bureaucracy and Self-Government.* Baltimore: John Hopkins University Press.

DeLeon, Linda, and Robert Denhardt. 2000. "The Political Theory of Reinvention." *Public Administration Review* 60(2): 89–97.

Denhardt, Janet V., and Robert B. Denhardt. 2003. *The New Public Service.* Armonk, NY: M.E. Sharpe.

Diver, Colin. 1982. "Engineers and Entrepreneurs: The Dilemma of Public Management." *Journal of Policy Analysis and Management* 1(3): 402–6.

Eagle, Kimberly. 1997. "Contract Monitoring for Financial and Operational Performance." *Government Finance Review* June: 11–14.

———. 2000. "Managed Competition in Charlotte-Mecklenburg Utilities." In *America's Water and Wastewater Industries: Competition and Privatization,* Paul Seidenstat, Michael Nadol, and Simon Hakim, eds. Public Utilities Reports.

———. 2004. "The Origins and Evolution of Charlotte's Corporate Scorecard." *Government Finance Review* October: 16–22.

Eikenberry, Angela, and Jodie Kluver. 2004. "The Marketization of the Nonprofit Sector: Civil Society at Risk?" *Public Administration Review* 64(2): 132–40.

Fox, Charles. 1996. "Reinventing Government as Postmodern Symbolic Politics." *Public Administration Review* 56(3): 256–62.

Frederickson, H. George. 1995. "Misdiagnosing the Orange County Scandal." *Governing,* April: 9.

———. 1997. *The Spirit of Public Administration.* San Francisco, CA: Jossey-Bass.

Goodsell, Charles. 1992. "Reinvent Government or Rediscover It?" *Public Administration Review* 53(1): 85–87.

Gore, Al. 1995. *Common Sense Government: Works Better & Costs Less. Third Report of the National Performance Review.* Washington, DC: U.S. Government Printing Office.

Hood, Christopher. 1991. "A Public Management for All Seasons." *Public Administration Review* 69(1): 3–19.

Hood, Christopher, and G.F. Schuppert, eds. 1988. *Delivering Public Services: Sharing Western European Experience.* London: Sage Publications.

Hughes, Owen. 2003. *Public Management and Administration: An Introduction.* New York: Palgrave.

Kaboolian, Linda. 1998. "The New Public Management: Challenging the Boundaries of the Management vs. Administration Debate." *Public Administration Review* 58(3): 189–93.

Kelly, Rita Mae. 1998. "An Inclusive Democratic Polity, Representative Bureaucracies and New Public Management." *Public Administration Review* 58(3): 201–9.

Kettl, Donald. 1993. *Sharing Power: Public Governance and Private Markets.* Washington, DC: Brookings Institution.

———. 1997. "The Global Revolution in Public Management: Driving Themes, Missing Links." *Journal of Policy Analysis and Management* 16(3): 446–62.

King, Cheryl Smirell, and Camilla Stivers. 1998. *Government Is US: Public Administration in an Anti-Government Era.* Newbury Park, CA: Sage Publications.

Kirlin, John. 1996. "The Big Questions of Public Administration in a Democracy." *Public Administration Review* 56(5): 416–23.

Klinger, Donald, John Nalbandian, and Barbara Romzek. 2002. "Politics, Administration, and Markets: Conflicting Expectations and Accountability." *American Review of Public Administration* 32(2): 117–44.

Kobrak, Peter. 1996. "The Social Responsibilities of a Public Entrepreneur." *Administration and Society* 28(2): 205–37.

Lynn, Laurence. 1996. *Public Management as Art, Science, and Profession.* Chicago: The University of Chicago.

———. 1998. "The New Public Management: How to Transform a Theme into a Legacy." *Public Administration Review* 58 (3): 231–37.

Maesschalck, J. 2004. "The Impact of New Public Management Reforms on Public Servants' Ethics: Towards a Theory." *Public Administration* 82(2): 465–90.

Moe, Ronald, and Robert Gilmour. 1995. "Rediscovering Principles of Public Administration." *Public Administration Review* 55(8): 135–46.

Moon, M. Jae. 2000. "Organizational Commitment Revisited in New Public Management: Motivation, Organizational Culture, Sector, and Managerial Level." *Public Performance and Management Review* 24(2): 177–94.

Moore, Mark H. 1995. *Creating Public Value: Strategic Management in Government.* Cambridge, MA: Harvard University Press.

Nagel, Jack. 1997. "Radically Reinventing Government." *Journal of Policy Analysis and Management* 15(3): 349–56.

Nalbandian, John. 1994. "Reflections of a 'Pracademic' on the Logic of Politics and Administration." *Public Administration Review* 54(6): 531–36.

Nathan, Richard. 1995. "Reinventing Government: What Does it Mean?" *Public Administration Review* 55(2): 213–15.

Niskanen, William. 1968. "The Peculiar Economics of Bureaucracy." *American Economic Review* 58: 293–305.

————. 1971. *Bureaucracy and Representative Government*. Chicago: Aldine-Atherton.

O'Looney, John. 1993. "Beyond Privatization and Service Integration: Organizational Models for Service Delivery." *Social Service Review*, December: 501–33.

Osborne, David, and Ted Gaebler. 1992. *Reinventing Government: How the Entrepreneurial Spirit is Transforming the Public Sector*. Reading, MA: Addison-Wesley.

Osborne, David, and Peter Plastrik. 1997. *Banishing Bureaucracy: The Five Strategies for Reinventing Government*. Reading, MA: Addison-Wesley.

Ostrom, Vincent. 1974. *The Intellectual Crisis in American Public Administration*. Tuscaloosa, AL: University of Alabama Press.

Peters, B. Guy. 1988. *Comparing Public Bureaucracies: Problems of Theory and Method*. Tuscaloosa: University of Alabama Press.

————. 1996. *The Future of Governing: Four Emerging Models*. Lawrence: University Press of Kansas.

Peters, B. Guy, and John Pierre. 1998. "Governance without Government? Rethinking Public Administration." *Journal of Public Administration Research and Theory* 8: 223–44.

Pollitt, Christopher. 1990. *Managerialism and the Public Services: the Anglo-American Experience*. Oxford: Blackwell Publishers.

————. 1993. *Managerialism and the Public Service*. 2nd ed. Oxford: Basil Blackwell.

————. 2003. *The Essential Public Manager*. Philadelphia: Open University Press.

Rohr, John. 1998. *Public Service, Ethics, and Constitutional Practice*. Lawrence: University of Kansas Press.

Romzek, B.S. 2000. "Dynamics of Public Sector Accountability in an Era of Reform." *International Review of Administrative Sciences* 66(1): 21–44.

Romzek, Barbara, and Melvin Dubnick. 1987. "Accountability in the Public Sector: Lessons from the Challenger Tragedy." *Public Administration Review* 47(3): 227–38.

Rosenbloom, David, and Robert Kravchuk. 2002. *Public Administration: Understanding Management, Politics and Law in the Public Sector*. 5th ed. New York: McGraw-Hill.

Russell, Gregory, and Robert Waste. 1998. "The Limits of Reinventing Government." *American Review of Public Administration* 28(4): 325–46.

Schachter, Hindy. 1995. "Reinventing Government or Reinventing Ourselves: Two Models for Improving Government Performance." *Public Administration Review* 55(6): 530–37.

————. 1997. *Reinventing Government or Reinventing Ourselves*. Albany: University of New York Press.

Slesinger, Ruben, and Asher Isaacs. 1968. *Business, Government, and Public Policy*. Princeton, NJ: D. Von Nostrand.

Sonenblum, D., J. Kirlin, and J. Ries. 1977. *How Cities Provide Services*. Cambridge, MA: Ballinger.

Stark, Andrew. 2002. "What Is the New Public Management?" *Journal of Public Administration Research and Theory* 12(1): 137–51.

Stivers, Camilla. 1990. "The Public Agency as Policy: Active Citizenship in the Administrative State." *Administration & Society* 22 (1): 86–105.

————. 1996. "Refusing to Get It Right: Citizenship, Difference, and the Refounding Project." In *Refounding Democratic Public Administration: Governance in a Postmodern Era*, eds. Gary L. Wamsley and James F. Wolf. Newbury Park, CA: Sage Publications.

Stivers, Camilla, Cheryl Smirell King, and Renee Nank. 1998. "Citizenship and its Discontents: The Political and Economic Context." In *Government Is US: Public Administration in an Anti-Government Era*, eds. Cheryl Smirell King and Camilla Stivers. Newbury Park, CA: Sage Publications.

Svara, James. 2001. "The Myth of the Dichotomy: Complementarity of Politics and Administration in the Past and Future of Administration." *Public Administration Review* 61(2): 176–83.

Terry, Larry. 1998. "Administrative Leadership, Neo-Managerialism, and the Public Management Movement." *Public Administration Review* 58(8): 194–200.

Thompson, Fred, and L.R. Jones. 1994. *Reinventing the Pentagon: How the New Public Management Can Bring Institutional Renewal.* San Francisco, CA: Jossey Bass.

Thompson, Fred, and Hugh Miller. 2003. "New Public Management and Bureaucracy versus Business Values and Bureaucracy." *Review of Public Personnel Administration* 23(4): 328–43.

Van Wart, Montgomery. 1998. *Changing Public Sector Values.* New York: Garland Publishing.

Wamsley, Gary. 1992. "Management Processes." Working paper cited in Clay 1994. Center for Public Administration and Policy, Virginia Polytechnic Institute and State University.

Williams, Daniel. 2000. "Reinventing the Proverbs of Government." *Public Administration Review* 60(6): 522–35.

Wolf, Patrick J. 1997. "Why Must We Reinvent the Federal Government? Putting Historical Developmental Claims to the Test." *Journal of Public Administration Research and Theory* 7(3): 353–88.

9

The Role of Performance Management in American Federalism

RICHARD P. NATHAN

In the information age, it has become all too easy for political leaders to make the assumption that computers, spreadsheets, and performance management systems can be used to direct public management from on high. The Bush administration's Program Assessment Rating Tool (PART) and the No Child Left Behind Law (NCLB) of 2002 are examples of how this can cause confusion and gaming and undermine policy purposes. The missing ingredient, *American federalism* (see also Keevey, chapter 10 of this volume).

Performance management systems carry out two vital and connected, yet different, functions. They improve management and inform the government, public, and media about government programs' effectiveness. In their second function, they serve government leaders as a tool for signaling and motivating agency personnel to achieve policy goals, often with reports or scorecards, ranking systems, and analysis of rates of change toward goal attainment.

This chapter discusses performance management in the context of U.S. federalism. It is my position, empirically grounded, that performance management systems are "naturally suited" (that is the dictionary definition of "proper") to the operational, close-to-the-ground levels of government, and that for a great many purposes this means *local*. I seek to influence people in the public management field to interject a federalism dimension to what is often a highly centralized view of the performance management movement.

The Local and State Role

In February 2005, the Rockefeller Institute held a policy forum to examine state and local roles in performance management.[1] Principal speakers were New York City and state officials and policy experts. Their statements reflected a positive view of what performance management systems can achieve by way of the twin purposes of oversight and motivation. At the same time, they demonstrated the need for a strong dose of federalism-realism on how hard it is to get good performance data on the purposes, conditions, and needs of particular public services, data that can be applied beyond the local level.

Initially, our attention in New York City was focused on the "CompStat" performance management system for the Police Department. Crime reduction is its goal. This is reflected in the baseline description of CompStat, written in 2001 by Dennis Smith and William Bratton, who was the New York Police Department commissioner when the CompStat system was established under Mayor Rudy Giuliani (Smith and Bratton 2001). Jack Maple, then Bratton's deputy, was the system's architect. Later, at the Rockefeller Institute's forum in February 2005, Dennis Smith presented an update on CompStat and expanded this analysis to include other New York City performance management systems, descendants of CompStat, if you will. New York City manages welfare-to-work through its JobStat performance management system and has a performance management system for child welfare services (called EQUIP), one for human service vendors (VendorStat), and others called HealthStat and ParkStat. There are also systems for corrections, traffic, and school safety. Under Mayor Michael R. Bloomberg, performance management systems were ratcheted up and expanded (Rutenberg 2005).

Swati Desai, executive deputy commissioner of New York's Human Resources Administration, talked about JobStat at the February 2005 forum. She described it as a management tool used to serve its Job Centers costumers and also as "a dynamic process."[2] Goals are changed according to the needs of the population served. Data are used both to improve performance and services and to develop new programs to meet client needs.

Fred Wulczyn, a leader nationally in the development and application of performance management for child welfare programs (foster care, adoptions, family preservation, and abuse-prevention programs), described his work at the February 2005 forum as designing and helping to operate New York City's EQUIP (Evaluation and Quality Improvement Protocol) system for child welfare. This system, which relies on procedures developed at the University of Chicago, has had extensive applications beyond New York City. Because it has been field-tested and operates with carefully reviewed data, it is used to make decisions about the capability and funding levels of the nonprofit agency that provides child welfare services. In his remarks, Wulczyn stressed outcomes. "If we focus exclusively on performance, we may miss the outcomes. We think that there is a link, but unless you are managing [for] outcomes and using performance to get to better outcomes, performance becomes an end in itself and it can be translated on to the organization in a way that doesn't translate down to the client" (Nelson A. Rockefeller Institute 2005, 61).

All three systems—CompStat, JobStat, and EQUIP—have developed over time and operate in real time. They are success stories where success is most critical, locally. CompStat spread to other cities. Baltimore's "CitiStat" approach has been applied to the police department and across city government. In Mayor Martin O'Malley's words, "The revolutionary feature of this open and transparent system of government is that it moves us from spoils-based patronage politics to results-based performance politics. A computerized map doesn't know if a neighborhood is black or white, rich or poor, Democrat or Republican." Mayor O'Malley established CitiStat in June 2000, soon after he took office, with Jack Maple as a principal consultant. Beyond law enforcement, O'Malley sought to improve the performance and accountability of every agency to assure that services were delivered in a timely fashion and efficiently. This is what Robert Behn (2005), who has studied local and state performance management, had to say about CitiStat.

> The Baltimore management strategy called "CitiStat" contributes to performance of individual city agencies because it keeps agency managers and employees focused on improving specific outcomes by:
>
> 1. the active engagement of the city's top executives;
> 2. the breadth, depth, disaggregation, and "nowness" of the data
> 3. plus the thoroughness of the analyses of these data;
> 4. the perseverance of the questioning, feedback, and follow-up (which is more persistent than relentless);
> 5. the consequences for both good, poor, and improved performance;
> 6. the focus on problem solving, continuous experimentation, and learning; and
> 7. the institutional memory of the city's top executives.

Other large municipal governments have followed suit—among them, Atlanta, Providence, St. Louis, and San Francisco. Behn says there are two pressures that may prevent mayors in the future from dismissing performance management as just a fad. One is political. The support that has built up within the city's business community for many of his management initiatives will make it difficult for a future mayor to do without it. Another is technological performance management provides much of CitiStat's data, allowing prompt response to citizens' requests and needs. "O'Malley," says Behn, "has established a '48-hour pothole guarantee.' What will the next mayor do? Create a 72-hour pothole guarantee? Simply forget about filling potholes?" (Behn 2005, 314).

For state governments, their proper role in performance management is to establish and implement systems for programs they are responsible for administering, and, second, to facilitate, advise, and assist local governments. This view was reflected in the presentations of three senior New York State officials at the Rockefeller Institute February 2005 forum on the role of local and state governments in performance management and budgeting. A five-state study by the Urban Institute came to the same conclusion (Urban Institute 2000).[3] The authors found Minnesota among the sample states to be most actively involved in aiding local governments. It does so by providing technical assistance, publishing reports on local government best practices, and providing matching funds for local governments to participate in the International City/County Management Association (ICMA) comparative performance management project (Urban Institute 2000, 7).

The Federal Role

As in the case of state governments, the federal government should have a leadership, catalytic, and teaching role—except for programs (like Social Security) where the national government has direct operating responsibility (Broadnax and Conway 2001). Unfortunately, there is a tendency in Washington to attempt to drill down in U.S. federalism and require the use of detailed performance management systems that misunderstand this federalism terrain. The 1993 law passed by Congress, the Government Performance and Results Act (GPRA), the Bush administration's PART, and NCLB all have this tendency (Nathan and Forsythe 1999).

When the Bush administration's PART system was established, officials of the U.S. Office of Management and Budget said that it was not intended as a budgeting tool. But events did not turn out that way. The administration's emphasis on results is reflected in budget documents, using PART scores to justify program reductions. Recently, the administration stepped up its effort to use PART for budgeting, proposing the creation of a "Results Commission" that would give the president new powers to restructure and (every ten years) sunset federal programs on the basis of their performance effectiveness (OMB 2005).[4] This misses a critical point. (Blanchard, in chapter 4 of this volume, discusses the use of PART scores in making budgetary decisions about programs.) The fact that a program is underperforming does not mean its goals are unimportant. To the contrary, maybe the purposes involved are so important that more money is needed, along with better managerial capability to carry them out.

At the agency level, employment and training offers an example of the pitfalls in trying to implement performance management from the center. These programs, going back to the 1970s, and most recently under the 1998 Workforce Investment Act (WIA), allow discretion to states and local entities while at the same time setting policy goals and establishing accountability mechanisms. The WIA law requires the use of specific measures to track outcomes for adults, youth, and dislocated workers and the collection of data on customer (participant and employer) satisfaction. State performance standards are determined through federal-state negotiations. Adjustments are only possible if a state appeal is filed and approved. Approaches to deciding when a job seeker becomes a participant or a former participant (exiter) are inconsistent. Incentives in the form of extra federal grant-in-aid payments and financial penalties are linked to state successes or failures in meeting performance measures. The problem with this, as many experts have pointed out, is that it can encourage "creaming," whereby states serve eligible individuals more likely to do well instead of those with greater labor market barriers. Under these conditions, measuring performance misses critical outcomes.

A Rockefeller Institute study on WIA implementation in eight states (Nelson A. Rockefeller Institute 2005, 49) concluded that:

> The current approach to measuring and managing performance under WIA has not been productive, nor does it fit well with the intergovernmental approach to

workforce policy that has evolved in recent decades. State and local officials and One-Stop Career Center staff were nearly unanimous in expressing displeasure with performance management and measurement under WIA. The predominant view was that prior to WIA, program participation and outcome data were of higher quality, performance standards negotiations processes were more balanced between the state and local WIBs, and there was more emphasis on managing programs for improved results as opposed to the achievement of what tended to be viewed as arbitrary numeric goals.

WIA service recipients have become progressively less disadvantaged. "An ever smaller share of exiters are poor, lack a high school diploma, are single parents, or rely on public assistance" (Center on Law and Social Policy 2005, 2). Although in April 2005, the U.S. Department of Labor issued guidance on negotiating WIA performance goals for program years 2005 and 2006 and provided states with analytical tools to better inform the negotiation process, it is too soon to determine "whether this new guidance will result in performance levels that better enable serving harder-to-employ adults" (Center on Law and Social Policy 2005, 5).

No Child Left Behind

President George W. Bush signed NCLB in January 2002, calling it "the cornerstone of my Administration." As is often the case, the law reflected a compromise between the leadership and enforcement roles of the federal government and the traditional strong roles of state and local governments (mainly school districts) in elementary and secondary education. It prescribes a regular testing regime to measure the fulfillment of fixed goals for student achievement and lists specific and increasingly more severe penalties for schools that fail to meet these goals. At first blush, this sounds like the feds grabbing the reins in a manner that breaks with forty years of federal school-aid laws that defer to the states and local school districts. But take a closer look.

The goals for mathematics and reading to be achieved by all students are set not by the federal government, but by the state, which also selects the tests to be administered and stipulates what the cut points are for achieving proficiency. Many supporters of the law, along with states and localities, are not happy with this arrangement. Pointing to the diversity among the states and the low levels of achievement defined by some of them as constituting proficiency, they have called for nationalization that would take the form of central definitions of proficiency and requirements for standardized national tests to measure whether they are achieved. It is argued that the U.S. economy, labor force, and schools are falling behind in the global economy. There is a tone of urgency to proposals for strengthening NCLB and making it more highly centralized. On the other side, describing what he called the unworkability of NCLB testing procedures and requirements, Charles Murray recently called NCLB "a disaster for federalism" (Murray 2006).

What to make of this controversy? Start with federalism: Is K–12 education properly a federal responsibility? Under the U.S. Constitution, each citizen is a citizen of two governments—national and state. Experts agree that a functioning federal system must have a democratic form at both levels that provides opportunities for access and participation by citizens, otherwise the idea of self-expression by state governments would not be meaningful. One way to read the NCLB experience is that the federal government has *overreached.* A solution might be not to tie things down more tightly with national standards, tests, and sanctions, but to go in a new direction—to consider creating a multilevel institutional mechanism for expertise and leadership for the assessment and measurement of K–12 educational achievement and progress.

There are precedents for such institutional inventiveness, for example, the partnership performance system of the Environmental Protection Agency (EPA) and the work and role of the Advisory Commission on Intergovernmental Relations, of which the author was a member. While EPA's structure and role are not an exact analog, there is also a long-standing precedent for industrial standards setting. Founded in 1910, the National Institute of Standards and Technology (NIST) is explicitly non-regulatory. It is located within the Department of Commerce, and has as its mission to "promote U.S. innovation and industrial competitiveness by advancing measurement science, standards and technology." NIST is not a small enterprise; with a budget of nearly $1 billion and 5,000 staff members, it sponsors research, operates a network of local centers as an "Extension Partnership," and holds working conferences with industry partners to navigate the complexities in aiding industrial advancement.

The Clinton administration in 1994 attempted to institute a similar and intergovernmental entity for K–12 education performance oversight, the National Education Standards and Improvement Council. Legislation to do this was enacted and signed. However, the controversy it engendered led to a decision not to appoint members to the council, and it languished. At the Rockefeller Institute, we are interested in a possible federalism intervention along these lines.

Conclusion

The balancing of accountability and flexibility has proven to be difficult for federal agencies and has created considerable tension in the intergovernmental system. As Beryl Radin has said, "It is not easy to craft a strategy for performance measurement activity that addresses the tensions surrounding the intergovernmental system. The approach that is taken must be sensitive to differences among policies and programs, differences among the players involved, and the level of goal agreement or conflict" (Radin 2006, 17). When I taught graduate students, I told them I worried that some of them would go off to work for a federal agency believing they could lay it on the line about a particular problem and, in effect, say to state, local, and nonprofit agency leaders, "Now you just go do it thus and so (smart like I just showed you)." In a similar spirit of caution and candor, this chapter is a plea for a more nuanced, federalism-sensitive view of performance management in Washington.

Notes

This chapter is based in part on a paper, "Performance Management in State and Local Government," available on the Rockefeller Institute website at www.rockinst.org, accessed October 2, 2007.

1. The forum was sponsored by the Rockefeller Institute, the New York State Division of the Budget, and the Manhattan Institute. See *Performance Management in State and Local Government* (Albany, NY: Rockefeller Institute Press, 2005) at www.rockinst.org/weinberg/pdf/PerformanceManagementReport.pdf, accessed January 25, 2007.

2. In the late 1990s Mayor Rudolph Giuliani implemented widespread reforms to the city's centralized welfare system. Welfare centers became job centers, as their primary outcome was self-sufficiency for welfare recipients. Job centers provide on-site access to job search and placement services; childcare information; vocational, educational, and training services; and referrals for Medicaid, food stamps, and other emergency assistance benefits.

3. See the remarks of Andrew S. Eristoff, commissioner of the New York State (NYS) Department of Taxation and Finance; Robert Fleury, first deputy commissioner of the NYS Office of General Services; and Chauncey G. Parker, director of the NYS Division of Criminal Justice Services in *Performance Management in State and Local Government,* 11–36.

4. Richard P. Nathan and Dall W. Forsythe, "Saving GPRA: The Role and Potential of Performance Management in America's Government," The Nelson A. Rockefeller Institute of Government, July 8, 1999. According to this conference paper, "One way to sum up what has been discussed so far is to view performance management in federalism terms: It is easiest to do locally since governments are more involved in physical and more measurable activities that they themselves finance and control. They are at the end of the intergovernmental food chain for grants-in-aid, which makes it reasonably feasible to gauge and oversee program performance. Experts who take this federalism view of performance management tend to see states as being in a better position than the national government to actually carry out these reforms" (p. 12). See also Dall W. Forsythe, "Performance Management Comes to Washington: A Status Report on the Government Performance and Results Act," The Nelson A. Rockefeller Institute of Government, February 25, 2000.

References

Behn, Robert D. 2005. "The Core Drivers of CitiStat: It's Not Just about the Meetings and the Maps." *International Public Management Journal* 8(3): 301.

Broadnax, Walter D., and Kevin J. Conway. 2001. "The Social Security Administration and Performance Management." In *Quicker, Better, Cheaper,* ed. Dall W. Forsythe, 143–76. Albany: State University of New York Press.

Center on Law and Social Policy. 2005. "Declining Share of Adults Receiving Training under WIA Are Low-Income or Disadvantaged." Washington, DC, December 14.

Murray, Charles. 2006. "Acid Test." *The Wall Street Journal,* July 25.

Nathan, Richard P., and Dall W. Forsythe. 1999. "Saving GPRA: The Role and Potential of Performance Management in America's Government." The Nelson A. Rockefeller Institute of Government, July 8.

Nelson A. Rockefeller Institute of Government. 2005. "The Workforce Investment Act in Eight States: Final Report." USDOL/ETA Occasional Paper 2005–01.

Office of Management and Budget (OMB). 2005. "White House Demands Power to Restructure Government." *OMB Watcher* 6(14) (July 11).

Peirce, Neal. 2006. "Less Secrecy, More Efficiency: Baltimore's Groundbreaking 'CitiStat,'" The Washington Post Writers Group. Available at http://www.postwritersgroup.com/archives/peir0112.htm, accessed May 17, 2006.

Radin, Beryl A. 2006. "Performance Management and Intergovernmental Relations." Prepared for delivery at the 2006 Annual Meeting of the American Political Science Association, August 30–September 3.

Rutenberg, Jim. 2005. "Bloomberg Lives by Statistics and Gives Aides a Free Hand." *New York Times,* October 18.

Smith, Dennis C., and William J. Bratton. 2001. "Performance Management in New York City: Compstat and the Revolution in Police Management." In *Quicker, Better, Cheaper: Management Performance in American Government,* ed. Dall W. Forsythe, 453–82. Albany, NY: Rockefeller Institute Press.

The Urban Institute. 2000. *States, Citizens, and Local Performance Management.* Washington, DC, September.

10

Maximizing Federal Performance with State and Local Partners

RICHARD F. KEEVEY

In our constitutional framework state and local governments provide extensive direct services to the public. It is the state or local governments, for example, that provide public education, roads, public safety, health services, and environmental protection. However, in many instances, the federal government provides some level of financial support in the form of grants, loans, and tax subsidies to assist states and local governments (see also Nathan, chapter 9 of this volume, on federalism). Because of the magnitude of these grants and loans the federal government bears some responsibility for ensuring that taxpayer-supported grant programs achieve their intended results.

Congress and successive administrations have approved laws and policies that stress the need to determine more fully the goals and objectives for all federal programs, including those that are executed at the state and local levels. Most recently, the executive, through the Office of Management and Budget, has implemented a Program Assessment Rating Tool (PART) to evaluate the performance of all government programs, including grants to state and local governments.

At the same time federal actions, such as unfunded mandates, implementation of "clawback" provisions of the recently enacted Medicare Part D law, unilateral federal changes to tax bases shared by the states, the accelerated pace of federal preemption of state and local taxation, and actions by the courts affecting tax bases have the effect of limiting the ability of states and localities to deliver necessary programs at expected levels of performance.

Federal Grants to State and Local Governments

Federal grant expenditures have risen dramatically in recent years. Between 1970 and 2000, federal grant outlays to state and local governments rose from a little over $24 billion to almost $285 billion, an average increase of 98 percent every decade. Budgeted grant expenditures of $459 billion in 2007 were almost double the 2000 total.

Four-fifths of the grant outlays go to education, social service programs, and health and Medicaid payments. The Office of Management and Budget (OMB)

178

also estimated that grant outlays to state and local governments for payments to individuals, such as Medicaid payments, would represent 65 percent of total grants in 2007, with physical capital investment (15 percent) and outlays for training, education, and social services (20 percent) making up the remainder.

Intergovernmental experts also point out that some tax expenditures—exemptions, deductions, and credits embedded in the federal tax code—constitute a form of federal aid to state and local governments. For example, deductibility of state and local personal income, sales and property taxes, and exclusion of interest earned on municipal bonds from federal taxation are major "tax expenditures" that provide indirect assistance to state and local governments. Curiously, however, while federal documents list tax expenditures (aggregating to approximately $77 billion) as forms of "federal aid," such documents do not include activities and policies of the federal governments that tend to lessen and have negative impacts on the revenue capacity of state and local governments and therefore hinder their ability to deliver services and/or provide high levels of performance. Some of these negative policies are discussed below.

Types of Grants

Federal grants are payments to support public purposes or national interests. Grants fall into two major categories. Competitive (or discretionary) grants are awarded to eligible grantees mostly on a competitive basis. They provide financial support for relatively clearly defined purposes and activities but leave considerable discretion to grantees to work out the details of how program goals will be accomplished. Discretionary grant program funding levels are usually determined annually through various appropriations acts. Examples include the Forest Legacy Program, the Department of Justice's Weed and Seed program, and the National Health Service Corps.

Block grant allocations to states and others (sometimes called formula grants) are determined in authorizing legislation; their amounts can only be changed by altering eligibility criteria or benefit formulas by law. The total amount available each year is sometimes set in the authorization, sometimes in the annual appropriation. Annual appropriations acts can, but do not often, modify allocations for formula grants. Examples of formula grant programs are state grants for vocational rehabilitation, elementary and secondary education, the Workforce Investment Act, and the Community Development Block Grant (see also Buss, chapter 11 of this volume). Federal administrative funds for these benefits are often appropriated separately as discretionary grants.

Sources of Tension

Sources of tension between the federal government and state and local governments lie in our intergovernmental system, which divides authority between the federal government and the fifty state governments. The Constitution reserves for the states any powers not granted to the federal government (such as border control and national defense). In the early history of the country, states and localities exercised sole responsibility for their own affairs without interference from the federal government. As the country matured and problems became more complex (particularly beginning during the Great Depression), however, the federal government assumed more power and responsibility for state functions, sometimes with state consent.

Notwithstanding this general shift in power, there were certain efforts, albeit brief, to provide significant grant autonomy and flexibility to state and local governments. The General Revenue Sharing Act of 1972 had as its goals more state and local discretion and less "interference." In effect, state and local governments were given a block of money that they could use for virtually any program; the only requirement was an end-of-year expense report.

Ultimately, the tide swung back to those groups within the Congress that argued for more accountability for federal taxpayers' dollars. General revenue sharing was eliminated because many state and local governments used the dollars as an augmentation or substitute for state or local funds—just as the law intended—and did not connect funds to accomplishments that could be measured. The law was repealed in 1986.

In general, the close federal supervision and control that accompanies most discretionary grants breeds resentment on the part of state and local officials, who typically prefer greater leeway in deciding how to use grant resources.

Three specific examples are noteworthy. First, states and localities act in some respects as agents of the federal government by implementing a wide array of federal programs and policies. They distribute grant funds to subunits and enforce rules and regulations for programs that have been developed by the federal government. States and localities have complained over the years that some of these programs conflict with their priorities and are inadequately funded—the issue of unfunded mandates, as most people refer to this phenomena. Examples include the Americans with Disabilities Act, environmental protection laws, and homeland security requirements. While these laws embody goals that all levels of government should pursue, states and localities have looked to the federal government for most, if not all, of the resources to support them.

There is no consensus on the proportion of federal versus state responsibility for certain policies and programs, specifically, who should fund what. Federal managers need to recognize that this conflict is inherent in our intergovernmental system and adopt approaches that work within this system.

Second, the federal government imposes matching requirements for many grants on states and localities; these can strain tight budgets. A 1997 Government Accountability Office (GAO) analysis found that every additional federal grant dollar results in less than a dollar of total additional spending on an aided program. Thus, one of the recommendations of the study was to require matching funds to obtain federal grant funding (GAO 1997). Matching requirements are imposed so that federal grant monies supplement rather than substitute for state and local spending on a particular program. For example, a matching grant may require states to spend from ten to fifty cents from their own revenues for each dollar of federal funds provided.

Some have argued that matching requirements are relatively small, often take the form of "in-kind" contributions, give states a financial stake in programs as befits their role as service providers, and also strengthens the states' negotiating position with the federal government.

Maintenance-of-effort requirements work in that state and local governments must maintain prescribed expenditure levels from their own sources to qualify for funding.

Third, to qualify for federal grants, states and localities must comply with certain conditions, including quarterly reporting requirements, often viewed as unduly burdensome and time consuming. Federal agencies have historically not done a good job of working with grantees to ease administrative burdens, obtaining state and local feedback in developing commonsense program performance measures, and reporting results. While timely and accurate reporting is essential, federal managers should do everything possible to (1) ensure that the reporting is a by-product of, rather than a new requirement on, state and local management systems, and (2) demonstrate the value of the reports to good management at all levels.

Government-Wide Federal Requirements

Several government-wide federal requirements are changing the way performance measures and outcomes are incorporated into federal, state, and local grants programs.

Government Performance and Results Act

The Government Performance and Results Act (GPRA) of 1993 placed the issue of program performance squarely on the agenda of every federal department, including those federal agencies that depend on grantees (usually state and local governments) to accomplish their objectives. Some program statutes always included some form of performance requirements, and for decades, succeeding administrations sought to impose government-wide performance management and budgeting requirements. GPRA, however, elevated the issue to a government-wide statutory requirement. Among other requirements, GPRA requires policymakers and managers in each federal agency to develop strategic plans, provide annual data on the performance of each federal program, and provide information to show whether grant programs are being implemented effectively and efficiently.

During development of the GPRA legislation, much discussion focused on how to treat federal agencies that rely on state, local, and nonprofit partners to implement grant programs. A significant area of debate related to how federal agencies could set goals, measures, and performance standards in policy areas where the federal government is a partner with a state or local government in program implementation.

Some—including state and local government associations, and even federal program managers—argued that it was not possible to do so as data were not available and the federal government would be creating another burden. Others argued that such data and information were critical in determining effectiveness of multi-million-dollar programs and that mechanisms could be developed that would link need for performance information with concerns of state and local governments. Through a series of initiatives, including the establishment of performance partnerships, the skillful use of incentives, and mutually developed and negotiated performance measures, these concerns have been addressed, if not yet eliminated.

Federal Financial Assistance Management Improvement Act

The Federal Financial Assistance Management Improvement Act of 1999 established a requirement for agencies to "establish specific annual goals and objectives" in cooperation with "recipients of federal financial assistance" and to "measure annual performance in achieving those goals and objectives" as part of the agencies' responsibilities under GPRA. This law in effect applied the statutory requirements of GPRA to grant programs in the federal government. OMB, through the Office of Federal Financial Management and the budget examiners, works with the grant-making agencies to ensure that grants are managed properly and that federal dollars are spent in accordance with applicable laws and regulations.

Program Assessment Rating Tool

In 2002, OMB developed the PART. This executive branch initiative is a management system that evaluates the performance of program activities across the federal government. By linking the GPRA and PART, the federal government has moved a long way toward assessing the performance of program activities and focusing on their contribution to an agency's achievement of its strategic and program performance goals. There is now much greater emphasis on developing performance measures according to outcome-oriented standards.

PART divides federal programs into: Direct Federal, Research and Development, Capital Assets and Service Acquisition, Credit, Regulatory, and two grant types—Competitive Grant, and Block/Formula Grant. The process then presents twenty-five questions, including additional questions tailored to the different program types. PART questions are divided into four sections—Program Purpose and Design; Strategic Planning; Program Management; and Results and Accountability—each of which is scored; the Results/Accountability section represents 50 percent of the overall score. Finally, each program can earn an overall rating of

effective, moderately effective, ineffective, adequate, or *results not demonstrated.*
On average, grant programs have received lower ratings than other types of federal programs. For example, to date, 41 percent of all grant programs received a rating of *results not demonstrated,* compared to 31 percent for all other programs (see Gilmour, chapter 2, and Blanchard, chapter 4 of this volume, for a comprehensive analysis of PART). It is perhaps understandable that grant programs would receive a lower rating because of their complexity, the breadth of purpose of some grants, and lack of consensus among grantees and federal agencies on the goals and purpose of the programs and the specific performance measures to be used.

Although the appropriate legislative initiatives and management tools appear to be in place to manage grant performance for results, issues remain. These include: What is the best method for collecting the data? How can the integrity of the data be ensured? What should be measured? Some grantees, for example, object to the federal agency's using their accomplishments as its own goals and suggest that the federal agency measure only what it controls—such as the time it takes to issue and process a grant. However, reporting only on process misses the key issue of Results and would not justify the expenditure of taxpayer dollars.

While the statutes governing the majority of federal grant programs do not explicitly include performance data collection and reporting requirements, recent federal laws (e.g., Temporary Assistance for Needy Families, No Child Left Behind) have done so. Also, joint state and federal program agreements (e.g., the National Environmental Performance Partnership System) have begun to focus increasingly on the collection of data and performance measurements at the program and operational levels.

Monitoring Grant Performance in an Intergovernmental Context

Two examples demonstrate how grants can be monitored in an intergovernmental context.

Department of Justice's Weed and Seed Program

Established in 1991, the Weed and Seed program is a Justice Department discretionary grant program. This joint federal, state, and local program provides funding to grantees to help prevent and control crime and improve the quality of life in targeted high-crime neighborhoods across the country. Weed and Seed grant funds support police bike patrols, community cleanups, youth and recreational activities, and computer training. A central program goal is for local Weed and Seed sites to develop partnerships with state and local governments as well as the private sector to leverage additional resources and eventually eliminate the need for federal support.

GAO conducted a management study of Weed and Seed, including whether the program has developed adequate performance measures to track program outcomes. The report found that while the program has started to develop measures to assess how well sites are meeting program objectives, it does not measure the extent to which grantees are weeding crime from neighborhoods and preventing it from recurring. In addition, no site's funding has been withdrawn as a result of its becoming self-sustaining in the program's eleven-year history (GAO 2004).

As a result of its findings, GAO recommended that the program clearly define criteria for assessing when sites are self-sustaining and apply those criteria to sites when making further funding decisions. GAO also recommended that the program develop outcome performance measures that can be used to track progress toward program outcomes.

In a letter commenting on the GAO report, the program office disagreed with GAO over the use of homicide rates as an effective indicator of program performance. It stated that external studies showed lower homicide rates in Weed and Seed sites when compared to host jurisdictions, and that program sites experienced a decline in homicides over a three-year period. GAO responded that the studies did not account for changes in population, used a faulty methodology in using host jurisdictions to compare performance in Weed and Seed sites, and evaluated program sites only on the basis of decreases in homicide when Weed and Seed was intended to reduce crime in general. This lack of federal/state agreement on performance measures and goals has persisted since the program began operation.

Weed and Seed also earned a PART rating of *results not demonstrated* in the FY2005 budget. PART indicated that a large number of project sites had "inconsistent oversight and results" and that the program had failed to establish baseline data for performance objectives such as homicide rates. PART also stated that only a small number of sites had been independently evaluated, thus making it difficult to assess program effectiveness.

Congress considered legislation in 2004 (H.R. 3036) that would impose more rigorous requirements on Weed and Seed program grantees, similar to other Justice programs like Community Oriented Policing Services and the Drug Free Communities Support Program. These include a matching grant requirement (currently none is required), a limit on the maximum number of years (proposed at ten) that a grantee can receive funding, and a "timely and effective" plan to sustain the program independently when federal funding ends.

Congress's action, while useful to improve program management, does not focus on results and thus falls short of what is necessary. Moreover, disagreement between GAO and Justice, as well as the program's mediocre rating on the PART, reflect a lack of collaboration among grantees and federal officials responsible for managing grant-funded programs.

Temporary Assistance for Needy Families Block Grant

The Temporary Assistance for Needy Families Block Grant (TANF) program was central for welfare reforms contained in the Personal Responsibility and Work

Opportunity Reconciliation Act of 1996, which replaced the federal entitlement program under Aid to Families with Dependent Children with block grants to the states. TANF had three broad goals:

- End the dependence of needy parents on welfare by requiring most recipients to work and prepare for self-sufficiency.
- Promote the preservation of two-parent families.
- Reduce the occurrence of babies born outside of marriage.

In addition, the law placed a five-year limit on welfare assistance to eligible parents and required recipients to participate in a job preparation program after two years.

TANF is one of the few programs that provided for performance goals and measurement within the statute. For example, the law required states to have one-half of their welfare recipients in "work programs" for at least thirty hours per week by 2000. In addition, TANF required the Department of Health and Human Services to report yearly performance measures, including work participation rates, average annual earnings of participants, demographic characteristics of families, and employment trends of needy families with minor children living at home.

GAO conducted a TANF review in 2001 and found that the program had gone a long way toward meeting its performance goals (GAO 2001). The report noted that "the states are transforming the nation's welfare system into a work-based, temporary assistance program for needy families." It found a 50 percent decline in the number of families receiving cash assistance, from 4.4 million in August 1996 to 2.2 million as of June 2000, and that most of the adults in families remaining off welfare rolls were employed at some time after leaving the program. Furthermore, states were training their "workfare" recipients to move off public assistance rapidly to paying jobs. The TANF program was not rated by the PART in the most recent reporting by OMB, but a number of independent studies have shown that this program has succeeded in moving individuals from welfare to work (Grogger et al. 2002).

TANF also includes provisions in the statute to improve performance. It rewards states that achieve the largest percentage reduction in the number of cash assistance cases, out-of-wedlock births, and abortions among program recipients. It also reduces grant funds to states that do not meet the requirements of the law by failing to provide data, failing to maintain specified levels of local funding, and failing to meet the work participation requirements of the statute.

As these examples show, managing for grant performance presents a mixed picture. Successful programs like TANF reflect a willingness of Congress and grant-making agencies to give guidance on what is required, and state and local grantees to cooperate and implement effective policies. On the other hand, programs like Weed and Seed reflect a lack of agreement between federal agencies and grantees over how to measure results. Federal leaders must be willing to resolve these differences.

State and Local Governments Should Be Viewed as Part of the Solution

Congress and the executive should not think that the federal government has a monopoly on the development of performance management tools like GPRA and PART. In fact, goal setting, strategic planning, and development and use of performance measures have long been in the tool kit of state and local governments. The National Association of Budget Officers and National Conference of State Legislatures have for many years been reporting on the progress made by their member states in governing for results. Furthermore, both the Government Finance Officers Association and the Association of Government Accountants have programs to review the annual financial and accountability reports of state and local governments against an established set of criteria, including the degree to which reports contain suitable performance metrics.

Since 2002, *Governing* magazine has reviewed and evaluated the progress that states, counties, and cities have made in performance management. State and local governments have taken different routes toward governing for results, and some governments have shown better results than others. Nevertheless, there is no doubt that state and local governments have been in the business of strategic planning, performance budgeting, outcome and output measurement, and reporting for as long as, or longer than, the federal government has.

How do you manage programs involving multiple levels of government? This issue has been a major challenge at least since the New Deal, but it has become even more important as performance has become the signpost for better public management. Furthermore, GPRA and more recently PART have placed pressure on federal managers to ensure that they work collaboratively with state and local governments to develop and implement effective performance measures for grant-funded programs.

Federal Actions and Policies Negatively Impacting State and Local Government Performance

As noted, there are actions by the federal government that have a negative impact on the flow of revenues to state and local governments—an impact that in the long run may have more of an impact on performance than does the positive flow of federal grant monies.

Intergovernmental cooperation is critical when deciding tax and spending policies. But, if the federal government takes unilateral actions that constrain or limit state and local fiscal flexibility and capacity to raise revenues and impose mandates on the expenditure side of the ledger, then intergovernmental cooperation is severely impacted. Some examples are illustrative.

Recently, tax legislation has resulted in unilateral federal changes to the tax code that have a negative impact on the state and local tax base. Changes to depreciation schedules or to the estate tax have either caused states to lose revenue or required them to decouple from the federal tax base. When states have decoupled, then there has been a negative impact on enforcement and tax administration.

Federal preemption (actions of the national government that either substitute nationwide policies for those of the states or localities or prohibit states and localities from exercising certain powers that had been their responsibility) has grown rapidly in the past forty years. In the past preemption tended to relate to just interstate commerce—now it impacts health and safety, banking and finance, natural resources, and other areas. Preemption can cost the states and localities money, limit their service capacities, and/or cause a loss of control over their own futures.

Federal courts have constrained the scope of state sales tax, excluding the collection of taxes on certain goods produced by remote sellers that are not located in the state and do not have a physical nexus to the state. In the same vein, Congress has banned states from taxing access to the Internet.[1]

The report by the President's Advisory Panel on Federal Tax Reform (November 2005) had numerous proposals to fix the U.S. tax system that would negatively impact state and local governments, including limiting deductions for mortgage interest, repealing the deduction for state and local taxes, limiting deductions on municipal bonds, and initiating a national retail sales tax. These recommendations illustrate the thinking permeating policymaking at the federal level as intergovernmental impacts are not considered. Incidentally, there was no representation from the state or local communities on the President's Tax Reform Panel.

Finally, the passage of the Medicare Modernization Act of 2003 (Medicare Part D), which provides prescription drugs for seniors, contains "clawback" provisions requiring the states to pay back to the federal government any savings the states might otherwise have enjoyed by not having to pay for prescription drugs for an estimated 6 million dual eligibles—people who were eligible for both Medicare and Medicaid. These clawback provisions represent an unprecedented mandate from the federal government. According to Trudi Matthews of the Council of State Governments, "this is a sea change in the state-federal relationship. Money generally flows down from Washington to the states, but in this case it's flowing upward, from the states to the federal governments" (Pear 2005, 12).

In any federal system a certain level of intergovernmental conflict is sure to exist, but most experts in the field would agree that the interests of all of the parties can be better achieved by having an active collaboration on fiscal policy. However, based upon the above actions, one might question whether this collaboration is currently taking place. Rather, these examples might very well be a preview of future state, local, and federal relations—a relationship that could have a negative impact on program and governmental performance at the state and local levels. Commenting on the federal actions related to the clawback provisions, Weissert and Miller hypothesize that such a trend could undermine states' long-standing role as policy innovators. States may be hesitant to experiment if they believe that they will be indefinitely required to bear the costs, and that federal mandates could leave them without the fiscal capacity to pursue innovation (Weissert and Miller 2004).

Working with State and Local Governments to Improve Grant Performance

The following observations are presented as a guide for current and prospective appointed and career federal agency officials, members of Congress, and their staffs to help all parties, including state and local grantees, focus more effectively on performance:

- Whether or not your program statute explicitly calls for it, reach out to state and local governments to develop mutually agreeable performance measures for grant-funded programs. Work cooperatively with state and local governments, as well as relevant interest groups such as national educational, environmental, and social service associations, to gain a better understanding of what is needed to develop better program goals and performance measures. These groups all have a stake in good management of public dollars. Federal managers can foster an environment that promotes a better understanding of the need for performance measures and shows how cooperation can benefit all parties.
- Emphasize to state and local government partners the mutual benefit of collecting good data on grant programs so that a central repository of measures will be seen as a valuable management tool. It is in the interest of state and local officials to operate programs based on sound data, so that they know that these programs are working effectively for their populations.
- Consult with your staff, representatives of grantees, and respected researchers to find best practices to help grantees improve results.
- Devise a series of incentives or rewards to promote the achievement of better results.
- Develop performance partnerships with like agencies in the states to foster and encourage the development of better performance measures and streamlined grants administration. Performance partnerships give states and localities more flexibility to solve problems the way they want to in return for being held accountable for results. They also eliminate federal micromanagement, share decision-making, and focus on public outcomes rather than outputs. A good example of such a strategy was developed by the Environmental Protection Agency (EPA) when it formed its National Environmental Performance Partnership System (NEPPS). Discussions with EPA program managers and state departments of environmental protection suggest that this is an excellent model.
- If your agency or program uses the same state or local agency for multiple programs, publish guidelines to standardize data requests for each program area within the states and localities. This will ensure that all states and local governments are reporting the same information, making comparisons more valid, enhancing data integrity, and reducing the paperwork burden.

To this end, the Department of Education has recently visited each state department of education to establish common measures and collect common data elements. This kind of up-front work will pay big dividends in the future.

- Ensure that the data being collected and reported by state and local grantees or third parties are accurate to the extent feasible. Even though agency inspectors general conduct internal audits of program and financial information, proactive leaders take the initiative to ensure that there are no surprises. The process of data verification is difficult for almost all grant program areas, whether it be education, social services, or the environment. But, if the data are flawed, all the benefits of benchmarking, best practices, and program performance will be negated and the conclusions will be invalid.

- Make alterations to performance metric requirements to facilitate data collection if you discover that the performance measures being used in your program do not accurately reflect program outcomes or results. State and local government program managers are often in a better position to know what kinds of data are available and what information is better suited to measure effectiveness. Your staff, GAO reports, and OMB are good sources. In such cases, federal, state, and local governments and associations should promptly negotiate a better set of performance measures. This will lead to better intergovernmental relationships, improved performance measures, and better program outcomes.

National actors need to play a role in the evaluation of the grant process as follows:

- Congress should step up to its oversight responsibilities by holding frequent hearings focused on federal grants to states and localities. (Public Law 97–258 makes provision for congressional review of grant programs to determine "the extent to which the purposes of the grants have been met.") To date, Congress has not fully used the data from GPRA and PART in its budget deliberations. Recently, the House Government Reform Committee passed the Program Assessment and Results Act, which would mandate that OMB review every federal program every five years. For this initiative to be truly effective, Congress should become more involved in the performance review process as part of its oversight responsibilities.

- Congress should ensure that taxpayer dollars are well spent by providing enough funding for high-quality data collection and program evaluations. It should make certain that federal grant-making agencies have the capacity to maintain and enhance existing performance data standards and analytical tools.

- Congress should give federal grant-making agencies the explicit statutory authority, if they don't already have it, to reward states and localities for achieving intended performance outcomes. TANF is a good model for how agencies can be given the power to sanction states and localities for failing to attain their performance objectives.

- Congress and the executive need to be much more careful when developing and considering tax reform proposals and spending policies that have an intergovernmental perspective. Some of the recommended actions that were suggested in recent publications of the National Academy of Public Administration include:
- Congress and the president should establish a permanent, independent organization to serve as a neutral convener to bring together officials from all levels of government to discuss common issues on tax and other intergovernmental fiscal issues.
- The federal government should observe forbearance when considering preemption proposals affecting revenues and taxes.
- Congress should amend the Unfunded Mandates Reform Act to include the intergovernmental fiscal effects of federal tax law changes as mandates.
- The president's budget should include a report on the status of the intergovernmental fiscal systems. The report should have a discussion of the prospective consequences of new revenue and spending proposals as well as recently enacted changes affecting all levels of government, including accounting for preemption and unfunded mandates.

These suggestions should be viewed not as a panacea for what ails the U.S. grants administration and implementation process, but as a guide to help decision-makers put in place a system based on accountability, cooperative partnership, and results; and just as important, a system that recognizes the whole-of-government perspective when developing and considering federal intergovernmental policies that affect state and local governments.

Effectively managing federal grant-supported programs and the entire intergovernmental systems for results is extremely difficult but exceedingly important. The size and complexity of federal programs mean that federal managers and Congress both bear responsibility for ensuring that taxpayer dollars support programs that produce results. Recent federal initiatives such as GPRA and PART move government in the right direction, but there is still a long way to go. The challenge for federal managers is to work cooperatively with state and local government managers who best understand local conditions and have been part of the effort to institute performance management in their communities.

And, the challenge for the president and Congress is to ensure that major policy and program problems do not develop at the state and local levels of government because of programs' failing to pay attention to the intergovernmental system, particularly as it relates to tax and revenue proposals and unnecessary funding mandates. Failure to adopt this whole-of-government perspective will have a significant negative impact on program performance.

Note

1. For a more detailed discussion see two reports by the National Academy of Public Administration, entitled "Financing Governments in the 21st Century: Intergovernmental Collaboration Can Promote Fiscal and Economic Goals" (July 2006) and "Beyond Preemption: Intergovernmental Partnerships to Enhance the New Economy" (May 2006).

References

General Accounting Office (GAO). 1997. "Federal Grants: Design Improvements Could Help Federal Resources Go Further." Washington, DC: GAO, GAO-AIMD-97–7.
———. 2001. "Welfare Reform: Progress in Meeting Work-Focused TANF Goals, Efforts to Improve Weed and Seed Program Management, Challenges Remain." Washington, DC: GAO, GAO-01–522T, March.
———. 2004. "Grants Management: Despite Efforts to Improve Weed and Seed Program Management, Challenges Remain." Washington, DC: GAO, GAO-04245.
Grogger, Jeffrey, Lynn A. Karoly, and Jacob Alex Klerman. 2002. "Consequences of Welfare Reform: A Research Synthesis." Santa Monica, CA: Rand Corporation.
Pear, Robert. 2005. "Cost-Cutting Medicare Law Is a Money Loser for States." *New York Times,* March 25: 12.
Weissert, William G., and Edward Alan Miller. 2004. "Punishing the Pioneers: The Medicare Modernization Act and State Pharmacy Assistance Programs." *Publius* 35(1): 117.

11

Performance Measurement in HUD's Community Development Block Grant Program

TERRY F. BUSS

Performance measurement systems can be difficult to execute in an intergovernmental context. The Department of Housing and Urban Development's (HUD) Community Development Block Grant (CDBG) program, which underwent major transformations from 2000 to 2007, exemplifies most of the performance issues that ought to be taken into account when decision-makers reengineer or design a system in which federal funding flows to states and communities. In this chapter, I present an overview of CDBG and the innovative process used to transform it; then, I summarize issues identified in reforming CDBG's performance measurement system, developing CDBG outcome and impact measures; and finally, I discuss concerns in constructing specific CDBG indicators or metrics. Because the system has yet to be fully implemented—as of late 2007—it is too soon to assess whether it will be an improvement over past efforts. But it is clear that CDBG learned much from current and past efforts at transformation.

1. Overview of CDBG

The CDBG program, administered by HUD's Community Planning and Development (CPD) office, is a $4-billion program that channels funding to entitlement communities (and counties) and states (see Table 11.1).[1] CDBG provides annual grants to develop viable urban communities by funding decent housing, a suitable living environment, and economic opportunities for low- and moderate-income persons. Grantees carry out a wide range of community development activities targeted at revitalizing neighborhoods, stimulating economic development, and improving community facilities and services, against grantee program and funding priorities. CDBG funds may be used for: acquisition of real property; relocation and demolition; rehabilitation of residential and nonresidential structures; construction of public facilities and improvements, such as water and sewer facilities, streets, neighborhood centers, and the conversion of school buildings for eligible purposes; public services, within certain limits; activities relating to energy conservation and renewable energy

Table 11.1

CDBG Budget, 2003–2006

	2003 Enacted	2004 Enacted	2005 Enacted	2006 Enacted	2006 Enacted vs. 2005 Enacted	Percent Change
Community Development Block Grants:						
Entitlement	3,037,677	3,031,592	2,876,923	2,592,790	(284,134)	–9.9%
Non–Entitlement	1,301,862	1,299,254	1,232,967	1,111,196	(121,771)	–9.9%
Insular	[6,955]	[6,959]	6,944	6,930	(14)	–.2%
Subtotal	4,339,538	4,330,846	4,116,835	3,710,916	(405,919)	–9.9%
Set Asides (see CDBG Set Asides)	565,371	603,469	584,946	466,884	(118,360)	–20.2%
Total CDBG	4,904,910	4,934,315	4,701,781	4,177,800	(524,279)	–11.1%

resources; and provision of assistance to profit-motivated businesses to carry out economic development and job creation/retention activities. HUD allocates grants through a statutory dual formula, using objective measures of community need, including: extent of poverty, population, housing overcrowding, age of housing, and population growth lag in relationship to other metropolitan areas.

2. CDBG's Performance Measurement Transformation Initiative

A variety of transformation initiatives are or were under way from many quarters, all with varying degrees of success.[2] The discussion of performance issues in this chapter was drawn from these efforts, especially the working group discussed below. Under continuing pressure from the Office of Management and Budget (OMB), CPD undertook several interrelated efforts to improve the performance of CDBG. CPD contracted with QED, Inc. to clean its databases so that data could be used in part for analyses to improve performance; with ESI, Inc. and the Urban Institute to conduct a best-practices study of communities with noteworthy performance measurement efforts; with the Urban Institute to determine the impacts of CDBG at the neighborhood level; and with the National Academy of Public Administration (NAPA) to recommend performance measures and suggest revisions to the management information system wherein performance data are reported. CPD also launched a pilot project to reform its Consolidated Plan, in which CDBG grantees report on their performance. At the same time OMB tried to force CPD to improve its performance by asking Congress to move its programs out of HUD to the Department of Commerce, then reduce their funding. Congress weighed in with hearings on the proposal, but legislation—Strengthening America's Communities Initiative (SACI)—was never passed. The Government Accountability Office (GAO), HUD, and others assessed the formula by which CDBG allocates funding to communities and states.

In addition, an outcome performance measurement system for CDBG, Emergency Shelter Grants (ESG), and the Housing Opportunities for Persons with AIDS Program (HOPWA), were developed by a joint *working group,* or stakeholders made up of representatives from the Council of State Community Development Agencies (COSCDA), National Community Development Association (NCDA), National Association for County Community Economic Development (NACCED), National Association of Housing and Redevelopment Officials (NAHRO), National Council of State Housing Agencies (NCSHA), CPD and HUD's Office of Policy Development and Research (PD&R), and OMB. This group eventually produced performance measures, which are in place.

3. Issues in CDBG Performance Measurement Systems

Many entitlement communities and states—in addition to researchers, practitioners, and advocates—during the initial stages of the transformation expressed concerns and doubts about developing and implementing a reengineered CDBG performance measurement system. Among the major challenges stakeholders considered were:

Competing Performance Measurement Systems

Many entitlement communities and states have advanced performance measurement systems that already serve state and local purposes, some more sophisticated than HUD's. These systems sometimes did not necessarily comport with the prospective HUD- or OMB-mandated performance perspective. Communities and states that excelled on their own had a legitimate complaint when asked to produce a new system for HUD or OMB that parallels an existing one. Under intense political pressure, CPD issued *Notice CPD-03–09,* in 2003, instructing grantees:

> The purpose of this Notice is to strongly encourage each CPD formula grantee to develop and use a state and local performance measurement system. Measuring performance at the state and local level is critical to the flexibility-driven formula programs. Since grantees are given the flexibility to make choices about how to use program funds, it is only logical that grantees be accountable, at the local level, for those choices.

In exchange for flexibility in maintaining their own systems, grantees agreed to report a minimum amount of performance data that would ensure that HUD satisfied its accountability requirements under the Government Performance Results Act (GPRA) and Program Assessment Rating Tool (PART).

Deficiencies in Capacity

Entitlement communities and states spend as much as one-fifth of their CDBG funding on administrative—depending on how this is defined—activities, translating into hundreds of millions of dollars in expenditures annually. Some estimates suggest that as much as $100 million annually goes into preparation of the CDBG consolidated plan, a statutorily mandated activity wherein grants establish goals, needs, and strategies under CDBG. All of this would be in addition to whatever grantees spend on their individual performance accountability systems. Whether these amounts are too much or too little is for policymakers to decide, but this illustrates that there is likely a great deal of capacity, at least for large cities and states, to produce and report performance measurement data. Nonetheless, small cities and states have much less capacity. To compound the issue further, entitlement communities and states often directly or indirectly contract with nonprofit, quasi-governmental, and governmental organizations with capacity to deliver services, but not as much administrative capacity to measure performance, especially long term. HUD invested in capacity building in those communities in need, in conferences, training and technical assistance.

Exorbitant Cost of Surveys

Some performance indicators may be too expensive to produce, not only for a single jurisdiction, but also nationwide. For example, survey research is an excellent methodology to gather data on how CDBG spending affects community beneficiaries. But, if communities and states were required to produce survey data for large numbers of neighborhoods and local units of government, it would be prohibitively expensive. Indeed, many already used surveys to determine community needs, further adding to the expense. Surveys were not imposed on grantees as a means for producing outcome data.

Past Problematic Efforts

Some believed HUD had not implemented (or had implemented ineffectively, inadequately, or differently) policies and procedures that it had previously promoted. The Integrated Disbursement and Information System (IDIS) management information system was an example raised by some grantees. HUD had gathered grantee input in the past, then proceeded to ignore it, creating much ill will. Some entitlement communities and states were suspicious when HUD, on its own or at OMB's direction, began to impose additional reporting burdens. As a solution, HUD reached out to grantees and their associations, eventually gaining buy-in for the system. HUD also actively participated in the working group as a show of good faith.

Lack of Control

Unemployment, mortgage rates, personal and business income, and even crime rates are a function of regional and national economic cycles. State and local officials have little or no control over these trends, even though they choose when, where, and how to spend CDBG funding. National and regional business cycles affect local employment. Entitlement community and state officials balked at supporting any performance accountability system in which they would have no way to directly influence indicators, either through policy or spending. HUD incorporated indicators more directly tied to program and policy intervention.

Duplicative Reporting

HUD's CPD and PDR offices have enormous amounts of data reported from the Census Bureau and other federal sources. Yet HUD asks grantees to acquire these data from HUD, then report them back again. For example, HUD knows how many low-income people live in neighborhoods across the country, but requires grantees to report this information back to HUD. This issue was never resolved in the new system, so grantees continue to report a lot of data that is already at HUD.

Conflicting Policy Goals

Cities and states are concerned that performance measurement systems will neither account for nor resolve conflicting policy goals. Some examples: Investing CDBG funding in affordable housing to improve home ownership may lead to renters' being displaced from targeted areas. Or, focusing minority home ownership in neighborhoods through CDBG contradicts HUD's housing voucher programs that "deconcentrate" low- to moderate-income minority families. Jurisdictions would be positively rated on one indicator yet negatively rated on the other, notwithstanding the fact that they attained their goals and objectives under CDBG. This issue was never fully resolved in the transformation initiative. Likewise, the issue of targeting funding to places most in need remained unresolved. OMB wanted targeting to encourage results, while grantees wanted discretion—even though some were already targeting—to channel funds to places according to their priorities. Targeting will never be universally accepted unless Congress decides to amend the legislation creating CDBG, something unlikely to happen.

Technical Difficulties

Several comprehensive reviews of possible performance indicators for CDBG were independently conducted by others (see NAPA 2005a). There were no measures that emerged as unbiased, unproblematic, valid, and reliable. Communities and states feared that they would be held accountable on faulty measures. In the end, stakeholders agreed that some measures were better than none, if they wished to demonstrate the value of CDBG. So, rather than striving for perfection, they settled for the best possible.

4. Issues in Measuring CDBG Outcomes and Impact

Stakeholders, not to mention researchers, analysts, and experts, acknowledge that the CDBG program faces among its most challenging obstacles in constructing a performance measurement system that satisfies the President's Management Agenda requirements, especially PART: moving beyond output to outcome measurement (somewhat feasible) and then into impact measurement (much more problematic).

After reviewing methodological issues associated with CDBG and community development performance measurement, stakeholders concluded that the potential to gather impact data that truly reflect program performance was remote. The issue is not gathering and reporting impact indicators, which is relatively easy and widely practiced. Linking impact indicators directly to programs, projects, and activities is very difficult and, in many cases, impractical. It is unlikely that CDBG program performance measurement reported by entitlement communities and states will satisfy rigorous, scientific criteria needed to conclude that the program had an

impact. Recognizing this, HUD funded an impact study to satisfy PART requirements, but shied away from requiring impact data from grantees.

Stakeholders had the following concerns about the possibility of establishing
impacts. None of these were ever really resolved in any transformation initiative.

Causal Links

The current state of the art in most community development impact studies is
to correlate every available social, economic, or demographic indicator against
CDBG expenditures for a geographical area. Past study results are methodologically unsound and, equally important, fail to demonstrate any but a few statistically
significant correlations. The Urban Institute conducted such a study, finding only a
handful of statistically significant relationships with no apparent significant policy
impacts. Although advances are being made in the field, methodologically, much
needed research on CDBG remains to be done in the view of stakeholders.

Before or After, With or Without

Impact assessments determine whether effects would have occurred independent
of some intervention—in this case, CDBG investment. In order to demonstrate
impact, baseline data would have to be gathered prior to CDBG investments being
made, and then compared with follow-up data afterward. Given that CDBG is three
decades old, it is difficult to establish baseline data that would not be affected by
past expenditures. In addition to before-and-after comparisons, CDBG investments
would need to be compared against similar communities where no investments
were made. Few locations with similar economies and demographics have eluded
CDBG investments.

Commingling of Funding

Most local community or neighborhood investments are an amalgam of funding
from federal, state, and local government; nonprofit and quasi-governmental organizations; and the private sector. Professional researchers and analysts have yet
to sort out funding impacts, except in rare cases. Disaggregating multiple funding
sources and linking them to impacts seem impossible on a wide scale. If this could
be done, adding them to a performance measurement system would be daunting.
Seattle reports having spent years trying to assign funding from all sources and
link it to performance indicators (see NAPA 2005a).

Magnitude of Expenditures

Although CDBG investments are important in communities and states, they represent a small share of overall investment—public and private. As such their impacts

can be easily dwarfed in any economy. Finding impacts—statistically at least in small areas with limited cases—is like searching for a needle in a haystack. For example: The payroll of a small manufacturing firm in a poor neighborhood effectively dwarfs investments made by CDBG.

"But For" Investments

Some argue that it is possible to establish impact by asking whether a given impact would have occurred without a CDBG investment—the "but for" test. Because entitlement communities and states have multiple funding sources for CDBG-like activities, an activity may be directly substitutable with a variety of other funding. Some critics find it difficult to see that any CDBG investment would satisfy "but for" criteria in establishing program impact. Yet CDBG investment is distinctive because it targets low- and moderate-income people, which is not necessarily the case with other federal programs, and certainly not the case with state and local spending. Even so, there is considerable overlap that likely cannot be unpacked for reporting purposes. PART allows programs to use "leverage" indicators as a way to satisfy the "but for" issue. In CDBG's case, private dollars leveraged would suffice.

Sporadic Investments

Although they vary greatly, most CDBG investments, as intended by Congress, are sporadic and widely dispersed frustrating efforts to measure impacts, an activity that depends on consistency over time. In many neighborhoods, investment can be miniscule. Furthermore, investments may be made one year but not the next, or even one time only; local investment patterns are virtually limitless. Some might argue that funding should be better targeted, not sporadic and dispersed, leaving an impression that funding is being dispersed for political reasons. This perception does not follow. Some city councils distribute CDBG by district or ward to satisfy their constituencies, but investments often are made one year to comply with a federal requirement that need not be funded in other years once the requirement is met. For example, states may spend heavily on their water infrastructure to meet revised EPA standards; once these are met, other community development needs can be addressed.

People and Place, Individual and Community

Although researchers and practitioners can measure impacts on individuals, they have not resolved how to definitively relate them to conceptual issues. The CDBG program typically invests in building or repairing structures or infrastructures. Its impact on a particular person is difficult to establish. So, how does a group or community benefit from such investments? CDBG may "rehab" a house of someone with limited means in order to bring it into compliance with building codes. The result is that the house is safe and decent, but what does this mean to the community in which the person resides and the house sits? Is community defined by political boundaries, as with a census tract or city ward, or is it defined along fuzzy boundaries, for example "uptown" or "downtown"? Is the community its people and, if so, do they comprise residents, commuters, and visitors? Or, is the community more than people; does it involve some level of interaction? In short, how do we measure community?

From a performance measurement perspective, it is highly problematic to create geographically based indicators at the local level that can be meaningfully aggregated to the national level while still measuring that geography. For example, it is unclear how HUD would aggregate a community that reports serving 100 people in a community center with one thousand other communities that serve people in neighborhoods, census tracts, census blocks, wards, districts, and the like. At best, HUD only could state that several thousand people were served nationally in the average census tract—a somewhat meaningless measure.

A good case for place-based reporting is when states award competitive grants to small, local agencies. Another good case is that grantees are asked for place-based census or survey-based information so that CPD can verify that funding was spent in places with high concentrations of low- to moderate-income people. Because this information is needed for compliance it does no harm to leave it in the performance measurement system. In addition, researchers can use these places to conduct place-based impact studies.

Crime Rate as an Impact Indicator: A Case in Point

Analysts and practitioners frequently propose "change in crime rate" as an indicator of CDBG's positive impact in people and places. The crime reduction program under former New York City mayor Rudolph Giuliani is illustrative. Upon taking office, Giuliani made crime reduction a top priority, replacing top police leadership and developing and adopting comprehensive management information systems to detect crime trends quickly and allocate resources to address them. His administration instituted one of the toughest zero-tolerance programs in the nation, placed more police officers on the street, and lobbied courts to hand out tougher sentences. Crime fell dramatically across the city.

New York City receives $218 million under CDBG, a relatively small amount of which is spent directly on crime reduction. A larger amount is allocated toward activities that might indirectly reduce crime, such as youth centers, training programs, and drug rehabilitation. Other federal, state, local, and private-sector initiatives fund activities that directly or indirectly relate to crime reduction. For example, the 1990s' unprecedented economic growth created jobs and reduced unemployment. Poverty rates fell, personal income rose, and the number of juvenile delinquents in the population declined.

Figure 11.1   **Impact of a Youth Center on Crime Rates**

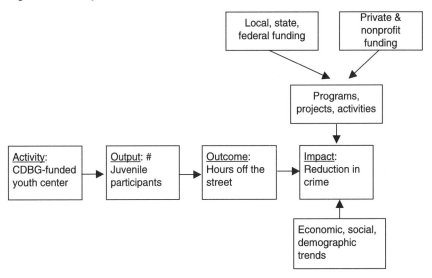

The question: How much of a contribution to decline in crime rate, if any, would a CDBG-funded youth center in a poor neighborhood make? Figure 11.1 scopes out this hypothetical. Suppose further that the youth center was funded with other federal, state, and local public monies, as well as private monies, and was part of a program that placed more police on the streets, instituted a neighborhood watch program, and attracted new employers to the area. When New York City–based CDBG program directors reported that crime rates fell, it seems unlikely that the result could be linked to the youth center. For a causal linkage to be made, policy analysts would have to address the issues enumerated above: "but for," "before-after, with-without," commingling of funds, small magnitude of funds, and exogenous effects including economy, socioeconomics and demographics, issues of place, and minimal effects. Entitlement communities or states do not have the resources necessary to carry out evaluation studies to assess impact. Even if they did, the studies would be more costly than the value.

Conclusion

It appears that using the language of cause and effect—that is, impacts as defined here—is misleading at best. It raises more questions than it answers and inserts a great deal of ambiguity and complexity into performance measurement, something antithetical to the enterprise. It is unlikely that any cause-and-effect analysis could be designed and executed.

5. Issues in Constructing Performance Indicators

In this section, I turn to questions surrounding construction of individual performance indicators. Stakeholders identified these challenges to be overcome or minimized. Nearly all of these issues were addressed satisfactorily, if not completely.

Cases

All performance measurement systems must enumerate cases—beneficiaries, non-beneficiaries, clients, patients, populations, residents, homeowners, and renters are just a few. They also must enumerate cases that are very complex or fuzzy—communities, households, and families. But this can be impossible to accomplish in many instances. For example, in impoverished neighborhoods, it is not unusual to find several families living illegally in a single-family dwelling. To complicate matters, the families may be illegal immigrants. If CDBG invests in improving the housing stock in a neighborhood, how many people actually benefit? We likely cannot count them; the best we can do is count the number of houses rehabbed.

Rates, Ratios, and Percentages

Many performance indicators use rates, ratios, or percentages to tie a baseline to an outcome. For example, a measure of unmet need is to divide the number of people receiving a benefit by the number of low- to moderate-income people eligible, yielding a proportion of those served or not served. Reporting data for this indicator, it is necessary to report the percentage along with the baseline or beneficiary if these are to be aggregated at the national level. The analyst would know little nor be able to extrapolate if the national performance measurement system reported only the percentage of people helped, but not the actual number that served as the basis. Other data used to derive that indicator need to be reported as well, greatly expanding the amount of information required. Averaging rates, ratios, and percentages also presents a challenge. A small community might report a ratio of 0.1 (1/10), as would a large one (10,000/100,000). Both ratios are equal, but the underlying calculations have much different implications. Yet this distinction can get lost when dissimilar things are lumped together.

Baselines and Benchmarks

Benchmarks are defined as indicators that represent a standard or performance level derived from another entity undertaking a similar task. For example, analysts might compare the health status of a CDBG entitlement community against that for the nation, or for communities of similar size or composition. The issue is what the benchmark should be. Does the community reporting data decide? Or, does HUD or OMB? Very few grantees use this measurement convention.

Baselines are defined as indicators that represent past performance levels, such as the performance of a CDBG activity in 2004 compared with the prior year. The issue is that CDBG programs do not invest in the same activities year after year. One year they may invest in affordable housing, and the next in infrastructure. That being the case, it may appear that CDBG was highly successful in some years but not in others. The performance measurement system would be too complex to annotate each measure with the CDBG investment strategy in effect for a given year. One way to manage this variance would be to report *moving averages*. Rather than reporting annual indicators separately by year, analysts could average three years together and, in subsequent years, drop the earliest year and add the latest year. This way, program effects would be smoothed, with spikes from changing investment strategies removed.

Time Parameters

A significant issue is determining the time that should elapse prior to reporting outcomes. How many months or years should pass from the time an entrepreneur is trained in a CDBG program to the time she is monitored for job creation? If the entrepreneur creates no jobs the first year, the program may appear to be a failure. The longer analysts must wait to see whether jobs were created, the more likely the data will be unavailable or problematic. A CDBG entrepreneurship training program offered as a one-shot effort would unlikely have the capacity to track entrepreneurs over several years. Entrepreneurs typically gain and lose members of their workforce at startup. How can these gains and losses be meaningfully reported? With CDBG investment, some activities are completed in days and do not have longer-term implications, while some, in which the same activity may occur in different ways over time, transcend fiscal or calendar years (e.g., a microfinance program may extend for one or five years).

Aggregation

It is necessary that indicator data for a national performance measurement system be aggregated from entitlement communities and states to a national level. Some observers would like to mandate or encourage entitlement communities and states to target CDBG investments in small geographical areas to maximize program outcomes. For the purpose of this report, such a policy prescription can be separated from the issue of outcome measurement. It may be too complicated or even meaningless to report indicators tied to geography. For example, CDBG might improve home ownership opportunities for low- to moderate-income persons by investing in distressed neighborhoods. Grantees would report the number of homeowners produced under CDBG, a statistic that can be aggregated to the national level. If the concept of distressed neighborhood is graphed onto the measure, grantees would first define a distressed neighborhood, and then how home ownership improved under CDBG. It seems there will be as many measures as there are grantees; distressed communities in rural North Dakota, inner city New York, and downtown Anchorage are different and how CDBG improved them will be too. It is difficult to see how this would be measured then aggregated to the national level. Even if grantees were to report that the number or percentage of distressed neighborhoods improved, such a statistic would be meaningless to the extent that cases added are not comparable.

Compatibility with Other HUD Programs

In addition to CDBG, CPD manages three other block grant programs—HOME, ESG, and HOPWA—and several competitive programs—Economic Development Initiative, Brownfields, Youthbuild, and Rural Housing and Economic Development. These programs invest in some of the same activities as CDBG, and sometimes they both leverage each other and match funds. Often, programs use the same indicators to measure outcomes for different activities. A performance measurement system should seek commonality across programs so that indicator data can be aggregated within and across programs to determine how CPD funding contributed to national goals and objectives.

Double Counting

Many projects have multiple purposes under CDBG. One investment might address safe housing, while another would address decent housing. Both activities might be made in the same housing unit. Is the number of safe and decent houses rehabilitated one or two? Clearly, double counting would be inappropriate in performance-based management systems. *This is no longer a problem in CDBG as was the case in years past.*

Reliability and Validity

Reliability asks whether an indicator would yield the same result when it is measured two or more times under the same conditions—in other words, consistency. Weather reporters often base their forecasts on "known" factors that often turn out to be incorrect. Pollsters attempting to predict elections may get different responses to the same questions asked a short time apart.

Validity asks whether an indicator measures what it is supposed to measure, in this case CDBG outcomes. For example, is the unemployment rate a valid measure of joblessness in a poor community? As an outcome, many consider it important to reduce unemployment using CDBG. Many stakeholders disagreed. Unemployment rates are calculated from unemployment compensation claims and population surveys for which a respondent must have actively sought work within the most recent two-week period to be considered unemployed. Those not looking for work for whatever reason are not considered unemployed for statistical purposes. In poor neighborhoods, where legions of people may not be looking for work, the labor force participation rate might be a better measure.

Political Concerns

All outcomes can be measured, but some may be "off limits" for political reasons. For example, some elected officials promote CDBG investments because they increase a community's tax base; investments increase housing values, which in turn increases property tax assessments. Tax increases are a byproduct of improved property values, seemingly a good outcome. Other elected officials may object to the notion of using federal tax dollars—specifically, CDBG funding—to increase the local tax take, seemingly a bad outcome. This also might be a factor when localities use CDBG to attract other federal funding as a form of leveraging.

Triangulation

Because indicators have associated methodological problems, it is desirable to use multiple sources to measure the same activity outcomes, known as *multiple measures*. For example, researchers could use employment and administrative survey data to determine whether they find the same level of performance. This is done at the national level when economists compare the Survey of Employers and the Household Survey to determine how many new jobs have been created. Having multiple indicators pointing to the same impact bolsters the analysts' confidence that certain activities very likely produced outcomes. Of course, triangulation is expensive, but might be worth the cost for some activities.

There are certain CDBG program characteristics that inhibit effective design and implementation of an outcome-based performance measurement system. Since CDBG is a block grant, recipients can delegate funds to sub-recipients within a broad range of program goals including housing, community, and economic development. This results in varied interpretations of goals, measures that indicate goal attainment, and definitions of outcomes versus outputs. Across communities, CDBG funds, in tandem with other federal, state, and locally appropriated dollars, vary considerably; making an assessment of whether funds were well spent difficult.

Difficulties in constructing performance measures stem from interrelated issues at the local, national, and program definition levels. Program flexibility, combined with the range of activities that CDBG funds, can be used to generate a series of issues that must be addressed in construction of useful performance measures.

6. Conclusion

The CDBG experience made major contributions to the merging field of performance-based management, especially in community development, not to mention intergovernmental transfers of funding. The stakeholder working group—comprising HUD, grantees, and OMB—serves as a model for achieving consensus on how to measure performance, then implementing it. Other efforts by OMB, associations, GAO, and researchers, in the end, also made positive contributions to performance in CDBG. Most importantly, the CDBG experience shows that most performance issues can be overcome if the will to do so is there. And even when issues cannot be fully overcome, there remains much merit in continuing to try to document results. Alas, there remain numerous other performance-related issues to overcome in this program.

Notes

1. Material in this section is drawn from HUD's website at: Community Planning and Development. 2007. Washington, DC: U.S. Department of Housing and Urban Development. http://www.hud.gov/offices/cpd/communitydevelopment/programs, accessed October 2, 2007. The program is authorized under Title 1 of the Housing and Community Development Act of 1974, Public Law 93–383, as amended; 42 U.S.C.-5301 et seq. Entitlement cities are defined as: principal cities of Metropolitan Statistical Areas (MSAs), other metropolitan cities with populations of at least 50,000, and qualified urban counties with populations of at least 200,000 (excluding the population of entitled cities), which are entitled to receive annual grants. Congress amended the Housing and Community Development Act of 1974 (HCD Act) in 1981 to allow each state to administer CDBG funds for non-entitlement areas—those units of general local government that do not receive CDBG funds directly from HUD as entitlement cities and counties. Non-entitlement areas have populations of less than 50,000 and counties have populations of less than 200,000.

2. The author, working for the National Academy of Public Administration, directed a project offering technical assistance to HUD to reengineer its performance management system. Final reports are available at NAPA 2005a and 2005b, from which much of the material in the chapter is drawn.

References

National Academy of Public Administration (NAPA). 2005a. *Developing Performance Measures for the CDBG Program.* Washington, DC: National Academy of Public Administration.
———. 2005b. *Integrating CDBG Performance Measures into IDIS.* Washington, DC: National Academy of Public Administration.

Part 3

The International Context

12

OECD Countries' Experiences of Performance Budgeting and Management

Lessons Learned

Teresa Curristine

Over the past two decades, enhancing public-sector performance has taken on a new urgency in Organization for Economic Cooperation and Development (OECD) member countries as governments face mounting demands on public expenditure, calls for higher quality services, and, in some countries, a public increasingly unwilling to pay higher taxes.

To address these challenges, OECD countries have sought to enhance their public-sector performance by adopting a range of new levers and approaches to management, budgeting, personnel, and institutional structures. Within government, these have included introduction of performance measures into budgeting and management, relaxation of input controls, delegation of responsibility to line ministries/agencies, and changes in public employment typified by the adoption of contracts for public servants and the introduction of performance-related pay. Examples of institutional changes include creation of executive agencies and the privatization or outsourcing of public services.

This chapter concentrates on attempts by OECD countries to introduce performance- or results-based budgeting and performance management. This reform lever moves the focus of budgeting, management, and accountability away from inputs toward results. Managers and/or organizations are given flexibility to improve performance and are then held accountable for results measured in the form of outputs and outcomes. Providing performance information is not an end in itself; rather, its overall objective is to support better decision making by politicians and public servants, leading to improved performance and/or accountability, and ultimately, enhanced outcomes for society.

The quantity of performance information provided to decision-makers has substantially increased but countries continue to struggle with issues of quality and with ensuring that the information is used in decision making. It takes time to develop performance measures and indicators, and even longer to change the behavior of key actors in the system (politicians and bureaucrats) so that they use this information and develop a performance culture adapted to their particular country. The performance movement is here to stay. Benefits of being clearer inside and outside government about purposes and results are undeniable. But to gain these benefits governments need a long-term approach, realistic expectations, and persistence. This chapter looks at the development of performance-based budgeting, management, and reporting in OECD countries and identifies trends, strengths, and limitations of approaches and future challenges. First, it discusses the wider perspective of government performance.

What Does Performance Mean for Government?

Performance, a term encompassing many different concepts, means the yield or results of activities carried out in relation to the purposes being pursued. Its objective is to strengthen the degree to which governments achieve their purposes.

The desire to improve government performance is not new. Governments have always wanted results from their spending and regulation. What is new is that increasingly, governments are facing spending constraints. With no new money to spend, more attention must be given to achieving better results from existing funds. At the same time, new ideas have emerged about how to reorganize and better motivate public servants to achieve results.

In traditional bureaucracy, performance was driven by ensuring compliance with set rules and regulations, controlling inputs, and adhering to the public-sector ethos. This system worked well when governments had less complex and more standardized tasks to perform—and when complying with the rules was considered more important than efficiency or effectiveness. The system has been criticized, however, because employees became more focused on process than on results, and there were weak incentives to use funds efficiently to achieve objectives. Public administrators not only have to serve collective interests of fairness and probity, but also have to meet individual needs and address complex social problems. Traditional public administrative systems were not designed to be flexible and adaptive in a modern society with customized services, need for constant adaptation, pressure for efficiency, and increased use of private agents. There is a call for sharper performance incentives than those provided by traditional bureaucracy. Furthermore, governments have taken on more challenging and complex tasks, which do not lend themselves to the traditional approach.

Performance information is important in assessing and improving policies in:

- managerial analysis, direction and control of public services;
- budgetary analysis;
- parliamentary oversight of the executive; and
- public accountability—the general duty on governments to disclose and take responsibility for their decisions.

Governments have adopted a number of different approaches to improving public-sector efficiency and effectiveness, including: strategic management; business planning; performance budgeting and management; devolved and delegated decision making; structural change, such as the creation of executive agencies; use of contracts; and introduction of competition and market-type mechanisms in service provision.

This variety of approaches toward improving public-sector performance is rich but confusing. Each approach has different strengths and weaknesses and the best choice of approach depends on its purpose. This chapter explores the introduction of performance measures into budgeting and management and their use in decision making.

Performance Budgeting and Performance Management

OECD countries use a variety of mechanisms to assess the efficiency and effectiveness of programs and agencies—performance measures, benchmarking, and evaluations. Evaluations can incorporate program reviews, cost effectiveness evaluations, and ad hoc sectoral and spending reviews.

"Performance information" includes evaluations and performance measures. While this chapter concentrates on examining the latter, it is important to acknowledge that evaluations have a valuable role to play in assessing the performance of programs.

The strongest trend in performance across OECD countries is introduction of performance-oriented budgeting and management. Many governments have adopted an approach to management and budgeting that shifts the emphasis of budgeting, management, and accountability away from controlling inputs toward achieving results. In theory, input controls are relaxed and managers are given flexibility to improve performance. In return, they are held accountable for results.

Moves to formalize targets and measurement in government management and budgeting systems have a long history. In fact, performance budgeting has existed in one form or another since the first Hoover Commission in the United States recommended it in 1949. Performance budgeting and performance management are used to describe a range of rather diverse interpretations and approaches. For example, they can simply refer to the presentation of performance information as part of the budget documentation or to a budget classification in which appropriations are divided by groups of outputs or outcomes. A more narrow definition of performance budgeting is a form of budgeting that relates funds allocated to results measured in the form of outputs and/or outcomes. Performance management also has diverse definitions: It can refer to corporate management or systems for evaluating and assessing individual or group performance. A more holistic definition, which is applied in this chapter, is a management cycle under which program performance objectives and targets are determined, managers have flexibility to achieve them, actual performance is measured and reported, and this information feeds into decisions about program funding, design, operations, and rewards or penalties.

Although various interpretations of performance budgeting and management exist, the common trend is that governments have sought to adopt a results-based approach, which shifts budgeting, management, and accountability away from inputs to a focus on measurable results.

Country Approaches to Implementing Performance Budgeting and Management

Many OECD countries have introduced performance measures into their management and budget systems. However, countries are at different phases of introduction and have varied objectives and approaches to implementing these reforms.

Different Phases

New Zealand was among the first to begin the present round of performance management and/or budgeting in the late 1980s, followed in the early to mid-1990s by Canada, Denmark, Finland, the Netherlands, Sweden, the United Kingdom, and the United States. A further phase began in the late 1990s to early 2000s for Austria, Germany, and Switzerland, while Turkey began a pilot phase of performance budgeting and management in 2004–2005.

Country approaches to performance management are evolving. New Zealand began by concentrating on outputs and is now moving to an outcomes approach. Denmark is changing its accounting and budgeting systems to focus on outcomes. France passed a law that requires the production of outputs and outcomes in budget documentation for the majority of programs.

Various Objectives

It is possible to discern four broad objectives for which countries have adopted the formalization of targets and measures in the government management process:

- Managing the efficiency and effectiveness of agencies and ministries and/or the internal control and accountability within individual ministries.
- Improving decision making in the budget process, and/or in the allocation of resources and accountability of ministries to the Ministry of Finance.
- Improving external transparency and accountability to parliament and the public and clarifying the roles and responsibilities of politicians and civil servants.
- Achieving savings.

Some countries have given attention to one or two of these objectives only. Other countries—Australia, Denmark, the Netherlands, New Zealand, the United Kingdom, and the United States—have embraced all four objectives, seeking to introduce performance-based management and budgeting across central government and to improve both performance and internal and external accountability to the legislature and the public.

Various Approaches

In some countries—the United States is a good example—ministries have developed strategic and performance plans that include performance targets. Other countries have adopted performance agreements either between a minister/ministry and a subordinate agency or between a minister and a department. Such agreements can also be between the Ministry of Finance and a ministry or agency.

In New Zealand there are purchase agreements between the minister and relevant departments setting out the agencies' agreed outputs. There are also formal performance agreements between ministers and department chief executives. In the United Kingdom, ministries approve agencies' annual business plans, which establish performance goals and targets. There are also performance agreements between departments and H.M. Treasury stating agreed objectives and targets. In Australia there are resource agreements between the Department of Finance and Administration and the relevant departments and agencies. In Denmark, there are performance contracts between ministries and agencies and between chief executives and ministries; these include links to performance-related pay.

Implementation

Some countries have adopted an incremental approach. For example, the United States had a four-year pilot phase before government-wide implementation of the Government Performance and Results Act (GPRA) of 1993. Other countries have chosen an incremental approach, allowing agencies to participate voluntarily in reforms without moving toward total implementation across government. Germany and Ireland use pilot schemes.

Australia, the Netherlands, New Zealand, and the United Kingdom have taken a top-down and total systems approach to implementation. Others—Finland in particular—have taken a more bottom-up and ad hoc approach, where agencies have been given freedom to develop their own methods with less enforcement from the top.

What Is the Current State of Play?

Despite differences in approach, a common trend in OECD member countries is to introduce a focus on measurable results in management and budget processes. This section examines current trends in OECD member countries using 2003 data obtained from twenty-seven countries in the OECD/World Bank Budget Practices and Procedures Database Survey.

Performance Information and Targets in Budget Documentation and the Budget Process

Among OECD countries, there is a strong trend of routinely including non-financial performance information in budget documentation:

- 72 percent of countries include nonfinancial performance data in their budget documentation.
- In 44 percent of countries, these data are available for more than three-quarters of programs.
- In 71 percent of countries, performance data include performance targets, although there is a wide variation in terms of program coverage.
- In 65 percent of countries, these results are included in the main budget documents and/or the annual financial documents.

While the introduction of performance information into budget documentation is becoming common, it has not been embraced by all OECD member countries. Over a quarter of countries surveyed do not include any nonfinancial performance data in their budget documentation. Iceland includes performance data but not performance targets.

The most common way of including performance targets in the budget process is a combination of outputs and outcomes. Only 27 percent of countries include mostly outcomes and no country has mostly outputs. Countries appear to have recognized the difficulty in following an approach that concentrates solely on either outcomes or outputs. Only concentrating on outputs can give rise to goal displacement as agencies lose sight of the intended impact of their programs on wider society and concentrate solely on quantifiable measures at the expense of activities that are less measurable. It can also result in less attention being paid to cross-cutting issues. While outcomes incorporate a wider focus on the impact of programs on society and have greater appeal to politicians and the public, they are very difficult to measure. As will be discussed later, in many cases a mix of outputs, outcomes, and inputs is desirable.

The Current Trends in Performance Budgeting

Some OECD countries have attempted to integrate performance targets into the budget process, but very few are carrying out "real" performance budgeting—including performance information in budget documentation and linking expenditure to outcome/output targets, reporting performance against these targets, and using the information to make decisions on future resource allocation. Using this definition, performance budgeting is rare. OECD surveyed the degree to which countries apply performance budgeting in this strict sense.

While 72 percent of OECD member countries routinely display targets in budget documentation given to the Ministry of Finance, linking of expenditure to output and outcome targets is not common among OECD member countries:

- 46 percent of countries either do not link expenditure to targets or only do so for a few programs.
- 35 percent of countries reported that they link expenditure to some targets.
- Only 18 percent of countries reported that they specifically link expenditure to all or most of their output or outcome targets.

A mixed picture emerges with regard to the use of performance results in determining budget allocations, with over 31 percent of countries stating that performance results are not used for this purpose. It is not common for politicians to use performance results in allocating resources between programs or in decision making. Forty-one percent of OECD countries reported that it was not common for politicians in the executive or the legislature to use performance measures in any decision making. This includes countries—for example, the United States—that have long experience in this area.

Very few countries engage in any form of direct performance budgeting, since many countries do not even link expenditure to output and outcome targets, let alone make the appropriation of funds an explicit function of performance. This form of budgeting is only applied to a limited number of functional areas and only in a few countries. It is mostly found in health and education, especially higher education. In Denmark, Finland, Norway, and Sweden, for example, it is the form of budgeting used to fund higher education.

As Figure 12.1 highlights, very few countries appear to have formal mechanisms in place that relate the success or failure in achieving a target to the reward or punishment of individuals or agencies:

- In 46 percent of OECD member countries, no rewards or sanctions are applied if a target is met or not met.
- In 20 percent of countries, rewards/sanctions are reflected in the size of the budget for the government organization.
- In 16 percent of countries, pay is sometimes linked to performance. In all these cases performance is linked to the pay of a civil servant or a number of civil servants. For example, in the United Kingdom, performance against organization targets is linked to the pay of the agency's chief executive.

Current Trends in Performance Management

Greater progress has been made in implementing performance management reforms than performance budgeting. This section examines whether OECD member countries have a system of performance management that incorporates the setting

Figure 12.1   **Are Rewards and/or Sanctions Applied if Performance Targets Are or Are Not Met?**

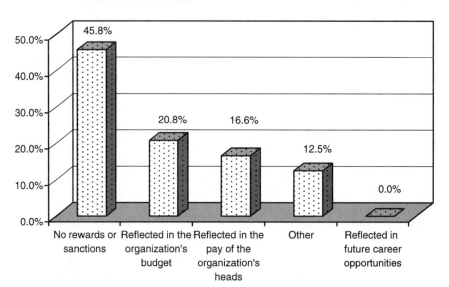

and reporting of targets and their subsequent use in the internal decision-making process of ministries and agencies:

- In 67 percent of countries, the relevant minister or the head of department is formally responsible for setting performance targets.
- In 56 percent of countries, performance against targets is continuously monitored internally in the relevant ministry.
- In 63 percent of countries, performance against targets is reported in a systematic annual report for some or most programs.

Performance results that feed into decision-making processes appear in a number of countries. In nearly 50 percent of countries, performance results are used internally within agencies/ministries to set priorities, to allocate resources, and to change work processes. Performance results are used by the parent ministry in approximately half of countries to set priorities and in over a third to adopt new approaches. This information is used least in setting individual staff performance plans.

While this information is used in the decision-making process, it is not clear what other types of information are used (if any) and how much weight is given to performance results compared to other types of information.

Approximately 50 percent of countries reported having a system of performance management. However, within a given country, there is variation in the number of programs and agencies to which performance management is applied. Australia, the

Netherlands, New Zealand, Norway, and the United States have taken a comprehensive approach and it is applied to nearly all ministries and agencies. In Belgium, Canada, and Germany it is only applied in approximately a quarter of programs.

The introduction of output and/or outcome targets as a system of management control requires relaxed input controls in order to give managers the freedom to use resources to achieve results and improve performance. To what extent has this trade-off between performance and controls been achieved in practice? In terms of the whole-of-government control processes, the information gathered from the OECD/World Bank Budget Practices and Procedures Database does not provide much evidence that this trade-off has occurred.

Among countries with a long experience of introducing performance indicators, there is variation in the degree of relaxation of input controls. Australia and the Netherlands appear to have relaxed central controls. Others—Denmark, New Zealand, and Norway—have also made substantial moves in that direction. However, in some countries—for example, the United States—introduction of performance indicators into management and budgeting does not appear to have been accompanied by a relaxation of central input controls.

Countries like Finland and Sweden register a high degree of management autonomy. This is to be expected given their long tradition of agencies. Equally, given that performance budgeting is a centrally driven device, they have only a moderate level of formalization of performance indicators in their budget system. Australia, the country that shows the strongest trend of substituting input controls for performance controls, is, according to recent advice from the Department of Finance and Administration, finding the current reporting from departments insufficient for whole-of-government purposes.

Accountability to the Public

As Figure 12.2 indicates, in OECD countries, the provision of information to the public on government performance is widespread.

In the survey, twenty-four OECD countries claimed to report to the public on performance results. This is strong evidence that transparency has improved. In presenting this information to the public, the aim is to improve trust in government by showing what government does and most importantly how well it does it. As improving public-sector performance becomes more important to citizens, in electoral terms it becomes increasingly necessary for governments to demonstrate that they are achieving these improvements.

The problem for governments is that improvements in performance take time to achieve but the electoral pressures are such that they need to show improvements in the short term. Some governments believe that the public will be more convinced that services have improved by the presentation of numerical performance information. However, even with numerical information there are questions about quality and accuracy. While governments present performance results as objective evaluations,

Figure 12.2   **Are Performance Results Made Available to the Public?**

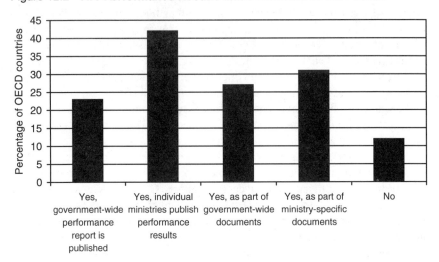

this information, depending on the nature of the political system, can become part of the political dogfight between the government and the opposition. This is more a problem in political contexts where the norm is adversarial rather than consensual politics. In this context, the opposition can use the very same results to discredit the government's performance and to raise questions about their objectivity. The media has a large role to play: If information is presented as party political propaganda and government spin, this could do more to increase public skepticism than trust.

A related issue is whether interest groups are willing to accept the government's presentation of performance results. Performance results are generally aggregated outcomes for the whole country, a region, or a single large institution. Even if accurate, the general conclusion may be at odds with some individual experience. Thus it is inevitable that performance results will be challenged on the basis of that experience. The views of the public are more likely to reflect personal experiences or views presented in the media rather than the government's performance reporting.

External Performance Auditing

Having externally audited performance information would help to assure the public of the quality and accuracy of the information presented in government reports. One might have expected that, with the great increase in the number of countries with performance information in their formal reporting systems, there would be a commensurate rise in the routine auditing of performance reports by supreme audit institutions. There is indeed some trend in this direction, but it lags behind the introduction of performance reporting.

Assuring credibility and quality of performance data is a key issue for OECD

Figure 12.3 **Is the Performance Data Externally Audited?**

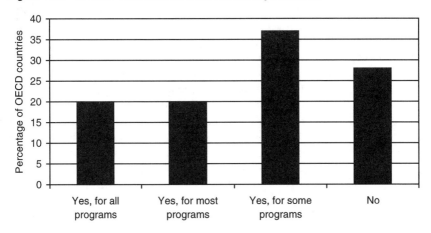

countries, taking performance information at face value can give a distorted picture. Threats to quality can come from poor practices in gathering and analyzing data and from political pressure to look good. Independent audits of performance data help reduce these problems (see Figure 12.3).

Auditing performance information is costly and it is also different from auditing financial information. Therefore, auditors must have the requisite expertise and training to conduct these audits. In addition, there is a danger that performance becomes compliance—that is, too much emphasis on compliance with rules and regulations can reduce the emphasis on flexibility and innovation needed to improve performance.

Summary of Trends

Across OECD countries, there is a strong trend of introducing performance indicators into management and budgeting. There is also a strong common trend of introducing a systematic approach to performance management. While many countries have reached the stage of introducing performance targets into their budget documentation, fewer countries have integrated this information into their budgetary decision-making process and even fewer have used it in the allocation of resources. There is also a strong trend of reporting this information to the public and the legislature, although the tendency is for legislatures not to make much use of this information. The performance budgeting movement seems at the moment to be stronger on process than on results.

Why Context Matters

Successful use of the formalization of performance in budgeting and management processes depends on other political and administrative factors. Reformers do not begin with a blank sheet; performance indicators and targets are introduced into existing and established systems of accountability and control, which have informal and formal components.

Performance is only one dimension of accountability. Other aspects include assuring that correct administrative procedures have been followed and that funds have been spent as allocated. Traditional accountability mechanisms designed around input controls have not been extensively relaxed in some countries. Accountability for performance will coexist alongside traditional mechanisms. The issue is not about replacing input controls with outputs/outcomes; it is more a question of how to find the desired mix of mechanisms within the system. Concentration on only one instrument of control can have distorting effects. For example, concentrating only on outputs can lead to goal displacement. Table 12.1 shows the different potential and limitations of control regimes for inputs, outputs, and outcomes.

The most appropriate balance of controls depends on the country context and problems these reforms seek to address. For example, if the problem is the susceptibility of a system or organization to corruption, then placing the stress on input controls is a more suitable approach than stressing outcomes. For other systems and organizations where the problem is inflexibility and lack of adaptation, a combination of outputs and outcomes could be a more suitable approach. Within each system it is necessary to find the desired combination of controls between outputs and inputs. Furthermore, it can be desirable to have some flexibility to allow for a different mix of controls for different organizations.

Whole-of-Government Approach: Changing the Behavior of Key Actors

Whatever the balance or mix of controls in a given country, when outputs and outcomes are introduced they have to be accommodated within the existing control system and this requires a realignment of relationships. In introducing these reforms it is important that governments take a whole-of-government approach—as the integration of performance measures into budgeting and management systems is not just about changing processes but is also about transforming the behavior of both public servants and politicians throughout the political system. This is the case if governments have taken a comprehensive approach and apply this reform across government to the majority of programs. Key actors in this case can include public servants and managers in ministries/agencies and in the Ministry of Finance, and politicians in the legislature and executive. Challenges in changing the behavior of public servants in ministries/agencies and in the Ministry of Finance have been discussed elsewhere. This section briefly examines challenges in changing political behavior.

Performance-oriented budgeting and management as a reform lever has wider governance implications: it has the capacity to help elected leaders to steer the public sector toward their policy objectives. It provides a mechanism for politicians to clearly

Table 12.1

Potential and Limitations of Different Management Control Regimes

	Potential	Limitations	Suitable contexts
Input	Easy and affordable; strengthens compliance.	Does not support efficiency; can be inflexible.	Low confidence and variable competence.
Output	Facilitates efficiency; facilitates control of aggregate expenditure; accountability for results.	Can distort focus; measurement problems; information overload.	Confidence, sound accounting, and professionalism.
Outcome	Supports policy formulation and coordination; long term.	Measurement problems; accountability problems; costs; information overload.	The above plus dedicated politicians and the ability to set clear objectives.

Figure 12.4 **Is It Common that Politicians Use Performance Measures in Decision Making?**

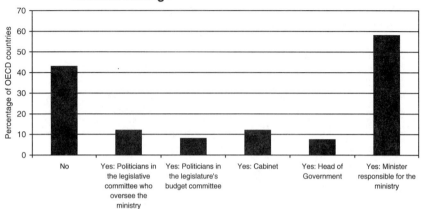

articulate their goals and objectives for the government as a whole or for the relevant ministry and the means to monitor progress toward achieving these goals.

In theory, this model should clarify the respective roles and responsibilities of ministers and public servants. Politicians set the objectives; these cascade down to the relevant ministry and/or organization and are translated into performance measures and/or targets. Results against these targets are used to hold agencies to account and to provide better information to be used in decision making on policy, budget, and management issues. For this model to succeed it is important that politicians use this information in decision making.

Motivating Politicians to Use Performance Information

Do politicians use performance information? The answer, according to Figure 12.4, is "not much," with the exception of ministers responsible for the department delivering a target.

In 72 percent of OECD countries, targets are routinely displayed in budget documentation presented to the legislature. However, in only 19 percent of countries do politicians in the legislature use performance measures in decision making. The percentage is even lower for politicians in the legislative budget committee, with only 8 percent using this information.

For countries that have introduced these reforms, a major challenge is to change the behavior of politicians and to create the right mix of incentives to motivate them to use this information. Table 12.2 summarizes the necessary, but not sufficient, behavioral changes that are needed from politicians in the executive and legislature if these reforms are to achieve their aims. The table lists some of the possible incentives that could motivate these actors to change their behavior and also the negative factors that discourage them from adopting this approach and using the performance information provided. This list of behavioral changes and incentives is not meant to be exhaustive.

The impact of these incentives will vary with political and institutional contexts and to some extent with the individual minister. In Westminster systems, accountability is focused on ministerial responsibility, and there can be strong emphasis on faultfinding and blame. In these systems, there is a danger that despite the formal system of accountability, which concentrates on performance, politicians may be more concerned with avoiding errors and managing public perceptions and will use the various accountability mechanisms selectively to that end. Systems where responsibility is more collective and the political system is less adversarial may offer more room for constructive use of performance information.

Despite these issues, according to the OECD survey, ministers with responsibility for a relevant ministry/entity have paid more attention to performance indicators than other politicians have. There is a problem, however, with getting politicians in the legislature interested in using performance results. Factors that can discourage them are listed in Table 12.2. They include questions about quality, readability, and relevance of information.

In a system of separation of powers with a strong legislature that has a say over the setting of objectives, like, for example, in the United States, there needs to be a high degree of institutional cooperation between the two branches of government. This need for strong cooperation is less of an issue in a country like the United Kingdom, which has a very powerful executive branch. Again, the behavioral changes required and the influence of incentives will vary to some extent with the political and institutional structures.

However, if performance management and budgeting is to have any impact in any political system it is important that the key actors in decision-making processes are provided with motivations and incentives to change. Without these provisions, performance information becomes a mere paper exercise. The combined experiences of OECD countries highlight the importance of taking a long-term approach. It takes time to change behavior and to see the benefits of this approach emerge.

Limitations and Tensions

This section considers some of the limitations and tensions that need to be considered when introducing performance budgeting and management.

Performance Measures: Only One Source of Information on Performance

Performance indicators and targets provide a snapshot of performance in time. They do not provide a guide to future performance nor do they explain why a target has been achieved. Therefore, when making decisions about the performance of an agency or a program, it is important to consider different types of performance information. To

Table 12.2

Incentives Influencing Performance Information in Decision Making

Key actors	Behavioral changes needed	Positive incentives and factors encouraging change	Negative incentives and factors discouraging change
Ministers and politicians in the executive	Provide leadership support for reforms. Set clear objectives and targets. Use performance results to hold agencies to account. Use performance results in decision-making processes on policies/programs or budgeting. Respect managerial freedom granted—by noninterference in delegated areas.	Process to set objectives and monitor progress in achieving them. Good quality information. Information relevant to political needs. Provide information to voters on achievement of political goals. Compatible with existing informal and formal mechanisms of oversight.	Concerns about quality of information. Information not relevant for real political issue and day-to-day concerns. Cost of being informed and monitoring. Lack of time to use information. Little or no influence on career advancement.
Politicians in the legislature	If applicable, set objectives. Use performance results for oversight purposes. Use information in decision making on programs and/or policy and/or budgeting. Respect managerial freedom.	Help to oversee government progress in achieving outcome goals. Good-quality information. Relevant to political needs. Presented in easily readable manner. Compatible with existing informal and formal mechanisms of oversight. Provide benefits over and above traditional approach.	Poor quality of information. Information less relevant to political needs. Cost of learning about new lever, continuing costs. Lack of time to use this information in decision making. Information presented in an unreadable manner. Receiving less detailed information. Concerns about having less control.

Source: OECD/World Bank Budget Practices and Procedures Database 2003.

obtain an encompassing picture of organizational and program performance, evaluations and performance indicators can be considered with other formal and informal sources of information and feedback. Unlike targets, evaluations can explain the results of a policy or program and what changes will improve its performance.

Not Everything Can Be Measured

Unlike financial information, with performance information it is difficult to apply a "one-size-fits-all" approach across government. Governments carry out a large variety of diverse functions, from building roads to providing advice on foreign travel. OECD country experience indicates that performance indicators and measures are more easily applied to certain types of functional and program areas than others. Three types of programs can be distinguished: tangible and non-tangible individually tailored services, and non-tangible ideal services. Performance indicators are more easily applied in programs that involve delivery of a tangible good or service with observable outputs, such as issuing passports or driver's licenses or collecting taxes. It is easier to create reliable unit cost measures for this type of activity. It is possible, although more difficult, to design performance measures for complex services to individuals such as education and health care. Performance indicators are difficult to apply to activities such as policy advice where the service is non-tangible and outcomes are not visible. In those areas where process is observable, a more obvious approach is to assess and control organizations on the basis of compliance with procedures. In some activities and organizations where neither outputs nor outcomes are observable, performance indicators are not a suitable option.

Given the different functions performed by government, consideration should be given to adopting an approach to performance management flexible enough to allow for the diversity of programs and also for the fact that for certain functional areas other methods of assessing accountability and evaluating performance are potentially more effective.

Limitations of Costs, Capacity, and Time

Public-sector performance information is, potentially, limitless, complex, and expensive to collect. Any formal system of information gathering must be selective. Complex areas of government are managed in the context of a well-developed professional culture. Performance targets and information are of value only insofar as they strengthen the performance orientation of that culture. Good management seeks to maximize the internal motivation of staff and to minimize the need for formal management controls. These controls are expensive to operate, and at a certain point formal management systems reduce internal motivation.

There are limits to how much information decision-makers can use; people have "bounded rationality" and so do organizations. Decisions are taken by busy, often distracted ministers and senior managers who operate under complex incentives.

Providing them with more information does not necessarily help their decision making and may actively hinder it.

Future Challenges

A great deal of rhetoric has surrounded the introduction of performance management and budgeting. Supporters claim that it has the capacity to transform governments. However, it is important that this reform should not be seen as a panacea and that governments have realistic expectations about what it can achieve and the time needed to reach these objectives.

Measurement

Even countries that have been using this approach for over fifteen years continue to struggle with issues of measurement; this is especially the case for outcomes. A key challenge for all countries is obtaining good-quality information that is valid, reliable, and timely. Numerous challenges can be encountered, including setting clear objectives, finding accurate measures of performance, and having good systems of data collection.

Setting Objectives: For some agencies or programs, even setting clear objectives can be a problem when there is no agreement on what the mission is, or there are diverse missions, overlapping and fragmented programs, and stakeholders with different interests.

Finding Accurate Measures of Performance: The design of measures is made difficult by finding measures for specific activities, and by relating what an agency or program contributes toward achieving specific outcomes. Output and outcome measures each present a different set of challenges. Outcomes are more difficult to measure; they are complex and involve the interaction of many factors, planned and unplanned. Also, there are problems with time lag issues and in some cases results are not within government control. Outcomes, however, have a strong appeal for the public and politicians. Most countries appear to have combined outputs and outcomes.

Establishing and Maintaining Data Collection Systems: To ensure quality there needs to be a process by which data collected are verified and validated. However, setting up and maintaining these systems can be complex and costly. As discussed above, the auditing of performance information can help to improve standards and provide some legitimacy for the reported results. It is challenging to assure the quality of these data when agencies are dependent on third parties to provide the information. This is a problem in federal systems.

Setting and Using Performance Targets

Performance targets help to clarify performance expectations for an organization for a given time period. Countries, however, continue to struggle with the issues of target level and numbers. There are problems with setting targets too low and/or too high. Setting targets too low means that agencies are not challenged to improve performance. Setting them too high, while it can motivate organizations, also creates unrealistic expectations and situations in which agencies will fail. It takes time to get the right level and to get the comparative data to realize that targets are set at too high or too low a level.

Too Many Targets: There is also an issue about how many targets to have. Too many targets create information overload and make it difficult to select priorities; too few targets create distortion effects. Again, it takes time to get a realistic balance. Several countries have started out with a large number of targets and reduced them. In the United Kingdom when performance agreements for departments were first introduced as part of the comprehensive spending review in 1998, there were 600 targets across government. By the time of the revised spending review in 2002, that number had been reduced to 130 targets.

Avoiding Distorting Behavior: This is a challenge for all governments. Possible perverse effects include goal distortion—that is, organizations' and managers' focusing on a few specific indicators and targets, usually the most achievable or "saleable," at the expense of the overall objectives or program. In extreme cases of goal distortion, agencies or staff, under pressure to meet targets, may deliberately present misleading information.

Challenges with Using the Budget Process to Improve Performance

In many OECD countries, the objective in introducing performance into the budget process is to improve budgetary decision making and to act as an incentive for agencies to improve performance. Most countries, however, continue to struggle with this approach. One issue is obtaining good-quality and reliable performance data. Briefly, other challenges include establishing some link between financial information and performance information. This is challenging for outcome measures. In many countries there are also problems with the structure of the budget and accounting issues. Budgets tend to be structured in accordance with institutional and functional boundaries and not according to results categories. Also if there is no system of cost recording, it is difficult to relate true costs to results.

Getting the Right Mix of Incentives: This is particularly important when countries use performance information in resource allocation. A fundamental question is whether financial rewards should be given for good performance and bad performance should be punished and, if so, how. Punishing failure by removing resources creates a clear signal to other agencies that performance is considered important. However, it does not address underlying causes of poor performance. Indeed in some cases failure to meet targets can be the result of lack of funding or other resources. While rewarding good performance is intuitively appealing, it does not take into account cost issues and government priorities. In a climate of budgetary saving, a question is whether to give additional funding to an agency, especially one that is not a government priority. In either case, there is the danger that linking results to financial resources can create incentives to distort and cheat in presenting information.

Changing the Behavior and Culture

One of the most difficult challenges is to create a results-based culture within organizations and throughout government. Changing behavior and culture across government requires a whole-of-government approach and creation of the right mix of incentives taking account of how key actors influence each other. Most countries continue to struggle with achieving change in the behavior of public servants and politicians; this is a long-term process.

Obtaining and maintaining the support of managers and employees within government organizations is crucial. This reform has the potential to improve the focus on organizational goals; to provide managers with better information for decision making on programs, budgets and policies; and to improve internal reporting and controls. Gaining these benefits is challenging because it requires technical as well as cultural change. In technical terms, it can be difficult to measure what an agency does and to link organizational objectives to individual goals. It is important to obtain the buy-in of frontline employees; this can be facilitated by the right mix of formal and informal incentives and controls. Obtaining the strong support of the organizational leadership and managers can be facilitated by giving them the necessary flexibility to achieve goals. Without this flexibility, managers will have the responsibility for achieving targets without the ability to deliver, and no one wants to be held accountable for targets that are not within his/her control.

Within the context of a government-wide approach, if and how the performance information is used by politicians and the Ministry of Finance can create incentives that impact on how managers behave. If performance information is required but not used by leaders or managers in decision making, there is a danger of its becoming a burden on organizations in terms of cost of information systems and staff time. Provision of this information, in addition to the requirements of the traditional control mechanisms, can interfere with getting the job done. If this happens, then performance management and budgeting can become a distraction, a distortion, or an expensive paper exercise rather than a means to transform organizations and an essential part of good management.

Obtaining and maintaining the support of politicians, as discussed above, is a key challenge facing reformers. The support of politicians in the legislature and the executive helps to reinforce the need for change and to push reform, although it is particularly difficult to obtain the support of politicians in the legislature.

Issues of horizontal and vertical coordination must be overcome. Many goals and outcomes cut across government organizations and involve the work of many agencies. While some OECD countries have established cross-governmental horizontal goals and targets, it is proving difficult to achieve coordination across departments and to hold them accountable for results. On a vertical plane there is an issue with different actors' wanting the same information for diverse purposes; their informational needs are not the same.

Expectations must be managed. Realistic expectations are needed about both what can be achieved by this reform and how long it will take. A long-term approach and persistence are needed: It takes time to overcome the technical issues and to change the behavior of public servants and politicians.

Findings and Conclusion

Government performance can be improved through a focus on results in policy advice, central and departmental management processes, and parliamentary and public accountability. It is important to first identify the relative priority of these areas in a particular country. What a government should do is different in each case.

The majority of OECD countries are implementing performance management and performance budgeting, although the extent and the approaches vary widely across countries. Introduction of performance management and budgeting appears to be an important and enduring innovation in public management. It is a strong device for horizontal priority setting, policy alignment, and cost analysis. These reforms have improved transparency through the provision of more information on government performance to the public. However, some initial hopes have been too ambitious.

Most countries continue to struggle with changing the behavior of public servants and politicians. This is a long-term process. To achieve change in behavior and culture across government requires a whole-of-government approach, the creation of the right mix of incentives and controls (formal and informal), and an understanding of the systems and how the actions of key actors influence each other.

There is no clear pattern of input controls being lightened as performance indicators are strengthened. This raises issues about balancing accountability and flexibility. Whatever the accountability systems in place, they need to be balanced against the freedom required by managers to do their jobs. Critics of traditional systems of accountability argue that rules had become ends in themselves, accountability stressed compliance, and hierarchical structures hindered efficiency and performance. Thus, critics emphasized the need to relax input controls.

There are obvious dangers in relaxing input controls too soon after the introduction of output and outcome measures. However, there are also dangers in failing to relax these controls sufficiently, with the possible effect that output and outcome measures become an expensive paper exercise, with little impact on managers' ability to improve performance. If the system has too many restrictions and managers do not have enough freedom to improve performance, then failure to relax input controls can result in inefficiency.

The common assumption that the performance information that is useful for the executive would also serve the legislature remains unproven. With a few exceptions, performance reporting has been neither welcomed nor used by OECD country legislatures in their oversight and decision making. Performance measures and targets are only one source of information about performance, and they are no substitute for the independent, in-depth qualitative examination of the impact of policies that evaluations can provide.

The combined experiences of OECD countries highlight the importance of taking a long-term approach and having realistic expectations about the capacity of performance management and budgeting to improve performance and account-ability. A long-term approach and persistence are needed to achieve the necessary technical and behavioral changes that this lever requires.

Finally, from a wider perspective, the design of cross-governmental performance interventions needs careful analysis and consideration of options. Broadly, these interventions are: leadership; strategic planning; performance management; the inclusion of targets and measures in the formal budgeting, management and over-sight processes; and policy evaluation. Each has different strengths and limitations. There is a danger of governments' becoming fixated on a particular formal solution to the problem of improving performance.

The performance orientation of public management is here to stay. It is essential for successful government. Societies are too complex to be managed only by rules for input and process and a public-spirited culture. The performance movement has increased formalized planning, reporting, and control across many govern-ments, improving the information that is available to managers and policymakers. But experience shows this can lead to a new form of bureaucratic sclerosis. More attention needs to be given to keeping performance transaction costs in check, and to making optimal use of social and internalized motivators and controls.

Note

This chapter is a revised version of a paper that originally appeared as "Government Performance: Lessons and Challenges," *OECD Journal on Budgeting* 2005, 5(1): 127–51. It is published here with permission of OECD. The views expressed in this chapter are those of the author and do not represent the opinions of the Organization for Economic Cooperation and Development (OECD).

13

Institutionalizing Monitoring and Evaluation Systems in Five Latin American Countries

Argentina, Chile, Colombia, Costa Rica, and Uruguay

ARIEL ZALTSMAN

This chapter compares the ways in which Argentina, Chile, Colombia, Costa Rica, and Uruguay have organized their monitoring and evaluation (M&E) functions. These five countries have structured their M&E functions in a variety of ways. In Colombia, Costa Rica, and Uruguay, the functions are concentrated in one single system. These systems are known, respectively, as the "Public Management Results Evaluation System" (SINERGIA), the "National Evaluation System" (SINE), and the "Results-Based Management Evaluation System" (SEV).

For the most part, the selection of national cases has been based on data availability. However, the fact that these five experiences are among the best-documented ones in the region is probably an indication of their relative importance. Analysis focuses on government-wide M&E systems only. That is, it does not cover sector-specific efforts that, at least in some of these countries, coexist with the initiatives examined here. Similarly, I reserve the phrase *M&E* for a variety of ongoing and retrospective policy, program, and agency assessments. Analysis does not include ex-ante appraisal systems, such as those that only rely on cost-benefit or cost-effectiveness analysis, or other prospective assessment methods.

The chapter is based on four information sources: (1) the relatively small number of studies that have been published on these country cases; (2) legislation that created and regulates the different M&E initiatives and their various components; (3) documents available on the M&E systems' websites or obtained directly from their coordination units; and (4) in-person and telephone interviews, and e-mail consultations with current or past M&E system officials or stakeholders from the five countries. Most interviews were conducted between January 2003 and October 2004 in the context of other projects.[1] These have been complemented with a new round of telephone and e-mail consultations that were done between May 2005 and March 2006.

The chapter consists of five sections. Section 1 describes how the M&E func-

Table 13.1

Government-Wide M&E Systems of Argentina, Chile, Colombia, Costa Rica, and Uruguay

Argentina	Chile	Colombia	Costa Rica	Uruguay
National Budget Office's Physical and Financial Monitoring System (PFMS)	Management Control System (MCS)	Public Management Results Evaluation System (SINERGIA)	National Evaluation System (SINE)	Results-Based Management Evaluation System (SEV)
System of Information, Monitoring and Evaluation of Social Programs (SIEMPRO)	Governmental Programming Monitoring System (SSPG)			
Results-Based Management System's monitoring scheme (RBMS)				

tion is organized in each of five countries. Section 2 discusses the M&E systems' origins and objectives. Section 3 outlines their implementation strategies and their subsequent developments. Section 4 contains a comparative characterization of the five countries' approaches to M&E, and Section 5 presents a number of lessons from these countries' experiences.

Configuration of the M&E Function

The countries included in this report have structured their M&E functions in a variety of ways (see Table 13.1).

In Chile, the M&E function is organized around two systems: "Management Control System" (MCS) and "Governmental Programming Monitoring System" (SSPG). Unlike the other M&E initiatives in Chile—created by the National Budget Bureau (DIPRES) in the Ministry of Finance—SSPG was established by the ministry general secretariat of the Presidency (SEGPRES). Notwithstanding its coordination with MCS, it remains a separate system.

Finally, in Argentina, the M&E function is structured around three systems, known as the National Budget Office's "Physical and Financial Monitoring System" (PFMS); the "System of Information, Monitoring and Evaluation of Social Programs" (SIEMPRO); and "Results-Based Management System's" (RBMS) monitoring scheme. These three systems were created by and remain under the control of different institutions, and operate without coordination.

The M&E Systems' Objectives and Origins

The eight M&E systems examined were created with a variety of objectives (Table 13.2), grouped under one or more of the following: (a) inform national planning; (b) support sector policy and program design and fine-tuning; (c) inform the budget allocation process; (d) encourage continuous management improvement; and (e) enhance transparency and accountability.

It is common for systems to emphasize some of their stated objectives over the others. In some cases, these differences in emphasis have changed over time. In general, the various degrees of attention that the systems have paid to their different objectives can be associated with the primary concerns of the broader reform initiatives of which they were part, and with the institutional and political environment in which they developed.

Thus, Argentina's PFMS was created in 1992 to inform the budget allocation process, encourage agencies' management improvement, and enhance transparency and accountability. The way in which it was conceived and set up, however, emphasized the budget allocation objective over the other two, which is arguably in line with the nature of the financial administration reform that brought it into being. The creation of both PFMS and the financial administration reform were part of the Menem administration's "First Reform of the State" which, like all "first-generation" reform programs, was much more concerned with attaining macroeconomic equilibrium, deregulating the economy, and reducing the size of the public sector than with enhancing the government's policymaking and management capacity.

On the other hand, the creation of SIEMPRO in 1995, also in Argentina, was part of a broader initiative to enhance the government's capacity to develop and implement effective antipoverty policies. In the context of this reform, SIEMPRO was entrusted with the mission of supporting the design and fine-tuning of social programs. Neither the emergence of SIEMPRO nor the broader initiative that inspired its creation were part of an across-the-board second-generation reform program comparable to the ones that gave birth to M&E systems elsewhere. After a frustrated attempt in the latter half of the 1990s, such a government-wide reform program launched in Argentina in 2000 and was effectively implemented.

Other M&E systems, like Chile's SSPG, Colombia's SINERGIA, and Costa Rica's SINE, emerged in the context of reform initiatives that were especially concerned with reinforcing the government's capacity to undertake effective national planning and to align government policies and national strategic priorities. More specifically, Chile's SSPG was first established as the so-called "Ministerial Targets" in 1990, with the objectives of assessing the ministries' and agencies' compliance with the president's policy priorities and serving as an accountability tool. Its creation took place shortly after the first democratic government in nearly two decades took office, as part of an ambitious series of reforms intended to strengthen the public sector's capacity to address society's needs.

Colombia's SINERGIA and Costa Rica's SINE were both created in 1994. When

Table 13.2

The M&E Systems' Stated Objectives

System's Objectives	Argentina			Chile		Colombia	Costa Rica	Uruguay
	PFMS	SIEMPRO	RBMS	SSPG	MCS	SINERGIA	SINE	SEV
National planning								
Policy and program design and fine-tuning		✓		✓	✓	✓	✓	
Budget allocation					✓	✓	✓	
Inducing management improvement	✓		✓		✓	✓	✓	✓
Accountability and transparency	✓		✓	✓	✓	✓	✓	✓

first launched, SINERGIA was entrusted with the five types of objectives identified above, and SINE with all but budget allocation. However, in line with the broader reform initiatives that led to their creation, for several years they emphasized national planning and accountability objectives over the others. For a relatively short period and due to relatively pragmatic reasons, SINERGIA placed emphasis on inducing public agency management improvement as well. Eventually, it redirected its attention to some of its other objectives. As to its budget allocation objective, SINERGIA only started to address it at the beginning of the 2000s. This appears to have been more the result of a lack of coordination between the institutional unit that it reported to and those units in charge of formulating the budget, than a conscious choice. Another expression of this lack of coordination was the use of a budgetary classification that does not make an explicit connection between the government's policy objectives and its budget allocations. SINE adopted the budget allocation objective in 2002, more or less at the same time that SINERGIA redirected its attention to it. In both cases, this development occurred in the context of new administrations that took the adoption of results-based budgeting as one of their core policy objectives.

Finally, the various M&E mechanisms that make up Chile's MCS were created between 1995 and 2002, Uruguay's SEV was created in 1995, and Argentina's RBMS between 1999 and 2004. The three systems emerged in the context of public-sector reforms that placed their greatest focus on improving the budget allocation process and modernizing the state's management practices. In the case of Chile's MCS, the system's stated objectives are informing the budget allocation process, supporting program fine-tuning, encouraging organizational management improvements, and enhancing transparency and accountability. In the case of Uruguay's SEV and, at the time of its creation, Argentina's RBMS (known originally as the "Expenditure Quality Evaluation Program"), their objectives were the same as for MCS, except for program fine-tuning. In the last three years, RBMS appears to have dropped its objective of supporting the budget allocation process. This changed after the reform initiative that had inspired its creation faded, the secretariat of finance stopped participating in the system's development, and the undersecretariat of public management became its only institutional sponsor.

In most of the cases, the development of the systems received financial and technical assistance from multilateral development agencies. This is likely to have affected the orientation the systems ended up taking, although it is not easy to ascertain in what ways. Thus, SINERGIA and the RBMS were supported by the World Bank; the PFMS and SEV drew on Inter-American Development Bank (IDB) assistance; SIEMPRO obtained funding from both sources; and SINE benefited from IDB, the United Nations Development Programme and World Bank assistance.

Systems Implementation and Development

Except for Uruguay's SEV and Chile's SSPG, where the authorities decided to launch the system across the board all at once, implementation of all the other initiatives followed a relatively gradual approach. Implementation began with a series of pilots in a small number of agencies, and was only extended to the remaining agencies and programs after the systems' methodologies and procedures had reached a certain level of maturity. Participation in the M&E systems was initially voluntary, and only became mandatory after a number of years. In all cases, the implementation of the M&E systems involved a significant capacity-building effort on the part of the coordinating unit. Such efforts included provision of training activities, manuals and other support materials, technical assistance, and ongoing support to the participating agencies' and programs' officials as well as to other stakeholders.

In some of the cases (e.g., Argentina's PFMS and SIEMPRO, and Uruguay's SEV), save for relatively minor adjustments that may have been needed along the way, the implementation process turned out to be relatively linear. Systems as they exist today resemble their original design quite closely.

Thus, in Chile, at the time of their creation, the various M&E initiatives that the government launched before 2000 were not part of a single and internally consistent plan. The first M&E mechanism to be created was SEGPRES's Ministerial Targets, in 1990. In 1994 DIPRES launched its Performance Indicators (PIs), and the so-called Modernization Agreements. In 1997, DIPRES began undertaking desk reviews, known as Evaluations of Governmental Programs (EPGs); and in 1998 it replaced Modernization Agreements with its Management Improvement Programs (PMGs) and merged PIs into them. For the most part, the creation of each new M&E mechanism came to add to the functions that the preexisting ones were already fulfilling. But they were not conceived nor were they managed as if they were part of a system. The first effective move in that direction occurred after the Lagos administration took office in 2000. That year, DIPRES's M&E mechanisms were merged under the newly established Management Control System (MCS), to be headed by a specifically created unit, known as the Management Control Division. From then on, three new M&E mechanisms were created. In 2001, the MCS established its Central Fund of Governmental Priorities (CFGP) and began undertaking impact evaluations, and in 2002 it conducted its first Comprehensive Spending Reviews (CSRs). And several M&E mechanisms underwent different degrees of refinement. More specifically, in 2000 the Management Control Division redefined PMGs and turned PIs into a separate M&E mechanism and, given the reduced availability of fiscal resources to finance new projects, it replaced the CFGP in 2004 with a simpler and less costly but analogous procedure that is based on the submission of Standardized Funding Requests for Programs' Innovation and Expansion (SFRPIEs). For their part, also in 2000, SEGPRES's Ministerial Targets were subject to several methodological improvements and became the Governmental Programming Monitoring System (SSPG). But, unlike the M&E mechanisms created by DIPRES, they remained a separate system and under SEGPRES's jurisdiction.

In the case of SINERGIA, the system's original design included an indicator-based monitoring scheme as well as a program evaluation component. However, the evaluation component did not become fully operational until 2002. In addition, the system was originally created to monitor and evaluate the implementation of the National Development Plan's strategic policies rather than as an organizational management support instrument. However, faced with a lack of the human and financial resources that they would have needed to create an external M&E system, the system's designers opted to base it on self-evaluations by entities. Their expectation was that the agencies' self-evaluations would provide them with the information they needed to produce the sector policy assessments that the system had been created to produce. Given the suitability of self-evaluation to support organizational strategic management, it did not take long for the system to adopt the encouragement of organizational management improvement as one of its core objectives as well. Eventually, for reasons that are not entirely clear, the system's coordinating unit began tightening its grip over the monitoring process and, in the early 2000s, stopped conducting organizational performance assessments and instead concentrated on program and sector policy assessment. The system made considerable progress in establishing a clear connection between its performance assessments and the budget. This effort is reflected in the presentation of the national investment budget bill on a results-oriented basis.

In Costa Rica, SINE's original design included both an external monitoring component (known as the "Strategic Evaluation" component) and a self-evaluation one. However, the latter component was not implemented. In 2002, those two originally conceived components were merged into one that combines external monitoring and diagnostic self-assessment by entities. This new development occurred in the context of an increasing coordination of actions between the Ministry of Planning (which is the system's institutional sponsor), the Ministry of Finance, and the Comptroller General's Office. The current arrangement allows them to centralize requests for the information they need from the evaluated agencies in one single instrument and procedure, as well as to facilitate information sharing among the three. At least as importantly, cooperation among the three institutions also made it possible to adopt a results-based budget classification that allowed SINE to attain a much more direct connection to the budget process.

In Argentina, the RBMS was first known as the "Expenditure Quality Evaluation Program" and enjoyed significant political support from the vice president's office. At the time, the development of the system was based on a joint effort among the National Secretariat of Modernization (which was created in 2000 and reported directly to the vice president), the Ministry of Economy's Secretariat of Finance, and the Chief of Cabinet's Office. The system's original plan included a "Program Agreement" component, which was meant to establish a clear link between the system's performance assessments and the budget cycle; and the "Management Results Commitments" and "Commitment-with-the-Citizen Charter" (CCC) components, both of which focused on improving organizational management. Had the joint effort among those three institutions continued, the system could have succeeded in attaining some degree of articulation with the National Budget Office's (ONP) PFMS. This might have helped reduce the profound disconnect that exists among Argentina's M&E efforts. However, following the resignation of the vice president at the end of 2000, the National Secretariat of Modernization and the Expenditure Quality Evaluation Program were moved to the Chief of Cabinet's Office and, shortly afterward, cooperation between the latter and the Secretariat of Finance came to an end. The Expenditure Quality Evaluation Program became the Chief of Cabinet Office's RBMS and, in 2003, following a period of deep political turmoil, the Program Agreement and the Management Results Commitment components were interrupted. Consequently, until 2004, all performance assessment activities revolved around the CCC program. In 2004, the RBMS began implementing its second monitoring instrument, known as the Management Information System (SIG). SIG is organized as an internet-based balanced scorecard monitoring scheme.

Two factors that affected the systems' developments most profoundly in the five countries were the evolution of the political environment and the government's level of commitment to the M&E systems over time. All of the M&E systems remained in operation despite the various changes in the political affiliation of the administrations that were in office; however, the degree of political support that they enjoyed was far from uniform. Several systems, like Argentina's three systems and Uruguay's SEV, appear to have attained their maximum impetus at the earliest stages of their development. Colombia's SINERGIA enjoyed substantial political support after its creation but deep political instability and the relative neglect that it experienced on the part of the subsequent authorities reduced its momentum dramatically, until the administration that came to office in 2002 directed attention to its rejuvenation. In Costa Rica, the system's support has reportedly been constant since its creation. But even in Chile, where the MCS enjoyed probably the highest levels of governmental commitment, the systems' level of support did undergo some fluctuations.

A second factor likely to have influenced the development of some systems is diagnostic studies of their operation that were undertaken at different times. Examples are: (a) a number of the internal appraisal studies that Argentina's RBMS coordinating unit undertook of its own functioning and results; (b) the frequent undertaking of ad hoc studies and different types of analysis that Chile's MCS coordinating unit commissions or conducts itself to assess the workings of its various components; and (c) a focus-group-based study and a World Bank review that Colombia's SINERGIA commissioned in the early years after its creation. Finally, in addition to the difficulty in obtaining the necessary level of political support following their creation, the development of the M&E systems encountered several other challenges, some of which they are still trying to overcome.

One of the first challenges that many of these initiatives needed to address, very early in the implementation process, originated in insufficient clarity with regard to missions, goals, and objectives of the agencies and programs that they were intended to evaluate. This made it extremely difficult to assess whether the agencies and programs were achieving their intended outcomes. Thus, implementation was preceded by different strategic planning processes that brought clarity not only to each specific agency's and program's objectives, but also to how those objectives related to higher- and lower-level objectives (e.g., how an agency's mission and objectives are connected to both the objectives of its responsible ministry's sector policies and those of its programs). For Uruguay, this process resulted in a redesign of many of the state's organizational structures.

Another prevalent problem was the limited receptiveness, if not open resistance, that the systems encountered in the agencies and programs that were to be monitored or evaluated. This unwillingness to cooperate was mainly caused by their apprehension toward the possible consequences of unfavorable evaluation. This fear turned out to be less pronounced when the systems' practices involved an important degree of joint work between the coordination unit and the agencies, as in Argentina's RBMS.

A third problem was the lack of baseline information. This problem disappeared progressively, as the subsequent performance assessment cycles began producing information that until then had been unavailable.

A fourth challenge originated in coordinating actions among different institutions. A number of systems attempted to overcome this problem by establishing inter-ministerial committees, but these have not always proven successful. A good case in point can be found in the frustrating experience of Argentina's Social Cabinet in the mid-1990s. The work of the cabinet was coordinated by the Secretariat of Social Development (SIEMPRO's running agency), which was neither as powerful as some of the other cabinet members nor had strong enough support from the highest political authorities to facilitate the M&E system's implementation. By contrast, the experience of Chile's MCS inter-ministerial committees appears to be more successful: The powerful DIPRES exerts the leading role and the other members of the committee help in ensuring an appropriate degree of articulation with other government institutions.

The fifth and last problem was the limited involvement of line agency senior officials, which has usually resulted in poor organizational awareness of the systems' objectives and practices. Some systems, such as Colombia's SINERGIA and Argentina's RBMS, are addressing this problem by requiring the direct participation of agencies' senior officials in the negotiations that open each monitoring cycle. Once agreement is reached, technical staff of both parties are able to prepare measurable targets. In the case of Chile's MCS, what attracted the attention of agencies' senior officials to the M&E system requirements and activities was the weight of DIPRES's committed sponsorship, and institutional and material incentives that accompany participation and compliance with the system.

M&E System Architecture

System Components and M&E Activities

The systems' approaches to M&E combine monitoring and evaluation, or rely on monitoring alone (Table 13.3). Monitoring consists of the periodic or continuous assessment of performance based on selected indicators. On the other hand, evaluation relies on a wider variety of methods to examine the evaluated programs or activities more closely, gain a better understanding of their nuances, and produce sounder assessments of their consequences (Rossi and Freeman 1993).

Given the relatively low costs that it entails, monitoring can measure the performance of programs frequently and for a large number of programs at the same time. However, it is unable to provide enough elements to understand the complexity of the processes involved or to distinguish the evaluated programs' effects from those of external factors. On the other hand, program evaluation is best equipped to establish the latter but, given the extended time and high costs involved, it can only be undertaken on a small number of programs at a time. The cost and duration of an evaluation will depend on its level of depth, rigor, and comprehensiveness. In any case, the level of coverage, promptness, and economy of monitoring are always greater than those achieved by evaluation. Because their respective strengths and weaknesses make them complementary, these approaches become effective when combined (Rossi and Freeman 1993).

Of the eight M&E systems analyzed here, only three rely on both monitoring and evaluation activities: Argentina's SIEMPRO, Chile's MCS, and Colombia's SINERGIA. The other five systems all base their assessments on performance monitoring alone.

The Systems' Monitoring Activities

The systems' monitoring schemes rely on a variety of indicators that track agency or program compliance with preestablished targets. In most cases, these indicators measure efficiency, effectiveness, economy, and/or service quality. They include a series of physical and financial input, unit cost, output, coverage, and outcome indicators. Given the difficulty of measuring outcomes, all the systems tend to over-rely on input, process, and output indicators. Some systems (especially Chile's MCS) have been slowly advancing toward a greater inclusion of intermediate and final outcome indicators. For Chile's MCS Management Improvement Program component and Argentina's RBMS Commitment-with-the-Citizen Charter program, what the monitoring schemes are oriented to assess is the extent of progress that agencies have made in the implementation of a highly structured agenda of organizational process improvements.

The systems differ, to some extent, in the level of public-sector performance that they monitor. Argentina's PFMS and SIEMPRO monitor program-level performance; Argentina's RBMS, Chile's MCS, and Uruguay's SEV focus on organizational performance; and Colombia's SINERGIA assesses program-and sector-level and policy performance. Finally, Chile's SSPG monitors both policy- and agency-level performance, and Costa Rica's SINE monitors institutional and program-level performance.

Table 13.3

The Systems' M&E Activities

System's Objectives	Argentina			Chile		Colombia	Costa Rica	Uruguay
	PFMS	SIEMPRO	RBMS	SSPG	MCS	SINERGIA	SINE	SEV
Indicator-based monitoring	✓	✓	✓	✓	✓	✓	✓	✓
Program, policy, or institutional evaluation		✓			✓	✓		

Except for Argentina's RBMS monitoring system, which is still in an early stage of implementation, all the monitoring systems have reached a relatively high, if not total, coverage. But there are two important challenges these monitoring schemes still face. The first of these challenges is in ensuring that the indicators cover all the core activities of the evaluated agencies and programs. Performance of some activities is much easier to measure than that of others and, therefore, the ones that are most difficult to assess tend to be neglected. In addition, the intent to be thorough in this regard usually conflicts with the need to keep the number of indicators manageable. The second challenge is improving the quality of the indicators used, such as their relevance, measurability, timeliness, and so on.

The Systems' Evaluation Activities

The three M&E systems with program evaluation components conduct evaluations of the following types: ex-ante appraisals (e.g., cost-benefit and cost-effectiveness analyses), desk reviews, program implementation evaluations, and impact evaluations. System impact evaluation studies usually rely on quasi-experimental designs and sophisticated statistical analysis techniques. In addition, Argentina's SIEMPRO and Colombia's SINERGIA complement their M&E activities with the undertaking of periodic diagnostic surveys and studies. In all cases, evaluations are commissioned from external consultants or institutions, selected through public bidding based on terms of reference defined by the systems' coordinating units.

SIEMPRO's evaluations concentrate on program-level performance. The MCS has three evaluation components, two of which are focused on programs while the third assesses institutional design and performance. Finally, SINERGIA undertakes evaluations of both programs and sector policies.

In the case of SINERGIA and MCS, the programs, policies, or agencies to be evaluated are selected on the basis of: amount of public resources involved; the size and characteristics of the policy's or program's target population; the program's relative importance for a specific sector policy; and the possibility of replicating the program in a different context or enlarging its scale. In addition, in the case of MCS, another criterion is the agencies' performance as measured by their Performance Indicators and desk reviews (i.e., Evaluations of Governmental Programs). In the case of SIEMPRO, selection criteria are not explicitly defined.

Chile's MCS has evaluated approximately 61 percent of what it defines as "evaluable expenditure." Colombia's SINERGIA, which began undertaking evaluations more recently, has evaluated 18 percent of the national investment budget, and expects to raise this percentage to 20 or 25 percent in coming years. Finally, in the case of Argentina's SIEMPRO, the last available estimate dates from 1999 and represented, at that time, 9 percent of the total budget of the ministries that run the evaluated programs. This percentage is likely to have increased.

Coordination between M&E Activities

One last important issue to consider relates to the extent to which each of the systems that conduct several M&E activities coordinate them with each other. In this regard, Chile's MCS seems to be the system that is dealing with this most effectively. Its various components (i.e., Performance Indicators, Management Improvement Program monitoring scheme, desk reviews, impact and institutional evaluations, and ex-ante appraisals) have been conceived explicitly with the intent to address different information needs and to complement each other. Moreover, DIPRES's assessment of agency performance—as measured through the system's two monitoring components together with the findings of the desk reviews—are stated to be some of the factors that DIPRES considers when deciding what programs it will evaluate in depth in the subsequent year. Evidence suggests that the M&E components of the MCS system are increasingly being used in this complementary manner.

In the case of Argentina's SIEMPRO, such complementarity among M&E activities has not been evident until recently. In Colombia, where the evaluation component was only recently implemented, it is too early to make such an assessment.

The intent to coordinate the different M&E activities becomes most challenging when such efforts are championed and administered by different institutional actors. Among the five countries, only Argentina and Chile present this situation. There is a stark contrast between the experiences of these two countries in terms of coordination.

In Chile, the M&E functions are organized around two systems: the MCS, which was created and is run by DIPRES, and the SSPG, which was established and remains administered by SEGPRES. At the time of their creation, the three M&E mechanisms that were merged into the MCS in 2000 emerged as separate DIPRES initiatives. They focused on fairly distinct aspects of agency or program performance, but they were not managed in a coordinated way. Nevertheless, at the beginning of the 2000s DIPRES decided to turn those three mechanisms into a system, and to then add a further three components to this system. Coordination between DIPRES's MCS and SEGPRES's SSPG has also been growing in recent years. Thus, to define the indicators and targets that it uses to track ministry and agency performance, the SSPG takes the MCS's scheme of institutional goals, objectives, and products—known as "Strategic Definitions"—as a basis. Similarly, the SSPG relies on DIPRES's Comprehensive Management Reports as a primary channel for the public dissemination of its findings. Arguably, one of the factors that may have contributed most to this increasingly harmonized approach is the high level of commitment that influential DIPRES authorities have invested in these reforms. All initiatives that make up DIPRES's MCS and the SSPG alike appear to be part of a common vision in the context of which empirically based decision making is regarded as a desirable practice.

In contrast, Argentina's government-wide M&E activities are concentrated in three systems that function independently of each other. The three systems are: the

PFMS, which depends on the Secretariat of Finance's ONP; SIEMPRO, originally created by the then Secretariat of Social Development and which now reports to the National Council for the Coordination of Social Policies; and the RBMS, which was developed through a joint effort among the then National Secretariat of Modernization, the Chief of Cabinet's Office, and the Secretariat of Finance and, since 2001, has been managed by the Chief of Cabinet's Office alone.

Lack of coordination among the three systems is reflected in at least two ways: (1) the PFMS and SIEMPRO, both of which assess performance at the program level, rely on different operational definitions of what "programs" comprise, which makes it very difficult to combine the information that each of them produces; and (2) there has been no systematic attempt, on the part of either the programs' authorities or the evaluators, to link those programs' objectives with the organizational goals and objectives that the RBMS has helped identify for some of the agencies responsible for these programs.

This high level of disconnect among the three systems keeps their transaction costs higher than necessary and undercuts the potential benefits. It does this by requiring the evaluated ministries and programs to respond to multiple information requests, thereby imposing an excessive burden on them, which, eventually, is most likely to conspire against the quality of the information they provide and the likelihood that they will end up using it.

Arguably, the fragmentation that prevails among Argentina's M&E efforts is associated with the fact that they developed under different conditions from the ones in Chile. In Argentina, efforts to enhance the institutional capacity and management practices of the public sector, and to enrich policy and decision making through ensuring that M&E and other empirical information are available, have not been given the same priority as they have in Chile. In addition, in a political context where, unless an initiative is championed by or at least openly blessed by the president, turf battles and inter-ministry rivalries outweigh the initiative's merits, the fact that the three systems had different institutional sponsors is most likely a serious drawback. Effects of these factors may have been exacerbated by periods of political instability and the high turnover of the senior officials who conceived or championed some of these initiatives.

Organizational Framework and Distribution of Roles

In order to be effective, M&E systems need to be organized in a manner that ensures both relevance and credibility of the information they produce. A way to ensure relevance of the systems' M&E assessments is by involving their expected users in the definition of what policies, programs, or aspects of performance are to be evaluated (Mokate 2000). On the other hand, to attain an acceptable level of credibility, it is desirable to maintain some substantive level of independence between those who control or manage an M&E system and those who have a direct stake in the evaluated programs. This second condition is important when the information's main expected users are external to the evaluated policy, program, or agency. When M&E findings are targeted at the agents responsible for the evaluated processes themselves, ensuring a high level of involvement and receptiveness on their part becomes more important than the information's external credibility (Ala-Harja and Helgason 1999).

One of the greatest challenges that M&E system designers face originates in the fact that these systems are usually created with the objective to address the information needs of a variety of stakeholders. And, as just noted, the conditions that need to be met to ensure the information's relevance and credibility tend to be specific to each user. For example, when a system's M&E activities are meant to address the information needs both of line ministries or agencies and of one or more central ministries, there are at least two alternatives. On the one hand, the control of the M&E processes can be entrusted to a central ministry, in which case the information's credibility may be ensured for all stakeholders but its relevance, usefulness, and acceptability to line ministries and agencies may be limited. On the other hand, the higher the level of control that line ministries or agencies exert over the processes, the more likely that the information produced is relevant to their needs but, given the direct stake they have in the activities being evaluated, the M&E findings' credibility may suffer. In short, there is an underlying tension between conditions required to ensure appropriate levels of information relevance and credibility to different stakeholders (Zaltsman 2006). As will be discussed below, there are different ways to address and reconcile these potentially conflicting requirements, but they involve trade-offs.

The eight M&E systems examined in this report have been set up and remain under the control of executive branch institutions. In the case of Argentina's PFMS, Chile's MCS, and Uruguay's SEV, the system coordinating units report to institutions that are responsible for the budget formulation process (such as Argentina's ONP and Chile's DIPRES) or, at the very least, play an important role in it (such as Uruguay's OPP). In Costa Rica, SINE depends on the ministry that is in charge of national planning (i.e., the Ministry of Planning, or MIDEPLAN), while in Colombia the institution that controls SINERGIA (the National Planning Department, or DNP) is responsible for both national planning and the formulation of the national investment budget. The coordinating unit of Argentina's SIEMPRO reports to an interinstitutional commission (the National Council for the Coordination of Social Policies) made up of all the ministries that run antipoverty programs. Finally, in the case of Argentina's RBMS and Chile's SSPG, the system coordinating units report to central government institutions with interministerial coordination functions (the Chief of the Cabinet Office and SEGPRES, respectively).

Based on their stated objectives, all the systems are expected to help hold governments accountable, but Costa Rica's SINE is the only one where a supreme audit institution (SAI) independent of the executive branch participates in the definition of the M&E agenda (see below). In Colombia, SINERGIA's authorities have plans to engage civil society organizations in the analysis and dissemination of the information that the system produces, which may result in the system's becoming subject to social control.

The Systems' Monitoring Activities

Except for Costa Rica's SINE, where this function is overseen by an interministerial committee, the definition of the basic elements of the M&E agenda always lies with the institution that is ultimately responsible for each system. Development of the systems' methodologies is always in the hands of their central coordinating unit. The definition of the indicators and targets that systems base their assessments on involve, to a greater or lesser extent, participation of both the assessed programs and institutions and the central coordinating units, and the information that feeds into the system is always provided by the assessed programs and institutions themselves. Finally, save for Argentina's RBMS, where participating agencies play a much more leading role in this regard, it is always also the coordinating unit that is in charge of issuing the final performance assessments.

The greatest differences across systems revolve around the level of leadership and control that they assign to their coordinating units and the assessed programs and institutions in the definition of the indicators and targets. On the one hand, some systems appear to be more concerned with ensuring the standardization and the impartiality of the process and, therefore, assign the coordinating unit a much more decisive role in this regard. Chile's MCS is a good case in point, as it is probably the system where the relationship between the coordinating unit and the assessed agencies follows the most vertical approach. More specifically, in addition to defining the overall performance monitoring agenda, the system's coordinating unit exerts a closer oversight role throughout the entire process than in any of the other M&E systems.

On the other hand, other systems seem to give higher priority to the sense of ownership and receptiveness to the M&E findings by senior officials in the assessed programs and agencies, rather than to the external credibility of the information produced. Therefore, they provide these officials a greater level of involvement in this part of the process. Among the eight systems discussed in this paper, Argentina's RBMS is the one that ensures the greatest involvement of the line agencies. In effect, one of its monitoring components leaves the definition of the aspects of performance to be assessed entirely up to the evaluated agencies while, in the other, except for the definition of the basic methodologies and the verification of the data (which are both conducted by the coordinating unit) and the proposal of performance targets (which is up to the agencies themselves to make), all the other steps of the process are undertaken on the basis of a joint effort between the line agency and the coordinating unit's experts. This also includes the assessment of agency performance and the preparation of the final monitoring reports, and may include the joint preparation of an action plan.

In the rest of the M&E systems, the distribution of roles between the coordinating unit and the assessed programs and agencies appears to lie somewhere between the tight external oversight characteristic of Chile's MCS and the more relaxed and horizontal relationship that exists between Argentina's RBMS's coordinating unit and the participating agencies. In the six cases, it is the assessed programs and agencies that propose both the indicators and targets. However, in Chile's SSPG, Colombia's SINERGIA, and Uruguay's SEV the programs and agencies appear to play a greater role in defining whether the indicators will be used than in the other systems. On the other hand, in Chile's SSPG, Colombia's SINERGIA, and Costa Rica's SINE, the coordinating units seem to have a greater level of involvement in the definition of the programs' and agencies' performance targets than in the other three systems.

Information on receptiveness and utilization of these systems' monitoring findings is rather scarce and, for the most part, merely anecdotal. Interestingly, the system where use of monitoring findings is most documented is Chile's MCS—a system where the coordinating unit exerts the tightest control over the assessment process, and not one of those that concede greater leverage to line agencies.

The most prevalent obstacle for the assimilation and eventual use of monitoring findings by line programs and agencies appears to originate from the lack of commitment and involvement on the part of their senior staff. It is common for all the activities associated with the monitoring process to remain concentrated on the line agency organizational unit that acts as a liaison with the system's coordinating unit. Consequently, the level of organizational awareness of the programs' or institutions' performance targets and assessments tends to be extremely low. This would seem to be true regardless of whether the coordinating unit's counterpart at the agency was specifically created to deal with this task or already existed to perform other functions (e.g., planning, budgeting, etc.).

In an attempt to secure the commitment of the ministries and departments to the negotiated performance targets, some systems, like Argentina's RBMS and Colombia's SINERGIA, require that the process that results in the definition of those targets begin with high-level negotiations between the two parties. On the other hand, in Chile's MCS, what appears to attract the high-level attention of programs and agencies to the assessment process and findings is the importance that the system's powerful institutional sponsor (DIPRES) assigns to them, and a concern that those performance assessments may end up impacting their budget allocations.

The Systems' Evaluation Activities

In the context of the evaluation components of the three systems that undertake this type of assessment, the distribution of roles among the different parties involved is relatively more uniform. In all cases, the decision as to what policies, programs, or organizations will be evaluated, and the type of evaluation approach to apply, is defined by the system's sponsoring institution and/or some other entity independent of the programs or institutions to be evaluated. In three systems, this critical decision lies with more than one single actor. More specifically, in the case of Argentina's SIEMPRO, the National Council for the Coordination of Social Policies (NCCSP) comprises all the ministries responsible for antipoverty programs. In the case of Chile's MCS, the decision is shared between DIPRES and Congress, whereas in Colombia, the Inter-Sector Evaluation Committee is made up of several central ministries. Except for SINERGIA, where the affected line ministries are engaged in the definition of the type of evaluation to undertake, the evaluated institutions are excluded from this other critical decision as well.

Although it is up to the systems' coordinating units to define the evaluations' basic methodological approaches, evaluations are commissioned to external consultants or institutions selected through open bidding processes to ensure independence. SIEMPRO and MCS finance these evaluations with their own resources, while SINERGIA cofinances them with the evaluated programs and ministries responsible for them.

SIEMPRO and SINERGIA entrust supervision of the evaluation process to their coordinating units. In the case of MCS, the system's coordinating unit oversees the process very closely but, in addition, there are two more actors involved. One of them is an inter-ministerial committee comprising the presidency and the ministries of Finance and Planning. This committee is also in charge of ensuring that the evaluations' development is consistent with the government's policies, that the necessary technical support and coordination are available, and that the evaluations' conclusions are passed on to the affected agencies. The second actor involved is the evaluated agencies and programs themselves, which (a) provide evaluators with the information that they need; (b) in the case of EPGs and CSRs, prepare the logframe that serves as a basis for the evaluation process; and (c) in the three types of evaluation alike, are given the possibility to react to both the intermediate and final evaluation reports.

Finally, the MCS requires that, at the end of the evaluation process, the coordinating unit and the evaluated agencies engage in formal negotiations to define the specific ways and timeline within which the agency will implement the evaluation's recommendations.

Information Flows and Reporting Arrangements

The systems have organized their information flows in a number of ways. To characterize their various arrangements, this section revolves around three issues. The first is the way in which each system has organized the different steps that precede the preparation of their M&E reports. Since the steps that these processes involve are specific to the type of M&E activity undertaken, this part of the discussion focuses on the monitoring and the evaluation processes separately. The second issue includes the reporting arrangements and overall dissemination strategy that the systems employ to ensure that the information they produce reaches their various stakeholders. The third issue is the incentives to use this M&E information, and the actual extent of utilization.

Process that Precedes Preparation of Monitoring Reports

The process that precedes preparation of the systems' monitoring reports can be conceptualized as consisting of four steps. The first step includes the identification of the indicators and performance targets that serve as a basis for assessing policies, programs, and agencies. Notwithstanding differences in the relative level of control that the coordinating unit and assessed institutions hold in this part of the process, it entails the first important exchange of information between these two parties, which prepares the ground for the subsequent stages. The second step concerns the dissemination of these performance targets. The third step involves obtaining information required by the system to produce its assessments, and the fourth, the procedures the systems employ to ensure the information's quality and credibility.

Submission of Performance Indicator and Target Proposals. Argentina's PFMS, Chile's MCS, Costa Rica's SINE, and Uruguay's SEV require that the assessed agencies and programs submit their indicator and target proposals as part of (or attached to) their budget requests. In most systems, these proposals are generally submitted through standardized forms that, in the cases of SINE, SEV, and the RBMS's SIG, also collect information on the institutions' mission, goals, strategic objectives, and operational plans. In the context of SINE, these forms also require an organizational diagnosis of the institutions' strengths and weaknesses. In Argentina's SIG, Chile's two systems, and Uruguay's SEV, the assessed agencies submit all this information electronically. SINE plans to adopt a similar information submission procedure shortly.

At least in some of the systems (e.g., Argentina's PFMS, Uruguay's SEV, and possibly Argentina's SIEMPRO as well), the identification of indicators and targets is undertaken with very little or no involvement on the part of the programs' or agencies' most senior officials, which most likely reduces their relevance to the operations of the agencies and programs. Colombia's SINERGIA and Argentina's RBMS are trying to avoid this problem by requiring that standards that serve as a basis for the performance assessments are defined through top-level negotiations between the assessed institutions and the M&E system authorities. Naturally, for this requirement to be enforced, the M&E systems need to possess sufficient institutional clout, which is usually a function of the level of commitment and power of their institutional sponsor.

Dissemination of the Performance Targets. After the M&E system coordinating units review and approve these proposals, the agency and program performance targets are agreed on and, in most cases, publicized. For the most part, the main means of public dissemination is the coordinating unit's website.

Provision of Monitoring Information. As already noted, the information that feeds the M&E system is provided, in all cases, by the line programs or institutions themselves. In Chile's two systems, Colombia's SINERGIA, Uruguay's SEV, and, at least to some degree, in Argentina's RBMS, the information reaches the coordinating unit through intranet or internet systems. Costa Rica's SINE is planning to reorganize this part of the process around a similar system shortly. In the case of Argentina's PFMS, information on compliance with physical output targets is delivered in the form of printed reports. The information on compliance with financial targets is provided through an electronic intranet system.

Control of Data Quality and Credibility. Data auditing is far from systematic and, in some of the systems, is not even a regular practice. Chile's MCS and Argentina's CCC program conduct randomized quality checks. In the case of MCS, when the agency or program concerned is considered to be of high public impact, these consistency checks extend to all information the system receives from them. In other systems, like Argentina's SIEMPRO and Colombia's SINERGIA, data quality controls are somewhat less methodical, and they are not conducted regularly in Argentina's PFMS, Costa Rica's SINE, and Uruguay's SEV.

Process that Precedes Preparation of Evaluation Reports

In the context of the M&E systems' evaluation components, the information flow cycle is different. In addition to the information obtained from the evaluated agencies and programs, the evaluation studies rely on ad hoc interviews and surveys and other sources to obtain needed data.

In the specific case of the EPG and CSR components of Chile's MCS, the evaluation cycle begins by asking the evaluated program or agency to provide some basic information following a standardized format. The EPG component requires programs to prepare their own logframe matrix. This matrix contains details on the program's goal, the general and specific objectives of each component, the program's main activities and performance indicators, and its assumptions. As part of the CSR component, evaluated agencies are required to prepare "preliminary evaluation matrices" containing details on government priorities that they intend to address; their mission, strategic objectives, and organizational structure; strategic outputs and outcomes associated with each specific objective; and so on. In both cases, these matrices are later assessed and, if necessary, adjusted by the evaluators, who use them as a basis for the entire evaluation process. In the case of impact evaluations—the MCS system's third evaluation component—the information that evaluators require from the evaluated programs is more complex and could not readily be summarized in a standardized format. This information is collected by a range of methods, depending on the nature of each evaluation. Even so, the information that the evaluated programs and agencies provide remains a fundamental input to the evaluation process.

Once the evaluators complete their studies, they submit a final report to the system's coordinating unit. For Chile's MCS, evaluators first submit a preliminary version of their evaluation reports to the coordinating unit and to the program or agency; the latter, in turn, review these reports closely and provide comments to the evaluators. Based on this feedback, the evaluators deliver a final report, which is also sent to the evaluated programs or agencies, to give them the opportunity to express reactions. These responses are added to the evaluation report in the form of a written statement.

Reporting Arrangements and Dissemination Strategies

The systems' M&E findings are always conveyed through different reports. Contents of these reports are tailored to the specific information needs of the intended reader. For example, Argentina's PFMS produces quarterly reports on each of the evaluated programs to be submitted to the program managers, their agencies and ministries, the ONP's authorities, and other divisions of the Secretariat of Finance. An annual report is submitted to the National Accounting Office, containing more abridged program information. This information is in turn used as a basis for preparing the Investment Account report, through which the executive branch reports to the Congress concerning its execution of government programs. In all cases, documents are made publicly available. Similarly, Chile's SSPG produces quarterly and annual reports containing information on the entire government's performance for the president, and ministry- and agency-specific reports are prepared for ministry and agency heads. Summary versions are disseminated through the MCS's Comprehensive Management Reports (see below).

In some systems, information on the compliance of evaluated institutions with their performance targets can be consulted through intranet and internet systems, which provide the various stakeholders with different levels of access. This is the case with Argentina's RBMS SIG, Chile's two systems, Colombia's SINERGIA, and Uruguay's SEV. The intranet system that Costa Rica's SINE is planning to launch will also serve this function. The internet system that SINERGIA uses gives citizens partial access. Access to the RBMS SIG is restricted to the evaluated agencies' officials and to certain other officials, but there are plans to make it partially accessible to the general public as well.

Some of the systems have begun experimenting with reader-friendly report formats. This is an attempt to overcome difficulties that many of the intended information users (citizens, legislators, policymakers, and public managers) have had in understanding and making use of the original reports, which they found exceedingly lengthy and written in too technical a language. Thus, Colombia's SINERGIA and Uruguay's SEV have begun relying on different bulletins and booklets written in plain language, and making extensive use of graphs. Similarly, for several years, Chile's MCS has concentrated its M&E information in its Comprehensive Management Reports (BGIs), which are more reader friendly than the system's individual performance assessment reports. In addition, MCS attaches summaries to all its final evaluation reports.

Finally, in the five countries, the Internet serves as the main channel of public dissemination. In addition, some of the systems also rely on other dissemination media. For example, in Argentina, the RBMS CCC program requires participating agencies to publicize their performance targets and assessments themselves, and it evaluates the agencies' efforts in this regard as part of its agency assessments. In Colombia, the president and the members of his cabinet take part in an annual TV program known as "telecast ministry councils," and in weekly town hall meetings around the country, in the context of which they make use of this information to respond to citizens' questions on the government's policy results. Finally, both in Colombia and in Costa Rica, M&E findings are also publicized through press conferences.

The Use of M&E Information

For the most part, the extent to which M&E findings are being used in all these M&E systems remains unclear. A study on the national M&E systems of Chile, Colombia, Costa Rica, and Uruguay conducted between 2001 and 2002 (Cunill Grau and Ospina Bozzi 2003), found that most of the systems' stakeholders were making limited use of the information. In 2004, a case study of Argentina's three M&E systems reported similar findings (Zaltsman 2004). However, since these studies were undertaken, there have been reports that, in some of these countries, M&E findings are beginning to influence decision making. The soundest evidence comes from Chile, where an MCS evaluation component review (Rossi and Freeman 2005) found that most of the stakeholders consulted (DIPRES budget analysts and section heads; ministry and agency budget officials; program authorities; etc.) reported that the information was being used for decision making.

Most of the systems have intended to foster the use of M&E information and performance improvement by establishing budgetary or institutional incentive mechanisms, but few have succeeded in operationalizing them. The system that has accomplished most is Chile's MCS, which has set up incentives targeted both at the evaluated programs and agencies, and at the Ministry of Finance, including: (a) the introduction of the so-called "Institutional Commitments," which are formal pledges through which evaluated agencies commit to implementing the evaluation recommendations within a given timeline; (b) the regular monitoring of agencies' compliance with these Institutional Commitments, as well as with their targets under the PI and PMG initiatives; (c) the explicit requirement that agencies and ministries justify their budget requests with information on past and planned performance; and (d) the explicit requirement that M&E information is used as part of the internal and external discussions that take place during the budget formulation process.

At least part of the success of the MCS can be attributed to the committed support that it has received from the powerful DIPRES over many years. Most of the other systems have not been able to achieve this level of support. Where these other systems have succeeded in creating incentives, they have lacked the political leverage required to enforce them. This is the case of the Program Agreement component of Argentina's RBMS, where a law of 1999 and a decree of 2001 enabled the Chief of Cabinet to use financial and institutional incentives to encourage good organizational performance. However, after the key officials who sponsored the creation of the system left the government, the entire initiative lost impetus, and the component's incentives were never enforced. Moreover, within two years, the component itself ceased operation. A second example can be found in Uruguay's SEV where, after a first frustrated attempt in 1995, the 2000–2004 Budget Law instituted a series of financial rewards for good institutional performance. However, these incentives never materialized because of fiscal constraints and insufficient political support.

Thus, in most cases, the incentive for assessed agencies and programs to pay attention to and make use of this information is the fact that their performance is now measured and tracked, and the resulting assessments are circulated both within government and publicly. However, the effectiveness of this type of incentive is highly sensitive to the degree of dissemination and the visibility of the systems' performance assessments.

Linkage between M&E and Budgeting

Very frequently, integration of M&E information into the budget decision-making process is hindered by the lack of an appropriate budget classification (Joyce and Sieg 2000). That is the case when the budget is organized around objects of expenditure and does not specify the objectives or intended outcomes that each of the budget allocations are meant to finance. But, as some of the cases below show, program budget classifications, in and of themselves, do not achieve an appropriate connection between types of information.

Argentina is one of the three countries included in this report with a program budget classification. However, the connection between M&E findings and the budget allocations is still difficult to attain, at least for two reasons. First, it is rather common for the budget's structure not to reflect the programs' actual production processes accurately: many programs are included as subprograms or as activities of other programs, or are completely merged under larger programs. Secondly, most M&E activities focus on federal programs, and the functioning of many of them involves the use of human and material resources that are financed by provincial and local governments. Because subnational governments' expenditures are not included in the national budget, the information on the program expenditures that it contains is far from complete.

In addition, agencies have a very short time span to prepare their budget requests, which hinders the appropriate connection between their financial programming and their physical output plans. This, in turn, is exacerbated in that coordination between the program authorities (who are in charge of developing physical output plans) and the budget divisions of the agencies that run the programs (who bear responsibility for financial programming) is rather poor.

By contrast, in the other two countries with program-based budget classifications (Uruguay and Costa Rica), the linkage between the M&E system performance assessments and budget allocations is much clearer. Before implementing SEV, Uruguay's government redefined the public sector's organizational structures so that each program would be ascribed to one single agency. This allows the budget to identify the expenditures associated with the attainment of the different program objectives without losing track of the organizational responsibilities over them. Moreover, since the beginning of the 2000s, agency budget requests have been required to specify the amount of resources that they plan to assign to the pursuance of each specific performance target, which facilitates the connection between the information that the SEV produces and the budget.

Costa Rica adopted a programmatic budget classification after 2001. Since then, cooperation between the ministry responsible for planning (MIDEPLAN) and the institutions in charge of formulating the budget (the Ministry of Finance and the Comptroller General's Office) has enhanced coordination between the two processes. As in Uruguay, agency budget requests take the form of strategic and operational plans that specify the amount of resources that they plan to assign to each goal and target. This allows budget decision-makers to weigh the alternative possible outputs of the financial resources that they are to assign. SINE's M&E findings inform them about the extent to which the targets that agencies propose in their strategic and operational plans are being met in practice.

For both Uruguay's SEV and Costa Rica's SINE, the greatest challenge facing the link between the M&E system and the national budget lies in ensuring that indicators that serve as the basis for monitoring represent assessed agencies' and programs' performance effectively, and that the cost estimates that they rely upon are accurate.

Colombia's national budget follows a line-item classification, which limits the potential for establishing a clear link between budget allocations and the M&E information that SINERGIA produces. As already noted, SINERGIA's assessments focus on the performance of specific policies and programs. In 2004, the DNP submitted a reform bill to Congress proposing the adjustment of the Organic Budget Statute so that, in addition to the functional, economic, and accounting classifications that it employs today, the national budget would adopt a program classification. This bill has not been approved by Congress, however. Nevertheless, the DNP has already begun moving in this direction. Since 2004, DNP has prepared the national investment budget bill using two parallel budget classifications: the legally approved one, and a newly developed "results-based" one. For the latter, most budget allocations have one or more performance indicators attached and, in all cases, they are linked to the pursuance of one or more of the National Development Plan's strategic objectives. On the other hand, the current expenditure budget, prepared by the Ministry of Finance and representing a greater share of the national budget, is still formulated according to the traditional line-item classification.

Like Colombia, Chile's budget is organized around a line-item classification by agency; this includes details on only some of the agencies' program allocations. A recent change in the budget classification has increased the number of programs identified in the budget, and the implementation of a new integrated financial management system will allow the intended outcomes and specific allocations to be linked much more clearly. But for the time being, the relationship between intended outcomes and budget allocations remains elusive.

Nevertheless, the MCS M&E findings are better integrated into the budget process than those of any of the other systems examined in this chapter. To some extent, this is facilitated by the fact that most of the performance information that MCS produces follows the same level of aggregation as the budget. More specifically, PMGs, CSRs, and PIs concentrate on agency performance and, in the specific case of PIs, many of the performance assessments can also be linked to specific agency expenditure items. On the other hand, many of the programs that the system evaluates with its EPGs or IEs are not identified in the budget. Therefore, the DIPRES evaluators and the budget coordinating units need to eliminate those programs' budgets ad hoc.

Another factor that appears to be critical in the success of MCS in integrating M&E information into the budget formulation process is the committed support that it receives from its powerful institutional champion, DIPRES.

In short, the experience of these five countries suggests that while in principle program-based budget classifications should be able to maximize the benefits of M&E information for budget decision-making purposes, simply having such a program classification does not produce performance-based budget decision making. On the other hand, Chile's experience demonstrates that, when the determination to integrate performance considerations into the budget process comes from the highest levels of government, this can be achieved even in the absence of program-based budgeting.

Lessons Learned

Similarities and contrasts that emerge from the comparative analysis of these eight government M&E systems suggest a number of valuable lessons, presented below.

Institutional Configuration of the M&E Function

In Colombia, Costa Rica, and Uruguay, M&E is organized around a single system, which, in principle, seems to leave them in a good position to ensure consistency among the different processes that the function entails. On the other hand, in Chile and Argentina, the function is configured around two and three different systems.

In Argentina, although the three systems focus on distinct (and therefore potentially complementary) aspects of public-sector performance, they operate in a totally uncoordinated manner, and with nearly no points of connection. This fragmented approach represents a lost opportunity, as it makes it difficult to use the information from the different systems in a complementary, synergistic manner. Moreover, because these uncoordinated systems require ministries, agencies, and programs to respond to multiple information requests, an unnecessary burden is imposed on them, which likely conspires against the quality of information they provide and the likelihood they will end up using it.

On the other hand, the two systems that exist in Chile have been functioning in an increasingly congruent manner. Having the M&E function structured in more than one system, in and of itself, is not necessarily an impediment to its effective operation. What appears to have made the difference between Argentina and Chile is that, in the latter, initiatives are grounded on a higher-level overarching vision that enjoys the support of powerful institutional sponsors. In Argentina, the only time when the initiatives came close to being coordinated was during a brief period when the Vice President's Office championed cooperation between the institutional sponsors of these initiatives. Shortly after the vice president left office that cooperation came to an end, and the development of the two initiatives ended up following different paths.

Approaches to M&E

The most prevalent performance assessment practice across the systems is indicator-based monitoring, which all eight systems conduct. Only Argentina's SIEMPRO, Chile's MCS, and Colombia's SINERGIA also include evaluation components. This provides these three systems with a wider range of options than the other five systems to adjust the level of depth of their performance assessments to the specific information need they are trying to address. Performance monitoring, in and of itself, represents a relatively crude way to inform decision making. In many cases, there is a need for a much more nuanced, in-depth understanding of the processes involved in particular programs or policies, which evaluations are much better equipped to provide.

Given that specific strengths and weaknesses of monitoring and evaluation are potentially complementary to each other, the ideal approach is one that relies on a balance between the two activities. Chile's MCS provides an example of how this can be done in practice.

The system includes two performance monitoring, and three evaluation, components—each of which is centered on different aspects of organizational and program performance. Monitoring information is used as one of the factors to consider when deciding on which agencies and programs the evaluations will focus. Moreover, one of the evaluation components relies on relatively short, less costly, and less sophisticated studies that, besides providing valuable performance information, are taken as a basis to determine the possible need for larger-scale, rigorous impact evaluations.

Relevance of M&E Information to M&E System Stakeholders

One of the best ways to ensure the relevance of M&E information to the needs of intended users is by engaging them in the definition of what policies, programs, and aspects of performance will be subject to monitoring and evaluation. Moreover, the greater their level of involvement in that first and essential stage of the process, and in the subsequent ones, the higher their sense of ownership and their likely receptiveness to the M&E findings. A challenge that M&E systems face is achieving a high level of participation by stakeholders whose information needs the systems are meant to address. The way in which the systems have been dealing with this issue varies from one case to another but, in general, it has entailed significant trade-offs.

For example, Colombia's SINERGIA is intended to serve the information needs of: (a) the National Planning Department, to inform its national planning activities and the formulation of the investment budget; (b) line ministries, to support the design and management of programs; and (c) the President's Office, Congress, audit institutions, and society in general, to enhance transparency and accountability. To ensure relevance to various stakeholders, the decision on what programs and policies to evaluate has been left in the hands of an interinstitutional committee that includes representatives from the presidency, the National Planning Department, and the National Budget Bureau (in the Ministry of Finance). However, the committee leaves several stakeholders outside these critical decisions: it does not include representatives from Congress, audit institutions, or civil society organizations. In the case of the line ministries responsible for the programs to be evaluated, the committee assigns them a role in helping the DNP decide on the type of evaluation to be conducted. However, they do not participate in the selection of the programs that will be subject to evaluation nor in the subsequent stages of the process.

Argentina's RBMS relies on a different approach. One of its components leaves the definition of the aspects of performance, indicators, and targets to be monitored to the agencies themselves, whereas the second component demands a high level of participation from the two main intended users of the assessments that it produces: the Chief of Cabinet's Office, represented by the system's coordinating unit, and the evaluated agencies themselves. Thus, the monitoring cycle engages both parties in the definition of the performance aspects to be assessed, the identification of indicators, the assessment of the agencies' performance, and the preparation of the final assessment reports. The expectation is that each of these steps of the process will be undertaken on a consensual basis. The system requires that the overall performance standards and targets that are set be agreed upon through high-level negotiations between the agencies and the Chief of Cabinet's Office.

The Systems' Impartiality and Credibility

It is widely considered necessary—to ensure the credibility of M&E findings—that the M&E system activities are conducted with some degree of independence from the agencies and programs being evaluated. This is important when the intended users of the M&E findings are external to the policy, agency, or program being assessed. However, when M&E findings are primarily targeted toward the agents responsible for the evaluated activities, ensuring a high level of involvement and receptiveness on their part becomes more important than the information's external credibility. The systems examined have relied on several strategies to ensure the impartiality of the assessments they conduct. One strategy used by all three evaluation systems is to contract out evaluations to external consultants or institutions selected through open and public bidding processes.

In the case of monitoring activities, all the systems have reserved at least some of the process's most sensitive steps to their coordinating units, which, in all cases, are independent from the agencies and programs whose performance is being assessed. These steps include, in all cases, the decision on what activities to assess, the systems' basic methodologies, and, except for Argentina's RBMS, also the analysis of the data gathered and the final assessments. In the case of the RBMS CCC program, the last step of the monitoring cycle is conducted jointly between the system coordinating unit and the assessed agencies, whereas in its SIG component it is left up to the agencies.

Although the managers of all the systems acknowledge the importance of auditing the information that they receive from the assessed agencies and programs, not all of them do so in a systematic way. At least three of them—Argentina's PFMS, Costa Rica's SINE, and Uruguay's SEV—currently do not audit the information on a regular basis, while those where data quality controls are done most methodically—that is, Chile's MCS and Argentina's RBMS CCC program—perform them on a random basis.

One of the stated objectives of most of these M&E systems is enhancing public-sector transparency and accountability, yet the control of all these systems always lies with executive branch institutions. Moreover, except for Costa Rica's SINE, none of them assigns supreme audit institutions (SAIs) that are independent of the executive branch any kind of role in M&E processes. SINERGIA's coordinating unit, in Colombia, has plans to engage civil society organizations in the analysis and dissemination of the system's findings, and this has been conceived as another way to reinforce the system's credibility.

Reporting Arrangements and Dissemination Strategies

The existence and availability of M&E information does not guarantee that the intended users will use it. The systems examined have been trying to facilitate and encourage utilization in various ways. One approach consists of tailoring reporting arrangements according to the expected needs of each type of user. This includes preparation of different reports for different audiences. Some of these reports focus on each assessed program or agency separately, while others present in one document a less-detailed overview of all the performance assessments. Other aspects by which reports are tailored to their intended users are the frequency with which the reports are issued, the complexity of the language with which they are written, and their format.

It is equally important that the key stakeholders are aware of the availability of this information and have easy access to it. For example, in many agencies there is a widespread lack of awareness of the organization's performance targets and assessments. This is the result of poor internal communication. This problem is often aggravated by the concentration of all of the agency's M&E functions in a single organizational unit, which may not communicate well with the agency's senior management.

In order for M&E systems to serve as a public accountability and transparency instrument, it is important that the information that the systems produce is publicly visible and easily accessible. The Internet is used as a primary dissemination channel in the M&E systems considered. The Internet offers the advantage of facilitating access to information but it is less effective as a means to achieve public awareness of the existence of this information. Several systems therefore rely on other dissemination strategies. For example, in addition to disseminating an abridged version of this information through its website, Argentina's RBMS CCC program requires participating agencies to publicize their performance targets and assessments themselves, and it assesses agency efforts in this regard as one of the dimensions that it considers as part of its broader agency appraisals. In Colombia, the president and the members of his cabinet take part in an annual TV program, and in weekly town hall meetings, in which they respond to citizens' questions on the government's policy results. Finally, in both Colombia and Costa Rica, M&E findings are also publicized through press conferences.

Most of the systems have tried to encourage use of M&E information and good performance by establishing budgetary or institutional incentive mechanisms, but few have succeeded. In most cases, the main incentive for the different stakeholders to pay attention to and make use of this information is the fact that performance is now being measured and tracked, and the resulting assessments are circulated both within government and publicly.

The system that has been able to advance most on this front is Chile's MCS. This system has set up a variety of incentives. These include: the requirement that the agencies responsible for the evaluated programs make a formal commitment to implementing the evaluation's recommendations; the close monitoring of agency compliance with these commitments and with the performance targets on which they have agreed; and the institutionalization of utilization of M&E findings during budget negotiations and preparation. The contrast between Chile's MCS experience and some other M&E systems suggests that committed support of a powerful institutional sponsor, as the MCS has from DIPRES, may be essential—not only to designing these incentives, but also to enforcing them.

Linkage between the M&E System and the Budget

One obstacle to integrating M&E findings into the budget process is lack of correspondence between intended outcomes of agencies and programs and the budget classification (which is generally organized by agency and type of expenditure). One way to address this disconnect is to adopt a program- or objective-based budget classification, and some countries have done so.

In contrast, Chile's budget is still largely organized around a line-item classification by agency. Nevertheless, the MCS M&E findings are arguably much better integrated into the budget process than those of the other systems examined in this chapter. This is facilitated by the fact that most of the performance information that MCS produces follows the same level of aggregation as the budget (that is, agency level). For the specific programs that are evaluated, the DIPRES evaluators and budget coordinating units link the evaluation findings and the budget estimates for individual agencies and activities. Another important factor has been the committed support that MCS enjoys from its institutional champion, DIPRES. In addition to having consistently supported the system's development, the senior managers of DIPRES have clearly signaled their determination to incorporate M&E considerations into the preparation of the budget.

Implementation Strategies and Subsequent Developments

Implementation of M&E systems followed a gradual approach, with the exception of Chile's SSPG and Uruguay's SEV. Implementation began with a series of pilots in a small number of agencies, and was only extended to the remaining agencies and programs after the M&E methodologies and procedures were judged to be sufficiently robust. Participation in the M&E systems was initially voluntary, and only became mandatory after a period of years. Implementation involved a capacity-building effort on the part of the M&E system's coordinating unit, which involved training, technical assistance, and other ongoing support.

Some systems resemble their original design very closely. In other cases, however, the final form of the system has little in common with the original plan. Two factors may have been behind these unforeseen developments. One was the evolution of the systems' political environment, which usually entailed changes in the government's priorities and in the system's level of political support. The second factor was a growing understanding of which elements of the M&E systems were working as intended, and which were not. In some of the systems (e.g., Chile's MCS, Colombia's SINERGIA, and Argentina's RBMS), this learning process was supported by the periodic undertaking of diagnostic studies and reviews, commissioned from outside experts or conducted internally.

Notes

This chapter is a revised version of a report, *Evaluation Capacity Development,* World Bank, Independent Evaluation Group, Working Paper No. 16, May 2006, published here with permission of the World Bank. The author would like to thank Keith Mackay (evaluation capacity development coordinator at the World Bank) and Yasuhiko Matsuda (senior public sector specialist at the World Bank) for their insightful feedback on an earlier version of this paper.

1. These interviews and consultations were done as part of the author's preliminary doctoral dissertation research, and a project for the Latin American Center for Development Administration's (CLAD) "Integrated and Analytical System of Information on State Reform, Management and Public Policies" (SIARE).

References

Ala-Harja, Marjukka, and Sigurdur Helgason. 1999. *Improving Evaluation Practices: Best Practice Guidelines for Evaluation.* PUMA/PAC (99) 1, OECD, París.

Cunill Grau, N. and Ospina Bozzi, S. (eds.). 2003. *Evaluación de Resultados para una Gestón Pública Moderna y Democrática.* Caracas: LAD, AECI/MAP/FIIAPP.

Joyce, P.G., and S. Sieg. 2000. "Using Performance Information for Budgeting: Clarifying the Framework and Investigating Recent State Experience." Prepared for the 2000 Symposium of the Center for Accountability and Performance of the American Society for Public Administration, held at the George Washington University, Washington, D.C.

Mokate, K. 2000. "El Monitoreo y la Evaluación: Herramientas Indispensables de la Gerencia Social." *Diseño y Gerencia de Políticas Sociales.* Banco Interamericano de Desarrollo. Instituto Interamericano para el Desarrollo Social (mimeo).

Rossi, P.H., and H.E. Freeman. 1993. *Evaluation: A Systemic Approach.* Newbury Park, CA: Sage Publications.

———. 2005. *Chile: Study of Evaluation Program. Impact Evaluations and Evaluations of Government Programs.* Washington, DC: World Bank

Zaltsman, A. 2004. "La Evaluación de Resultados en el Sector Público Argentino: Un Análisis a la Luz de Otras Experiencias en América Latina." *Revista del CLAD Reforma y Democracia* 29.

———. 2006. "Credibilidad y Utilidad de los Sistemas de Monitoreo y Evaluación para la Toma de Decisiones: Reflexiones en Base a Experiencias Latinoamericanas." In *Evaluación para el Desarrollo Social: Aportes para un Debate Abierto en América Latina,* ed. M. Vera. Ciudad de Guatemala: Instituto Interamericano para el Desarrollo Social, Banco Interamericano de Desarrollo. Magnaterra Editores.

14

The Millennium Challenge Account

A New High-Performance Program

TERRY F. BUSS

Many bilateral and multilateral donors in recent years have imposed discipline on their aid programs by holding developing countries accountable. Some donors[1] now require that developing countries meet standards and attain goals before they become eligible for assistance or to determine whether assistance will be continued. Donors monitor progress in spending by or for developing countries to ensure that goals are met and projects are on track. Once completed, aid projects and programs are evaluated to assess whether they yielded intended impacts. In spite of attempts to hold developing nations accountable, many aid recipients are chronically plagued by war, civil war, revolution, uprisings, natural disasters, pandemics, and much more. Even the most brutal dictatorships—for example, North Korea—receive aid. Neither donors nor recipients can control much of what happens in the third world, although control is a prerequisite for good performance.But bilateral and multilateral donors are increasingly holding aid agencies accountable for performance in the same way that agencies engaged in domestic work are. If donor agencies make bad investment decisions or are poorly managed, they, along with developing countries, may find themselves in trouble—reduced budgets, redefined or circumscribed missions, or increased oversight. Agencies may not have control over developing countries, but they do have control over their own operations, more or less.The Millennium Challenge Act (MCA) of 2003 is an attempt by the federal government to learn from past mistakes in foreign aid allocation and management of aid agencies. This chapter looks closely at the use of performance, capacity assessment, capacity building, and monitoring as the foundations of the MCA program (Part I). Then it goes on to assess MCC's performance as a government agency (Part II). Because MCC had only been in operation for three years as of this writing, it had yet to develop a track record, but much about performance-based management can be learned.

Background

Early in George W. Bush's first term as president, policymakers decided to reengineer a large part of the U.S. foreign assistance effort not only in making awards to developing countries, but also in the way aid agencies operate. On March 22, 2002, arising out of a global commitment at a conference in Monterrey, Mexico, Bush proposed a radically new, innovative approach to bilateral aid (UN 2002). Aid would flow to countries demonstrating progress in poverty reduction, democracy, free markets, rule of law, human rights, and anticorruption, measured objectively on a standard set of indicators. Aid would be distributed only after an eligible country prepared a plan—including performance goals and objectives—mutually agreed to by the United States, and then demonstrated that it had the financial management capacity to spend and control aid, and account for aid spending. Countries also would be required to promote widespread participation from citizens, civil society organizations (CSOs), and nongovernmental organizations (NGOs); demonstrate commitment at the highest levels of government; ensure transparency in the entire process; and pursue sustainability. Congress passed the Millennium Challenge Act of 2003, funded as the Millennium Challenge Account (MCA) and administered by the Millennium Challenge Corporation (MCC).[2] MCC was launched as a government corporation, operating more like a private-sector business, in the belief that it would do a better job in provisioning aid than traditional government agencies did. MCC was designed to be a high-performance operation that could organize its operations in any way it saw fit, with highly flexible human resource authorities, allowing it wide latitude in hiring and firing, promotion, and compensation. MCA resulted in large part from dissatisfaction with the way foreign assistance was allocated under the U.S. Agency for International Development (USAID), and from operations of USAID itself.[3] In 2006, the Bush administration began the long process of folding the agency into the State Department, much as Bush's predecessors had done with the now-defunct U.S. Information Agency (USIA).

Part I: Foreign Aid Reengineered

Improving on Past Aid Programs

MCC policymakers designed MCA to: (1) *Reduce Poverty through Economic Growth*—promoting sustainable economic growth and development, reducing poverty through investments in agriculture, education, private-sector development, and capacity building; (2) *Reward Good Policy and Governance*—Using objective indicators developed by the World Bank, countries will be selected to receive assistance based on their performance in governing justly, investing in their citizens, and encouraging economic freedom; (3) *Operate as Partners*—Working closely with MCC, countries receiving MCA assistance will eliminate barriers to development, ensure civil society participation, and develop an MCA program. MCA participation will require a high-level government commitment. Each MCA country will enter into a public compact that includes a multiyear plan for achieving objectives and identifies responsibilities for achieving those objectives; and (4) *Focus on Results*—MCA assistance will go to countries that have developed well-designed programs with clear objectives, benchmarks to measure progress, procedures to ensure fiscal accountability, and a plan for effective monitoring and objective evaluation of results. Programs will be designed to enable sustainable progress, even after funding under the MCA Compact has terminated.[4]

Indicators Approach

Selection of Candidate Countries

The World Bank annually sets GNI per-capita income thresholds for developing countries in late June. Based on these data, MCC's board approves a list of *candidate* countries that meet income qualifications and are not otherwise ineligible to receive funding by law or policy. Even though MCA is intended as a departure from current foreign aid practices, major provisions in law, including the Foreign Assistance Act of 1961, remain in place. Other laws prohibit aiding countries with human rights problems, drug trafficking, terrorism, nuclear weapons proliferation, military coups, debt payment arrears, and human trafficking. Of course, even in the face of these issues, the United States continues to aid countries when it appears politic to do so. But it will be more difficult to do so under MCA because of the transparency of the process and requirements for funding. MCC then submits the candidate list to Congress.[5] For FY2007, each candidate country had to meet one of two income tests: (1) per-capita income equal to or less than $1,675 gross national income (GNI) to be considered as a Low Income Country or (2) income greater than $1,675 but less than $3,465 GNI per capita to be considered as a Lower-Middle Income Country. Countries must also be eligible for assistance under the World Bank's International Development Association (IDA) program.

Selection of Eligible Countries

From the list of candidate countries, MCC determines which countries are *eligible* for aid, according to each country's demonstrated commitment to "ruling justly, investing in people, and promoting economic freedom," measured by performance on sixteen policy indicators within each country's income peer group (MCC 2005c; 2005d; 2006a). Indicators come primarily from a database assembled and maintained by the World Bank.[6] MCC bases its eligibility determination on objective, quantifiable indicators of a country's commitment to the principles above. MCC also considers whether a country performs above the median on at least half of the indicators in each of the three policy categories and above the median on the corruption indicator. A country's inflation rate, however, need only be under a fixed ceiling of 15 percent.

Selection of Threshold Countries

MCC's Threshold Program assists countries deemed ineligible but nevertheless showing commitment to MCA objectives. MCA authorizes some assistance to candidate countries to help them achieve eligibility in subsequent years. Candidate countries must (1) meet FY2007 requirements for MCA candidacy and (2) demonstrate a significant commitment to meeting the act's eligibility criteria, but fail to meet those requirements. MCC transferred administration of the Threshold Program to USAID in an effort to partner, and perhaps cut administrative expenses. The program may consume up to 10 percent of MCA funding.

Developing Bilateral Compacts

MCC invites eligible countries to submit proposals, developed in consultation with CSOs, the private sector, and NGOs, not to mention citizens. Eligibility does not guarantee a compact. MCC encourages eligible countries to propose projects and programs complementing national development strategies, including those required by the World Bank *Poverty Reduction Strategy Papers* (PRSP).[7] MCC staff discuss the proposal with country officials during compact development. MCC conducts an assessment of the proposal, utilizing its own staff, contractors, and employees of other U.S. government agencies to examine: (1) potential impacts of the proposal's strategy for economic growth and poverty reduction, (2) consultative processes used to develop the proposal, and (3) indicators for measuring progress toward the proposed goals. MCC staff then seek approval from the Investment Committee to conduct due diligence. Due diligence includes an analysis of the proposed program's objectives and its costs relative to potential economic benefits. Plans for program implementation, as well as monitoring and evaluation, fiscal accountability, and coordination with other donors are also reviewed. Country assessments are not audits but diagnostic reviews of systems, operations, procedures, and practices of a country's designated fiscal agent, pointing to strengths and weaknesses in fiscal agent capacity; risks to which MCA funds might be exposed; and government efforts to correct deficiencies. Assessments yield one of three outcomes: (1) a proposed country's fiscal agent has the capacity to properly manage MCA funds against MCC expectations; (2) a recommendation of ways for the government to build capacity in the proposed fiscal agent to meet MCC needs; or (3) a new, alternative fiscal agent that might better meet expectations. Once in operation, assessments determine whether expectations were warranted. Country fiscal agents should manage under the following principles: transparency, accountability, sustainability, integrity, stability, efficiency, and effectiveness. In addition, because the United States is not the only donor distributing aid, recommendations flowing from assessments must take into account the need to harmonize U.S. fiscal agent requirements with those required by other multilateral and bilateral donors (see also Buss and Gardner 2007). On-site assessments of eligible countries involve most of the following tasks:

- *Evaluation of Fiscal Accountability Capacity:* MCA assessments of fiscal agent processes and practices are to be guided by the following: (1) funds control and documentation, (2) separation of duties and internal controls, (3) consistent accounting methodologies and systems, (4) ability to generate timely and meaningful reports, (5) the practice of making information available in a timely and meaningful fashion, (6) cash management practices, (7) procurement systems, (8) timely payment of vendors, and (9) an audit plan.
- *Assistance in Creating an Alternative Fiscal Agent Mechanism:* When fiscal agents are found wanting, MCC will help countries create the appropriate capacity.
- *Post-Compact Review of Fiscal Agent:* Once eligible countries enter into a compact, a subsequent follow-up site visit will be undertaken to verify claims in the compact.
- *Evaluation of Compact Procurement Practices:* MCA guidance for the assessment of procurement processes and practices includes: (1) ethical standards, (2) acquisition planning, (3) competition, (4) contractor selection, and (5) contract administration.

MCC's Investment Committee must approve due diligence work before notifying Congress that MCC intends to begin compact negotiations. After negotiations, the Investment Committee then decides whether to approve submission of the compact text to MCC. In the final step, MCC reviews the compact draft. Before signing the compact and obligating funds, MCC must approve the draft and notify Congress of its intention to obligate funds. MCC approves compacts with governments for three to five years. Congress does not specify which projects or countries MCA shall fund. Un-obligated money can be used in subsequent fiscal years.

MCC Individual Country Assessments

As of FY2007, MCC had awarded eleven compacts (see Table 14.1) (MCC 2006a, 2006b). An additional sixteen countries had been designated as threshold countries, and another twelve countries had become MCA eligible. In FY2005, MCC committed $905 million in funding, or an average of $181 million for five countries. In FY2006, MCC funded six countries at about $1.7 billion, or $283 million on average. In FY2007, MCC planned to fund nine to twelve countries at $3 billion, or $365 million on average (MCC 2006a, 4).

MCC's Critics

MCC is not without its critics, and this was especially true at its inception. Issues included: Would MCC reject aid applicants? Are better-off countries likely to be aided at the expense of those worse off? Is growth potential a fair criterion for granting aid? Should investments be transformative?

Table 14.1

Status of MCC-Eligible Countries, FY2007

Compact Executed	Threshold Country	MCA Eligible	Suspended
Armenia	Albania	Bolivia	The Gambia
Benin	Guyana	Burkino Faso (also threshold)	Yemen
Cape Verde	Indonesia	East Timor	
El Salvador	Kenya	Jordan	
Georgia	Kyrgyz Republic	Lesotho	
Ghana	Malawi	Mongolia	
Honduras	Niger	Morocco	
Madagascar	Paraguay	Mozambique	
Nicaragua	Peru	Namibia	
Vanuatu	Philippines	Senegal	
Mali	Rwanda	Sri Lanka	
	Sao Tome & Principe	Tanzania (also threshold)	
	Uganda		
	Ukraine		
	Zambia		
	Moldova		

Source: Millennium Challenge Corporation, available at www.mca.gov/countries/index.php (accessed 1-8-07).

Rejecting Aid Applicants

In the end, the "proof of concept" for MCA is whether countries are turned down for aid when they do not demonstrate their commitment to MCA principles. Early in the program, MCC awarded aid to Armenia even though it had major elections problems (Dugger 2005b). This raised questions about whether MCC would really be different from USAID. But, in June 2006, MCC rejected Gambia's proposal because the government continued to arrest members of the opposition. Congressman Henry Hyde, a strong advocate of the program, took this as an indication that the United States would no longer reward poor governance with foreign assistance (Hyde 2005). MCC suspended Yemen in FY2004 and FY2005 from the Threshold Program because its performance on eight of sixteen socioeconomic indicators declined, and four represented a failed performance. MCC appears to have taken out much of the politics of foreign aid as intended.

Eligibility Criteria

The FY2007 candidate countries list included Cape Verde, Namibia, and El Salvador, all Lower-Middle Income Countries (LMICs). MCC awarded Cape Verde and El Salvador compacts. Critics claim that the inclusion of LMICs in the selection process will stretch MCA funds even thinner with a lower profile for MCA in compact countries and potentially less country buy-in for aid programs, not to mention less chance for a major transformation (see below). Others counter convincingly that effective development policies like those advocated by MCA propelled LMICs into the higher income group and countries should not be penalized for their successful efforts fighting poverty. LMICs still have significant numbers of people living in poverty, and would benefit from MCA aid. Furthermore, a few LMICs also have important political and strategic ties with the United States—for example, Egypt, Jordan, Colombia, Turkey, and Russia.

Targeting Growth Potential

MCA is predicated on the idea that countries with sound policies are more likely to grow and develop than are others. Growth and development then benefit everyone. Countries will not benefit from increasing amounts of aid invested if sound policies are not in place. World Bank researchers, David Dollar and Paul Collier, to name the most widely noted, soundly argue that aid should be invested where it will do the most good (Burnside and Dollar 1997; Collier and Dollar 1999). There is not much support for continuing to pour money into dysfunctional countries any longer. Representative Jim Kolbe, chairman of the House Appropriations Foreign Operations Subcommittee, calculated that ninety-seven countries received $144 billion (in constant dollars) since 1980, and as of 2000, the median income of these countries actually declined (Kolbe 2002). Much of the initial criticism of MCA questions the program's focus on growth and development at the expense of other more pressing needs. Some criticism appears political—that growth and development as goals are the Bush administration's attempt to impose a "conservative" vision on the developing world. These critics fail to realize that this is not a conservative agenda but rather the widely accepted market-based economics approach—in place of the failure of planned economies in developing poor countries. Other criticisms are theoretical: Is development best pursued by promoting growth or providing for basic needs? Others counter that humanitarian aid creates dependency, not self-sufficiency. Some critics want aid to be invested in sustainable projects—meaning protecting the environment (Purvis 2003). Many environmentalists are against sacrificing the environment for development. Developing countries often oppose protecting the environment when it means they cannot compete in world markets. China, for example, one of the world's largest polluters, was exempted by the Kyoto environmental treaty because it needed to exceed emissions limits to develop. The most advantageous approach is somewhere in between these two extremes. Madagascar's MCA proposal requested funding to develop a land tenure system. Such a system establishes legal ownership to land, allowing owners to sell it, improve it, or use it for collateral, something they cannot now do because much land is in disputed ownership. Critics question this investment, asking why villagers lacking running water, health care, and schools would care about land tenure. But many economists argue that it is precisely this lack of title to property that has hampered development (De Soto 2000). It may not be possible to resolve issues of growth and development until MCA and similar efforts are evaluated. Many believe that aid has been ineffective in many developing countries, and it is time to try something new. There is enough aid available internationally for each country to pursue its own objectives. None of the aid investments made under MCA thus far (see below) are onerous and all have extensive country support.

Transformative Investments

Given the restrictive U.S. budgetary climate, considerable disagreement exists over the merits of signing smaller compacts with many countries or larger compacts with only a few. MCC CEO John Danilovich highlighted MCC's role of ensuring that U.S. aid dollars have a *transformative* impact (Danilovich 2005, 2006; Fletcher and Bluestein 2006). Both sides of the debate have credible arguments. Some say investing boldly in a few countries is the only way to ensure transformational impact (Radelet and Herrling 2005). Indeed, in its FY2005 and FY2007 Congressional Budget Justifications (CBJs) (MCC 2005a, 2006b), MCC emphasized providing countries with significant policy incentives to "galvanize the political will essential for successful economic growth and sustainable poverty reduction" (MCC 2005a, 2005e). Initial reports from countries in the proposal process indicate that governments may be less willing to undertake reforms if MCC funding levels are lower than anticipated. Others seek more equity among those eligible MCC countries—spreading the wealth. Investing modest amounts in more countries is a viable approach because it would create fewer hard feelings among those excluded, and more support for the program in Congress. As the smaller compacts demonstrate success, Congress will likely invest more in MCA, so that other countries might participate, receiving more aid. It seems that MCC is leaning toward awarding larger compacts to fewer nations (see Table 14.2). In a January 2006 interview with the *Washington Post,* CEO Danilovich said that MCC was "focusing on fewer countries with larger compacts, because [it] wants to have a transformative impact" (Fletcher and Bluestein 2006). In the same interview, Danilovich also outlined his plan to give recipient countries greater sums of money at the outset of their development projects to step up the pace of disbursements. Apparently the new CEO has decided that demonstrating success with a few well-funded, transformative compacts will generate the best results—in recipient countries as well as on Capitol Hill.

Indicators

Although much has been made of the use of socioeconomic indicators as an objective way for MCC to determine country eligibility, MCC has discretion in including or excluding countries for participation. The indicators approach has attracted criticism about their use in country selection and their validity. Inclusion or exclusion of countries related to either indicator rankings, legislative aid prohibitions, or foreign policy concerns also attracted criticism. Some of these criticisms appear justified; others do not. GAO (2005) and World Bank (Kaufmann and Kraay 2002) staff have criticized MCC for using quantitative indicators in selecting eligible countries for MCA, noting significant data problems. Scores or rankings were not available for some countries. Errors or missing data caused some countries to score higher than they should have and others to score lower. Numerous countries clustered around median scores, making it difficult to discriminate among them. While these criticisms are valid from a statistical perspective, they beg an important question: If such data are not to be used to rank countries, on what "objective" basis can countries be ranked? In fact, much data are wanting in most cases, and not just for developing countries. Proponents rightly claim that at least MCC made a transparent effort to rank countries on what data was available. These criticisms, at least by World Bank researchers, seem a little disingenuous. Why would the World Bank develop these databases, maintain them annually, present legions of reports and press releases based on them, and then turn around and suggest that they should not be used? Some critics facetiously suggest that perhaps the millions of dollars the World Bank spent on data programs might be better spent assisting developing countries.

Part II: MCC as a Government Corporation Assessed

It is premature for the MCA program to have any track record under the Government Performance and Results Act (GPRA), President's Management Agenda (PMA), or

Table 14.2

Descriptions of MCA Compacts as of January 8, 2007

Country	Amount	Program Description
Madagascar	$109,773,000	Helps raise incomes by bringing the rural population from subsistence agriculture to a market economy by securing formal property rights to land, accessing credit and protecting savings, and receiving training in agricultural production, management, and marketing techniques.
Honduras	$215,000,000	Reduces poverty and spurs economic growth by increasing productivity of high-value crops and improving transportation links between producers and markets.
Nicaragua	$175,000,000	Reduces poverty and spurs economic growth by funding projects in the regions of León and Chinandega aimed at reducing transportation costs and improving access to markets for rural communities; increasing wages and profits from farming and related enterprises in the region, and increasing investment by strengthening property rights.
Cape Verde	$110,078,488	Makes sizable investments in water resources, agricultural productivity, major port and road improvements, and initiatives to promote the private sector, including investment climate and financial-sector reforms.
Georgia	$295,300,000	Reduces poverty and stimulates economic growth in the regions outside of Georgia's capital, Tbilisi, by focusing on rehabilitating regional infrastructure and promoting private-sector development; the program will directly benefit approximately a half-million Georgians.
Armenia	$235,650,000	Reduces rural poverty through a sustainable increase in the economic performance of the agricultural sector.

Program Assessment Rating Tool (PART). Nonetheless, it is interesting to note that MCC got off to a poor start but has made an impressive comeback. It is tempting to attribute the slow start to fairly common problems in starting any new federal program, but in retrospect, it appears that MCC's first CEO was ineffective and that his replacement turned the program around (Dugger 2005a).Under start-up leadership, according to a GAO audit, MCC had not completed "the plans, strategies, and time-frames needed to establish corporate-wide structures for accountability, governance, internal control and human capital management" (GAO 2005, 4). MCC had no strategic plan, annual performance plans and goals, performance measures, or reporting mechanisms as required by law under GPRA and by policy under PMA (34). MCC lacked an internal control environment, process for ongoing risk assessment, and process for correcting weaknesses (35). On the human capital side, MCC had not developed an effective human capital infrastructure, an assessment of critical skill needs, a recruitment plan aligned with corporate goals and plans, or a system linking performance to compensation (35). As far as procurement—recall that the mission of MCC is to dole out billions of dollars in a rigorous procurement process—MCC had few procurement policies and processes in place, and only a skeletal staff to execute them. Organizationally, the divisions within MCC made no sense, so much so that operations became very inefficient. As evidence of its dysfunction, MCC was able to conclude compacts with only four countries—Madagascar, Cape Verde, Nicaragua, and Georgia—from January 2004 through November 2005, when a new director was appointed. Congress, disappointed in MCC's initial performance, held numerous hearings on why the program was floundering, and denied the Bush administration's appropriation request. Program critics wondered how MCC could assess management capacity in developing countries when its own operations were in disarray. Now MCC appears to be well functioning, and criticism has nearly disappeared. All of the problems at start-up appear to have been resolved. But the proof is in the performance: from November 2005 to November 2006, MCC signed seven compacts with others in the pipeline. Congress is supporting continued and expanded funding for MCC. MCC has sorted out the aid allocation process. What remains to be seen is whether the results expected from MCC countries are attained.

Notes

1. Other countries have made their foreign assistance agencies more performance oriented. Canada (CIDA 2002) and the United Kingdom (see www.dfid.gov.uk/aboutdfid/performance.asp, accessed January 8, 2007) are models for development.

2. MCC and MCA background documents are found at www.mcc.gov (accessed January 8, 2007). An excellent overview of the program is found in Tarnoff 2006.

3. In 2004, under Secretary of State Colin Powell, USAID and State issued a joint Strategic Plan. In 2006, State began approving budget allocations that were once the province of USAID.

4. The report is no longer posted on the web.

5. The country selection process is found at http://www.mcc.gov/selection/index.php, accessed January 8, 2007.

6. A description and analysis of World Bank governance indicator databases is found in Kaufmann, Kraay and Mastruzzi 2006, and on their website at: http://info.worldbank. org/governance/kkz2005/, accessed January 8, 2007.

7. Aid harmonization initiatives are discussed at: http://www.aidharmonization.org/, accessed January 8, 2007.

References

Burnside, Craig, and David Dollar. 1997. "Aid Spurs Growth in a Sound Policy Environment." *Finance and Development,* December.

Buss, Terry F., and Adam Gardner. 2007. "Why Aid to Haiti Failed." In *Foreign Assistance and Foreign Policy,* eds. Louis A. Picard, Robert Groelsema, and Terry F. Buss, chapter 9. Armonk, NY: M.E. Sharpe.

Canadian International Development Agency (CIDA). 2002. *Canada Making a Difference in the World.* Hull, QC: CIDA. www.acdi-cida.gc.ca, accessed January 8, 2007.

Collier, Paul, and David Dollar. 1999. "Aid Allocation and Poverty Reduction." Washington, DC: World Bank, January.

Danilovich, John. 2005. *Speech at InterAction's Annual CEO Retreat.* December 6. http:// www.mcc.gov/public_affairs/speeches/120605_CEOretreat.shtml, accessed January 8, 2007.

———. 2006. Keynote Speech at a conference hosted by the American Enterprise Institute to mark the second anniversary of the MCC. Washington, DC, January 23, 2006.

De Soto, Hernando. 2000. *The Mystery of Capital.* New York: Basic Books.

Dugger, Celia W. 2005a. "Foreign Aid Chief Pledges Reforms." *New York Times,* November 13.

———. 2005b. "US Approves Grant to Armenia, But Urges Greater Political Rights." *New York Times,* December 20.

Fletcher, Michael A., and Paul Bluestein. 2006. "With New Leader, Foreign Aid Program Is Taking Off." *The Washington Post,* January 31: A15.

Government Accountability Office (GAO). 2005. *Millennium Challenge Corporation.* Washington, DC: GAO, April 26, 05–455T.

Hyde, Henry. 2005. "Millennium Challenge Account." U.S. House of Representatives, Committee on International Relations, April 27.

Kaufmann, Daniel, and Aart Kraay. 2002. *Governance Indicators, Aid Allocation, and the Millennium Challenge Account.* Washington, DC: World Bank.

Kaufmann, Daniel, Aart Kraay, and M. Mastruzzi. 2006. *Governance Matters V—1996–2005.* Washington, DC: World Bank.

Kolbe, Jim. 2002. Remarks to the Advisory Committee on Voluntary Foreign Aid, October 9 (as cited in Nowels 2003).

Millennium Challenge Corporation (MCC). 2005a. *FY2005 Congressional Budget Justification.* Washington, DC: MCC. www.mcc.gov/about_us/key_documents/FY05_Budget_Justification.pdf, accessed August 1, 2006.

———. 2005b. *FY2006 Congressional Budget Justification.* Washington, DC: MCC.

———. 2005c. "Report on the Criteria and Methodology for Determining the Eligibility of Candidate Countries." *Federal Register* 70, (173), September 8: 53392–95.

———. 2005d. "Report to Congress in Accordance with Section 608(a) of the Millennium Challenge Act." Washington, DC: MCC. http://www.mcc.gov/countries/candidate/ FY05_candidate_report.pdf, accessed August 1, 2006.

———. 2005e. "FY2006 Budget Justification." Washington, DC: MCC. www.mcc.gov/ about_us/key_documents/FY06_Budget_Justification.pdf, accessed August 1, 2006.

———. 2006a. *Congressional Notification Transmittal Sheet—2007.* Washington, DC:

MCC. www.mcc.gov/selection/reports/FY07_candidate_report.pdf, accessed November 3, 2006.

———. 2006b. *Budget Justification, 2007.* Washington, DC: MCC.

Nowels, Larry. 2003. *The MCA: Congressional Consideration of a New Foreign Aid Initiative.* Washington, DC: Congressional Research Service, January, RL31687.

Purvis, Nigel. 2003. "Greening U.S. Foreign Aid through the MCA." Washington, DC: Brookings Institution, policy brief no. 119.

Radelet, Steven, and Sheila Herrling. 2005. "The MCC between a Rock and a Hard Place: More Countries, Less Money and the Transformational Challenge." Washington, DC: Center for Global Development, October 26.

Tarnoff, Curt. 2006. "Millennium Challenge Account." Washington, DC: Congressional Research Service, no. RL32427, August 1.

United Nations (UN). 2002. *Report of the International Conference on Financing Development: Monterrey Consensus.* New York: United Nations, March 18–22.

15

Reforming Accountability in the United States and the United Kingdom from Rule-Bound to Performance-Based Accountability

Case Studies of the Highways Agencies

Teresa Curristine

In the late 1980s and the early 1990s, governments on both sides of the Atlantic faced problems of economic recession, budget pressures, and a public increasingly disillusioned with government. Both governments introduced similar civil service reforms. In the United States, reforms consisted of the National Performance Review (NPR) (see especially Radin, chapter 6 of this volume) and the Government Performance and Results Act (GPRA) (see Posner and Fantone, chapter 5) and in the United Kingdom, Next Steps Agencies. These reforms sought the replacement of traditional rule-bound structures of accountability by performance-based forms of accountability. Performance-based accountability concentrates on holding civil servants to account for results. Civil servants are given managerial flexibility to improve the efficiency and/or the effectiveness of their agencies and programs. They are then held accountable for results, measured in the form of outputs and/or outcomes. Both governments claim that these reforms have improved civil service efficiency and accountability.

This chapter argues that the introduction and successful implementation of performance-based accountability (PBA) is highly related to the following conditions: First, the institutional frameworks, the Westminster system in the United Kingdom and the separation of powers system in the United States, have historically established incentive structures and traditional mechanisms for achieving accountability. The success of PBA is related to the ability of both institutional structures and the traditional accountability mechanisms to accommodate shifts in accountability relationships. Second, politicians must allow managers the freedom to manage and refrain from interfering in operations. Third, performance measures are a competent means of holding agencies to account. For this to be the case accurate measures must be produced. This requires the objectives of an agency to be clear and for it to be possible to measure the agency's contribution toward achieving these objectives (Deleon 1998). This article contends that the existence of accurate measures is not sufficient to improve accountability. These measures must be used by politicians to hold agencies to account.

Based on empirical research, this article examines the attempts to introduce performance-based accountability into the Federal Highways Administration (FHWA) in the United States from 1993 to 2000 and the Highways Agency (HA) in the UK over the period from 1993 to 1998. Ninety face-to-face interviews have been conducted with officials in both the United States and the United Kingdom. Interviews were carried out with former ministers; with officials in FHWA, HA, Office of Management and Budget (OMB), and Government Accountability Office (GAO); and with committee staff in Congress and Parliament. All interviews were given under the condition that the interviewees would not be named.

This chapter asserts that the institutional framework within which these bureaucracies operate not only shapes the current accountability relationships with politicians in the legislature and the executive but also places inherent limits on how these relationships can change. The dominance of the executive in the UK institutional structure facilitates the introduction of PBA, resulting in improved accountability to the executive. However, the traditional mechanisms for achieving accountability, ministerial responsibility and parliamentary questions, hinder the ability of the reforms to enhance accountability to Parliament for the politically sensitive HA. In the United States, the institutional structure and partisan political environment have hindered the introduction of the reforms and those aspects of NPR aimed at improving accountability at a federal level. Even when reforms are introduced, such as GPRA, old accountability structures impede the effectiveness of new accountability mechanisms. Successful changes in accountability will demand the support of Congress, the presidency, and the bureaucracy. In both countries real changes to the traditional accountability relationships will require changes in the behavior not only of civil servants but also of politicians. The reforms have been fed into existing political structures that have not altered. The incentives, which already exist in the political system, especially the legislature, make it difficult for politicians to change their behavior and to move away from their concentration on ensuring responsiveness to them and highlighting administrative failure toward using performance measures. For PBA to succeed this transformation needs to take place.

This chapter is in three sections. Section 1 describes how both political systems have attempted to introduce PBA. It also discusses the possible tensions between PBA and traditional accountability mechanisms. Section 2 examines the implementation in the United States of the accountability aspects of NPR and GPRA in the FHWA and their impact on FHWA's accountability to the legislature and the executive. This section then strives to make some general conclusions about the impact of the reforms on accountability to Congress and the executive. Section 3 examines the effect of the creation of the HA on accountability to ministers and Parliament in the United Kingdom.

Performance-Based Accountability

Civil service accountability has traditionally concentrated on responsiveness to politicians and administering government programs in a lawful manner. In both countries the main traditional mechanisms used to hold civil servants to account were hierarchical structures, rules, and regulations.

PBA involves delegating responsibility to civil servants in order to increase their flexibility to improve services, while holding them to account for achieving these improvements through performance measures. Delegation is a key to improving efficiency. Reformers perceived the traditional mechanisms for achieving accountability, rules and regulations and long lines of hierarchical structures, as obstacles to efficiency. The NPR Status Report argues that "the old methods of achieving accountability have often served to tie up the government in endless reams of useless and expensive red tape" (Gore 1994, 72). A corresponding sentiment is expressed in the Efficiency Unit's Next Steps Report. It claimed that improved performance was hindered by central rules and managers' lack of control over factors such as staffing and resources on which results depend (Efficiency Unit 1988, 5–6). The reforms seek to hold civil servants accountable for achieving results not for following rules, regulations, and procedures (Hood 2001, 300–301).

In the United Kingdom, delegation of authority has taken place through the creation of Next Step Agencies. They separate policy from operations to provide managers with the delegated authority to achieve results. Agencies' chief executives are held accountable for achieving results in the form of annual performance targets set by ministers. The government maintains that Next Steps Agencies improve accountability to Parliament by clarifying lines of responsibility within government while maintaining the principle of ministerial responsibility. It also asserts that it supplies more information to Parliament in the form of an agency's business plan and annual performance report. Chief executives answer written parliamentary questions on operations, and they appear before parliamentary select committees to answer questions on agency operations.

In the United States, attempts have been made to delegate authority through NPR initiatives that concentrate on removing layers of middle management, cutting red tape, and empowering frontline employees. Employees are held accountable for achieving results through GPRA and the Presidential Performance Agreements between the president and department cabinet secretaries. These set out the president's major goals for the department for the coming year. In theory, these agreements should cascade through the organizations, connecting political and career employees for the first time in an unbroken chain of accountability to achieve results. In accordance with GPRA, all departments developed five-year strategic plans by September 1997. Each year since 1998 they have produced annual performance plans, containing their goals, performance measures, and performance targets for the upcoming fiscal year. Beginning in March 2000, all departments were required to submit an annual performance report to Congress and the president presenting their progress against their annual performance targets. It is hoped that Congress will use the performance information contained in these plans to hold agencies to account and to make funding decisions.

Problems with Performance-Based Accountability

A tension arises between these new mechanisms for achieving accountability, which emphasize results, and the traditional mechanisms, which stress responsiveness to politicians and the law. First, there is a strain between political accountability on the one hand, which requires responsiveness to the demands of politicians, and managerial flexibility on the other. The reforms claim to be nonpolitical, as they seek to create a more results-oriented bureaucracy. They aim to limit the intervention of politicians in administration in order to provide managers with the flexibility to improve efficiency. However, for a variety of reasons politicians can be reluctant to loosen their grip on agencies. They may want to ensure that an agency is achieving their desired policy objectives. Politicians in the legislature, through their demands for responsiveness, can pressurize the executive to control agencies. Politicians in the executive may also intervene if they fear that civil servants will make mistakes for which they could be held to account. All politicians may intervene in agencies to ensure that constituency gains are obtained even if they are questionable on value-for-money terms. Simply put, politicians can be more concerned with ensuring responsiveness to them than with managerial flexibility and efficiency.

Second, some commentators fear that the reforms will undermine accountability by reducing rules and hierarchical structures (Moe 1994). They are concerned that performance measures are an inadequate replacement for traditional accountability mechanisms. Third, the above points are related to the ability of the institutional structures and the traditional accountability mechanisms to accommodate shifts in accountability relations. If PBA is to succeed, politicians must refrain from intervening in agency operations and politicians in both legislatures must use performance measures to hold agencies to account. It is not clear that incentives exist within the institutional structures to achieve these changes. In this instance, institutional structures affect whether or not reforms are implemented and how they are implemented.

Reforms in the United States

In the United States, the separation of powers system results in joint control of the bureaucracy, which hinders the introduction of the reforms as both branches of government compete for control over the bureaucracy. To introduce major aspects of the NPR, the president needed the support not only of Congress but also of the agencies involved and the interested groups affected by these changes. This was a difficult balance to achieve. The results of NPR varied greatly depending on the agency in question. However, many of the aspects of the reforms relating to enhancing accountability have not been passed by Congress, such as Performance-Based Organizations (PBOs) or civil service personnel reform. Other aspects have failed to be fully implemented in some agencies, such as the removal of middle management and rules and regulations, the delegation of responsibility down to the lower levels, the empowerment of employees, and the introduction of Presidential Performance Agreements (Kettl 1998). The institutional difficulty in implementing the reforms was compounded by a partisan divide over how to reform government. Both the Republicans and the Democrats agree that government needs to be reduced and reformed, but they have different ideas about how to reform government and, more fundamentally, about the role of government. NPR has been seen by the Republican Congress as a political gambit by the Democrats to gain public support by reducing the size of the bureaucracy. Thus the reforms that claimed to be nonpolitical and emphasized the managerial aspect of government have become part of the political battle between the Republicans and the Democrats.

Institutional and political environments within which the Agency operates and the traditional accountability structures adopted by these institutions have limited the NPR impact on the agency. In 1995, the Department of Transportation (DOT) proposed to restructure its organization by consolidating its ten existing agencies into three. Despite DOT's claim that the new structure would result in efficiency gains, Congress did not pass the proposed bill. The proposal faced strong opposition from interest groups. As one agency official explained, they feared that without an agency representing their areas of interest their voices would not be heard. Further attempts to change the department through the creation of PBOs for the St. Lawrence Seaway and the Federal Lands Division of the FHWA stalled in Congress. Congress refused to approve these PBOs for fear that it would weaken their oversight of the agencies in question.

The NPR has had only a minor impact on the FHWA. There has also been a removal of rules and middle management, but most of these changes have been more a matter of appearance than substance. Most middle managers were merely given a new title but kept the same job description. The greatest impact of NPR on FHWA has been through cutbacks in personnel; between 1992 and 2000 the FHWA reduced its full-time staff by 1,789. However, even before NPR there had been reductions in personnel because of the completion of the interstate highway system.

Mostly, NPR has taken credit either for changes that were already on the way or for changes that have occurred as a result of other factors. The traditional accountability structures, especially the authorization and appropriation processes, have both preceded and superseded the reforms in terms of introducing change into the agency. They have played a more significant role in transforming the agency than either NPR or GPRA. The agency has completed its original mission to build the interstate highway system. This, combined with pressure from the states, has led to changes within the agency.

Since 1991, there has been increased delegation of authority from FHWA headquarters to its regional and divisional offices. This has occurred not as a result of NPR but because states through ISTEA (the 1991 five-year transportation reauthorization bill) pushed for delegation of authority to their own highway departments and FHWA regional and divisional offices. Reflecting the completion of the interstate, ISTEA delegated authority to state highway departments and FHWA regional offices. Subsequently, the states continued to press for delegation from FHWA's regional offices to its division offices. This pressure resulted in the House Appropriation Committee's requiring the agency to evaluate its organizational structure with a view to reducing the number of regional offices (House Report 105–188). The subsequent report called for the replacement of nine regional offices with four resource centers.

The DOT did introduce Presidential Performance Agreements. The president signed an annual Performance Agreement with the Transportation cabinet secretary stating the objectives of the department for the coming year. The cabinet secretary in turn signed an agreement with the head of each agency in the department including FHWA. Performance agreements between the secretary and the agency heads have now been integrated with GPRA annual performance plans. Both Congress and the administration have praised the department's GPRA strategic and performance plans. In congressional evaluations the DOT's plans received the highest grade of all agencies. These integrated agreements are mainly a tool of the department. Agency heads have monthly meetings with the deputy secretary to discuss their progress. In an interview, a senior DOT political appointee stated that he felt these agreements provided him with more information and enhanced the responsiveness of agencies to the department.

Within the FHWA, GPRA has had more of an influence than the NPR. It is being used as a supplement to the traditional structures of accountability. However, interviewees in FHWA expressed concern about the increase in paperwork and that political appointees would use the additional information provided in these integrated agreements to micromanage the agency.

It remains to be seen whether in the long term GPRA performance information will be used by FHWA's managers and political appointees to make managerial and funding decisions. Early indicators are not encouraging; in a recent survey less than half of managers at DOT stated that they used performance information in undertaking key management functions (GAO 2001, 184). Political appointees, when disposing of discretionary highway funds and funds for the public lands program, were no longer taking the advice of officials who recommended the most efficient project. Instead, they made these decisions on the basis of political information. A GAO report criticized this blatant use of political criteria to make these decisions (GAO 1997b).

FHWA's Accountability to Congress

A staff member of the House appropriations subcommittee on transportation stated, "Highways has a long standing reputation as being responsive and very professional."

In terms of improving accountability to Congress, the reforms have not had an extensive impact. They made no difference to FHWA's reputation for being responsive to Congress. GPRA will provide Congress with more information. The reports accompanying the House and Senate appropriations bills for 1998 and the Senate bill for 2000 refer to GPRA and praised the department's strategic plan and performance plan.

However, receiving information is very different from using it to make funding decisions. The indicators from interviews with the appropriators show that they will not use performance measures in making funding decisions for highway programs. One staff member of the House appropriations committee commented on the likelihood of appropriators using performance measures, "It is hard to teach an old dog new tricks. The political reality is such that it is not going to change. There may be short term changes but over the long term it will go by the graveside, like zero-sum budgeting. It [GPRA] is a fashion, a fad." In a system where funding decisions are strongly influenced by political criteria and constituency interests it is not apparent what role performance measures will play. Congressmen are concerned with reelection and decisions are based on political and constituency criteria. TEA-21 is a major example of making funding decisions on the basis of constituency interests. It contains a total of 1,850 earmarked constituency projects costing $9.5 billion over six years. It is a clear indication of how the interests of efficiency can be secondary to political concerns. Even if congressmen and appropriators wished to use these performance measures it is hard to find measures that provide an accurate picture of FHWA's performance. Since the states implement the majority of FHWA's programs many of the factors that influence the results of FHWA performance targets are not within its control.

Effects on Accountability to Congress

The NPR has had little impact on accountability to Congress. The GPRA has had more of an influence because it has been enacted into legislation and has bipartisan support. One staff member of a congressional committee explains, "it [NPR] is so politicized because NPR equals Al Gore. You will have members in the Republican Party that may support the concepts, but they would prefer to use the Result Act [GPRA] because one, they created it and it is the law, and two, it is something that does not have Al Gore's name written on it. And so I think there is a political difference." GPRA has been more successful than previous reform initiatives in obtaining the attention of Congress. However, the U.S. political system, with its institutional conflict between the legislative and executive branches, and the fragmentation of responsibilities in Congress, make it difficult for GPRA to succeed (Radin 2000, 120).

In the partisan context of the late 1990s with intense electoral competition for control of Congress and the presidency, GPRA has become part of the traditional battle between the legislative and the executive. Both parties support it; however, both wanted to use GPRA not as a management tool, but as a political tool. The act required that agencies submit their five-year strategic plans to Congress by 1997.

Republican House Majority Leader Richard Armey's office directed the grading of these strategic plans. The final average grade for the plans came to only 46.6 out of a possible 100. Armey was severely critical of the general standard of the plans. Some departments claim that the evaluation was a partisan exercise, with the Republicans giving low grades so that they could engage in political point scoring. Over the objections of the Clinton administration, Congress evaluated agencies' performance plans in March 1998. The average score was 42.5. The Republican leadership claimed that the act had a long way to go before it could produce dependable performance data that would be useful to congressional decision-makers. The House Democrats accused the Republicans of giving failing grades to most agencies in an attempt to embarrass the administration.

Despite questions about the accuracy of the performance data, Armey's office encouraged appropriation committees to use GPRA as a tool for cutting back government in the areas in which the Republicans wish to see it reduced. However, there was a further division within Congress itself between the appropriators and other congressional committees and the majority leader's staff. The key to whether the GPRA affects accountability is whether the performance information is used to make budget decisions. The indications are that the appropriators are very reluctant to use performance measures to make budget decisions. A staff member of the House Government Reform Committee described the situation: "We have a long way to go especially with appropriators who are used to receiving information on an annual basis for budget justification . . . they are resisting to some extent and it is a slower change to get the appropriators but that will be the key." There are no clear incentives for congressmen or appropriation committees to use performance data. It is not obvious how using this data to make budget decisions will help congressmen with reelection. The appropriators wish to retain the present system, which provides them with extensive control over the funding process of agencies. It is too early to come to a firm conclusion about GPRA, however; to date the indications are that these measures will not be used by appropriators in making decisions and thus will not make a substantial change in the operations of accountability (Radin 2000, 122). It remains to be seen whether Congress will use performance information to hold agencies to account. Failures to meet targets could be used, like the evaluations of strategic and performance plans, for the political purpose of embarrassing the executive.

Effect on Accountability to the Executive

In most cases, NPR has not enhanced accountability to the cabinet secretary or the president, as Performance Agreements have not been introduced extensively. In the first two years, only ten agreements were signed between the president and cabinet secretaries. The DOT was one of the few departments that used these agreements. Even in DOT, they were integrated with GPRA annual performance plans and remained one of many mechanisms that political appointees used to hold agencies to account.

The GPRA, which has been extensively implemented, has provided political appointees with more information about the operations of the department. However, many political appointees spend most of their time dealing with Congress and the president over political issues involving their department. Thus, they may not have the time for or the interest in management issues. After four years of government-wide implementation of GPRA there were no indications that political appointees' interest in using performance results had increased. A GAO survey of federal managers noted, "top leadership's commitment to achieving results—a critical ingredient in managing for results—remained stagnant" (GAO 2000, 2).

The performance measures may be more used by senior career officials. According to the GAO, to improve programs it is vital that performance information be used by senior managers to make decisions. However, only one-fifth of federal managers surveyed in 1997 reported that performance information was being used to help make funding decisions, legislative changes, or program changes (GAO 1997a, 10). The GAO 2000 survey indicated that more performance information was provided in 2000 than in 1997. However, the report stated, "the significant reduction in the reported use of performance information in making most of these critical management decisions is disturbing. It suggests that efforts to increase the focus on results and the use of performance information are not penetrating the federal bureaucracy" (GAO 2000, 11).

Critics' fears that the reforms would undermine accountability have mostly proven unfounded because in many agencies, the traditional rules, regulations, and hierarchical structures have largely remained intact. Performance measures will at best be an addendum to traditional accountability structures rather than a replacement for them, as the reformers intended. The GPRA provides the opportunity for improving accountability to the executive. However, if political appointees and managers do not use performance data to make decisions the danger is that it will become an expensive paper exercise adding another layer to an already extensive reporting system. This would result in PBA's having the perverse outcome of contributing to the very problem of excessive red tape that it hoped to solve.

The reforms in the United States have been difficult to introduce successfully because of the institutional structure and the partisan divide. Even when the reforms are implemented, in many cases they fail to change the traditional structures of accountability and the behavior of bureaucrats and politicians. Where these new mechanisms of accountability have been introduced, such as GPRA's performance measures, they are not the objective criteria the reformers sought. They have become subject to political partisan estrangement.

The United Kingdom

The constitutional and institutional structure in the United Kingdom facilitates the introduction of the reforms, but these same structures hinder enhancing accountability to Parliament and yet improve accountability to the executive. The United

Kingdom's executive-dominated system, with its unitary structure and centralized bureaucracy, facilitates the introduction of reforms. Legislation was not required to establish Next Steps Agencies. However, in politically sensitive agencies such as highways and prisons (Barker 1998), Next Steps Agencies' call for separation of policy from operations is more appearance of reform than reality. Given that the traditional accountability system, that is, ministerial responsibility, provides incentives for politicians to intervene in politically sensitive areas, it is difficult to maintain this separation. It is, however, in the interest of the executive to claim it exists, as they can avoid taking responsibility for administrative failures.

Effects on Accountability to the Executive

According to Massey, agency status enhances accountability to ministers by clarifying the role and function of officials and by improving ministers' knowledge of what takes place in departments and agencies (Massey 1995). Ministers now have an official, the chief executive, who is responsible for operations within a department. This makes it easier for ministers to communicate their demands and clarifies the lines of responsibility within large departments. Ministers can obtain more information on the performance of an agency through the provision of annual performance reports. They also have the ability to set annual performance targets and to reward or punish chief executives for the achievement of these targets. Interviews with former transport ministers confirmed Massey's view. All ministers stated that they felt the HA's agency status had improved responsiveness to them.

The HA was created in April 1994 as an agency of the DOT. Before agency status, ministers controlled the operations of the road program. Agency status has not resulted in the expected distancing of ministers from operations. While delegations were given to the agency in the Framework Document, ministers felt they could intervene in operations at any stage and did. Ministers' interest in the day-to-day operations of the agency reflected the high political profile of roads. The former Conservative government's 1989 Road to Prosperity Programme put roads back onto the political agenda. New road construction was political because members of the public and MPs were either in favor of or against certain road schemes and bypasses, while the environmental lobby took direct action over controversial road projects and raised political questions about the viability of road construction. Ministers thus came under pressure from MPs and the media to take action.

As one would expect, ministers inevitably became immersed in the details of road schemes that received a high level of media and parliamentary interest, such as the Salisbury bypass, the Newbury bypass, and the A30. However, ministers also became involved in aspects of the agency's business that one would expect would remain within the agency. These were relatively minor issues such as the agency logo. According to an official, ministers showed tremendous interest in expressing a preference for the color of the agency's logo.

Ministers were also interested in more substantive sectors of the agency's operations such as road maintenance and new construction. Traditionally ministers would decide on the building of roads costing more than £3 million. Decisions on road schemes costing less than £3 million were exclusively delegated to the agency's regional offices. When cutbacks extensively reduced the more expensive road schemes (more than £3 million), ministers became more interested in the details of minor projects. They required the publication of a list of projects costing between £3 million and £100,000 and eventually of projects between £100,000 and £50,000. Ministers took an interest in the projects included on this list. An agency official stated "And they [ministers] usually wanted a bit more than the list. They wanted to know what is being done and what the local response might be. For example, a mini-roundabout close to a village. What do the locals think? What does the local MP think? Could there be a backlash? Or alternatively is it something people are very keen to see? Will it work?" Politicians now influenced decisions formerly made by the regional offices on the basis of technical criteria, such as safety and congestion. At a time when the rhetoric calls for greater delegation, in this case the reality was greater intervention.

Ministers were very concerned with having a close hand on operations because of the potential political backlash if things went wrong. A picture emerges of a gray area where it was not clear who was responsible for what. The agency structure improved the responsiveness of highways to ministers. However, the requirement of ministers to be responsive to MPs and the media created the incentives for them to intervene in the operations of the agency. This intervention undermined the managerial flexibility of the agency.

Accountability to Parliament

According to the government, Next Steps Agencies enhance accountability by making the lines of responsibility clearer. This clarity is supposedly achieved by separating policy from operations. The traditional practice for answering parliamentary questions has been altered to reflect this division. In theory, the agency chief executive answers parliamentary written questions on operational issues, and ministers answer questions on policy. Chief executives appear before select committees on behalf of ministers to answer questions on operational issues. The government claims that annual performance and business plans provide Parliament with more information on agencies' performance. Each of these accountability mechanisms—parliamentary questions and select committees—will be examined in turn to see whether the reality matches the theory.

In order to show the level of parliamentary interest in highways the number of parliamentary questions answered by the agency over a four-year period has been determined. The HA is among the half-dozen agencies that Hogwood identifies (through his analysis of the number of parliamentary questions) as attracting the most interest from MPs (Hogwood, Judge, and McVicar 1998, 13). Table 15.1 shows the number of questions asked of the chief executive of the HA from 1994 to 1997. Due to the 1997 election the 1996/97 session ended in March.

Table 15.1

Number of Parliamentary Questions, 1994–1997

Parliamentary session	Number of written parliamentary questions answered by HA chief executive
1993/94	100
1994/95	137
1995/96	170
1996/97	44

It is important to note that political interest in roads existed before the agency was established and this interest continued throughout the agency's first three years. Written parliamentary questions are varied and can reflect the diverse interests of individual MPs. In the case of highways a large proportion of these questions were concerned with individual roads, reflecting MP's constituency issues. A different set of questions was about environmental issues and included high-profile cases such as the Newbury bypass. The opposition spokespeople took advantage of these controversies to highlight contested government decisions and to emphasize the costs of government mistakes.

The political interest in the agency and the sensitivity of some parliamentary questions meant that the ministers had a stake in the content of the agency's answers. In the 1994–1997 period, the ministers responsible for roads were Mr. Key (1993–1994) and Mr. Watts (1994–1997). Both insisted on viewing all of the chief executive's responses before sending them to the relevant MP (HC 313-III 1996, 84). One former minister explained that the political interest in roads made this a necessity. He remarked that he had only found it necessary to change approximately 5 to 10 percent of answers. The appearance that the chief executive had answered the questions created the illusion of open government and the separation of policy from operations. In reality, little had changed. Ministers were reluctant to lose control over the agency; thus they viewed and vetted all answers. This served to blur accountability rather than to clarify it.

Although it was not part of the agency's performance targets, responding to MPs' demands and being at the "beck and call" of ministers was important in determining how politicians viewed a chief executive. This responsiveness costs time and money. However, the problem was not the time taken to answer questions or letters but the fact that responding to questions and informal inquiries from MPs got ministers involved in agency operations, which distracted from the business of managing the agency. MPs behaved very much as they did before the creation of the agency. They would go to ministers to place their requests and to make known their views, knowing that the minister would interfere if necessary in any aspect of the agency's business. One HA official, in comparing the situation of the Prison Service Agency with that of the HA, stated, "the reason Howard [Michael Howard, former home secretary] got involved is because it suddenly got high political profile, and he interfered. This is happening in the HA, far more often and on a more day to day basis, because they [ministers] could not sit back and let the Agency get on with things, because the world out there, in the form of MPs, wanted the programme changed to suit them and ministers responded to that . . . and that is where the Agency has not in my view operated successfully." This intervention blurs the lines of responsibility. It restricts the agency's managerial freedom and undermines the very justification for creating the agency in the first place.

Select Committees

The Transport Committee did not appear to use the information provided in the Department of Transports agencies' annual reports. Over the period from 1994 to 1997, the committee had only one session to examine the annual performance of the Drivers and Vehicles Licensing Agency. The committee did not examine the overall performance of the HA or its annual reports. A great deal of the Transport Committee's work prior to 1997 concentrated on railway policy. This reflected members' interests, which tended to be in areas of policy and policy changes. One staff member of the Transport Committee explained: "it is difficult to get members enthusiastic about having a session or two on the performance of an agency; the Committee is quite reluctant sometimes to look in detail at how agencies work." As well as not having the interest, the Transport Committee did not have the resources to investigate the performance of all the agencies under its remit. The committee had at most a staff of four or five special advisers to assist them. However, the chief executive of the HA has appeared with the permanent secretary before the Transport Committee in relation to issues other than the agency's business plans.

The other means by which the government claims that accountability has been improved is by the provision of agencies' business plans and annual reports. Giddings claims that these plans provide the opportunity for greater accountability to Parliament (HC 313-I 1996, para. 105). The existence of this information is not sufficient for accountability to be improved. The information must accurately reflect agencies' performance. The HA targets do not provide an accurate picture of its performance. All the agency's officials interviewed agreed that most of the performance measures did not demonstrate what it actually contributed toward achieving its objectives. A large number of its targets are set in milestone measures, which merely record the completion of certain actions. There are no real outcome measures and only minimal output measures. It remains difficult to measure what the agency does. In this the HA is not unusual. Talbot argues that the information provided in the majority of agencies' annual reports is completely inadequate to be used to judge agency performance by Parliament (HC 313-I 1996, para. 106).

Individual MPs, through parliamentary questions, have demonstrated only limited interest in the HA's annual reports and in its achievement of performance targets. Neither the Public Accounts Committee (PAC) nor the Transport Committee had an inquiry into the overall performance of the HA or examined its business plans or annual reports. The PAC inquiries have traditionally been based on National Audit Office reports and this continues to be the case. These reports tend to relate to broader issues rather than the specific performance of an agency. Examining these broader issues such as road maintenance tends to involve both the department and the agency; it is not clear that an accurate division can be drawn between their areas of responsibility.

This lack of interest in agencies' performance is not unusual. Despite the requests of the Liaison Committee (HC 323-I 1997), MPs do not appear to be interested in holding inquiries to examine agencies' performance, the exception being when an agency comes to the public's attention because of serious failings. The existence of agencies' annual reports and business plans has not altered the way select committees operate, what issues they investigate, or how they use information. No committee routinely examines the annual reports or business plans of agencies. Even if committees did examine these reports, they do not have the power to reward or punish chief executives or the agencies.

The government has attempted to squeeze the agency structure into an existing institutional framework. Next Steps Agencies establish accountability systems, which concentrate on holding civil servants to account for achieving performance targets. But the traditional accountability mechanisms—parliamentary questions and the principle of ministerial responsibility—emphasize responsiveness to politicians and continue to place demands on ministers and agencies. Politically sensitive agencies face a vicious cycle. MPs have a political interest in the issues they deal with; they want to ensure both responsiveness and clear lines of responsibility. MPs' demands for responsiveness result in ministers' intervening in agency operations and a blurring of the very lines of responsibility the agency concept seeks to clarify.

Conclusion

The institutional and constitutional structure in the United States and the traditional accountability structure hinder the introduction of the reforms and their ability to enhance accountability to the executive and the legislature. NPR and GPRA have become part of the partisan political battle between the Republicans and the Democrats. This has resulted in many of the NPR initiatives' not being passed. The constitutional and institutional structure in the United Kingdom facilitated the introduction of the reforms and the enhancement of accountability to the executive. However, for the HA, a politically sensitive agency, the reforms are more rhetoric than reality.

The traditional accountability mechanisms through the principle of ministerial responsibility limit the ability of the reforms to enhance accountability to Parliament. Neither NPR nor GPRA have enhanced accountability to Congress to date. Although the U.S. Congress will receive more information through the GPRA, initial indications are that appropriators will not use this performance information to make budget decisions. In the UK, Parliament receives more information from Next Steps Agencies, but MPs are not interested in using it. Even if they did, Parliament does not have the ability to employ this information to hold civil servants to account.

However, some of the failure to enhance accountability must remain with the reforms themselves. The reforms try to introduce a concept of accountability that emphasizes performance measures and efficiency and de-emphasizes politics in what is, in essence, a very political environment. Accountability is about politics, and the process of accountability is itself political and by no means neutral or transparent.

While there are benefits to a system where decisions are made on the basis of so-called objective performance criteria, the process of achieving such a system requires the political actors to come out of their partisan boxes to take a wider view of what would benefit government as a whole. In the United States, institutional actors tend to view the government from their narrow institutional perspectives.

Real changes in accountability will require changes in the behavior of politicians. In both countries, the incentives in the legislatures encourage opposition politicians to emphasize the failures in administration and to highlight the cases of fraud and abuse in order to embarrass the executive and to score political points. The incentives are for the executive to hide administrative mistakes or to exaggerate administrative successes and to try to control politically sensitive agencies in order to minimize potential embarrassments. These structures are not conducive to systems of performance-based accountability that aim to delegate control to civil servants, and emphasize efficiency above political concerns and institutional structures. Performance measures can at the most be used to inform decisions in nonpolitical areas. It is more likely that rather than being objective standards of performance they could become another tool in the political game of point scoring between the legislature and the executive. While the incentive structure for politicians remains unchanged, accountability remains political.

Note

The views expressed in this chapter are those of the author only and do not represent the opinions of the Organization for Economic Cooperation and Development (OECD).

References

Barker, A. 1998. "Political Responsibility for UK Prison Security—Ministers Escape Again." *Public Administration* 76(1): 1–23.

Deleon, Linda. 1998. "Accountability in a 'Reinvented' Government." *Public Administration* 76(3): 539–58.

Efficiency Unit. 1988. *Improving Management in Government: The Next Steps*. London: HMSO.

Gore, Al. 1994. *Creating a Government that Works Better and Costs Less: Report of the National Performance Review—Status Report*. Washington, DC: U.S. Government Printing Office.

General Accounting Office (GAO). 1997a. *The Government Performance and Results Act 1997 Government Implementation Will Be Uneven*. Washington, DC: GAO.

———. 1997b. *Transportation Infrastructure: Review of Project Selection Process for Five FHWA Discretionary Programs*. Washington, DC: GAO.

———. 2000. *Managing for Results: Federal Managers' Views Show Need for Ensuring Top Leadership Skills*. Washington, DC: GAO.

———. 2001. *Managing for Results: Federal Managers' Views on Key Management Issues Vary Widely across Agencies*. Washington, DC: GAO.

HC 323-I. 1997. *The Work of Select Committees. First Report from the Liaison Committee*. London: HMSO.

HC 313-I. 1996. *Ministerial Responsibility and Accountability. Second Report of the Public Service Committee*. London: HMSO.

Hogwood, Brian, David Judge, and Murray McVicar. 1998. "Agencies and Accountability." Paper presented at Whitehall Programme Conference, Birmingham.

Hood, C. 2001. "Public Service Managerialism: 'Onwards and Upwards,' or 'Trobriand Cricket' Again?" *The Political Quarterly* 72(3): 300–309.

Kettl, Donald. 1998. *Reinventing Government: A Five Year Report Card*. Washington, DC: Brookings Institution.

Massey, Andrew. 1995. *After Next Steps: The Massey Report*. London: Office of Public Service and Science.

Moe, Ronald. 1994. "The Reinventing Government Exercise: Misinterpreting the Problem, Misjudging the Consequences." *Public Administrative Review* 54(2): 111–22.

Radin, Beryl. 2000. "The Government Performance and Results Act and the Tradition of Federal Management Reform: Square Pegs in Round Holes?" *Journal of Public Administration Research and Theory* 10(1): 111–35.

Part 4

Tools for Performance Management and Budgeting

16

Results-Based Budgeting

HARRY HATRY

"Look at life through the windshield, not the rearview mirror."

(Hatry 2006, 229)

Budgeting is the annual (sometimes biennial) process by which organizations estimate their resource needs and allocations for the future. This chapter focuses on how performance measurement information, particularly outcome data, can be used to assist budget formulation and review. For many governments, making the budget process more results based has been the primary motivation for legislating performance measurement. A budget process should encourage, if not demand, a performance orientation.

Results-Based Budgeting: Widely Acclaimed, But Is Anyone Doing It?

Results-based budgeting, frequently called performance-based budgeting, gives outcomes central attention in the budget process. It emphasizes the importance of outcome data in both formulating and justifying proposed budgets. Much lip service has been paid to the topic. Unfortunately, it is not clear how much real attention has been devoted to the actual use of outcome information in budgeting. Suggestions in this chapter identify procedures for incorporating outcomes into a budget process. Agencies will need to refine the process.

Results-oriented performance measurement provides information to formulate, and subsequently justify, a budget. The information helps locate problems and successes that may need more or fewer resources. *The key element of results-based budgeting is that it attempts to consider, if only roughly, the future values of performance indicators—the amount of outcomes expected from proposed resources—and projected outputs.*

Agencies preparing performance budgets project values for each performance indicator for the forthcoming year(s). Projections of outputs and outcomes are intended to reflect the estimated consequences of resources budgeted. *Data from an agency's performance measurement system should provide basic information for developing budget proposals and subsequently help justify the budget proposals that have already been developed.* This information has even greater weight if linked to strategic plans.

293

By focusing systematically on the results sought, results-based budgeting should better enable decision-makers to achieve the following:

- *Identify poorly performing programs,* thereby signaling the need to make changes and allocate less or more funds. (Other information is needed to determine which changes to make.)
- *Identify programs that are performing well* and presumably need no significant changes. (Even here, other information is needed to determine what, if any, changes may be desirable.)
- *Assess new programs* for what they are expected to accomplish, not just their costs or general statements of expected value. Are new programs worth expected costs?
- *Compare different proposed options* on their expected outcomes and costs.
- *Help identify agency activities that have similar outcome indicators* and, thus, are candidates for coordination and perhaps revised funding needs.
- *Justify budget choices more effectively* to agency and elected officials—and the public.
- *Provide the basis for greater agency accountability,* if reasonable performance targets are set for the budget year and achieved values are subsequently compared to targets.

Results-based budgeting supports an agency focus on outcomes, for example:

> The Massachusetts Department of Environmental Protection sought to obtain funding from the state legislature to line unlined landfills. It justified the expenditure by reporting the product of the expenditure as *the number of acres expected to be lined.* This did not move the legislature, which turned down the request. The department then switched to a more outcome-based approach and justified the request in terms of *gallons of leachate prevented.* Legislators asked for a definition of *leachate.* When they found that it referred to potential pollutants leaked into the groundwater and water supply, they approved the funding request.[1]

The U.S. Office of Management and Budget (OMB) has instituted probably the most extensive use of outcome information as part of its Program Assessment Rating Tool (PART) process (PART is extensively analyzed in chapters 2 to 6 of this volume). OMB reviews each major federal program on a number of performance factors, including results achieved. OMB has emphasized that ratings are not the only factor in decisions and that low (or high) scores do not necessarily mean decreased (or increased) funding. Nevertheless, ratings appear to have affected, or at least supported, some funding decisions.

In a performance-based budgeting system, agencies select targets (make projections) for the budget year for each output, outcome, and efficiency indicator, as well as for expenditures.[2]

A key problem for results-based budgeting, especially at the state and federal levels, is to persuade legislators and legislative staffs to switch from primary dependence on line-item budgeting to an outcomes focus. At the very least, legislators and their staffs need to address outcomes during appropriation hearings. The executive branch is responsible for providing meaningful, reliable, important outcome information to its legislators—in a user-friendly format. When some state governments initiated their results-based budgeting efforts, they loaded legislators with large numbers of indicators and data—sometimes including outputs and outcomes mixed in together—presented unattractively, thus discouraging their use.

Key Issues in Results-Based Budgeting

1. Need to Increase Focus on Outcomes, Not Only Inputs and Outputs

Using outcome information for budgeting seems quite sensible on the surface, but in fact, its use in budgeting for agency operations is controversial. It has been, for example, the major subject of debates comparing the New Zealand to the Australian and U.S. approaches to budgeting at the federal level (see Curristine, chapter 12 of this volume, for a discussion of Organization for Economic Cooperation and Development approaches). New Zealand's approach had been to hold its operating departments responsible for outputs but not outcomes—and to use performance agreements with department heads to hold them accountable for outputs. New Zealand's rationale was that agencies control outputs, but too many other factors beyond the control of the operating departments affect outcomes. Only ministers were held responsible for outcomes. New Zealand has recently changed back to including outcomes in department responsibilities.

The counterargument to the view that agencies should be held responsible only for producing outputs is that outcomes are the fundamental reasons for establishing an agency in the first place. The activities of operating agencies clearly contribute to program outcomes, even if no single group of people, whether operating personnel or the policymakers themselves, fully controls results. Take as an example income maintenance and public assistance programs. Primarily policy issues are who is eligible for assistance and what level of payments is to be provided. These decisions are made by the legislature and the upper echelon of the executive branch of government. However, if the policy is not implemented well—if program personnel do not execute the policy properly and get the correct checks to the right people quickly—the desired outcomes will be compromised, and program personnel can be at least partly responsible for the failure.

Encouraging agency personnel to work to improve service outcomes seems a much better way to go. Many, if not most, outcomes are produced by many agencies and sectors of the economy, and responsibility is thus inherently shared. This is the implicit philosophy of the Australian and U.S. governments. Agencies can rate the extent of their influence over individual performance indicators in their performance reports. This alerts users to the inherent limitations of outcome information while retaining a degree of responsibility for each agency.

The controversy over output versus outcome responsibilities has been less an issue at lower levels of government—especially at the local level (see chapters 7 to 11 on state and local issues).

2. Limitations in the Usefulness of Performance Information for Results-Based Budgeting

Performance measurement looks *backward.* It attempts to provide the best possible data on what happened in the past. Past outcome data provide important information for projections, *but estimating future outcomes differs radically from assessing past performance.* Past trends are only one among many influences on future outcomes. The future effects of those other influences are inevitably a matter of uncertainty, particularly in cases where little is known about the *quantitative* relationship between inputs and outcomes. For uncertain outcome forecasts, analysts might provide a range of values. This range is likely to be more reaiistic and informative.

3. Time Frame to Be Covered by Results-Based Budgeting

Budgets typically only present data for the current budget year(s). Some central governments, such as those of the United States and Australia, now also include out-year funding estimates (perhaps for three additional years) but not outcome projections, except in separate long-run strategic plans. Including out-year forecasts for outcomes can be important, particularly in the case of federal and state programs, for three reasons:

- It reduces the temptation for agencies and their programs to focus all their funding decisions on the short term.
- For some programs, achievement of the hoped-for outcomes will require funds not only from the current year's budget but from future budgets as well.
- When important outcomes will not occur until after the proposed-budget period, the outcome targets for the budget year will not reflect those effects.

Therefore, budget proposals, especially those of higher levels of government, should include out-year estimates for some outcomes, regardless of whether this information is included in the final appropriation document. For many programs, organizations will be able to better allocate resources when they explicitly consider expected costs and outcomes for out-years. For example, results of funding a new federal or state program to reduce alcohol abuse might not be apparent for two or more years.

Even for intermediate outcome indicators, measurable effects may not be expected until after the budget year. Another example: Road construction can reduce accidents and congestion over several years. Should not estimates of the magnitude of these future improvements be included in the budget justification?

A partial solution is to build into the budget process any important expected outcomes because of the proposed new funding. Programs would be asked to estimate the values for each outcome indicator for each out-year the proposed budget funding is expected to significantly affect. Requiring outcome projections in the budget development process is likely to encourage agencies to consider multiyear effects.

For some programs, this forecasting can be done readily. For example, a federal program to help residential housing might request funds for rehabilitating the homes of a certain number of families. The program can probably predict the years in which those rehabs will occur and the number of families occupying the housing units. A program that provides drug treatment funding will find it more difficult to estimate the number of clients who will become drug free and in which years. Performance measurement data on past success rates will help in preparing or reviewing budgets to estimate outcomes.

A less demanding option is to ask for estimated future outcomes without requiring that they be distributed by year.

The need to consider future outcomes of the current year's budget is less frequent for local than for federal and state programs. But even at the local level, some programs, such as school and health programs, will have long-term outcome goals. Most governments have not addressed the problem of long-term outcomes. A partial exception is that some state governments separate expansion requests (including new programs) from requests for continuation of programs. For expansion requests, these require out-year projections of future outcomes.

4. Whether Proposed Inputs Can Be Linked to Outputs and Outcomes

In analyzing performance information for budgeting, a critical step is to link information on proposed costs to the projected amount of output and outcomes. Results-based budgeting and similar resource allocation efforts (including strategic planning) enter into this new dimension—*estimating the link between inputs and expected future results.* Such estimates can be subject to considerable uncertainty.

Part of the uncertainty relates to lack of good historical cost, output, and (particularly) outcome information. This problem is potentially curable. More difficult is estimating *future* costs. Even more difficult is estimating the amount of expenditures needed to increase outcomes, especially end outcomes, by specific amounts. Typically, programs do not know with any certainty how much more (or less) funding or staffing is needed to increase (or reduce) an end outcome by a certain amount. As programs gain experience with their outcome data, they should be able to better estimate this relationship, although it will never be as predictable as the relationship between funding or personnel and output indicators.

Projecting accurately becomes increasingly difficult and uncertain as programs move from linking inputs to outputs, to linking inputs to intermediate outcomes, and, finally, to linking inputs or outputs to end outcomes. The following sections discuss links between inputs, outputs, intermediate outcomes, and end outcomes. Little research has examined these latter relationships.

Linking Inputs to Outputs

The amount of output expected in the budget year can be used to estimate the associated costs and personnel requirements or vice versa. If the amounts of dollars and personnel are the starting point for the budget, the amount of output achievable can be estimated. Many, if not most, programs can estimate somewhat accurately how much workload they are likely to have, and thus the amount of output they can accomplish, given particular amounts of staff and funds. Programs will likely have reasonably accurate counts of past outputs and the direct costs of employee time. If they do not currently record such information, they can obtain it.

If funding needs are developed from estimates of the workload, estimates of future expenditures of employee time and money will be affected by the program's ability to estimate accurately the magnitude and character of the budget year work-load and effects of any new service procedures or technology. For example, school systems try to estimate the next year's school population in order to decide about school buildings, classrooms, teachers, and purchases of books and other teaching materials. Inaccurate projections have been known to embarrass school officials.

Performance measurement information from earlier years normally provides the basis for projecting the relationship between inputs and outputs for the current budget year. However, if the *complexity of the workload* during the forthcoming budget year is likely to differ substantially from that in previous years, this change needs to be considered when developing the budget. For example, the Internal Revenue Service can tabulate the number and complexity of tax returns that come in each year. However, many factors—such as revisions to the tax code—can alter the future mix of tax-return difficulty and thus the amount of time required to review and process returns.

External factors can also affect future workload. For example, at the state and local levels, weather conditions, such as freeze-thaw conditions, can have sub-stantial effects on costs, outputs, and outcomes. Agencies can obtain projections of these for the budget year, affecting such performance indicators as estimates of future roadwork and costs, and accident and injury rates. Similarly, the number and characteristics of incoming clients, such as their need for employment, health, and social service programs, can be highly unpredictable because they are affected by many economic and social factors—and projections based on past data are by no means certain. For some programs, agencies can use reasonably reliable estimates of their client populations, but these are also subject to uncertainties, such as in-creased immigration from countries in crisis.

Linking Inputs to Intermediate Outcomes

Precise relationships between past input data and past intermediate outcome data can be developed for some outcome indicators. Even so, past relationships between the intermediate outcomes and inputs will usually provide only rough indications of what will happen in the budget year. For example, federal agencies such as the departments of Education, Housing and Urban Development, Health and Human Services, and Labor as well as the Environmental Protection Agency provide much of their assistance to state and local agencies rather than to the ultimate customers. If these state and local agencies undertake promising steps that the federal department has encouraged, the steps can be considered intermediate outcomes for that department. Data on the past relationship between the amounts of federal funds and assistance, on the one hand, and the extent to which the state and local governments undertook promising initiatives, on the other, are likely to be useful. But the past relationship provides only a rough estimate of what state and local agencies will do in the budget year.

Some intermediate outcomes can be estimated relatively accurately. For example, agencies can make fairly accurate estimates of such intermediate outcomes as future response times, given particular amounts of staff and dollar resources.[3] Even here, however, a number of outside factors over which the program has little control can intervene. For example, an unexpectedly large number of requests for service or changes in the proportion of complex requests can have major effects on response times.

Here are some examples of difficult-to-predict intermediate outcomes:

- Number of businesses (or households) that alter their handling of waste to be more environmentally prudent after receiving assistance from state or local programs.
- Number and percentage of parents who take special parenting classes and then alter their behavior in ways that encourage their children's learning in school.
- Customer satisfaction.

All these outcomes are driven not only by agency efforts to seek certain customer behaviors and perceptions but also by many aspects of the behavior and circumstances of the customers themselves, as well as outside factors.

The bottom line is that agencies should expect historical data on costs and intermediate outcomes to be useful in preparing cost and intermediate outcome information for budgets. In many cases, however, agencies will be able to make only rough projections about the future relationship between costs and intermediate outcomes.

Linking Inputs to Outcomes

As a rule, agencies should not expect to have solid, known relationships between inputs and end outcomes, no matter how good the historical data are. (In more economic terms, little information is available about the production function that relates the inputs to the end outcomes.) Nevertheless, these relationships are important and need to be considered, *at least qualitatively,* in any budget process.

Some end outcomes are easier to relate to inputs than others. For example, the number and percent of a state or local jurisdiction's roads that are in satisfactory condition can be considered an end outcome indicator for road maintenance services. These numbers relate closely to the funds that the agency applies to road maintenance and repair. Past data on this relationship can be used to estimate the expenditures needed in order to achieve a certain value for this outcome indicator (or, conversely, to estimate the percent of road miles in satisfactory condition given a particular funding level). In contrast, how much a client's condition is improved by expenditures of particular amounts of federal, state, local, or private funds to reduce substance abuse or to enhance elementary education is considerably more difficult to estimate.

Projecting how well budgeted resources will achieve *prevention* (whether of crime, disease, family problems, or so on) is extremely difficult. At best, the historical data will provide very rough clues about the relationship between resources and prevention. In-depth studies can provide evidence, but decision-makers may need to rely more heavily on qualitative information and subjective judgments on the prevention outcomes expected from a particular level of budgeted resources.

In general, the more direct a program's influence over an outcome, the greater the program's ability to develop numerical relationships between inputs and the outcome. Local governments and private agencies generally have more direct influence on end outcomes than state or federal agencies do; therefore, the relationships between their inputs and outcomes (both intermediate and end) are likely to be clearer. Nevertheless, for many end outcome indicators, the relationship will be imprecise. How many more resources would be needed to increase the percentage of customers satisfied with their recreation experiences by 5 percent (such as from 65 percent to 70 percent)? The answers to questions like this usually can be estimated only very roughly, at best.

If identifying the quantitative (or even qualitative) relationships between size and type of input, type of intervention, and amount of outcomes achieved is likely to be crucial to future major budget decisions about an existing program, agencies should seek an in-depth program evaluation.

Agencies can track changes in resources to assess the differences on outcomes and then use that information to help make future budget estimates. Agencies might also be able to intentionally alter the amount of input to certain activities to see how more or fewer resources affect outcomes—and then use the information for future estimates.

Linking Outputs to Outcomes

Outcomes presumably flow from outputs. For example, the number of calls answered is an output for a service—whether these calls relate to police, fire, sewage backups, travel information, or any other service request. This output leads to outcomes, such as what resulted and whether the requests were fulfilled to the customers' satisfaction. Some outcome indicators explicitly relate outputs to outcomes, such as "the percent of those to whom services were provided (an output) who had successful outcomes."

Staff preparing or reviewing budget proposals should examine the amount of output expected in the budget year and assess what outcomes can be expected from that number—and when. If x customers are expected to be served during the budget year (an output), how many customers (and what percent) can be expected to be helped to achieve the desired outcomes that year and in future years (an outcome)? For example, How many persons are expected to find employment after receiving training services, and when? And, what percentage of babies born to low-income women who received appropriate prenatal care will be healthy?

Those preparing budget requests and those subsequently examining them should *ascertain that outcome numbers make sense relative to the amount of output*. For services that have lengthy lag times between outputs and outcomes, outcome numbers for the budget year need to be compared to output numbers *in the relevant previous years*.

Linking Intermediate Outcomes to End Outcomes

It is likely to be difficult to provide quantitative relationships between intermediate and end outcomes, but it is often easier than directly estimating the relationships between input and end outcomes. For example, a state agency might provide funds or technical assistance to local agencies to undertake an environmental protection regulation designed to lead to cleaner air. The relationship between the local agency's successfully getting businesses to adapt better practices for handling hazardous wastes (an intermediate outcome for both the state and local agencies) and the extent to which cleaner air results (an end outcome for both agencies) is uncertain. Some relationships are clearer, such as the extent to which increased percentages of children vaccinated against a disease can be expected to lead to reduced incidence of the disease among the vaccinated population.

How to Make These Links?

For most programs, knowledge about most of the above links is lacking. Historical data from the performance measurement process, even if they have been implemented for only one or two years, can provide clues. But there will almost always be uncertainty about projections of outcomes, especially end outcomes, for given budget levels. A key is to make *plausible* connections between the amount of budgeted funds and the outcomes projected. These connections can be based on past performance and modified by information on changes in either internal or external factors expected in the budget year.

5. The Role of Efficiency Indicators

Efficiency is an important consideration in the budget process. As noted, efficiency is measured as the *ratio of inputs to outputs*. The new indicator added in results-based budgeting is *ratios of inputs to outcomes*. An example of this is "cost per person served *whose condition improved significantly after receiving the service.*" The more traditional output-based efficiency indicator is "cost per person served."

When reasonably solid numerical relationships exist between outputs or outcomes and the associated inputs, past data can be used to develop historical unit-cost figures, such as the "cost per lane-mile of road maintained" or the "cost per lane-mile rated as in good condition." These figures can then be used to make estimates for the budget year. Likely future factors need to be factored in. For example, road maintenance budget estimates should consider any planned price changes, any new technologies that might be used and their cost, and any indications that repairs will be more extensive or more difficult than in past years.

Some outcomes, such as road condition, can reasonably be numerically related to outputs, such as the number of lane-miles expected to be repaired during the budget year for a given dollar allocation. Budget preparers and reviewers can then examine various levels of the number of lane-miles to be repaired for various levels of expenditures and estimate the number of lane-miles that will be in satisfactory condition for each expenditure option. *These estimates will inform decision-makers of the trade-offs between costs and outcomes, so they can select their preferred combination.*

In police investigative work, "number of cases cleared per police dollar or per investigation hour" is an outcome-based efficiency indicator. Past data on clearances can be used to make estimates for the forthcoming budget. However, the number and percent of crimes cleared in the budget year will also depend significantly on the number of crimes reported (many more crimes may mean investigators have less time to spend on individual cases), types of crimes (for example, burglaries have substantially lower clearance rates than robberies), and amount of evidence available at the scene. Factors largely outside police department control (such as case difficulty) as well as internal factors (such as the amount of investigator turnover and the quality and quantity of investigative effort) can affect clearance rates. Trends in such factors should be considered when projecting clearance rates from past efficiency data.

Use of unit costs in which units are *outputs* is common in budgeting. However, use of unit costs in which units are *outcomes* is rare. One reason for this is that outcome data have not often been part of the budget preparation process. In the future, the primary reason for limited use of costs per unit of outcome will be not lack of outcome data but rather lack of solid numerical relationships between inputs and outcomes.

6. Setting Performance Targets in Budgets

The projected values for individual outcome indicators are important numbers in results-based budget submissions. In view of the considerable uncertainty surrounding future conditions and links between agency resources and indicator values, how should agencies develop these targets? Two special target-setting options are available to programs that are highly uncertain about the future values of one or more outcome indicators: variable targets and target ranges.

The *variable target option* applies to outcome indicators whose values are believed to be highly dependent on a characteristic of the incoming workload *and* where major uncertainty exists about that characteristic. In this procedure, the expected relationship between the characteristic and outcome is identified first. The final outcome target is determined *after the fact,* depending on the workload characteristics that occurred in the budget year. For example, if an outcome is expected to be highly sensitive to the mix of workload (e.g., customers) coming in, and the mix for the budget year is subject to considerable uncertainty, the program can set targets for *each category* of workload without making assumptions about the workload mix. The *aggregate target* is determined after the budget year closes and the mix is known.

For the indicator "percent of people who leave welfare for work," the program might set separate targets for groups defined by their amount of formal education. Suppose the program estimated that 75 percent of people coming in with at least a high school diploma would find jobs and get off welfare in the budget year, but only 30 percent of those with less than a high school education would do so. These targets would be presented in the budget. The aggregate percent, which might also be included, would be based on the program's estimated mix of clients.

At the end of the year, the aggregate target for the year would be calculated for the actual education mix and compared to the aggregate percent. If 420 people who had not completed high school and 180 people who had completed high school entered the program during the year, the aggregate target would be 44 percent—30 percent of 420 (126) plus 75 percent of 180 (135), equaling 261. Dividing 261 by the total number in the program that year (600) yields the aggregate target for the share expected to go off welfare, 44 percent.

The target might also be linked to the national unemployment rate. For example, the program target might be 15 percent of enrollees off welfare if the national unemployment rate turned out to be over 5.4 percent and 25 percent off welfare if the national unemployment rate turned out to be less than 5.0 percent. The program would not know if it had achieved the target until the national figure became available. Another option is to use a formula that relates expected outcome to the value of the external factor—in this example, a formula that relates the expected percentage off welfare to the unemployment rate.

The *target range option* applies to any outcome indicator with highly uncertain future values. A range of values, rather than one number, is given as the target for the indicator. Many programs might benefit from this approach, especially for their end outcomes. Here are some examples of target ranges: customer satisfaction level is expected to be in the range of 80 percent to 87 percent, or percentage of clients who will be off illegal drugs twelve months after program completion is expected to be between 40 percent and 50 percent.

As higher-level administrators and elected officials begin to use targets in budget documents, the temptation to game targets will inevitably grow. Such gaming can occur at any level. Program managers and upper-level officials might set targets so their projected outcomes will look good. (This is an argument for legislators to ask independent audit offices to review and comment on proposed budget targets, especially at the state and federal levels.) Elected officials might manipulate targets for political purposes.

Setting targets that are easy to achieve will be tempting to those whose funding or compensation is based on achieving targets. The opposite—setting very optimistic, if not impossible, targets—is tempting to those seeking support for high budgets.

Gaming may be alleviated by:

- Establishing a multilevel review process in which executive personnel check targets to identify values that appear overly optimistic or overly conservative.
- Examining the past relationships between inputs, outputs, and outcomes to see if the proposed targets are consistent with those relationships.
- Using one of the special target-setting options noted above to avoid a single-number target. These ranges can still be gamed, but the effects of gaming should be reduced.
- Explicitly identifying in performance reports any future outcomes that are particularly difficult to estimate. Budget documents should also identify new outcome indicators, pointing out that setting targets for them is particularly difficult because there is no experience on which to base estimates.
- Asking programs to provide explanations for unusual-looking targets.
- Reducing reliance on major incentives that link funding or salary compensation to target achievement. However, pressure to link compensation to target achievement is likely to increase as agencies switch to outcome-based target-setting procedures. In such cases, an in-depth examination of the reasons for successful or unsuccessful outcomes should be undertaken before funding or salary decisions are made.

In some instances, executives and elected officials will prefer unclear, fuzzy goals. For example, school districts have debated whether they should include precise objectives on student test improvement (such as increasing the overall scores by 5 percent or reducing the difference in performance between the minority and majority student populations by 7 percent during the year). These officials might accept a target range.

Agency staff sometimes are reluctant to provide targets lower than the previous year's targets, even if budget-year resources are lower in real terms (i.e., after allowing for cost increases). They fear this will make them look bad. Even so, it is important that agencies and programs realistically estimate the consequences of reduced resources. Agencies should encourage such reporting if it can be justified. Not being able to do everything they did in the previous year is not a basis for applying blame to programs if resources are cut. Upper management may believe that productivity improvements can make up for the reduced resources (and this may be true—up to a point). If political pressure requires that a program establish published targets that are higher than the program believes are achievable, the distinction should at least be made clear internally.

Setting performance targets is an excellent management tool for agencies, particularly if the targets are provided and progress is examined periodically during the year, such as monthly or quarterly. Even if an agency does not use outcome targets in its budget process, the agency can choose to retain an internal outcome-targeting process.

7. Use of Explanatory Information

Agency programs should provide explanatory information along with their past performance measurement data when developing and submitting budget requests. Staff preparing budgets should examine such information for insights into why the program performed well or poorly and for any suggestions about what is needed to improve it. This information can also identify program changes likely to affect cost and outcome estimates.

As already noted, the results of any relevant program evaluations should be part of budget preparation and review. Findings on outcomes and the extent to which the program has been instrumental in producing the outcomes are important for judging the value of the current program. Persons who review the program's proposed budget can use later performance data to assess whether the proposed budget reflects the changes suggested by the evaluation. *Program evaluation findings should typically take precedence over findings from the agency's performance measurement system.* Preferably, an agency would sponsor evaluations for each of its major programs, say, once every few years. New programs might be required to provide an evaluation strategy. Unfortunately, in-depth evaluations are expensive and time consuming. Agencies and programs with limited resources might schedule periodic, but less comprehensive, reviews of each program to learn more about how well they are working and why.

For target values that deviate substantially from past results, agency programs should be encouraged to provide explanations for those targets, especially on key outcome indicators. Such information should identify the basic assumptions used to develop the outcome projections and any important external factors expected to make the outcome value deviate from past performance levels.

Explanatory information on past performance, including any available findings from recent program evaluations, can help identify the reasons for success or lack of it—that is, program strengths and weaknesses. Budget preparers and reviewers can then assess the extent to which steps have been taken, or are needed, to correct problems.

8. Strength of Program Influence over Future Outcomes

Agency managers are apprehensive about including outcome indicators as a part of performance measurements. Managers often have only partial control over outcomes, especially end outcomes. To alleviate this concern in budget preparation, and to give budget reviewers a better perspective on the projected outcome data, agencies *should consider categorizing each outcome indicator by the extent of the agency's influence over it.* This will identify the extent to which the agency can affect each indicator relative to outside factors likely to affect the program's outcomes. Note, however, that *agencies and their programs may have more influence than they think.* In many instances, innovative approaches to their missions might influence outcomes in meaningful ways, including making recommendations for legislative changes.

Indicators can be slotted into a small number of broad categories, such as considerable influence, some influence, or little influence. If the program has no influence over the value of a performance indicator, then it should not be considered a performance indicator. For budget examination purposes, however, programs should be asked to identify the reasons they think they have no influence. *Lack of influence may indicate that the program is not doing the right things, perhaps requiring major program changes.*

9. Using Performance Information in Formulating and Examining Budget Requests

The budget preparation and review process is intended to help ensure that needed resources are budgeted for the most cost-effective purpose. Data on past inputs, outputs, outcomes, and efficiency, as well as explanatory information, allow analysts to formulate and examine program budget proposals much more comprehensively and meaningfully than in the past. Outcome information, even if crude and partial, enables analysts to consider both resource needs and likely outcomes from those resources—and under what conditions results have been good or bad. This adds more substance to a budget process.

10. Applying Results-Based Budgeting to Internal Support Services

All governments and private agencies support a variety of administrative functions, such as building maintenance, facilities maintenance, information technology, human resources, risk management, purchasing, and accounting. The link between products of such activities and public service outcomes is distant and difficult or impossible to determine, even roughly. Costs of support services, however, need to be considered when analyzing the total costs of a program and comparing its costs to its benefits.

These activities are nonetheless important in providing needed support for operating programs. Good management requires that administrative services track their own internal intermediate outcomes (such as the quality of their services to other agency offices). Agency records, customer surveys, and trained observer ratings can be used to obtain data on service quality.

11. Using Results-Based Budgeting for Capital Budgeting

Many state and local governments prepare separate capital budgets, sometimes in the form of multiyear capital improvement programs. Capital budgets typically list proposed projects and the estimated capital funds required for each project in the budget year. Multiyear plans usually contain such information for each out-year. These plans may include general statements about the purposes of the expenditures, *but they seldom contain information about their expected effects on outcomes.*

Results-based budgeting should apply to capital budgets. The agency should gain experience with results-based budgeting, then call for the explicit estimation of effects of major capital expenditures on outcomes. For example, planned capital expenditures for road rehabilitation might be justified in terms of expected effects on future road conditions, such as added rideability and safety, compared with conditions that would occur without the capital expenditures. Similarly, funds for water and sewer purposes should be related to projected improvements in water quality and health protection. For capital projects that benefit segments of the community, estimates should be provided on which, and how many, citizens are expected to benefit.

Many agencies are also faced periodically with the need to invest in information technology. These investments should be assessed not only on their costs but also on their expected benefits. For example, how does the proposed technology reduce response times to customers or change the accuracy of service delivery?

Some capital expenditures, such as those for administrative services, do not link well with end outcomes. New construction of office buildings is a good example. For this construction, a performance measurement system might track such internal outcomes as work completed on time, work completed within budget, ratings of the quality of facilities built, and any added efficiencies or improved working conditions for employees.

12. "Budgeting by Objectives" and "Budgeting for Outcomes"

Conceptually, it makes sense for a department to submit budgets with proposed funding grouped by major objectives—budgeting by objectives.[4] For example, child abuse prevention, alcohol abuse reduction, unemployment assistance, and traffic accident reduction might be major objectives. All activities related to the particular objective would be included, regardless of which program or agency is involved.

The major question that confronts organizations that try this approach is how to sort out objectives and programs. Most programs have multiple objectives, and their personnel and other resources simultaneously affect more than one objective. The crosswalk between objectives and programs or agencies can be cumbersome. If some activities simultaneously affect more than one objective, how should costs be split between them, or should they be split at all? For example, transportation programs can influence multiple objectives across a wide range of policies: making transportation quick and convenient, enhancing health and safety, and protecting the environment.

A recent variation of budgeting by objectives is "budgeting for outcomes." Here, service organizations estimate how much outcome they will provide and at what cost. The focus is not on programs but on the results the organization says it will achieve. Budgeting for outcomes encourages innovation in the way outcomes will be produced, and can even encourage providers outside the government to "bid." The government might also preselect the major outcomes it wants and establish a total expenditure level for each outcome.[5] The State of Washington has experimented with this approach, but it is too early to assess its long-term success. The approach has some major hurdles, including the need to have good outcome information and be able to judge the claims of bidders. In addition, most government organizations seek many outcomes, and sorting them all out and determining allocations for each outcome (and what to do about outcomes that are not considered "major") present difficulties.

At this point, it is by no means clear whether budgeting by objectives or budgeting for outcomes can be made practical. *Providing crosswalks linking activities to each outcome, however, does seem a reasonable approach* for modern information technology (as has been done by North Carolina and Oregon and by Multnomah County, Oregon). Programs that contribute to several outcomes can be coded to identify which contribute to what outcomes. Such crosswalks can at least trigger the need for coordination and cooperation among programs, and they will help budget examiners detect the need for across-program budget reviews.

13. Special Analytical Techniques for Projections

Budgeting, like strategic planning (and unlike performance measurement), involves projecting costs and outcomes into the future. Estimating future costs, and especially future outcomes, can be very difficult, as already emphasized. Program analysis (sometimes called cost-effectiveness analysis) and cost-benefit analysis can help agencies select service delivery variations. Findings should help the agency select the service option that should be budgeted, help estimate outcomes, and then justify the budget proposal. These techniques have been around for many years, but their use in budget preparation and review is rare.

Program (Cost-Effectiveness) Analysis

This term applies to special quantitative analyses used to estimate the future costs and effectiveness of alternative ways to deliver a service. While program evaluation is retrospective, program analysis is prospective. The Department of Defense is one of the few agencies in the country that has designated personnel to undertake regular program analysis. Otherwise, systematic program analysis has not taken hold in the public sector or in nongovernmental organizations. The Department of Health, Education, and Welfare (now the Department of Health and Human Services) and the State of Pennsylvania had special offices with such expertise in the 1960s, but later discontinued them.

While some agencies have policy analysis shops, these are qualitative. Program evaluation offices, which examine past performance, may sometimes take on this role, since some of the same technical skills are involved. Information from program evaluations can be valuable when past data can be used to help decide about the future.

For results-based budgeting, program analysis is helpful when an agency proposes to introduce a new service delivery approach or a significant variation of an existing approach. Unless the delivery approach proposed closely resembles an approach for which relevant past data are available, projecting costs and outcomes from past data may not be useful.

Agencies can consider doing pilot tests or experiments, using the performance measurement system for data on the old and the new service approaches, and then using that information as the basis for estimating outcomes and costs. These procedures are worthwhile if the agencies can wait to make their final decision until the test has been completed and the findings have become available. Agencies should use the findings from such analyses and experiments to help formulate and justify budget proposals.

Cost-Benefit Analysis

Cost-benefit analysis goes one step further than program analysis. It provides a *monetary estimate of the value of a program.* (Cost-benefit analysis can also help evaluate the value of a program's past performance.) Its key characteristic is that it translates nonmonetary outcomes into monetary ones. Costs are compared to the estimated dollar benefits to produce cost-benefit ratios and estimated differences in monetary values of costs and benefits. Before the calculations into monetary values can be performed, the basic outcome values, usually measured in nonmonetary units, are needed—that is, program analysis needs to be done first. Cost-benefit analysis adds an additional, difficult, step to the process.

The monetary value of outcomes has to be *imputed* in some way. For example, an estimate that *x* number of traffic accidents could be avoided by a particular activity might be converted into monetary estimates of the costs of those accidents, including damage repair, hospital and other health care, time lost from work, and the economic value of any lives lost. Costs of the activity being considered would then be compared to these dollar valuations and a cost-benefit ratio calculated.

Sound cost-benefit analysis, whether of past program accomplishments or projected program value, can provide major backup information for program budget requests. Such calculations can also appeal to public and private officials, because most outcomes are converted into dollars and summarized in one number (the cost-benefit ratio), which can be interpreted as the program's value. One summary number is much easier for decision-makers to handle. The usual application is to compare options within a single service area, but it could also be used to compare programs across services.

Cost-benefit analysis has its drawbacks. The calculations of monetary value usually require numerous assumptions that can be quite controversial. For example, how should the value of lost work time or of deaths be determined? (The value of lives lost has sometimes been estimated based on the economic potential of human beings at particular ages. This approach sounds reasonable, but giving older people little or no value in the calculations implies that it is all right to "knock off" the elderly.) Another problem is monetary values often accrue to different populations from the populations that pay the costs. For example, revenues for most government expenditures are raised by taxes, but benefits often accrue to particular groups.

If performed and used carefully, cost-benefit calculations can provide insights into the expected value of the proposed budget for a program. However, cost-benefit analysis reports should *always* spell out the value assumptions used so readers can better understand the basis for the findings.

Cost-benefit analysis tends to be time consuming and expensive. As a result, it has been used very selectively. The Army Corps of Engineers has undertaken many such studies when selecting major water and other construction projects. Cost-benefit analysis has also been used, and sometimes mandated, for federal regulatory programs.

14. The Role of Qualitative Outcome Information in Results-Based Budgeting

Not all outcomes can be adequately measured in quantitative terms. An agency's budget process should at least *qualitatively* consider the implications of the budget for desired (and undesired) outcomes. Even if outcomes can only be expressed qualitatively, explicitly including them in the budget, and in the political debate over amounts and allocations, can help improve decisions on expenditures.

Steps for Examining Performance Information in Budget Reviews

Some basic steps for developing and examining budget requests are discussed below. Together, these steps represent a heavy workload for those reviewing or developing budget requests. However, these steps can be used selectively. They are also likely to be appropriate at any time during the year when a program seeks additional resources.

1. Examine the budget submission to ascertain that it provides the latest information and targets on workload, output, intermediate outcomes, and end outcomes—as well as the funds and personnel resources requested. The budget submission should include past data on each indicator, the latest available outcome data for the current budget year, and the targets for the fiscal year(s) for which the budget is being submitted. If an indicator is too new for data or targets to be available, the submission should note this and indicate when data will be available (both actual data and targets). If staff do not believe they can obtain numerical values for important indicators, then it should explain why and provide qualitative information on past and expected future progress.

2. Assess whether the outcome indicators and targets are consistent with the mission of, and strategies proposed by, the program and adequately cover that mission. If the agency's programs do not have explicit mission statements that adequately define their major objectives (such as those included in strategic plans) or descriptions of the strategies the programs propose to use to achieve the objectives, the reviewers will need to ask the program to construct these or construct these themselves—discussing them with program personnel as necessary.

For example, federal, state, or local litigation offices may emphasize deterrence of crime in their formal mission statements. Litigation programs, however, usually have not included indicators that explicitly address deterrence. The outcome indicators tracked will focus on bringing offenders to justice. From the program's viewpoint this focus is reasonable, but reviewers should consider whether it is feasible to track deterrence using counts of non-deterrence as a surrogate (i.e., the amount of reported criminal behavior) or whether they should be content to seek qualitative information. Reviewers might also decide that the litigation program does not in fact have the responsibility or the capacity for estimating prevention. They might determine that the mission statement was overstated and the program's focus on the number of offenders brought to justice is appropriate.

3. If the program is seeking increased resources, assess whether it has provided adequate information on the amount each output and outcome indicator is expected to change over recent levels. Changes might be expressed as a table showing pluses or minuses for each affected indicator. Programs need to make clear what effects their special proposals are expected to have on outputs and outcomes—not merely on funding and personnel resources.

4. Examine the program's projected workload, outputs, intermediate outcomes, and end outcomes, as well as the amount of funds and personnel. Make sure these numbers are consistent with each other (e.g., that the amount of output is consistent with the projected workload). Determine whether the program has included data on the results expected from the outputs it has identified. Output indicators normally should be included in the budget submission for each major category of workload.

Intermediate outcomes should be consistent with outputs and end outcomes consistent with intermediate outcomes. If such information has not been included, the program can be asked to provide the needed data.

Data on outputs and outcomes should be checked for consistency with each other. For example, do the number of successes exceed the number of cases completed during that reporting period? Note, however, that substantial time lags can occur between the time a customer comes in for service and the outcomes. For example, the outcome indicator "percent of cases that were successful" should be derived by dividing the number of cases expected to be successfully completed by the number of cases completed during the year, regardless of the year the case was initiated, not by the number of cases worked on or started during the budget year. Another example: A budget-year estimate for the outcome indicator "percent of child adoption cases in which the child was placed with adoptive parents within twenty-four months of the child's entry into the system" would need to be based on the number of children that came into the child welfare system two years before the budget year. Where appropriate outcome indicators and/or outcome data have not been provided, ask the program to provide them. Two reminders:

- Outcomes can result from activities undertaken before the budget year. Also, some outcomes intended to result from the proposed budget might not occur until after the budget year. The budget submission should identify such situations.
- In the initial years of the performance measurement system, programs may not be able to provide data on some outcome indicators.

5. Compare past data on workload, output, intermediate outcomes, and end outcomes with the proposed budget targets. Identify unusually high or low projected outputs or outcomes. This can be done in at least two ways:

- Compare the latest data on actual performance to those for previous reporting periods and to the proposed budget targets.
- Compare historical data on individual outcome indicators to the past targets set for those indicators *to assess the program's accuracy in setting targets.* In light of this past experience, assess the program's proposed targets. Some agencies may have a pattern of being optimistic about their ability to achieve outcomes; others may have a pattern of overly conservative targets. Budget analysts should take this into account as they interpret target achievement. Ideally, targets should be set at a level that encourages high, but achievable, performance.

Where projected performance values differ considerably from past values, or appear otherwise unusual, seek explanations. Has the program provided any other information that explains this? If not, ask for explanations. For example, if a program has the same targets it had last year, and it fell far short of those targets in the current year, ask what has changed to make the targets more achievable. If the program is requesting a considerable increase in funds without increasing outcome targets over previous years' results, ask why the added funds are needed. If a program projects lower values for outputs or outcomes, find out why. The program might report, for example, that the reason was reduced workload, unusually difficult or complex workload, or reduced efficiency or effectiveness in delivering the service.

6. *Examine the explanatory information, especially for outcome indicators whose past values fell significantly below expectations and for any performance targets that appear unusually high or low.* This step should be given special attention when any of the earlier steps indicate that the performance levels projected need further examination. Explanatory information should be examined before any conclusions are drawn about the performance of the program and its resource implications. Explanations can be substantive or merely rationalizations or excuses. To assess the value of the explanations, analysts may need to follow up to clarify and/or obtain more information.

7. *For programs likely to have delays or backlogs that might complicate program services, be sure the data adequately cover the extent of delays, backlogs, and lack of coverage.* Buildups of such problems can be a justification for added resources. The size of any delays or backlogs, and how these may be growing, can be important customer-focused, quality-of-service performance indicators for social, health, welfare, loan, licensing, and many other programs. For legal prosecutions and court cases, "justice delayed is justice denied."

Conversely, if a program's indicators show no evidence of significant delays, then existing resource levels appear adequate for the future—unless the program provides evidence that a significant buildup of its future workload is likely. Programs, where possible, should categorize incoming caseloads by level of difficulty or complexity. Programs should also project the size of their caseload by difficulty or complexity as a factor in determining their proposed budget. Is there any evidence that the program is now getting or expects to get more complex and/or more difficult cases? Such changes would offer justification for additional resources.

Indicators that programs can be asked to provide include:

- Counts of the number of cases pending and projected at the end of each year (tracked over time, this will indicate buildups).
- Indicators of the time it has taken and is expected to take, given proposed budget resources, to complete various activities.
- Estimates of the number of cases that will have to be turned away (for programs that have the discretion to turn them away).

8. *For regulatory programs, be sure that adequate coverage is provided for compliance outcomes (not merely numbers of inspections).* Examples include environmental regulation programs, work-safety programs, civil rights programs,

and regulatory boards. Analysts should ascertain that the outputs and intermediate and end outcomes of compliance-monitoring activities are identified. For example, does the budget proposal report on expected outputs (such as the number of needed inspections that are expected), and the intervals at which they are projected to be done? Do the indicators provide past data on such outcomes as the number of organizations found in previous years not in compliance and then the number and percent that subsequently were found to have fully corrected the problems? Do the indicators include the incidence of problems that occurred despite the regulation activities? Do the budget-year projections include such estimates for the budget period? Do the monitoring resources proposed in the budget appear too little or too large compared to the expected outcomes?

9. Ascertain that the program has sufficiently considered possible changes in workload that are likely to affect outcomes (such as higher or lower proportions of difficult workload). Programs may not report such breakouts in their budget submissions, but they are often able to supply such information. (Programs should be encouraged, for their own data analyses, to break out their outcome data by various work and customer characteristics, such as type of case, its difficulty, and different locations or facilities.) For example, federal and state correctional facilities will have internal reports on individual facilities and facility categories, such as security level and type of prisoner. Health and human services programs can provide service data on individual facilities or offices and on demographic groupings of clients.

Examine whether the outcomes differ for some service characteristics (such as for some facilities or regions) over others. If so, examine why. This information can be helpful in interpreting a program's projected outcome data. For example, certain locations or cases may be more difficult to handle than others, suggesting that lower-than-desired projected performance is the result of an increase in the proportion of difficult cases and thus providing a supportable case for lower outcomes. Budget reviewers should look for evidence that more cases that are difficult (or easy) are likely to come in during the budget year.

Comparing outcomes among demographic groups is also important in assessing equity and fairness. Are some groups underserved? Should additional resources be applied to those groups? Even though identifying who loses and who gains can be a political hazard, the information is basic to resource allocation. It needs to be addressed.

10. If recent outcomes for a program have been substantially worse than expected, make sure the program has included in its budget proposal the steps it plans to take and the resources it plans to put toward improvement. If the program projects improved performance, are resources and planned steps commensurate? If not, why not? (For example, substantial time may be needed between the time funding is approved, implementation, and consequences of the funded activities for achievement of outcomes.)

11. Examine findings from any program evaluations or other special studies completed during the reporting period. Assess whether these findings have been adequately incorporated into the budget proposals. This includes studies produced by other organizations. Such information may support activities and budgets proposed by the program, or it may contradict the findings produced by the program to support its proposed activities and budget.

12. Determine whether the program has developed and used information on the relationship between resource requirements, outputs, and outcomes (e.g., the added money estimated to increase the number of successfully completed cases by a specified amount). Assess that information for plausibility. Few programs are likely to have undertaken much analysis of this relationship. Programs should be encouraged to do so to help substantiate future budget requests.

Relating expenditures and resources to outcomes (both intermediate and end outcomes) is usually difficult and uncertain. However, to the extent that additional dollars and staff enable the program to take on more work (more customers, more investigations, more road repairs, more inspections, etc.), the program can estimate roughly how much additional work it can handle based on past performance information. For example, a program may be able to estimate the percent of cases or incidents it might not be able to handle (such as identifying illegal immigrants) without the added funding requested.

Many, if not most, programs will be unlikely to have investigated the cost-to-output and cost-to-outcome relationships that underlie their budget requests. However, these relationships are at the heart of resource allocation decisions, implicitly if not explicitly, and the program should be pushed to be as explicit as possible. After all, *the projected targets the program sets each year based on its outcome indicators by definition imply such relationships, however rough the estimates may be.*

A program seeking additional resources will tend to be overly optimistic about the outcomes that will result. Budget analysts should look for supportable estimates of the relationships between resource requirements (dollars and personnel) and at least approximate values for each outcome indicator.

Over the long run, programs should be encouraged to develop information about these relationships. The analysis needed for such studies requires special background, however, which is not likely to be in place in most programs. Analytical staff, whether attached to each program or to a central analysis office, should be helpful.

13. Identify indicators with significantly reduced outputs or outcomes projected for the budget year (compared to recent performance data) and no decrease in funding (adjusted for projected price increases) or staffing. Identify and assess the program's rationale. Reduced funding or staffing projections are obviously plausible rationales for reduced outcome projections, as is a more difficult or complex workload in the new year. If the program has been categorizing its incoming caseload by level of difficulty or complexity, it should be able to provide evidence supporting a reduction. The program might have in its pipeline many difficult cases. For example, litigation or investigation programs may be working on cases that are complex and require additional resources.

Other possible reasons for lower outcome targets include (a) an unexpected jump in workload during the budget year without an accompanying increase in resources, leading to reductions in the percent of cases for which the program can produce successful outcomes; (b) new legislative or agency policies that add complications or restrictions, reducing the probability of successful outcomes in certain categories of cases; and (c) external events that would impair outcomes, such as the expected departure of key industries from a community, affecting local employment and income.

14. Identify outcome indicators with significantly improved outcomes projected by the program for the budget year (compared to recent performance data) and no increase in staffing, funding (adjusted for projected price increases), or output. Identify and assess the program's reasons for these increases. Budget reviewers should ask the program how it expects to achieve the improved performance—to check the plausibility of the higher targets. Such improvements might occur if the program plans to improve the efficiency of its operations. Another reasonable rationale is that the program expects its workload to be easier or less complex. The program may already have in its pipeline cases that it expects to be successful in the budget year.

15. Identify what, if any, significant outcomes from the budgeted funds are expected to occur in years beyond the budget year. Assess whether they are adequately identified and support the budget request. As noted, many programs and activities affect outcomes beyond the budget year (particularly federal and state programs that work through other levels of government and any investment funding). To justify expenditures for such activities, programs should project expenditures' effects on outcomes for years beyond the budget year. The program should also provide rationales for such projections. Budget analysts should review these rationales for plausibility.

16. Identify any external factors not considered in the budget request that might significantly affect the funds needed or the outcomes projected. Make needed adjustments. The persons examining the budget request may be privy to information not available to those preparing it. For example, newly proposed or passed legislation or recently released economic forecasts can have major effects on the outcome projections.

17. Compare the latest program performance data to those from any other programs with similar objectives for which similar past performance data are available. Assess whether projected performance is compatible with that achieved by similar programs. This point and the next are resource allocation issues that cross program lines. Agency budget analysts should consider the performance experience of other, similar programs even if the programs are in another agency. Are the program's past accomplishments poor relative to similar programs? If so, work with program personnel to determine why and identify what can be done to improve future performance. Make any resource judgments that such future actions might entail. Does the program complement or overlap other programs' efforts? If they are complementary, check whether the data are consistent among the programs. If they overlap, consider whether altered resource allocations are appropriate to reduce the overlap.

18. *Identify any overarching outcome indicators that can provide a more meaningful and comprehensive perspective on results. Consider coordinating with other programs, other agencies, and other levels of government.* Few programs produce outcomes alone, especially end outcomes. This is a core concern in performance measurement. Programs related to employment, youth development, substance abuse, crime, and so on generally involve scores of other programs that also influence the desired ends. For example, crime control involves investigation, apprehension, adjudication, punishment, and probably a variety of social services. Each component is critical to success, and each is handled by different programs and agencies.

Look for, and examine, consolidated outcome indicators that apply to all such programs. The budget examiners should make recommendations for any needed coordination and collaboration among programs and agencies. This would include the use of common cross-cutting outcome indicators and determining the roles and responsibilities of each program in achieving jointly targeted outcomes.

For example, reduced drug and alcohol abuse involves many different programs, agencies, and sectors. Each agency with a substantial role in helping reduce substance abuse should track the overall incidence and prevalence (but one agency would normally be responsible for data collection)—recognizing that their responsibility is shared. Each program will likely have its own intermediate outcome indicators and focus on one part of the overall problem (such as on reducing drug abuse by one age group).[6]

In Summary

Primary uses of performance data in budgeting help to formulate the budget and to make a more convincing case for budget recommendations. Performance information, especially if it includes credible outcome data, should lead to better choices and more convincing choices than are possible in its absence. Outcome targets for the budget year establish a baseline for accountability, encouraging reviews of actual accomplishments throughout the year and at year's end.

Performance measurement of outputs, outcomes, and efficiency for past years is important for budget allocation decisions. First, the performance information provides baseline data on outcomes, fundamental for making decisions. *If you do not know where you are, you will have difficulty determining where you need to go.* Second, historical data are usually a primary *basis* for budget projections of future accomplishments.

Making projections for the budget year and beyond is considerably more difficult and is subject to *much* more uncertainty than measuring past performance. The future is very hard to predict, even if for only one or two years, because of the many external factors that can affect results. This problem becomes particularly troublesome if the program is suggesting significant new program variations or new programs to tackle its mission. Then past data will be a much less adequate guide to the future.

However uncertain the data, addressing the relationship of inputs to outcomes should be a major issue in making resource allocation decisions and budget justifications in any budgeting system. *Even if such discussions are heavily qualitative and judgmental, they are far better than nothing, because they encourage those making budget decisions to focus on what is most important to achieve.*

The budget review effort should be viewed as an opportunity for both the program and the agency's budget review staff to develop the best possible budget, to make the best possible case for budget requests, and to focus on maximizing outcomes for a given amount of resources. The inherent tension between budget analysts who perceive their primary job as keeping costs to a minimum and program personnel who want to obtain as many resources as they can will inevitably pose problems. The two groups will find the process much less difficult and less contentious if they work to make it as much of a partnership as possible. The interests of both groups are best served if the final resource allocation decisions forwarded to higher levels are presented as effectively as possible. These days, that means proposals need to be justified, at least in part, based on outcomes—the potential benefits to the public.

Notes

This chapter is a revised version of materials presented in Harry Hatry, *Performance Measurement: Getting Results,* 2nd ed. (Washington, DC: Brookings Institution, 2006). It is published here with permission of Brookings.

1. Personal communication with David Strauhs, commissioner of Massachusetts Department of Environmental Protection, December 4, 1997.

2. The word *target* is not always used in this context. The Government Performance and Results Act of 1993 uses the term *annual goals.* Another terminology problem arises for programs, such as law enforcement, in which the word *targets* for some outputs or intermediate outcomes might be interpreted as establishing quotas, such as on the number of arrests, prosecutions, or collections. For this reason, programs whose missions are investigative, such as criminal investigation activities, might use another, more neutral, label, such as *projections.*

3. Those readers who do not believe that response times to requests for services should be labeled an outcome might prefer a label such as *quality-of-output indicator.*

4. This approach is discussed in Mark Friedman, 1997, *A Guide to Developing and Using Performance Measures in Results-Based Budgeting* (Washington, DC: The Finance Project, May).

5. An example of this is the crosswalk developed by the Oregon Progress Board and the Department of Administrative Services, 1999, *Benchmark Blue Books: Linking Oregon Benchmarks and State Government Programs* (Salem, May).

6. The U.S. Office of Drug Control Policy has been a leading agency in attempting to work out such cooperative efforts among federal, state, local, and foreign governments. See, for example, "National Drug Control Strategy: FY 2007 Budget Summary" (Washington, DC: The White House, 2006).

17

Rigorous Program Evaluation Research

Key to Major Improvements in Government Effectiveness

JON BARON

In the field of medicine, public policies based on rigorous evidence have produced extraordinary advances in health since the mid-twentieth century. By contrast, in many other areas of policy—such as education, poverty reduction, welfare and employment, health care financing and delivery, crime and justice, substance-abuse prevention, and foreign aid—government programs often are implemented with little regard to evidence, costing billions of dollars yet failing to address critical needs of our society. However, in these areas rigorous evaluations have identified a *few* highly effective interventions (i.e., programs, practices, and strategies), suggesting that a concerted government strategy to develop such interventions, and spur their widespread use, could bring rapid progress to many key policy areas similar to the way in which policies transformed medicine.

This chapter advocates a major government effort to (1) increase the number of rigorous evaluations, in order to build the knowledge base of interventions proven to produce meaningful improvements in participants' lives; and (2) facilitate and/or incentivize the widespread use of these research-proven interventions. This chapter focuses on government social policy, but similar concepts could potentially be applied to other policy areas where rigorous evaluations are now rare or nonexistent—areas such as environmental policy, defense procurement, homeland security, and intelligence policy.

1. In Many Policy Areas, Progress Is Thwarted by Government Interventions that Are Not Based on Rigorous Evidence, and Research that Is Not Scientifically Rigorous

Illustrative examples of such policy areas include federal crime and substance-abuse policy, education policy, and international development assistance, discussed as follows.

Federal Crime and Substance-Abuse Policy

Widely used crime and substance-abuse interventions have been shown ineffective or harmful in rigorous evaluations—including well-designed randomized controlled

319

trials, which are discussed later and are considered the strongest measure of a program's effectiveness. For example:

- In-school-based substance-abuse prevention, the nation's most widely used program, operating in 75 percent of U.S. school districts, has been found ineffective in randomized controlled trials (Ennett et al. 1994; Perry et al. 2003). At the same time, government data show that the United States has made little overall progress since 1990 in decreasing adolescent use of drugs or alcohol (Johnston et al. 2005). The program—Drug Abuse Resistance Education (D.A.R.E.)—is now testing revised curricula.
- The nation's juvenile justice system frequently places severely delinquent adolescents in group homes or other congregate care settings—a practice that actually appears to backfire. Randomized controlled trials have shown that such group treatments may *increase* adolescent problem behavior and negative life outcomes, possibly because in a group setting deviant behavior receives positive reinforcement from peers (Dishion, McCord, and Poulin 1999; Howell 1995).
- Another crime prevention program that appears to backfire is Scared Straight, in which at-risk or delinquent children are brought into prison to participate in a realistic and confrontational rap session run by prisoners serving life sentences. A review of nine randomized controlled trials of Scared Straight found that these programs either did not affect, or in some cases actually caused a small *increase* in, subsequent criminal activity by program participants (Petrosino, Petrosino, and Finckenauer 2000).

The vast majority of existing crime and substance-abuse interventions, however, have never been rigorously evaluated, and no one knows how effective they are. For example, in the area of youth violence and substance-abuse prevention, a recent systematic review of over 600 interventions by the respected Blueprints Initiative at the Center for the Study and Prevention of Violence at the University of Colorado at Boulder identified only eleven that have been found effective in scientifically rigorous evaluations.

Similarly, in the area of drug control enforcement, where the federal government spends $12 billion annually, a National Academy of Sciences report in 2001 found that there exists a "woeful lack of investment in programs of data collection and empirical research that would enable evaluation of the nation's investment in drug law enforcement. . . . [B]ecause of a lack of investment in data and research, the nation is in no better position to evaluate the effectiveness of enforcement than it was 20 years ago . . ." (Manski, Pepper, and Petrie 2001).

And the central conclusion of the Justice Department's 1997 report to Congress on a systematic review of over 500 program evaluations in crime prevention was as follows: "The effectiveness of most crime prevention strategies will remain unknown until the nation invests more in evaluating them. That is the central conclusion of this report. The inadequacy of that investment to date prevents a judgment for or against the effectiveness of the $3 billion in federal crime funds, at least to a reasonable degree of scientific certainty. . . . By scientific standards, there are very few 'programs of proven effectiveness'" (Sherman et al. 1997, 10).

Federal Education Policy

Currently, knowledge about "what works" in education, based on rigorous evaluations, such as well-designed randomized controlled trials, is small, as described by Cook (2001, 63):

> Very few of the major reform proposals currently on the national agenda have been subjected to experimental scrutiny. I know of no randomized evaluations of standards setting. The "effective schools" literature includes no experiments in which the supposedly effective school practices were randomly used in some schools and withheld from others. Recent studies of whole-school-reform programs and school management have included only two randomized experiments, both on James Comer's School Development Program, which means that the effects of Catholic schools, Henry Levin's Accelerated School program, or Total Quality Management have never been investigated using experimental techniques. School vouchers are a partial exception to the rule; attempts have been made to evaluate one publicly funded and three privately funded programs using randomized experiments. Charter schools, however, have yet to be subjected to this method. On smaller class size, I know of six experiments. . . . On smaller schools I know of only one randomized experiment, currently under way. In fact, most of what we know about education reforms currently depends on research methods that fall short of the technical standard used in other fields.

Slavin describes the problem in a similar way (Slavin and Fashola 1998, 1):

> Change in educational practice more resembles change in fashion; hemlines go up and down according to popular tastes, not evidence. We do give lip service to research in education. Yet practices from use of phonics in beginning reading to use of ability grouping in secondary schools go in and out of fashion, often in direct contradiction to well-established evidence, but more often in the absence of adequately rigorous and compelling research.

In 2002, the U.S. Education Department began a major shift in its education research agenda, greatly increasing funding for rigorous evaluations, including randomized controlled trials, to evaluate K–12 educational interventions in areas ranging from reading comprehension to charter schools to educational technology (Angrist 2004). The goal of the department's Institute of Education Sciences is to transform education into an evidence-based field.

However, this shift is a recent development, and a major departure from a long history of education research in which rigorous evaluations were a rare phenomenon. For example, a review by Boruch and others of the 144 contracts awarded by the department's Planning and Evaluation Service for evaluation studies during 1995–1997 found that fifty-one addressed the impact of federal programs, yet only five used a randomized controlled design to measure impact. Similarly, their review of the eighty-four program evaluations and other studies identified in the department's Annual Plan for FY2000 found that sixteen addressed federal program impact, yet only one used a randomized controlled design (Boruch, DeMoya, and Snyder 2002).

Boruch and Leow also carried out a hand search of every article in every issue of the *American Educational Research Journal* since the journal's inception in 1964, in search of articles reporting on the effectiveness of interventions in mathematics and science education. Of the 1,200 articles they identified, only thirty-five concerned randomized controlled trials (3 percent), and there was no obvious increase in this percentage over the period from 1964 to 1998 (Leow and Boruch 2000).

International Development Assistance

The World Bank and other multilateral development banks make tens of billions of dollars in grants and loans each year to help the world's poor, with little attention to rigorous evidence on what works. For example, according to an internal World Bank review, less than 2 percent of World Bank projects funded since 2002 have been properly evaluated for whether they make a difference ("World Bank . . ." 2004). A number of senior bank officials recognize this problem, and several rigorous evaluations using a randomized controlled study design have recently been funded by the bank. However, much more needs to be done to expand and institutionalize this work to provide a rigorous evidence base for the bank's work.

Furthermore, the trend among the World Bank and other multilateral development banks toward funding "community-based development" projects—where the target community participates in project design and implementation—is unsupported by rigorous evidence. This finding ("not a single study establish[ing] a causal relationship") was the conclusion of a systematic review by senior World Bank economists—which also found that these projects account for approximately $7 billion annually in World Bank loans (Mansuri and Rao 2004).

More generally, since the mid-twentieth century, the main poverty reduction strategies supported by the World Bank and other multilateral development banks have shifted back and forth with little basis in rigorous evidence—from promoting business and economic development (1950s–1960s), to supporting projects directly targeting the poor (1970s–1980s), and at least partway back to promoting economic development (1990s–2000s, through microenterprise lending).

2. The Study Designs that Are Typically Used to Evaluate Government-Funded Interventions Often Produce Erroneous Conclusions

As noted, evaluations that use scientifically rigorous designs are uncommon. These rigorous designs include, first and foremost, well-designed randomized controlled trials, which are widely recognized as the "gold standard" for evaluating an intervention's effectiveness across many diverse fields, such as welfare and employment, medicine, psychology, and education (e.g., OMB 2004).[1] This is because the process of randomly assigning a sufficiently large number of individuals into either an intervention group or a control group ensures, to a high degree of confidence, that there are no systematic differences between the groups in any characteristics (observed and unobserved) except one—namely, the intervention group participates in the intervention, and the control group does not. Therefore, the resulting difference in outcomes between the two groups can confidently be attributed to the intervention and not other factors.

When a randomized controlled trial is not feasible, evidence suggests that well-matched comparison-group designs—that is, studies in which the intervention and comparison groups are matched in their key characteristics—can be a rigorous, second-best alternative (OMB 2004).

However, the study designs used to evaluate government-funded interventions fall well below the rigor of either a well-designed randomized controlled trial or a well-matched comparison-group study. These less-rigorous designs include "pre-post" studies and comparison-group studies without careful matching. Such designs often produce erroneous conclusions and can lead to ineffective or harmful practices (OMB 2004):

"Pre-Post" Study Designs

Pre-post studies, frequently used to evaluate government-funded interventions, examine whether participants in an intervention improve or become worse off during the course of the intervention, and then attribute improvement or deterioration to the intervention. The problem with this type of study is that, without reference to a control group, it cannot answer whether the participants' improvement or deterioration would have occurred anyway, even without the intervention. This often leads to erroneous conclusions about the effectiveness of the intervention. For example, a pre-post study of Even Start—a federal program designed to improve the literacy of disadvantaged families—found that the children in the program made substantial improvements in school readiness during the course of the program (e.g., an increase in their national percentile ranking on the Picture Peabody Vocabulary Test from the ninth to the nineteenth percentile). However, a randomized controlled trial of Even Start carried out by the same researchers found that the children in the *control* group improved by approximately the same amount over the same time period. Thus, the program had no *net* impact on the children's school readiness. If the researchers had carried out only the pre-post study, and not the randomized controlled trial, their results would have suggested erroneously that Even Start is highly effective in increasing school readiness (St. Pierre et al. 1996).

Comparison Group Study Designs without Close Matching

A comparison group study (also known as a "quasi-experimental" study) compares outcomes for intervention participants with outcomes for a comparison group chosen through methods other than randomization. In social policy (e.g., welfare and employment, education), a number of "design replication" studies have been carried out to examine whether and under what circumstances comparison-group studies replicate the results of randomized controlled trials. The most commonly used comparison-group study designs—which do not include very close matching of the intervention and comparison groups—often produce inaccurate estimates of an intervention's effects, because of unobserved differences between the intervention and comparison groups that differentially affect their outcomes. This is true even when statistical techniques are used to adjust for observed differences between groups (see Bloom, Michalopoulos, and Hill 2005; Glazerman, Levy, and Meyers 2002).

The field of medicine also contains important evidence of the limitations of most comparison-group studies. The following is illustrative: Over the past thirty years, more than two dozen comparison-group studies have found hormone replacement therapy for postmenopausal women to be effective in reducing the women's risk of coronary heart disease, typically by 35 to 50 percent. But when hormone therapy was recently evaluated in two large-scale randomized controlled trials—medicine's gold standard—it was actually found to do the opposite—namely, it *increased* the risk of heart disease, as well as of stroke and breast cancer (e.g., Manson et al. 2003; NIH 2002; MacMahon and Collins 2001).

3. Rigorous Evaluations Have Identified a *Few* Highly Effective Social Interventions, Suggesting that Policy Based on Such Findings Could Spark Rapid Progress

Although they are rare, the very existence of these research-proven interventions suggests that a concerted government effort to build the number of such interventions, and spur their widespread use, could increase government effectiveness in improving people's lives. Illustrative examples include:[2]

- *Nurse-Family Partnership*—a nurse visitation program for low-income women during pregnancy and children's infancy (at fifteen-year follow-up, produces a 40 to 70 percent decrease in child abuse/neglect, and arrests/convictions of children and mothers, compared to controls).
- *High-quality one-on-one tutoring for at-risk readers in grades K–2*—at the end of second grade, one such program raises reading achievement to about the thirtieth percentile versus the twentieth for controls; another reduces grade retentions and severe reading failure by 50 percent versus controls.
- *Portland JOBS Training Program*—to move welfare recipients into high-quality, stable jobs through short-term job search and training activities (at five-year follow-up, increases employment and earnings, and decreases welfare receipt, by 20 to 25 percent compared to controls).
- *Minnesota Family Investment Program*—requires long-term welfare recipients

to participate in employment/training activities and provides those who do find jobs with a sizeable earnings supplement (at the two- to three-year follow-up, increases employment of single-parent recipients by 35 percent compared to controls, reduces poverty by 12 percent, increases percent married from 7 to 11 percent, reduces incidence of mother being abused by 18 percent).

- *Life Skills Training*—a substance-abuse prevention program for junior high school students that teaches social and self-management skills, including techniques for resisting peer pressure including drug refusal skills, and consequences of drug use (at the five-year follow-up—the end of high school—reduces smoking by 20 percent and serious levels of substance abuse by 30 to 50 percent, compared to controls).

- *Good Behavior Game*—a low-cost classroom management strategy for first graders that rewards students for positive *group* behavior (at age nineteen to twenty-one, reduces substance abuse by 30 to 60 percent; at age eleven to thirteen, reduces school suspensions, conduct disorder, and smoking/hard drug use by 25 to 60 percent, compared to controls).

- *Treatment Foster Care*—a program that provides severely delinquent teenage boys with foster care in families trained in behavior management, and emphasizes preventing contact with delinquent peers (at two-year follow-up, reduces the rate of criminal referrals for violent offenses by 45 percent, compared to controls).

- *High-quality, educational child care and preschool for low-income children*—by age fifteen, reduces special education placements and grade retentions by nearly 50 percent compared to controls; by age twenty-one, more than doubles the proportion attending four-year college and reduces the percentage of teenage parents by 44 percent. Further research is needed on how to translate these findings into broadly replicable programs that will work in typical classroom settings.

4. The Fields of Medicine and Welfare Policy Show that the Funding and Effective Use of Rigorous Evaluations Can Produce Remarkable Advances

Precedent from Medicine

In 1962 Congress enacted legislation that, as implemented by the Food and Drug Administration (FDA), required the effectiveness of any new pharmaceutical drug to be demonstrated in randomized controlled trials before the FDA would approve the drug for marketing. That policy change, along with parallel support for randomized trials by the National Institutes of Health (NIH), transformed the randomized trial in medicine from a rare and controversial phenomenon—which had first appeared in the medical literature only fifteen years earlier (1948)—into the widely used gold standard for assessing the effectiveness of all new drugs and medical devices.

Between 1966 and 1995, the number of clinical research articles based on random-ized trials surged from about 100 to 10,000 annually (Chassin 1998).

Since then, randomized controlled trials required by the FDA and/or funded by the NIH and other agencies have provided conclusive evidence of effectiveness for most major medical advances, including: (1) vaccines for measles, hepatitis B, and rubella; (2) interventions for hypertension and high cholesterol, which in turn helped bring about a decrease in coronary heart disease and stroke by more than 50 percent over the past half-century; and (3) cancer treatments, which have dramatically improved survival rates from leukemia, Hodgkin's disease, breast cancer, and many other cancers. Such advances have improved life and health in the United States over the past half-century.

In 1945, President Roosevelt died from a stroke caused by malignant hyperten-sion, and earlier in his life he had been crippled by polio. Today, as a result of the evidence-based revolution in medicine over the past half-century, hypertension can easily be treated and polio prevented, and it can truly be said that the average American receives far better medical care than the president did sixty years ago (Gifford 1996).

Precedent from Welfare Policy

In welfare policy, the Department of Health and Human Services' Administration for Children and Families has, since the 1980s, consistently funded and facilitated randomized controlled trials of welfare-to-work programs and other employment, income supplementation, and related programs for the poor. That support, along with support for such trials from the Office of Management and Budget in the more recent years, has resulted in the implementation of more than eighty-five randomized trials in this policy area—many of them large-scale, well-designed trials that provide convincing evidence about the effectiveness of particular pro-grams and approaches. Studies showed conclusively that welfare reform programs that emphasized short-term job-search assistance and training, and encouraged participants to find work quickly, had larger effects on employment, earnings, and welfare dependence than did programs that emphasized basic education. Work-fo-cused programs were also much less costly to operate (Manpower Demonstration Research Corporation 2001). Studies showed that welfare-to-work programs often reduced net government expenditures. Studies also identified a few approaches that were particularly successful (e.g., the Portland, Oregon, and Riverside County, California, welfare-to-work programs).

These findings were a key to the consensus behind the 1988 Welfare Reform Act and helped shape the major 1996 Welfare Reform Act, including its strong work requirements (Haskins 2002). These acts led to dramatic changes in state and federal programs, and helped bring about reductions in welfare rolls and gains in employment among low-income Americans.

5. A Major Government Effort to Increase Rigorous Evaluations, and Apply Their Results, Could Spark Similar Rapid Progress in Many Areas of Policy

As an important next step, Congress might consider incorporating the following two evidence-based components into the statutory authorization and grant-making procedures of U.S. social programs: (1) allocation of a small portion of program funds toward rigorous evaluations to determine which interventions currently or potentially funded by the program produce meaningful improvements in participants' lives; and (2) strong incentives and assistance for state and local grantees to adopt the interventions proven effective in such studies, and put them into widespread use (incentives such as a competitive priority in the proposal selection process).

As discussed, such reforms could greatly increase government's effectiveness in addressing educational failure, poverty, crime, substance abuse, and other problems that damage or destroy the lives of millions of Americans each year.

Notes

1. See also U.S. Department of Education, "Scientifically-Based Evaluation Methods: Notice of Final Priority," *Federal Register* 70(15), January 25, 2005, 3586–89; the Food and Drug Administration's standard for assessing the effectiveness of pharmaceutical drugs and medical devices, at 21 C.F.R. §314.12; "The Urgent Need to Improve Health Care Quality," Consensus statement of the Institute of Medicine National Roundtable on Health Care Quality, *Journal of the American Medical Association* 280(11), September 16, 1998, 1003; "Criteria for Evaluating Treatment Guidelines," American Psychological Association, *American Psychologist* 57(12), December 2002, 1052–59; and *Standards of Evidence: Criteria for Efficacy, Effectiveness and Dissemination,* Society for Prevention Research, April 12, 2004, at http://www.preventionresearch.org/sofetext.php, accessed October 2, 2007.

2. A more complete description of these research-proven interventions, including citations to the original research, is contained on the *Social Programs That Work* website—www. evidencebasedprograms.org, accessed October 2, 2007.

References

Angrist, Joshua D. 2004. "American Education Research Changes Tack." *Oxford Review of Economic Policy* 20(2): 198–212.

Bloom, Howard S., Charles Michalopoulos, and Carolyn J. Hill. 2005. "Using Experiments to Assess Nonexperimental Comparison-Groups: Methods for Measuring Program Effects." In *Learning More from Social Experiments: Evolving Analytic Approaches* Howard S. Bloom, ed. New York: Russell Sage Foundation.

Boruch, Robert, Dorothy DeMoya, and Brooke Snyder. 2002. "The Importance of Randomized Field Trials in Education and Related Areas." In *Evidence Matters: Randomized Trials in Education Research,* eds. Frederick Mosteller and Robert Boruch. Washington, DC: Brookings Institution Press.

Chassin, Mark R. 1998. "Is Health Care Ready for Six Sigma Quality?" *The Milbank Quarterly* 76(4): 574.

Cook, Thomas D. 2001. "Sciencephobia: Why Education Researchers Reject Randomized Experiments." *Education Next* (Fall): 63–68.

Dishion, Thomas J., Joan McCord, and Francois Poulin. 1999. "When Interventions Harm: Peer Groups and Problem Behavior." *American Psychologist* 54(9) (September): 755–64.

Ennett, Susan T., et al. 1994. "Long-Term Evaluation of Drug Abuse Resistance Education." *Addictive Behaviors* 19(2): 113–25.

Gifford, Ray W. 1996. "FDR and Hypertension: If We'd Only Know Then What We Know Now." *Geriatrics* 51(January): 29.

Glazerman, Steve, Dan M. Levy, and David Myers. 2002. "Nonexperimental Replications of Social Experiments: A Systematic Review." Mathematical Policy Research discussion paper no. 8813–300, September.

Haskins, Ron. 2002. *Rigorous Evidence: The Key to Progress in Education? Lessons from Medicine, Welfare and Other Fields.* Washington, DC: Coalition for Evidence-Based Policy, Council for Excellence in Government, November 18.

Howell, James C., ed. 1995. *Guide for Implementing the Comprehensive Strategy for Serious, Violent, and Chronic Juvenile Offenders.* Washington, DC: National Council on Crime and Delinquency and Developmental Research and Programs, Inc., May.

Johnston, Lloyd D., Patrick M. O'Malley, Jerald G. Bachman, and John E. Schulenberg. 2005. *Monitoring the Future: National Results on Adolescent Drug Use, Overview of Key Findings.* Washington, DC: National Institutes of Health.

Leow, Christine, and Robert Boruch. 2000. "Randomized Experiments on Mathematics and Science Education: Results of a Hand Search and a Machine-Based Search." A report of the Campbell Collaboration and the Third International Mathematics and Science Study, University of Pennsylvania.

MacMahon, Stephen, and Rory Collins. 2001. "Reliable Assessment of the Effects of Treatment on Mortality and Major Morbidity, II: Observational Studies." *The Lancet* 357 (February 10): 458.

Manpower Demonstration Research Corporation (MDRC). 2001. *National Evaluation of Welfare-to-Work Strategies: How Effective Are Different Welfare-to-Work Approaches? Five-Year Adult and Child Impacts for Eleven Programs.* Washington, DC: U.S. Department of Health and Human Services and U.S. Department of Education, November.

Manski, Charles F., John V. Pepper, and Carol V. Petrie, eds. 2001. *What We Don't Know Keeps Hurting Us.* Washington, DC: National Academy Press.

Manson, J.E., et al. 2003. "Estrogen Plus Progestin and the Risk of Coronary Heart Disease." *New England Journal of Medicine* 349(6): 519–22.

Mansuri, Ghazala, and Vijayendra Rao. 2004. "Community-Based and -Driven Development: A Critical Review." Washington, DC: World Bank Policy Research Working Paper no. 3209, February.

National Heart, Lung, and Blood Institute of the National Institutes of Health (NIH), and Giovanni Lorenzini Medical Science Foundation. 2002. *International Position Paper on Women's Health and Menopause: A Comprehensive Approach.* Washington, DC: NIH Publication No. 02–3284, July.

National Research Council of the National Academy of Sciences. 2001. "Informing America's Policy on Illegal Drugs." In *What We Don't Know Keeps Hurting Us*, eds. Charles F. Manski, John V. Pepper, and Carol V. Petrie. Washington, DC: National Academy Press.

Office of Management and Budget (OMB). 2004. *What Constitutes Strong Evidence of Program Effectiveness.* http://www.whitehouse.gov/omb/part/2004_program_eval.pdf, accessed January 24, 2007.

Perry, Cheryl L., et al. 2003. "A Randomized Controlled Trial of the Middle and Junior High School D.A.R.E. and D.A.R.E. Plus Programs." *Archives of Pediatric and Adolescent Medicine* 157 (February): 178–84.

Petrosino, Anthony, Carolyn Turpin-Petrosino, and James O. Finckenauer. 2000. "Well-Meaning Programs Can Have Harmful Effects! Lessons from Experiments of Programs

Such as Scared Straight." *Crime and Delinquency* 46(3) (July): 354–79.

Sherman, Lawrence W., et al. 1997. *Preventing Crime: What Works, What Doesn't, What's Promising.* A Report to the United States Congress, prepared for the National Institute of Justice.

Slavin, Robert E., and Olatokunbo S. Fashola. 1998. *Show Me the Evidence! Proven and Promising Programs for America's Schools.* Thousand Oaks, CA: Corwin Press, Inc.

St. Pierre, Robert G., et al. 1996. "Improving Family Literacy: Findings from the National Even Start Evaluation." Washington, DC: Abt Associates, September.

"The World Bank Is Finally Embracing Science." 2004. *Lancet* 364 (August 28): 731–32.

18

Strengthening the President's Management Hand

Budgeting and Financial Management

F. STEVENS REDBURN AND PHILIP G. JOYCE

A president has powerful tools in hand to more effectively manage and direct financial resources. In recent years, thanks in part to the Government Performance and Results Act (GPRA) (see especially Posner and Fantone, chapter 5 of this volume) and legislation intended to improve financial management and reporting, much better information has been developed about the government's finances and how effectively they are being used for intended purposes. The Bush administration's Program Assessment Rating Tool (PART) (see chapters 2 to 6) process lends system and transparency to the traditional Office of Management and Budget (OMB) career staff's role in assessing program management and performance.

Gaps remain, however, in the information base for policy choices and program management. Better information on costs, benefits, and relative returns on investment can help the president make better choices.

In addition to better information, institutional adjustments affecting how the president's budget is developed and presented may strengthen the president's hand. The changes most needed are those that will permit the public to hold both the executive branch and Congress accountable for responsible budgeting and effective use of budget resources.

Many helpful changes can be instituted by the president alone; others will require congressional action. In both cases, however, their effectiveness will be multiplied if the president gives priority to addressing the nation's long-term structural budget imbalance, identified by so many observers. Congress must be engaged and prepared to cooperate in making changes to the process that will make it easier to pursue difficult policy choices. This will not be an easy sell even with strong presidential leadership; without it, effective management of looming budget problems may be impossible.

Additional Budget Information

Three proposed changes would improve the informational base for budgeting, and, by doing so, would change the incentives facing budget decision-makers. The first

330

of these is to change the budgetary treatment of certain costs in the budget so that they are treated on an accrual basis, rather than a cash basis. This would send a more appropriate signal concerning the long-term costs of federal budget items at a point at which these costs could be controlled. Second, tax expenditures could be more fully integrated into budget decisions. This would place benefits provided through the tax code on roughly the same budgetary footing as spending programs. Third, further progress could be made on the production and use of performance information in the budget process. This should increase the probability that budget decisions will be informed by sound knowledge of their implications for performance.

Recognize Accruing Costs as They Arise

The U.S. budget is generally presented on a cash basis, but since passage of the Federal Credit Reform Act as part of the Budget Enforcement Act of 1990, the costs of extending and guaranteeing credit have been estimated on an accrual basis—that is, the expected net costs of making or guaranteeing loans are recorded on a present value basis in the budget and are disbursed in the year when loans are made. Congress must appropriate funds for the cost of a year's loans in advance, if the expected cost is positive. The same principles could be extended to certain non-credit programs for which the timing of outlays on a cash basis does not provide a good measure of current costs. The International Monetary Fund's (IMF) commentary on the U.S. budget system suggests that "accrual budgeting . . . be considered over the long term" as a way to give better signals about the macroeconomic effects of budget proposals "at decision-making time" (IMF 2003, 35). IMF staff advise that this change be approached carefully because of the risk of a loss of transparency given the complexity of such calculations and therefore their vulnerability to manipulation. This IMF advice is consistent with some of the experience under credit reform, where accurate pricing of credit subsidy costs has proven elusive. Nonetheless, improved signals that could be sent concerning budgetary costs may make the benefit worth the measurement complexity. With this in mind, here are short-term actions that could be taken to move toward an accrual approach:

1. Improve actuarial estimates for insurance and social insurance programs. Improved estimates will increase confidence of policymakers and the public in the shift to an accrual system of budgeting and accounting.

For programs that have sufficient history, homogeneity, and stability to permit it, statistical models should be used to derive estimates, as they are now, for example, for the Federal Housing Administration's (FHA) single-family mortgage insurance program. Cost estimates should not be based on a single economic forecast as they are today but instead on a probability distribution of economic scenarios that include low-probability scenarios; without using that approach estimates will be biased downward because they do not capture extreme events that may occur over the life of a loan. OMB has responsibility for the quality of estimates and, after more than a decade of experience with credit reform, can demand more sophistication and consistency from the agencies.

2. Legislate to extend credit reform, at a minimum, to federal insurance and pension guarantee programs.

The same principles that motivated credit reform should be extended to federal insurance programs—including deposit insurance, PBGC, and flood insurance. If the change were made, the budget would show the estimated year-to-year change in the government's liability as a component of outlays. For example, if large corporations whose pension liabilities were guaranteed by the Pension Benefit Guarantee Corporation (PBGC) drifted toward possible bankruptcy, the budget would reflect this as an increase in the PBGC's liability that year, creating a scoring incentive for prompt consideration of remedial action. If the costs of the savings and loan debacle had been recorded in the budget as hundreds of thrifts became hopelessly insolvent, Congress and the administration would have been forced to confront them years earlier, and the eventual cost of resolving the problem would have been in all likelihood far less. Such a change would require legislation.

3. Consider recognizing changes in accrued liability for social insurance and pensions on the budget in a similar fashion.

The application of accrual principles to social insurance and pension programs would be more controversial. For one thing, Social Security and some other social insurance programs do not represent legal obligations at the time costs arise, making it inappropriate to include a change in expected liability in the budget as a current expenditure. For another, the challenge of estimating long-term costs for social insurance combined with the scale of these programs could lead to large estimating errors and volatility, which would cause uncertainty about the size and proper interpretation of the deficit (Redburn 1993, 233–34).

Even if a formal change to accrual budgeting and accounting is determined to be beyond reach for social insurance programs, budget presentations and alternative deficit estimates and projections could reflect estimates. Presidents could use the information about accruing costs to highlight long-term budget problems and thereby create public pressure and congressional incentives for early remedial action.

Fully Incorporate Tax Expenditures in Budget Reviews and Presentation

Tax expenditures, which represent foregone tax revenue from benefits that are provided to individuals and corporations through the tax code, are often inefficient and frequently lack transparency. If these are reviewed, this review typically occurs in isolation from related program choices. This means that tax expenditures are seldom evaluated for their cost-effectiveness relative to alternatives. For example, a tax break for a corporation to encourage the provision of more affordable housing would not typically be compared to spending programs (grants or loans) that have similar goals. Given their magnitude individually and collectively, these tax breaks deserve greater scrutiny and integration into normal budget processes. The following steps could be taken:

1. More fully integrate the review of tax expenditures into budget formulation.

These reviews should be grouped by policy area and included in area budget reviews along with programs administered by executive departments and agencies. These important program equivalents receive only cursory attention in isolation from programs with similar policy objectives. This change would require a shift of responsibilities from the Treasury Department to OMB, initiated years ago but never completed. Treasury, in turn, could improve its attention to producing reliable models for revenue estimation, including improved estimates for tax expenditures. The current isolated presentation of tax expenditures in the budget obscures their contribution to particular policy goals. OMB should experiment with crosscutting reviews by policy areas and on alternative presentations in the budget until consensus is reached on the most effective integration of these program equivalents with other parts of the budget.

2. Selectively assess major tax expenditures using the PART and other rating tools.

To date OMB has only experimented with application of the PART to tax expenditures. It may be wise to focus performance ratings initially on provisions of the code that have an important administrative component, since some of the PART deals with management concerns that do not apply otherwise. However, the most important elements of the PART—focus on strategic goals, long-term and short-term performance measures, and demonstration of results—logically apply to tax expenditures just as much as to programs whose spending is included in the budget.

3. Reach agreement internally and with Congressional Budget Office (CBO) and the budget committees on conventions for defining and estimating tax expenditures.

This will include agreement on a tax expenditures baseline, developing cost estimates for individual provisions (ways of addressing both baseline and interactions) and estimating the cost of continuing or changing provisions of the code.

Continue to Improve Performance Information and Its Use

Since the 1990s, presidential budgets have moved from a near-exclusive, one-sided focus on costs to a more balanced consideration of costs and expected results. A great amount of work has been required to develop adequate information about program performance and to integrate it into the budget formulation processes of the agencies and OMB. However, better information is needed on *both* costs and benefits, in order to establish where a marginal application of additional resources will achieve the best returns relative to the goals pursued by an administration. A larger investment is required in adequately rigorous evaluations of major programs, for which reliable impact estimates are generally lacking still; this is one category of spending that has been routinely starved and where substantial increases—while hardly noticeable in the larger budget picture—could pay for themselves by helping policy officials and Congress understand which programs work and which do not. Recommended next steps include:

1. Increase investments in rigorous program evaluation.

Evaluations should simultaneously examine sets of programs used in combination, strategically, and coupled with state and local resources to address major public objectives and should meet the "gold standard" of the independent, randomized controlled trials.

2. Improve estimates of marginal benefits and return on investment.

More emphasis should be placed on developing reliable estimates of the marginal benefits of additional spending, and on developing reasonable methods of estimating economic returns on investment in programs that are properly categorized as investments.

3. Analyze and present consumption and investment as separate spending categories.

The president's budget should differentiate between programs that provide primarily near-term benefits (consumption) and those that represent long-term investments—including education and other human capital investments—justifiable based on expected returns. For the latter, estimates should be made of expected returns, including effects on future economic performance estimated on a present-value basis.

4. Expand the budget presentation to highlight the federal government's broader role in the economy.

A broader alternative budget presentation, building on that in the current *Analytical Perspectives* volume, should be presented alongside the traditional budget format for comparison (cf., "Stewardship," *FY 2007 Analytical Perspectives, Budget of the U.S. Government,* 175–201). This would serve to highlight long-term policy challenges and whether the president's proposals can be expected to address those challenges adequately under a range of assumptions.

Institutional Reform

Better budget information can do much to strengthen the president's management of budget challenges and the government's finances, but institutional reforms can help a president do more. Among institutional changes that would assist the president with budgetary management are taking a more long-term focus toward the budget, embracing improved financial management through full cost accounting, emphasizing the use of performance information for management, strengthening the president's hand in controlling spending, and giving citizens a more formal role in providing budgeting advice.

Return to Multiyear Budgeting

In recent years, as part of a general relaxation of budget discipline, budget development has become myopic. Most (if any) attention is paid to the deficit for the budget year; the president's budget estimates for out-years are a mechanical rather than a policy forecast, calculated to hit an arbitrary deficit level. De-emphasis on multiyear decision making and real estimates for the out-years arose within the president's budget process and is correctible without legislation. Nevertheless, a long-term budget agreement between the branches, such as that reached in 1990, would provide a more stable institutional framework and incentives for developing "real" out-year spending and revenue estimates. Steps to correct the budget process's "nearsightedness" include:

1. Require that the president's budget include real five-year estimates of the spending effects of decisions made annually regarding ongoing discretionary programs.

This is straightforward and would be a return to previous practice. It would focus choices on the question of whether a new commitment can be sustained and whether policy goals can be achieved at realistic levels of future spending. Right now these questions are obscured by a process that applies mechanical across-the-board cuts in the out-years to most discretionary programs without regard to policy consequences.

2. Encourage Congress to undertake parallel reforms to appropriations.

Currently, only the first-year allocation to the appropriations committees is enforceable, encouraging decisions that may create substantial costs outside of this one-year window. This encourages congressional response to short-term pressures through expediency and gimmicks that give short shrift to longer-term policy objectives.

Congress can enforce a multiyear regime by requiring through the budget resolution that appropriators produce five-year estimates that are consistent with multiyear allocations, thus discouraging the adoption of spending that has relatively modest costs in the first year but creates increasing costs in the long term.

Strengthen Financial Management through Improved Full-Cost Accounting and Reporting around Agency Strategic Objectives

Prodded by a series of legislated reforms such as the Chief Financial Officers Act, the Federal Managers Financial Integrity Act, and the Federal Financial Management Improvement Act, executive departments and agencies have produced improved, more timely annual financial and performance reports that provide much useful—and increasingly reliable—information about how agencies use financial resources and with what results. A number of additional steps to improve executive branch financial management would build on the improvements to date:

1. Develop a new budget structure aligning budgets with accounting and strategic planning.

Improvements in information about both costs and results have set the stage for a fully integrated accounting presentation of how the government uses its resources. However, currently most agencies face significant misalignment between the way information about cost and performance is maintained in their systems and the way it must be organized for strategic planning and performance-driven budget decision making. The National Academy of Public Administration workgroup recommends that CBO, OMB, and the appropriate congressional committees work together on a proposed realignment. This could be accompanied by restructured annual Performance Accountability Reports that better integrate information on finances with that on major program outcomes.

2. Study the merits and feasibility of a simplified approach to agency accounting and accounts presentation.

A layering of reforms and requirements has produced a system that is "confusing, costly, difficult to implement . . . [and] badly in need of reform" according to the academy workgroup. They outline a recommended streamlined approach that "would simplify accounting, reduce opportunities for error, and be less costly to operate" (NAPA 2006b).

3. Demand further improvements in the accuracy and reliability of agency cost accounting.

The academy panel argues that the best way to achieve better cost information—critical to adequate analysis of marginal returns from increased spending—is for

OMB to use the PART process to press agencies for efficiency measures. In many cases this will require investments to build better cost accounting systems capable of tying costs to results.

Continue the Shift to Performance-Driven Program Management

The PART process—which makes public the assessments of OMB career examiners—highlights weaknesses in the way many programs are designed and administered. Budget development has taken advantage of newly systematic, newly public, more detailed information about program performance to focus decision-makers on the effects of possible reforms and to demonstrate how shifts in spending priorities may alter what programs can achieve. Indeed, budget execution represents one area in which there is a great deal of potential for making decisions that are more informed by performance considerations (Joyce 2004). Grant programs—especially traditional block grants that lack clear focus and performance requirements—score poorly in PART ratings. Using such information, administrations could develop stronger performance-based program models that hold both federal managers and recipient organizations accountable over time for achieving expected results. Here are examples of what can be done:

1. Most grants should be replaced with annual or multiyear performance contracts.

Some program designs make it difficult to hold funds recipients accountable for results. The low PART scores received by many block grant programs provide evidence of this. A general review of grant programs may be in order, to determine whether their designs can be modified to measure and reward effective use of funds or whether, as a general matter, it would be wiser to employ a different model—such as a performance-based contract. The latter would provide much stronger incentives for achieving maximum benefit by specifying up front the performance standards that must be met before a lower level of government or other federal government partner receives full cost compensation and, when exceeded, would yield bonus funding or other rewards. A broad shift from grants to performance-based contracting could result not only in improved public productivity but also in greater public satisfaction with government's use of budget resources. Directly tying spending to demonstrated results will strengthen the president's ability to ensure effective program management and therefore provide more confidence that budget decisions will have the intended effect.

2. Program and agency scorecard processes can continue to focus attention on management improvements that will lead to improved performance.

The President's Management Agenda (PMA) and the PART process together have put unprecedented focus and sustained pressure on executive agencies to improve performance. Whatever other measures a future administration takes to improve management, they should continue to employ these or similar devices to draw both agency and public attention to weaknesses in program design and administration and to identify remedial actions.

Enact Automatic Triggers and Delegated Spending Control Authority

The president's interest and ability, along with that of the Congress, to address the long-term budget challenge will require a political sea change from the status quo, where it seems that neither the Congress nor the president has the incentive to lead the country in making tough choices. Assuming that a future president wants to lead the public in addressing the long-term budget challenge before it becomes a crisis, these steps could be taken:

1. Seek legislation giving the president certain discretion to address increases in the government's long-term liabilities in the absence of congressional action.

In anticipation of but prior to an actual budget crisis, legislation could be proposed by the president that would authorize proactive action to trim certain entitlement commitments as needed to control long-term liability growth. This legislation could, for example, provide authorities that are triggered when the projected deficit problem deteriorates beyond a certain point and Congress fails to act to alter this projection. Such a reform might allow limited changes affecting benefits for future entitlement recipients to correct the problem. This authority would permit action only when and until Congress took its own corrective action, whether the president chose to sign the resulting legislation or not. Congress would be very reluctant to give any president such authority; but a Congress that finds itself unable to act to head off a crisis may find that letting a president take the heat is its best option.

2. Seek legislation that would strengthen and extend the "Medicare fund warning" provision of the 2004 prescription drug bill (Penner and Steuerle 2004).

This provision establishes a procedure mandating proposed reforms when the condition of the Medicare fund worsens. Specifically, if the Medicare trustees project that, in the fiscal year in which their report is made or in any of the succeeding six fiscal years, general revenues will be required to finance more than 45 percent of the total costs of all parts of Medicare, they must report this fact. If such a report is made in two consecutive years it is to be treated as a "Medicare funding warning," requiring the president to respond with a legislative proposal within fifteen days of submitting a budget. According to House rules, if the House does not vote on the legislation by July 30, there is a procedure for discharging the legislation from the relevant committees and considering it in an expedited manner. Similar discharge procedures are used in the Senate and debate on the legislation is limited. While this is no substitute for presidential and congressional will, it may create the political preconditions for responsible leadership to address long-term problems short of an actual fiscal or financial crisis.

Give Citizens a Formal Role in Assessing Performance and Providing Advice on Budget and Policy Alternatives

This set of reforms is the most fundamental and is likely to be the key to the success of all others. Citizens now have free access to a new wealth of information about program finances and effectiveness, provided they have Internet access. This new information sets the stage for testing new ways to engage citizens meaningfully in the policy process. Experience shows that this will not occur automatically or in a representative fashion without procedures to structure that involvement and a belief on the part of citizens that their voices can be heard. If they are seen as legitimate rather than manipulative, efforts at engagement may strengthen the president's hand relative to narrow interests and, by creating a new source of constituency pressure, increase congressional interest in the new wealth of information about government's performance and finances as a basis for legislation and executive oversight. Steps to give citizens a meaningful role could include:

1. Enlarge the window into executive decision-making by publishing tentative policy directions and spending/revenue options for public comment early in the annual budget process.

The PART process and PMA scorecards have opened a window into OMB's institutional assessments of agency and program performance. For citizens to provide informed, meaningful feedback on policy directions and potential budget choices, they need to have an earlier opportunity to consider and react to policy options. While not binding policymakers in any way, such early engagement may lead to greater understanding of and support for difficult policy choices such as those required to address the long-term deficit problem. Moreover, greater citizen input prior to final budget choices can provide a counterweight to the already potent expressions of well-organized, well-financed interests.

2. Organize representative policy forums around major policy choices.

A president can do more than any other individual to strengthen democratic participation by organizing and leading national discussions on major policy questions. The goal should be to give more people effective means to influence decisions. This will require a period of testing and evaluating new institutional forms to see whether they lead to improved decisions, including those made by a more responsible Congress (Buss, Redburn, and Guo 2006).

Experience suggests that budgeting and financial management will not be re-formed—or reform efforts will not be sustained—without public engagement in and commitment to the goals of reform. The public is aware that the federal govern-ment is not a fiscally responsible financial manager. Large elements of the public appear to want a better-performing, more efficient, responsibly managed federal government that will deal with long-term budget imbalances. However, if citizens do not have regular, effective means of expressing and enforcing accountability for results—and given that there is always pressure to serve other, more immediate priorities—reform efforts will fail. A president who wants to strengthen his/her administration's control of financial resources and address long-term budget chal-lenges responsibly and successfully must find new ways to engage the public and obtain broad public support for this agenda.

References

Buss, Terry F., F. Stevens Redburn, and Kristina Guo, eds. 2006. *Modernizing Democracy: Innovations in Citizen Participation*. Armonk, NY: M.E. Sharpe, 29–48.

IMF. 2003. United States, Report on the Observance of Standards and Codes (ROSC), Fis-cal Transparency Module. http://www.imf.org/external/pubs/cat/longres.cfm?sk=16782, accessed August 5, 2006.

Joyce, Philip. 2004. *Linking Performance and Budgeting: Opportunities in the Federal Budget Process*. Washington, DC: IBM Center for the Business of Government.

National Academy of Public Administration. 2006a. *Ensuring the Future Prosperity of America: Addressing the Fiscal Future*. A report by a committee of the Academy (November).

———. 2006b. *Moving from Scorekeeper to Strategic Partner: Improving Financial Man-agement in the Federal Government*. A report by a workgroup of the Academy for the U.S. House of Representatives, Committee on Government Reform, Subcommittee on Government Management, Finance and Accountability (October).

Office of Management and Budget. 2006. "Stewardship." FY2007 *Analytical Perspectives, Budget of the U.S. Government,* chapter 13 (February): 175–201.

Penner, Rudolph G., and C. Eugene Steuerle. 2004. "Budget Rules." Washington, DC: The Urban Institute, July 23.

Redburn, F. Stevens, and Terry Buss. 2006. "Expanding and Deepening Citizen Participa-tion, A Policy Agenda." In *Modernizing Democracy, Innovations in Citizen Participa-tion,* eds. Terry F. Buss, F. Stevens Redburn, and Kristina Guo, 29–48. Armonk, NY: M.E. Sharpe.

Redburn, F. Stevens. 1993. "How Should the Government Measure Spending?" *Public Administration Review* 53 (3): 228–236.

U.S. Department of the Treasury, Financial Management Service. 2005. *Financial Report of the United States Government*.

U.S. General Accounting Office. 2004. *Results-Oriented Government: GPRA Has Estab-lished a Solid Foundation for Achieving Greater Results*. Washington, DC: GAO-04–38 (March).

About the Editors and Contributors

Jon Baron founded the nonprofit, nonpartisan Coalition for Evidence-Based Policy in fall 2001, and currently serves as its executive director. The coalition is sponsored by the Council for Excellence in Government. Since its founding, the coalition has built a strong track record of success in working with top executive branch and congressional policymakers to advance evidence-based reforms in major U.S. social programs. A recent independent evaluation of the coalition's work, conducted for the William T. Grant Foundation, found that the coalition has been "instrumental in transforming a theoretical advocacy of evidence-based policy among certain [federal] agencies into an operational reality." Based on this work, Mr. Baron was nominated by the president, and confirmed by the Senate in 2004, to serve on the National Board for Education Sciences, which helps set the research priorities and agenda for the U.S. Education Department's Institute of Education Sciences. Prior to establishing the coalition, Mr. Baron served as the executive director of the Presidential Commission on Offsets in International Trade (2000–2001); program manager for the Defense Department's Small Business Innovation Research (SBIR) program (1995–2000); and counsel to the House of Representatives Committee on Small Business (1989–1994). Mr. Baron holds a law degree from Yale Law School, a master's degree in public affairs from Princeton University, and a Bachelor of Arts degree from Rice University.

Lloyd A. Blanchard is executive assistant to the chancellor of Louisiana State University, where he is also adjunct associate professor of public administration. His academic background includes faculty positions at the Maxwell School of Citizenship and Public Affairs at Syracuse University and the Daniel J. Evans School of Public Affairs at the University of Washington. He earned his Ph.D. in public administration, with concentrations in public finance and urban policy, from Syracuse University's Maxwell School, and has taught graduate-level courses in budgeting, economics, quantitative analysis, urban policy, and executive leadership. Dr. Blanchard's research focuses generally on the resource tradeoffs of policy considerations. His coauthored publications include "Tax Policy and School Finance" in the *Handbook on Taxation;* "Market-Based Reforms in Government" in *Administration and Society;* and "Equity vs. Efficiency in the Provision of Educational

Services" in the *European Journal of Operations Research.* In 2006, the IBM Center for the Business of Government published his report entitled "Performance Budgeting: How NASA and SBA Link Costs and Performance."

Terry F. Buss manages projects at the National Academy of Public Administration in Washington, D.C. He earned his Ph.D. in political science at Ohio State University. He has held high-level policy analyst and adviser positions at the U.S. Department of Housing and Urban Development, World Bank, Congressional Research Service, and Council of Governor's Policy Advisors. He has also served as director of the School of Policy and Management at Florida International University in Miami, chair of Public Management at Florida International University in Miami, chair of Public Management at the Sawyer School of Business at Suffolk University, and director of research centers and graduate programs at Ohio State, Youngstown State, and Akron Universities. Buss has published twelve books and nearly 300 professional articles in many public policy fields.

Teresa Curristine works for the Budgeting and Public Expenditure division of the OECD Public Governance Directorate. She leads the project on governing for performance and heads the OECD's Senior Budget Officials Network on Performance and Results. She has managed projects and teams working on accountability and control issues, executive-legislative relations, and the OECD Latin American database on budget practices and procedures. She has been responsible for conducting a survey on the issue of performance information in the budget process in OECD countries, the results of which will appear in an article entitled "Performance Information in the Budget Process: Results of the OECD 2005 Questionnaire" in the *OECD Journal on Budgeting* (volume 5 no. 2). She planned and coordinated a directorate-wide project on public-sector modernization. She edited the book *Modernizing Government: The Way Forward,* which resulted from this project and was the main book for the recent OECD meeting for ministers of public-sector reform. She has also worked as lecturer at Oxford University, where she received her Ph.D.

Kim S. Eagle is the evaluation manager for the City of Charlotte. She has worked in local government administration over ten years and has published on topics including public finance, managed competition, administrative reform, and performance measurement. Her primary research interests include new public management and local government budgeting. Dr. Eagle received her Ph.D. in public administration from the Center for Public Administration and Policy at Virginia Tech. She has a master's degree in public administration from Appalachian State University.

Denise M. Fantone worked for local government and a public utility in California before she began her federal government career at the Department of Justice in the charter class of the Presidential Management Intern program. Following her internship, she joined the U.S. Office of Management and Budget's Budget Review Division, where she monitored appropriations legislation, led a budget execution and apportionment team, and supervised teams in the annual preparation of the president's budget. Prior to coming to GAO, she was progressively budget director, deputy director for Planning and Budget, and assistant inspector general for Oversight at the Peace Corps. At GAO, she is primarily responsible for agency budget execution issues. Her work includes two reviews of OMB's Program Assessment Rating Tool (PART) and best practices in state performance budgeting. Ms. Fantone is currently on a rotational assignment as part of GAO's Executive Candidate Development and Assessment Program.

John B. Gilmour is a professor of government and associate director of the Public Policy Program at the College of William & Mary. He teaches courses on U.S. politics, public policy, and budgeting. He is author of two books, *Reconcilable Differences? Congress, the Deficit and the Budget Process* and *Strategic Disagreement: Stalemate in American Politics.* He has also published articles in scholarly journals such as the *American Journal of Political Science,* the *Journal of Politics, Legislative Studies Quarterly,* and the *Journal of Public Administration Research and Theory.*

Harry Hatry is a distinguished fellow and director of the Public Management Program for the Urban Institute in Washington, D.C. He has been a leader in developing performance management/measurement and evaluation procedures for federal, state, and local public and private agencies—both in the United States and in developing countries.

Philip G. Joyce is a professor in the School of Public Policy and Public Administration, George Washington University. Dr. Joyce is also a former assistant professor of Public Administration, Maxwell School of Citizenship and Public Affairs, Syracuse University; principal analyst, Special Studies Division, Congressional Budget Office; adjunct professor, School of Public Affairs, American University; assistant professor of Public Administration, Martin School of Public Administration, University of Kentucky; executive assistant, Department of Corrections, State of Illinois; staff, Bureau of the Budget, Executive Office of the Governor, State of Illinois.

Richard F. Keevey is a professor at the Woodrow Wilson School at Princeton University, teaching graduate courses on state and local finance. He also is currently an adjunct professor at American University and the University of Maryland, teaching graduate courses in public finance. He was the chief financial officer for the U.S. Department of Housing and Urban Development; the deputy undersecretary for Financial Management and then the director of the Finance and Accounting

Agency for the U.S. Department of Defense. He served two governors as the state budget director and as State Comptroller for the state of New Jersey. In the private sector, he was a director at Unisys Corporation and a practice director for Arthur Andersen, LLP. He also served for two years as a first lieutenant in the U.S. Army. He received the DOD Medal for Distinguished Service, the DOD Medal for Outstanding Service, and the Ken Howard Lifetime Achievement Award in the field of budgeting and financial management from the National Association for Budgeting and Financial Management. He is a graduate of La Salle College and the Wharton Graduate School of the University of Pennsylvania.

Richard P. Nathan is codirector of the Nelson A. Rockefeller Institute of Government, the public policy research arm of the State University of New York, located in Albany. Formerly he served as provost at Rockefeller College of Public Affairs and Policy, State University of New York; deputy undersecretary for Welfare Reform, U.S. Department of Health, Education, and Welfare; assistant director of the U.S. Office of Management and Budget; professor of public and international affairs; and director at the Urban and Regional Research Center, Woodrow Wilson School of Public and International Affairs, Princeton University.

Paul L. Posner is the director of the Public Administration Program at George Mason University. He has recently completed a career with the U.S. Government Accountability Office (GAO), where he led GAO's work on the federal budget and intergovernmental finances. Dr. Posner has published articles on public budgeting and federalism issues in various academic journals and books and is the author of *The Politics of Unfunded Federal Mandates,* published by Georgetown University Press in 1998. He received his Ph.D. in political science from Columbia University. He chairs NAPA's Federal Systems Panel and was elected vice president of the American Society for Public Administration.

Ednilson Quintanilla is a research associate at the National Academy of Public Administration. He earned his B.A. from the University of California, Santa Cruz, and his M.P.A. from American University. He previously worked as a supervisor's analyst at the Santa Cruz County Board of Supervisors. He also served as alternate county planning commissioner, alternate county transportation commissioner, and chair of the Central Coast Energy Services and Women's Crisis Support~Defensa de Mujeres board of directors.

Beryl A. Radin is scholar-in-residence at the School of Public Affairs at American University and managing editor of the *Journal of Public Administration Research and Theory.* Formerly, she was a professor of government and public administration at the University of Baltimore; professor of public administration and policy at Rockefeller College, State University of New York at Albany; special adviser and consultant to the Assistant Secretary for Management and Budget, U.S. Department of Health and Human Services; professor of public administration and director at the Washington Public Affairs Center, University of Southern California, and assistant professor at LBJ School of Public Affairs, University of Texas at Austin.

F. Stevens Redburn is former chief of the Housing Branch at the Office of Management and Budget (OMB), Executive Office of the President. He and his staff helped coordinate administration policy and review the budget and management of the Department of Housing and Urban Development (HUD) and other federal agencies. He joined OMB in 1986. He earned his Ph.D. in political science from the University of North Carolina at Chapel Hill. Redburn's scholarly contributions include coauthoring a book, *Responding to America's Homeless,* that helped shape the nation's understanding of a complex problem by delineating subgroups within the homeless population and differences in approaches to service delivery required for each group. He has published twice in *Public Administration Review,* once on models for integrated delivery of human services, and again on how to account for the cost of insurance programs in the federal budget. His federal service began in 1979 at HUD, where he led field studies in the Office of Policy Development and Research to evaluate major programs. His most recent book is a collection of essays, coedited with Terry Buss, *Public Policies for Distressed Communities Revisited.* He is an elected fellow of the National Academy of Public Administration.

William C. Rivenbark is an associate professor in the School of Government at the University of North Carolina at Chapel Hill. He specializes in local government administration, focusing primarily on performance and financial management. He is the coauthor of *Performance Budgeting for State and Local Government* and has published numerous articles in academic and professional journals. Dr. Rivenbark also has worked in local government in various management positions. He earned his B.S. from Auburn University, his M.P.A. from Auburn University at Montgomery, and his Ph.D. from Mississippi State University.

Robert J. Shea is associate director for management, U.S. Office of Management and Budget; former counsel to the Controller, Office of Management and Budget; counsel, Senate Committee on Governmental Affairs, U.S. Senate; legislative director, Office of Representative Pete Sessions; and special assistant/professional staff member, House Committee on Government Reform and Oversight, U.S. House of Representatives.

Pamela A. Syfert is the city manager at City of Charlotte, North Carolina. Former positions with City of Charlotte include deputy city manager; assistant city manager; budget/evaluation director; assistant budget and evaluation director; evaluation supervisor; and program analyst/research assistant. Ms. Syfert has a master's degree in political science from Michigan State University. She completed the Program for Senior Executives in State and Local Government at the John F.

Kennedy School of Government at Harvard University and the Senior Executive Institute at the University of Virginia. She also serves as a fellow of the National Academy of Public Administration. In 1999, *Governing Magazine* named her a Public Official of the Year.

David M. Walker is the comptroller general of the United States. He is a former partner and global managing director of Arthur Andersen, LLP; public trustee, U.S. Social Security and Medicare Trust Funds; Assistant Secretary of Labor for Pensions and Welfare Benefits Programs, U.S. Department of Labor; acting executive director, Pension Benefit Guaranty Corporation.

Ariel Zaltsman is a Ph.D. candidate in Public Administration at the R.F. Wagner School of Public Service at New York University. His dissertation examines the utilization of monitoring and evaluation information during the budget allocation process in Chile. He has performed work in the area of evaluation capacity building for the World Bank, and for the Latin American Center for Development Administration (CLAD), and conducted evaluation research at New York University's Institute for Education and Social Policy. He is author/coauthor of several publications on the institutionalization of monitoring and evaluation systems in Latin America, and on the evaluation of New York City's Chancellor District educational program.

Index

Page numbers in **bold** refer to figures and tables.